International studies in the history of sport
series editor J. A. Mangan

Playing the game

This third part of Sir Derek Birley's comprehensive social history of British sport takes the story from the end of the Edwardian era to the Second World War. By interweaving sporting developments with the social, political and cultural background of this turbulent period, the study offers original and enlightening insights in the changing nature of Britain's obsession with sport.

Playing the Game explores a sporting golden age darkened by the shadows of economic crisis, mass unemployment and mechanised war. As its themes unfold there are dramatic episodes – the suffragette Emily Davison killed by the King's horse in the 1913 Derby; Edgar Mobbs leading his men into battle by punting a rugger ball toward the enemy; Larwood and the bodyline tour of Australia; Eric Liddel at the 1924 Olympics – and plenty of heroes – 'Dixie' Dean, Fred Perry, Henry Cotton, Gordon Richards, Tommy Farr – but it is essentially about the British and their ruling passion.

In the aftermath of the Great War, Britain faced profound social and political changes – sometimes dramatic, sometimes insidious. As commercialism and democracy eroded privilege old assumptions were disturbed – about amateurism, women players and the very function of sport. It was a new Britain that faced the Second World War and Sir Derek Birley's history shows how sport helped to make it a 'people's war'. The book covers the whole range of sport and games, traditional field sports, blood sports, team games, suburban recreations, virile sports, athletics and the Olympics, horse-racing and gambling addictions like greyhound racing and the pools.

This well-researched but accessible social history will appeal not only to students and scholars but to the general reader.

Sir Derek Birley is a former Vice-Chancellor of the University of Ulster

Playing the game

Sport and British society, 1910–45

Sir Derek Birley

MANCHESTER UNIVERSITY PRESS
Manchester and New York

Distributed exclusively in the USA and Canada by St. Martin's Press

Published by Manchester University Press
Oxford Road, Manchester M13 9NR, UK
and Room 400, 175 Fifth Avenue, New York, NY 10010, USA

Distributed exclusively in the USA and Canada
by St. Martin's Press, Inc., 175 Fifth Avenue, New York, NY 10010, USA

British Library cataloguing in publication data
A catalogue record for this book is available from the British Library

Library of Congress cataloguing in publication data
Birley, Derek.
     Playing the game : sport and British society, 1914–1945 / Derek
Birley.
        p.   cm. — (International studies in the history of sport)
     Includes bibliographical references and index.
     ISBN 0–7190–4496–0. — ISBN 0–7190–4497–9 (pbk. : alk. paper)
     1. Sports—Social aspects—Great Britain.   2. Sports—Great
Britain—History—20th century.   3. Great Britain—Social
conditions—20th century.   I. Title.   II. Series.
GV706.5.B57   1995
306.4'83'0941—dc20   95–49566
                                                                CIP

ISBN 0 7190 4496 0 *hardback*
      0 7190 4497 9 *paperback*

First published 1995

99 98 97 96 95   10 9 8 7 6 5 4 3 2 1

Photoset in Linotron Palatino by
Northern Phototypesetting Co Ltd, Bolton
Printed in Great Britain by
Redwood Books, Trowbridge

CONTENTS

SERIES EDITOR'S FOREWORD

In this third part of his very readable trilogy on the evolution of sport in Britain, Sir Derek Birley considers the 'confusing and contentious' period from 1914 to 1945 when, on most fronts, professionalism, commercialism and sponsorship began their now seemingly inexorable and unstoppable ascent to power – gremlins grown into monsters?

The long-running confrontation between amateur and professional self-interest is the central theme of this final volume, with the professionals by 1945, to use an appropriate sporting metaphor, firmly in the driving seat.

Of course, Sir Derek Birley's narrative embraces much more than this. As in his earlier volumes, in this consideration of 'the encroachment of modernity', politics, religion, class, gender, nationalism, imperialism and inter-nationalism and their relationship to the sports of Britain receive shrewd, and sometimes usefully iconoclastic, attention.

'Progress' came at different speeds to different sports. Amateurism fought a long, energetic and committed rearguard action. Oarsmen, protected by lack of commercial appeal, were free 'to concentrate on the burning issue of fixed or swivel pins', and for athletes the British equivalent of the intensive regimes of Nazi training camps was 'the prolonged leisure of an Oxbridge education'.

In the unfolding saga there was both continuity and change – arguably more change than continuity. Arcadian dreams mostly gave way to urban pleasures. The romantic ideals and self-indulgent life-styles of 'the sports-mad leisured classes, the "flanneled fools and muddied oafs" and the huntin, shootin and fishin aristocracy' gave ground steadily to the frenetic escapism or self-promoting ambitions of a sports-mad Lowrian proletariat, money con-scious entertainers and a commercial and industrial oligarchy. Herbert Sutcliffe, proletarian professional and 'imitation Oxonian', who eschewed the broad vowels of Pudsey for the accent of Mayfair, was one of the few who were out of step with the times.

The rise of professionalism, of course, continues as rugby union football bears topical witness, and it is to be hoped that Sir Derek Birley has the enthusiasm for a fourth volume to take the story of British sport on to the millenium.

J.A. Mangan

ABBREVIATIONS

AAA	Amateur Athletics Association
ABA	Amateur Boxing Association
ABF	Amateur Boxing Federation
AEWHA	All-England Women's Hockey Association
AFA	Amateur Football Association
AFC	Amateur Football Club
AFS	Auxiliary Fire Service
ARA	Amateur Rowing Association
ARP	air-raid precautions
ATA	Auxiliary Territorial Service
BBBC	British Boxing Board of Control
BC	Boating Club
BEF	British Expeditionary Force
BFSS	British Field Sports Society
BMA	British Medical Association
BOC	British Olympics Committee
BSJA	British Show Jumping Association
BWSF	British Workers' Sports Federation
CCPRT	Central Council of Physical Recreation and Training
CIGS	Chief of Imperial General Staff
C-in-C	Commander-in-Chief
DORA	Defence of the Realm Act
DUCAC	Dublin University Central Athletics Committee
FA	Football Association
FIFA	Fédération Internationale de Football Association
FIH	Fédération Internationale de Hockey
FISA	Fédération Internationale des Sociétés d'Avirons
FL	Football League
FSFI	Fédération Sportive Feminine Internationale
GAA	Gaelic Athletics Association
GC	Golf Club
GWR	Great Western Railway
HMI	His Majesty's Inspector
IAAF	International Amateur Athletics Association
IFA	International Football Association
IFWHA	International Federation of Women's Hockey Associations

ILTA	International Lawn Tennis Association
IOC	International Olympics Committee
IRA	Irish Republican Army
IRFU	Irish Rugby Football Union
lbw	leg before wicket
LGU	Ladies Golfing Union
LMS	London, Midland and Scottish Railway
LTA	Lawn Tennis Association
LCC	London County Council
MCC	Marylebone Cricket Club
MFH	Master of Foxhounds
MFHA	Master of Foxhounds Association
NARA	National Amateur Rowing Associations
NCSS	National Council of Social Service
NCU	National Cyclists' Union
NFC	National Fitness Council
NH	National Hunt
NHC	National Hunt Committee
NSC	National Sporting Club
NWSA	National Workers' Sports Association
OTC	Officers' Training Corps
PE	Physical Education
PGA	Professional Golfers' Association
PT&R	Physical Training and Recreation
PTI	physical training instructor
R&A	Royal and Ancient Golf Club
RAC	Royal Armoured Corps
RAF	Royal Air Force
RC	Rowing Club
RBCB	Racecourse Betting Control Board
RFU	Rugby Football Union
RHA	Royal Horse Artillery
RIC	Royal Irish Constabulary
RL	Rugby League
RSPCA	Royal Society for the Prevention of Cruelty to Animals
RYA	Royal Yacht Association
RYS	Royal Yacht Squadron
SRA	Squash Rackets Association
TA	Territorial Army
TRCA	Tradesmen's Rowing Clubs Association
TUC	Trades Union Congress

Abbreviations

USLTA	United States Lawn Tennis Association
WAAA	Women's Amateur Athletics Association
WAAC	Women's Auxiliary Army Corps
WARA	Women's Amateur Rowing Association
WCA	Women's Cricket Association
WRAF	Women's Royal Air Force
WRNS	Women's Royal Naval Service
YC	Yacht Club
YRA	Yacht Racing Association
YWCA	Young Women's Christian Association

To Edgar Mobbs and Hedley Verity –
and to my grand-daughters
for whose freedom they gave their lives

INTRODUCTION

I

'Serious sport has nothing to do with fair play. It is bound up with hatred, jealousy, boastfulness, disregard of all rules and sadistic pleasure in witnessing violence: in other words it is war minus the shooting.'[1] George Orwell was reflecting on the visit of the Moscow Dynamo football team to Britain in 1945. Despite countless confirmatory examples, before and since, the British continue to dismiss these as unrepresentative aberrations from a generally blameless norm. Football hooligans are 'a minority', the media blow things up out of all proportion, other countries are worse, British athletes don't take drugs, not many boxers are killed, and so forth. And there is general agreement, especially amongst the elderly, that money – professionalism, abetted by commercialism and its cohorts of agents – is at the root of the problem. This book begins in an age of relative innocence when such monsters were tiny gremlins, and ends in Orwell's time when, notwithstanding his lambent half-truth, sport had been a vital part of the unifying myth that saw Britain through the Second World War.

II

The Edwardians believed that it was their love of sport and the qualities it bred that set them apart from other nations and fitted them uniquely for the task of governing their vast Empire. They had their own heretics, notably Rudyard Kipling who had incurred great odium by listing preoccupation with sport among the principal causes of Britain's poor showing in the Boer War. How, he had asked the leisured classes, would they face the real test – against the Kaiser's Germany – when it came?

> Will the rabbit war with your foemen – the red deer horn them for hire?
> Will ye pitch some white pavilion and hastily even the odds
> With nets and hoops and mallets, with rackets and balls and rods?[2]

Kipling was contemptuous not only of the old aristocratic passion for 'beasts of warren and chase' but the caperings of the newer breed of 'flannelled fools at the wicket' and 'muddied oafs at the goals'. He also despised the 'witless learning' of the public schools that were supposed to produce the nation's leaders, disliking their arid classical scholarship as much as their games cult. But the lesson the British took from the Boer War was not so much the poor

1

example set by the leaders of society as the inadequate physical condition of their followers. The subsequent attempt to improve the health and fitness of children in the state elementary schools, though desirable in itself, begged the question of the intrinsic merits of sport and the purposes to which it could usefully be put.

Like the media of today Kipling was thought a sensationalist scaremonger by sports-lovers. When asked by two enthusiasts if he had not exaggerated he replied, 'You have to hit an Englishman more than once on the jaw before he will take anything seriously.'[3] He had not hit hard enough. The spirit that imbued those who led the nation into battle in 1914 was not the serious, puritanical commitment to the defence of Empire that Kipling demanded, but the altogether more romantic enthusiasm Sir Henry Newbolt had invoked back in 1898 when Kitchener was avenging Gordon's death by crushing the Khalifa at Omdurman:

> The river of death has brimmed his banks,
>   And England's far and honour a name;
> But the voice of a schoolboy rallies the ranks:
>   'Play up! play up! and play the game.'[4]

Kipling's own son, a keen footballer, was one of the first to volunteer – and to lose his life.

III

Industrialisation, an élitist education system and the growing commercialism of the adult world of sport had already in Edwardian times produced a culture clash that had sharpened class distinctions and widened the 'north–south' divide. The Great War drew people together only after a fashion and only for the duration. Women had helped win it, and their right to a share in the evolving democratic process was recognised. A start was made on improvements to housing, public health and state education. Otherwise the social changes it brought, though painful to the old order, were limited, and they were soon over-shadowed by international political and economic developments.

These obtrusive reminders of the alien influences that beset the modern world had their effect on sport. The MCC in particular were sorely troubled by Bolshevism. This apart the lesser breeds were not only playing good old British games, with annoying success, but were modifying them to suit their own, usually half-baked, purposes. FIFA showed scant understanding of true amateurism for instance, and the lax attitude of the IOC brought distress to well-bred middle-distance runners and Henley oarsmen alike. Worst of all were the Americans. Their sports scholarships had long been thought a vulgar debasement of the gentlemanly Oxbridge approach, and now American commercialism had created a situation in which Olympic gold medals were merely a passport to professional contracts or even Hollywood stardom. The first screen Tarzan was a swimming champion. Even superior sports like golf were not immune: Henry Cotton, who had gone to a decent school, had left it to turn pro in the wake of the irreverent Walter Hagen. Soon Fred Perry, the Wimbledon champion, had been seduced.

Italy and Germany, seeking to rescue sport from American showbusiness by state sponsorship, seemed to many enthusiasts – often in high places – to offer an attractive alternative, with the added advantage of being anti-communist. But dirigisme was not the British way: and the governing bodies of the leading sports, united only in opposition to government interference, had become entrenched long before such new-fangled foreign notions had gained currency. Britain sought a middle way between the American-capitalistic and the European state-controlled approaches, extremes exemplified by the successive Olympic Games at Los Angeles and Berlin. Even England's highly professional soccer team was chosen and managed by amateurs. And her gentlemen cricketers shook the foundations of the Empire by trying to put upstart Australians in their place.

It was a confusing and sometimes contentious era at home, too, with the imperatives of 'Brave New World' jostling those of the slump, Arcadianism contending with the craze for speed and records, hiking and keeping fit with the decadent pleasures of the dog-track and the ultimate solace of the football pools. A new class was emerging. Its values, some said, were a cheap, mass-produced imitation of decent native traditions, but it was an increasingly dominant force. Yet the men and women of the new Britain did not seek to sweep away the old. This was not a revolutionary country. Hunting and equestrian sports were reborn and yachting was becoming almost as popular – and as cheap – as motoring.

IV

The disparate elements of this changing nation had sporting values in common. The notion that sustained its uncertain progress towards democracy was that of fair play. It was, George V told his mother, the entitlement of the first Labour government despite its strange beliefs. Hitler's disregard for it was an important reason for Britain's embarking on her second war in twenty-five years. And in the process of serving together it came to seem the right of everyone when peace returned. Even Kipling, in condemning excess, had never questioned that fair play was an essential and valuable ingredient of

British sport. Orwell's outburst was the first warning punch on the jaw for our own generation. Playing the game, despite the lingering hypocrisy, was still a reality for our predecessors, and they may have been the better for it.

Notes

1 G. Orwell, *Tribune*, 14 December, 1945.
2 For the full text see *Definitive Verse of Rudyard Kipling*, London, 1940, pp. 301–4.
3 Recalled by P. F. Warner, *The Cricketer*, March 1936.
4 H. J. Newbolt 'Vitaï Lampada'. See Derek Birley, *Land of Sport and Glory*, Manchester, 1994, Chapter Eight.

CHAPTER ONE

King and country

The Edwardian era was over. In the early evening of 6 May, 1910, the dying King learned that his horse, Witch in the Air, had won the 4.15 at Kempton Park. Soon afterwards he fell into a coma. By midnight the shutters were down and the nation was plunged into gloom. The death of this self-indulgent yet much-admired monarch seemed the more portentous because the other two pillars of the British constitution were wobbling, and Parliament was in disarray. The House of Lords was no longer content, Gilbertian fashion, to do nothing in particular and do it very well: it was asserting itself.

After the Liberal landslide of 1906 the Tories had unsportingly begun to use their natural majority in the unelected upper chamber to thwart the government's policies. Things had come to a head in 1909 when, sniffing socialism, the Lords rejected the Budget, an act without precedent since the seventeenth century. In the general election that followed the constitutional issue was inevitably obscured in a welter of other contentious questions – tariff reform, taxation and, of course, Ireland. The Liberals' support for Home Rule lost them many English seats and they became more dependent than ever on the support of Irish nationalists. This further stiffened the resolve of the House of Lords. Then in the middle of the crisis the King was snatched away.

His successor, George V, did his best to fill the gap, but no impartial referee could have reconciled the fierce partisan loyalties that now gripped the warring factions. Politics, the nostalgic complained, was no longer a civic duty undertaken by the nobly born: it had become a career for aspirant professionals, like the Chancellor of the Exchequer Lloyd George, a Welsh demagogue, and the Prime Minister Herbert Asquith, a social-climbing northerner. Gentlemanly agreement was out of the question. A second election still left stalemate, but the lapse of time had cooled the Lords' ardour for confrontation. Asquith chose the right moment to spread the alarming intelligence that he had the royal backing, if all else failed, to create 500 radical peers, and gradually the die-hards' resistance crumbled. The Lords' right of veto was replaced by delaying powers but they remained uncontaminated by brash newcomers, anachronistic and proud of it.

Britain was democratic, but only just. Every male householder now had a vote.[1] However, this left a significant part of the population without one and even amongst men the common people had advanced further politically than socially. Of the population, 2.5% enjoyed 65% of the national wealth. Only one in nine earned more than £160 a year, the sum at which they had to pay income tax. The average male wage-earner in industry got some £75 a year, his counterpart in agriculture £40, women £30. Skilled men and clerks got £100 or so. Above them was a salaried class, which averaged £340 a year, with a few earning as much as £5,000, and a parallel hierarchy of the self-employed – lawyers, doctors, farmers and shopkeepers – and gentlemen of independent means. At the very top was the handful of really rich, the inheritors of wealth, the landowners and financiers, the top industrialists and businessmen. Incomes apart, the underlying social structure was little changed by the inroads of capitalism and industrialisation. Birth and breeding expressed the order of things God had intended. In His eyes some 2% were unmistakably upper class, 80% lower class and the remaining 18% an array of middle classes with a multiplicity of gradations.

He also dwelt in the country. Over three-quarters of the 45 million population now lived in urban sprawl, but relatively few of the better sort were town dwellers and fewer still lived in industrial areas – the 'north' of the great divide. The growth of large industrial firms had thrown workers closer together, creating an awareness of class divisions of a new, impersonal kind. There was increasing friction in the work-place. Emigration had risen to fresh heights, with the Irish still maintaining their disproportionate share. Yet this, outside Ireland at least, was not a society on the brink of revolution, for the British remained highly respectful of their betters. They were temperamentally inclined to tolerance and great believers in individual liberty. Inequality was accepted, for the most part, as the price of freedom. Above all they were convinced that British ways were best. This unswerving patriotism, for which they endured much, was characteristically expressed in loyalty to the throne.

Country matters

The new incumbent, George V, was not an inspiring figure, and he lacked his father's easy affability. But he possessed, so we are told, 'the range of qualities best calculated to appeal to Englishmen[2] of all classes, not least in his mistrust of cleverness, his homespun common-sense, his dislike of pretension, his ready sense of the ludicrous, and his devotion to sport.'[3] Such devotion was now obligatory for anyone with claims to represent the British, as George V was well aware. The public man 'did not like to miss a good Rugby match at Twickenham, a cup-tie final at Wembley, a Test match at Lord's or the lawn tennis championship at Wimbledon', but '[in] private life the King's interests lay in the pursuits associated with the English country gentleman'.[4]

These, though élitist and often barbaric, were still widely admired in Britain. Nevertheless there was an unimaginative excess about some of George V's artless pleasures. As his biographer said of his life as Duke of York: 'For seventeen years he did nothing at all but kill animals and stick in stamps.'[5] His large and valuable stamp collection was harmless enough, but the shooting was another matter. He was, if possible, even more addicted to it than his father, and, because he was a better shot, even more lethal. His passion for the kill did not subside when he assumed the throne. On the contrary he took the opportunity to widen his experience, insisting, for example, on including a week's tiger shooting in the programme of his Coronation Durbar at Delhi. As the Secretary of State, Lord Crewe, later observed, 'it is a misfortune for a public personage to have any taste so simply developed as the craze for shooting is in our beloved sovereign'.[6]

In one respect – and one for which the blue-blooded were truly grateful – he did not resemble his father, for he did not consort with ill-bred plutocrats, exotic Jews and brash Americans. In fact, neither George V nor Queen Mary had any time for the smart set, whatever their background. The King was more comfortable in the company of older landowning traditionalists like the Earl of Derby and the Dukes of Devonshire and Richmond. But high society was, by this time, hopelessly riddled by the new men. Nouveaux-riches like the Guinness millionaire Lord Iveagh and the building contractor Lord Cowdray were buying up the grouse moors. A new wave of opulent patrons brought their insensitive city manners and their motor cars to the old rural sports. By 1914 *Punch* was deploring the conquest of the countryside by 'the weekend merchant prince'.

There was much hypocrisy about all this. It had been the aristocrats and the squires themselves, forsaking the old method of stalking game for the fashionable battue in the early nineteenth century, who had shaped the modern fashions in shooting. And the expert shots of the day included aristocrats like the Marquess of Granby, Lord Ashburton, the Hon. A. E. Gathorne-Hardy, and the two most famous of all, Earl de Grey, second Marquess of Ripon, and the seventh Baron Walsingham. Walsingham, who had once single-handedly killed over 1,000 grouse in a day, ruined himself by his addiction, being obliged to sell up and go abroad in 1912. Whatever the social standing of twentieth-century shooters, their passion for big-scale butchery was prodigious. In 1913 a new record of 2,843 grouse were killed by nine guns in one day at Broomhead in Yorkshire, and George V himself once with a single companion accounted for over 4,000 pheasants, the ordinary gun-fodder of the day.

Indeed contrary to conventional wisdom (which held that it was the urban bourgeoisie who debased true venatorial values) a more fastidious shooting fashion arose amongst weekend sportsmen liberated by the railways. Wildfowling, hitherto considered a bucolic curiosity, acquired a cult status amongst those town dwellers who thrilled to the fascination of wild and solitary places, enjoyed natural history, fieldcraft and a certain amount of discomfort, and saw it as a positive virtue that 'bags' were not huge or artificially contrived for slaughter. To the wildfowler 'the secrets of nature are disclosed,' wrote the sport's first promulgators in 1911. 'On the far saltings on the lonely marshes of the sea he has wonderful moments. Downs that are august in their splendour rise for him in his lonely eagerness.'[7] Other more tangible attractions were that in most localities, unlike game shooting, it was legal on Sundays and it was free.[8]

Similarly 'the solitude of Nature and the presence of the immeasurable'[9] were the magnet for increasing numbers of weekend sailors that were coming into yachting, once the most exclusive sport of all and in its most opulent form a particular favourite of Edward VII. As a young naval officer George V had graced the Corinthian scene, sailing the more modestly-sized craft in which owners played a bigger part in the proceedings than occasionally being photographed with their hands on the wheel. As King, however, and approaching fifty, he was more than happy to take over the huge Royal Yacht *Britannia*, built for his father back in 1893 and still capable of stirring patriotic blood. He kept a meticulous record of her performances, and sailed on her himself from time to time, but he was constrained by Queen Mary's known dislike of the sport. This apart George V was temperamentally unfitted to adopt his father's role of jovial master of ceremonies at Cowes, and it lost something of its old magic after Edward's death.

One cloud on the horizon was the mounting evidence that the Germans, always something of a nuisance, were now becoming a serious menace. Britain's share of the world's yachting tonnage was declining. In the early 1890s it had been over two-thirds: now it was less than half, and Germany's share by contrast had increased dramatically. This naturally cast gloom over the proceedings at the Royal regatta, where the Kaiser's boasting and pretentiousness, encouraged by the equally ostentatious fifth Earl of Lonsdale, had been so irksome to Edward VII and so amusing to everyone else. It was no longer a laughing matter: yachts, after all, could be mobilised in time of war to act as submarine-spotters and coast-watchers.

There was also much head-shaking over the decline of the old Big Class yachting, which had become too expensive for all but the most capacious purses. Most of the remaining few belonged to the 'new money' men rather than the nobility who had created the sport. So many aristocrats had been forced into economies that the new 57-footers were known as the 'belted earl' class. Whatever its social effects the shift in economic power to the plutocrats did no discernible harm to the sport's moral standards, for the British aristocrats had compared badly in both sportsmanship and boat design with the Americans who were their principal rivals. But though the general public, the boat-builders and the sporting press might rejoice to learn that the grocery mogul Sir Thomas Lipton intended to resume his challenges for the America's Cup, the news was less welcome to the blue-blooded who had steadfastly denied him membership of the élite Royal Yacht Squadron, despite his intimacy with Edward VII.[10]

The trend towards smaller yachts did not greatly diminish their owners' desire for exclusiveness. By 1914 there were 120 clubs in England and Wales, ranging from the 32 metropolitan or county foundations which had acquired 'Royal' status to pretentious imitators in seaside resorts, and most of them were as keen as the RYS itself on keeping out the wrong sort. They were not always successful. Desire for membership was greatest in the London area, at places within reach of the weekend sailor. Southend, an accessible but socially undistinguished resort, had five yacht clubs by 1913, with 1,150 members and some 350 unattached yachtsmen. The oyster fishing village of Burnham on Crouch was transformed by the coming of the railway to a crowded yachting centre, becoming the headquarters of the Royal Corinthian and the Eastern Yacht Clubs, and giving birth to a new foundation, the Burnham Yacht Club, which grew from 51 members in 1895 to 217 in 1910, after which a halt had to be called. The concern here was that the tone set by the London gentlemen of independent means and the higher professions who founded it would be lowered by the process of expansion. Elsewhere it was sometimes the advent of bounders from the city that upset the local members, as for instance at the Royal Cornwall YC which first split apart and then conducted a purge of the interlopers.[11]

Most clubs were now preoccupied with racing, and the ability to stage a successful regatta was the hallmark of a superior watering-place and the envy of lesser resorts. However, regular competition was too demanding in skill, time and nervous energy for most weekend sailors, especially as convention still forbade Sunday racing. This apart, cruising had an intrinsic attraction, which some maintained, in another twist of the sport's snobberies, was the true delight of sailing. Here was sport as escape from the real world, not only literally in the quest for solitude and peace, but spiritually, rejecting the competitive values associated with industry and commerce, of which they saw quite enough during the week.

At the other extreme the trendier sort of weekend sailor was no longer content to rely on 'natural' methods of propulsion for his excitements. Steam yachts had long been the preferred alternative of the sybaritic, to the derision of purists, but the motor boat offered an altogether different challenge. Since 1903 the annual Harmsworth Trophy, originally sponsored by the *Daily Mail* in 1888, had become the premier team-race for international competition. In 1910 the British hydroplane 'Pioneer' caused a sensation by reaching 40 mph (before breaking down) and was the forerunner of the hydrofoil designs that transformed the sport. The craze for motorised speed was anathema to many traditionalist yachtsmen, but it was an irresistible modern phenomenon. And there was convenience as well as novelty in the new technology: soon many were talking learnedly of outboard motors, self-starters for boat engines and 'quenched spark' wireless telegraphy. By 1910 *Yachting Monthly* had added '*and Marine Motor Magazine*' to its title.

The expansion of yachting also brought more women to the sport. There was nothing new in having them on board for ornamental purposes. But in the smaller modern boats there was less room, actual or metaphorical, for passengers. Women's role in racing was constrained by the male belief that competition was intrinsically unfeminine and that women were physically and temperamentally unfitted for it. Mrs Frances Clytie Rivett-Carnac, part of her husband's crew on the winning 7 metre yacht in the 1908 London Olympic Games, had been a remarkable exception. Nevertheless, as in hunting, ladies of this class enjoyed great freedom, provided they observed local conventions. These, even for spectators, could be very strict when it came to dress: German girls created an unfavourable impression at pre-war Cowes when they displayed such over-enthusiasm to see the start of a race that they ran outside without their hats. On board there were severely practical problems, rarely openly discussed, to do with sanitary arrangements especially on smaller cruising yachts. But few yachtsmen saw the advent of women as a serious threat, not least because it seemed a better outlet for their energies than politics.

Since achieving a publicity coup in 1905 by interrupting a meeting, getting themselves arrested and being sent to prison for refusing to pay the fine, radical elements in the movement for female suffrage had adopted disruption as a regular tactic. Liberals were the chief targets of attack, since the only hope of advance was while they were in office, and Lloyd George, who was a supporter, was attacked as much as Asquith, who was not. Various Bills were discussed and sometimes introduced, but as nothing came of them frustration mounted and the moderates were brushed aside. Hunger strikes by those arrested leading to force feeding aroused great publicity and required skilful tactics by the authorities to avoid creating martyrs. Failure of the Franchise and Registration Bill in 1912 and another version the following year brought a fresh wave of violence. A bomb wrecked part of Lloyd George's house. There were two attempts to set fire to the stands and spoil the lawns at Wimbledon. Hence in a 1914 article entitled 'Boats for Women' the editor of *Yachting Monthly* expressed himself entirely in favour of women taking up sailing: 'Both now and for all time, the country would be the better for it.' [12]

This was part of a wider masculine view, now gaining adherents, that 'suitable' outdoor activity was a good way of diverting women's attention from less profitable pursuits. One benevolent Edwardian male, for example, had recommended angling as a desirable mind-broadening influence, a good cure for 'the petty habits of gossip and littlemindedness which too often mar the character of home-keeping girls'. [13]

The argument was more often heard in relation to game-fishing, more socially restricted and less openly competitive than coarse fishing which was predominantly a working-class affair. In families with limited income and no domestic servants the male breadwinners, particularly in the industrial environment, tended to take their sport with fellow-workers and leave their womenfolk behind. Thus even in angling, in which there were no inhibiting factors to do with physical or sartorial propriety, there was a marked difference between the participation of women in the rarefied atmosphere of fly fishing, in which they were encouraged, and vulgar coarse-fishing circles in which they were not. Local coarse-fishing competitions attracted a good deal of betting, though usually small-scale and informally arranged. Money prizes were rare compared with 'useful items such as china, clogs, blankets and sacks of flour' and even betting transactions might be conducted in commodities like sacks of potatoes, crates of oranges or, it seems, black puddings. This utilitarian flavour, possibly designed to reconcile fishermen's wives to their absence, [14] was one of coarse fishing's few concessions to femininity.

Of the 200,000 or so serious coarse-fishermen most were clustered in the cities and conurbations. Apart from London (geographically in the south but with its own 'northern' masses) the biggest single group was in Sheffield, where there were over 21,000 members in the 200-odd clubs affiliated to its Angling Association. These clubs, usually pub-based, were characteristically much given to Sunday excursions and organised competitions on 'pegged' sections of river banks. Since their start in 1906 the National Federation of Anglers' annual championships – sponsored by the populist *Daily Mirror* – had been dominated by northern clubs. Even game-fishing had greatly changed by this time. Urban middle-class enthusiasm had led to intensive demand for salmon and trout waters, and consequent high rents, syndicates, game licensing, pressure on stocks and the beginning of pisciculture (much like pheasant-breeding) for sporting purposes. Equipment manufacturers were thriving. But competition took discreet forms involving solemn debates about the ethically correct weight of rod for the size of fish and the superiority of 'dry-fly' methods.

The growth of interest in fishing was a characteristic example of industrialised Britain's Arcadianism. Another was continued reverence for the horse. George V, in the oldest of all royal traditions, was a keen horseman: even in London he was 'commonly to be seen in the summer riding in Rotten Row with a friend before breakfast'.[15] In 1911 he wrote sternly to Prince Edward, the future Edward VIII, 'You seem to be having too much shooting, and not enough riding or hunting . . . You must learn to ride and hunt properly.'[16] This, he made clear, was not a mere matter of recreation: 'In your position it is absolutely necessary that you should ride well . . . The English people like riding and it would make you very unpopular if you couldn't do so. If you can't ride, you know, I'm afraid people will call you a duffer.'[17] And by the time Edward, now aged 18 and Prince of Wales, left Naval College and went up to Oxford in 1912, his father decided it was high time his education was properly completed and assigned to an equerry the task of teaching him to ride. Edward at first thought it all very dull but soon developed a taste for it, going out with the South Oxfordshire hunt and appearing on the polo field.

By the second year George V was grumbling, 'You certainly have been doing a good deal, hunting two days, out with the beagles twice, golf and shooting one day, besides all your work, which seems a good deal for one week. I hope you are not over-doing it in the way of exercise.'[18] Not having been to public school the Prince did not play cricket and rugger or row, but he found plenty of companions to share his interest in field sports even in the great age of team games. The two traditions, for one thing, co-existed happily in the older public schools, particularly Eton. For another the image of the country gentleman, however much his field sports might offend the susceptibilities of middle-class radicals or resentful proletarian demagogues, had a powerful hold on the imagination of people at all levels of society. Hunting, in fact, had not merely found it possible to survive the incursions of modernity, but, at the cost of some social sacrifice, real or imagined, had enjoyed a remarkable resurgence. Of the 178 fox-hunting packs in England and Wales in 1912, 53 had been founded since 1850 and 14 since the turn of the century. Inevitably some of the recruits were socially-ambitious 'persons in trade': hunting's traditions conveyed the sort of cachet such people were anxious to buy. But there were also public school men from the gentrified or professional middle classes who were deeply conscious of the old aristocratic values. One such was George Sherston, hero of Siegfried Sassoon's fictionalised autobiography,[19] who exemplified the continuance of the old tradition alongside the new.

In 1913, having left Cambridge without taking a degree, Sherston, after a summer of cricket and a winter with one of the better hunts in his native Kent, decided to follow his friend Denis Milden, an Oxford man who had devoted his life to hunting, when he left to become Master of the famous Packlestone in the Shires.[20] For this Sherston needed four horses, and he took his own groom with him. The funds required, £10 a week for four days' hunting apart from capital outlay and the cost of socialising, was nothing compared with Milden's expenses of well over £2,000 a year, but it was more than Sherston could afford. He economised all summer, but needed a subsidy from his aunt. He was determined to enjoy at least one good season, but it was hard going keeping up with the Packlestone members who were almost all well-to-do. There was, of course, 'the newly-rich manufacturer who lived in a gaudy multi-gabled mansion' asking Sherston, "'Ow many 'orses do *you* reckon to keep?' But there was also a good deal of 'old money': Captain Harry Hinnycraft, an 'old-world grandee' and as despotic a hunt secretary as he was feudal overlord on his estate; Mrs Oakfield of Tharrow Park, daughter of a former Master, 'the feminine gender of a jolly good fellow'; Sir Jocelyn Porteus-Porteous with his 'deliberately majestic variation of spelling'; the grey-bearded Squire Wingfield 70 years old but still riding as hard as he had at 40; jolly Judge Burgess commuting from London; and the exquisitely polite old bachelor Mr Jariott.

The younger set included the intrepid Miss Amingtons. Women had long been accepted on the hunting field – so long as they were content to ride side-saddle and did not otherwise impair their femininity by becoming too much 'of the horse, horsey'. Propriety was reinforced by orthodox medical opinion which warned against straining or displacing vital organs: in 1914 a doctor explained that straddling was dangerously insecure for female riders since 'women's thighs, being round and fat, do not grip the saddle like the long flat ones of men'.[21] The Amingtons were as bold and dashing as any man, even side-saddle. Also disturbing to the hunting purists were Jack and Charlie Peppermore, well-known gentlemen steeplechase riders and a good deal too competitive for some tastes. Sassoon's characters were drawn from real life. The Peppermores were Frank and Harry Atherton Brown, sons of a wealthy landowner and property developer. These were not bourgeois interlopers but Etonians, 'fine specimens of a genuine English traditional type that has become innocuous since the abolition of duelling'.[22]

Flat-race riding had, of course, long been given over to the under-sized working-class professional jockeys. Amateurs, in varying degrees of purity, still contended successfully at the heavier weights in National Hunt racing. This was an uneasy amalgam of point-to-points, steeplechasing and hurdle-racing (variously end-of-season entertainments or fashionable showpieces for hunts and cavalry regiments, sidelines for farmers and publicans, virility tests – with a bet into the bargain – for sprigs of the aristocracy, a minor diversification for flat-race trainers and a specialism for Irish ones). The National Hunt Committee of the Jockey Club had been struggling ever since its formation in 1866 to bring order and a measure of respectability into its domain, a task not entirely consonant with its anxiety to maintain its social standing.

Preserving the socially-important link with the hunts brought its own hazards. It was one thing for the NHC to require horses taking part in hunter 'chases to be genuine hunters but quite another to implement the rule. Apart from crafty owners and trainers, the hunts, many of which had been around long before the NHC was heard of, had an innate resistance to bureaucratic interference. They were happier after 1913 when the Masters of Foxhounds Association was given more responsibility for enforcing the rules. It was still hard to persuade some hunts to register their winners (very necessary for purposes of handicapping and eligibility) but 132 out of 144 were doing so in 1914.[23] Apart from the unspeakable drag hunts, which were ineligible to hold meetings but got round the regulations by setting themselves up as clubs, the biggest continuing nuisance was Masters' carelessness in issuing Hunt Certificates. The NHC was not pleased to receive certification on 21 November 1913 that four horses had been hunted regularly in the 1913–14 season, which had scarcely begun.

The NHC and its Stewards, over-reliant on the gentlemanly code of honour as a warranty of integrity, had a poor record in dealing with the bigger swindles that took place regularly in steeplechases and hurdling. The few offenders that were disciplined were the smaller fry: those of higher standing 'used to get off scot-free'.[24] Things improved when Captain (afterwards Brigadier) F. C. Stanley, younger brother of the seventeenth Earl of Derby, became Senior Steward in 1910, showing an aristocratic impartiality in his approach to the misdoings of both minor gentry and celebrated professionals. Mr George Gunter, leading amateur rider of 1909 and a considerable swell in Yorkshire sporting circles. was severely cautioned in 1912, as was the admired professional Percy Woodland, 'Lucky Percy', who had ridden the 1903 Grand National winner. (He won it again the following year, presumably reformed.) More drastically, in 1913 Tom Coulthwaite, trainer of two Grand National winners, was warned off and it was 13 years before his sin was purged.[25]

The Grand National, by now a great popular festival, overshadowed all other races. The public found the lesser races attractive enough, especially when there were well-known riders like 'Tich' Mason, Arthur Nightingall, Ernie Piggott or Mr Jack Anthony (all winners of the National) but the prizes were pathetically small, so that owners and trainers tended to regard the season as a build up for the one big race. It did not always live up to its reputation. There were always plenty of runners but rarely as many survivors. In the appallingly muddy conditions of 1911 only one of 33 got round without falling. The connoisseurs had their first reward for years when Jerry M won in 1912 for Sir Charles Asheton-Smith and the immigrant Irish trainer Bob Gore. Sport apart, there had always been a highly articulate section of urban middle-class opinion which objected to steeplechasing on humanitarian grounds, and the Aintree fences were particularly dangerous. Furthermore for the purposes of betting – the principal reason why most people were interested in racing – the fences were just an undesirable complication. Flat-racing had infinitely more appeal.

Drumming hoofbeats

There was, of course, no need to go to the races at all to place a bet. Part of the excitement, and the mystique, for the punters who actually did go, as distinct from studying form in the newspapers, was to see the horses in the parade ring and the jockeys in the flesh. Some undoubtedly also got pleasure from the proximity of their social superiors in the more expensive rings and grand-stands. Middle-class moralists and revolutionary socialists stayed away. A common enthusiasm for gambling and a love of horses united the rest as it had done since the eighteenth century when foreign visitors had marvelled at the way all classes from the highest to the lowest had mingled together at Newmarket.

For George V it was a great opportunity to display that most-admired quality in a monarch, the common touch, for by happy chance racing was one of his favourite sports. The melancholy amongst fashionable race-goers at the death of Edward VII had been deepened by anxiety about the sporting intentions of the new King, who seemed a dull enough fellow. Yet, though he was not one for the social whirl, and hence was something of a disappoint-ment to the livelier Ascot set, George V went down better at Newmarket. Indeed he knew more about horses and the actual racing than his father, and when, to the general relief, he announced his intention of keeping on the Royal Stud it was a serious commitment. He was no great gambler – £10 was his usual limit – but he enjoyed, in a dour, calculating sort of way, the challenge of ownership and kept a keen eye on the Stud.

This was a critical time for the British Turf, both socially and in terms of national prestige, or so at least it seemed to the old order who regarded themselves as the custodians of such matters. The establishment had not yet entirely come to terms with the changes brought by the enclosure of courses 30 years before. Greater income from spectators had given a fillip to prize-funds – they rose to over £500,000 by 1910 – which in turn had attracted better fields and better competition, still bigger crowds and so on. This had certainly broadened the Turf's economic base, and made it easier to keep out the riff-raff, but traditionalists were not convinced that the benefits outweighed the disadvantages. It was no coincidence, they felt, that the influx of new money had brought in so many foreigners with dubious habits. The worst of the shady jockeys and trainers who had assisted the 'American invasion' earlier in the century had been repelled by sharp if arbitrary action on doping and crooked dealing. But sceptics noted the ominous return of Johnny Rieff as the 1912 Derby winner, and the more sustained success of the highly res-pectable but nonetheless American Danny Maher who became champion jockey the following year. Steve Donoghue, already a gnarled veteran of 30, who replaced him in 1914, was regarded as something of a 'wide boy' – he was a northerner with Irish blood – and more popular with the punters than with the establishment.

The Jockey Club's chief concern was to prevent the leading professional riders, whose scarcity value gave them inflated incomes, from getting ideas above their station. The Jockey Club was an eighteenth-century foundation and its outlook had not greatly changed in the meantime. Its gubernatorial task had been hindered in the past by the close links, of social class and often of family ties, between jockeys and the trainers who had day-to-day charge of both horses and riders. In recent years a wedge had been driven into this often unholy alliance by the emergence of the gentleman trainer. The first, the Hon. George Lambton, brother of the third Earl of Durham, had caused eyebrows to raise in 1893 by becoming trainer to the sixteenth Earl of Derby, but he had soon been followed across the social divide by the Anglo-Irish H. S. 'Atty' Persse, formerly a leading amateur National Hunt rider and a Master of Foxhounds. Soon an influx of public school men – often from Eton which had an old, aristocratic horsey (and gambling) tradition – and ex-officers from good regiments had created a new layer in the Newmarket hierarchy.

The great Victorian trainers – Scottish immigrants like the three Dawson brothers, Jimmy Ryan and Jimmy Waugh, as well as locals like Tom Jennings, Jem Godding, Tom Leader and Bill Jarvis – and their descendants and successors, such as the royal trainer, Richard Marsh, had become highly prosperous but they had remained essentially tradesmen. By 1910 Bedford Lodge, built up by Matt Dawson, mentor and father-in-law of Fred Archer, was presided over by Captain R. H. Dewhurst. Next door was Captain Percy Bewicke and nearby another military type, Peter Purcell Gilpin, whose new stables were called after the winner of the 1900 Cesarewitch, Clarehaven, which he had backed at favourable odds. The Jockey Club now rarely gave training licences to former flat-race jockeys, and the gentrification of the profession was further assisted by a system of pupillage. Thus the Anglo-Irish Cecil Boyd-Rochfort had gone straight from Eton as pupil of 'Atty' Persse before becoming assistant to Captain Dewhurst.

Lambton himself was more than once leading trainer and in 1911 he netted no less than £49,769, most of it for the seventeenth Earl of Derby, whose winnings of £42,781 that year raised hopes for a renascence of the old owner–breeder aristocracy. But whereas professional trainers might nowadays be gentlemen they could not afford to be selective about those for whom they trained. When in 1912 Cecil Boyd-Rochfort became racing manager to the naturalised German–Jewish financier, Sir Ernest Cassel, one of Edward VII's dubious friends, he was taking a bolder step than going into trade. He took it nevertheless. Meanwhile Mr J. B. Joel, one of two South African diamond-rich brothers, showed the way of the future, winning the Derby in 1911 and becoming leading owner in 1913 and 1914. American, French, South African, Australian and similarly exotic owners became more and more prominent, alongside the English nouveaux-riches. The English Turf, which had long been more of a business than a sport, and in which money, new or old, had always talked in its own special language, was becoming internationalised whether the Jockey Club liked it or not.

It certainly did not like it much, particularly with the prospect of American-bred horses flooding the market. In 1913 leading Jockey Club members used their influence to persuade the British government to introduce restrictive legislation. The Jersey Act (named after its proposer, the sixth Earl of Jersey, landowner, banker and former colonial governor) provided that only horses whose ancestry could be traced to sires and dams previously registered in the Stud Book could be accepted for future registration. It was presented as a conservation measure, born of concern for the purity of British bloodstock. To the Americans, however, it seemed a blatant protectionist move, born of snobbery and chauvinism, aimed at keeping British and Irish prices up. Though deeply resented and producing ludicrous anomalies it was to remain in force for many years until finally shown to be absurd by the numerous American and French 'half-breeds' that performed better than the thoroughbreds.

The horses George V had inherited were, alas, not very successful. He had only one winner during the whole of 1911 and 1912, but he enjoyed his occasional trips to Newmarket and took a keen interest in Richard Marsh's training schedules. The 1913 Derby might have led a less stolid monarch to give up racing altogether for it was the occasion when the suffragette Emily Davison was killed by his horse. In fact his diary entry for what he called 'a most disappointing day' first set out the facts concerning the disqualification of the favourite Craiganour and the awarding of the race to the 100–1 outsider Aboyeur before turning to Miss Davison's involvement.[26] This was, he recorded, 'a most regrettable, scandalous proceeding' and his chief concern was for the Royal jockey, Herbert Jones, who had been injured in the fall. Jones, a public spirited young man who ran the Newmarket Boy Scouts, was very put out by the affair. He resented keenly the tone of some of the letters he received as he lay on his hospital bed, particularly those that suggested that he should go to the suffragette's funeral. No doubt he was better pleased with the telegram from the Queen Mother's Comptroller and Treasurer, General Sir Dighton Probyn, VC, which read 'Queen Alexandra was very sorry to hear of your sad accident through the abominable conduct of a brutal and lunatic woman.'[27] George V took a similar though more detached view. When Harold Heath, a zoologist who had been overcome by the poignancy of it all, also threw himself under the royal hooves at Ascot, the King wrote in his diary, 'He is a lunatic who wished to commit suicide and not a suffragist, but it caused great excitement.'

For Ascot itself 1913 was the latest in a series of bad years: 1910 had been clouded by the death of Edward VII; 1911 by a coal-strike and other labour disputes. The profits had gone down again in 1912 because of the general unrest in the country; and apart from the Heath incident technical problems with the course had marred 1913. Throughout this time, at first behind the scenes but later in the law-courts, an unseemly dispute had gone on between the Trustees, the King's representative, Lord Churchill, and the Jockey Club about who should control the reserve funds that had been discovered. The Trustees won their case in court, but Lord Churchill outflanked them, joining forces with the Jockey Club to persuade Parliament that the time was ripe to set up a new Ascot authority. On some things at least, those that really mattered, state intervention was expected. After all these miseries and anxieties Royal Ascot 1914 was a welcome relief. Indeed the occasion, by common consent, quite equalled, in attendance, in sunshine and in fashion, anything seen in the past. *The Times* playfully called it the Parasol Ascot: 'Pink and blue, yellow, scarlet, mauve and apricot – with every intermediate shade and combination of tints – to look down upon the sunshades from an upper tier in one of the stands was like gazing down on a gorgeous flower garden where every flower was mushroom-shaped.'[28] No-one suspected that war was only six weeks away.

Anxieties

Britain had been uneasily contemplating the prospect of a war since her humiliating performance against the Boers. There was widespread agreement that the physical condition of the rank-and-file needed to be improved if the Empire was to be properly defended. The Empire was an important emblem of British superiority. What had initially been a source of cheap raw materials and ready markets was now more an attractive career outlet for public school men, and their salaries were a non-productive burden on the British tax-payer. But pride in Empire was strong – 80% of emigrants were now going to the Dominions instead of the USA – and few grudged the expense of presiding over it, still less of defending it.[29] These were facts of political life. The Liberal government was as aware of them as the Unionists had been: the radical MP Josiah Wedgwood, commented acidly in 1911, 'The foreign policy of the Government is . . . not merely a continuation, but . . . an accentuation, of the foreign policy of our predecessors.'[30] The cost of the eight battleships demanded by popular clamour following rumours of German naval expansion had inflated the notorious 1909 Budget as much as the new old-age pensions.

A succession of international incidents made it clear that Germany, inspired by Kaiser Wilhelm II's dreams of making her a world power, was now by far the greatest menace. Asquith's government, forsaking traditional principles, had reorganised the Army, focusing on possible deployment in Europe. The government was opposed to compulsory national service – much too serious an infringement of the liberty of the subject – but had founded the Territorial Army and now urged the National Rifle Association to inject greater realism into its sporting activities, such as firing at figure-shaped targets. It was rather like a boxer preparing for a fight by taking occasional strolls in the park, but scaremongering was best left to the popular press.[31]

Germany was not only a military threat but an economic one. Britain's share of world trade, some 30%, was still the biggest, but it was diminishing. Germany had been putting up protective tariffs since 1879 and her industry had flourished mightily behind them. As country after country had followed Germany's lead, exporting had grown harder for Britain and imports more expensive. This was a vote-losing situation, yet government intervention in industrial matters was an alien concept, literally and metaphorically. The arch-exponents of state intervention were the Germans. The British wanted no such jack-booted oppression, preferring to rely on free enterprise and competition. In consequence industry embarked on a series of expedients, some more successful than others, selling whatever was to hand without much regard to added value. Exporting coal, for instance, though it brought great prosperity (and many English immigrants) to South Wales, provided fuel for foreign factories to turn out mass-produced goods at highly competitive prices. Exporting textile machinery brought a flood of Asian cotton goods that undercut Lancashire's own.

Despite the complacent assumption that British manufacture was best, industry was often held in low esteem even by its own leaders. The activities over which they presided were seen as a mere source of income rather than an important and inspiring way of life. The rejection of industrial values in favour of rural myths, supported by the liberal and humane studies of the public schools and older universities, left Britain ill-equipped to meet the challenges of the future. Technology and applied science, on which industrial development depended, had distinctly inferior social connotations. Samuel Smiles and self-help had, in the end, proved less compelling than Matthew Arnold's vision of sweetness and light. Amongst the proliferating professional classes that had begun to dominate British society the two decades from 1891 to 1911 brought a sharp increase in the number of actors, authors, editors and journalists, and a decline in the number of civil engineers. Aesthetic yearnings apart, the growing distaste for industry often simply indicated the discovery that there were more congenial ways of making money: the number of stockbrokers also rose by some 220%.[32]

Family tradition, gentrification, the easier paths of capital investment and the pervasive anti-industrial culture stifled innovation. There were equally conservative, not to say reactionary attitudes amongst the workers. The most skilled, whose privileged position was buttressed by a medieval craft-based apprenticeship system, were seriously threatened by modern methods of production: factories were great employers of unskilled and semi-skilled labour, including women. Trade unions had assumed a new importance since the 1890s, and, as opportunity offered, they began to play their part in slowing the pace of production, with a principal objective of seeing that as many of their members as possible were employed according to established custom and practice.

In happier times the Liberal government had passed the Trade Disputes Act of 1906 restoring striking unions' old exemption from actions for damages. It was some time before the unions gathered confidence in using the legislation, but now in the heated political atmosphere they began to flex their muscles. Industrial unrest started at the end of 1910 with a series of skirmishes, unofficial stoppages and narrowly-averted strikes. Disaffected miners attacked the pit-head at Tonypandy, South Wales, and the Home Secretary, Churchill, sent in troops. That summer strikes by seamen, London carmen and dockers all brought violence in varying degrees, with savage rioting at the Liverpool docks and two men killed by the Army. A threatened national railway strike brought disorder in many parts of the country and, again, widespread use of troops.

Britain was in distinctly edgy mood by 1911 when Lloyd George introduced his remarkable National Insurance Bill, a contributory scheme to insure the working population against sickness. Humiliated by their defeat over the

Parliament Bill, the Tories had turned on their leader, Balfour. He was succeeded, amid mutterings of the need for 'direct action', by Bonar Law, a Glasgow iron-master, Canadian born of Ulster stock, fierce in his defence of the Union and in the cause of efficiency. When they could not defeat the Bill in Parliament, the Tories tried to stir up prejudice against it. 'Duchesses visited the Albert Hall to exhort the public not to "lick stamps"; mistresses organised domestic servants in the same crusade; wage-earners of every kind were urged to resist the deductions from their wages as a monstrous oppression by the government.'[33] The Bill passed and the country survived the shock, but it left its mark.

There was much other legislation in 1911, including the Shops Act which introduced the principle of a legal weekly half-holiday, a further milestone in the history of working-class leisure. But the wave of strikes, continuing into 1912, created an atmosphere of turbulence that was not conducive to social reform. The industrial unrest aroused excited anticipation amongst international revolutionaries that the British worker was at last rising from his torpor to shake off the shackles of capitalism. Lenin, writing from exile in Switzerland, broke the good news to the readers of *Pravda*: 'Since the miners' strike the British proletariat is no longer the same. The workers have learned to fight.'[34] But the miners, having secured a guaranteed minimum wage, returned to work, disconsolate and divided, and when the dockers, trying to repeat their success of the previous year, found a pretext to strike, they achieved nothing except public hostility, and were obliged to surrender.

Not all the proletariat engaged in industrial strife, let alone class warfare. The young Neville Cardus, born in the slums of Manchester and a professed socialist, was sustained less by Marxist or even Fabian notions of future plenty than by an Arcadian vision of a disappearing but still reclaimable Britain. 'In 1911,' Cardus recalled, 'I reached the age of twenty-one. My income was one pound weekly from marine insurance.'[35] He was not complaining. Rather than toiling to achieve a niche in the commercial world his first priority had been to make up for his lack of formal education by reading, always voraciously and latterly systematically, in pursuit of a 'cultural scheme'. A pound a week, furthermore, was enough to allow regular visits to the theatre and to concerts at the Free Trade Hall. And when, improbably, he was offered the post of assistant cricket professional to Shrewsbury School at £2 10s a week for the summer term he saw it as a chance of saving money. 'I could live in Shrewsbury on a pound a week and put the rest into the post office savings bank. By the end of the term I would have accumulated at least £18. I would have capital on which to fall back when summer had gone and I had to return to Manchester. Why, with £18 I would safely be able to launch into literature and music as a full-time winter study and occupation.'

This frugal project was so successful that it lasted five years. Apart from the light it casts on what it was possible to do in those distant days on a restricted budget, Cardus's Shrewsbury venture is of rich social interest. The cricket professionals, appointed by the captain of the XI not the school authorities, occupied a lowly place in the scheme of things. William Attewell, who had played a dozen times for England and made three Australian tours, was required not only to coach but to mark out the pitches and perform similar chores. The qualities Cardus admired in Attewell were those of the cricketing rustics employed by the great patrons of the eighteenth century: 'he had the soil in him and without the slightest loss of dignity he would raise a forefinger and say, "Mornin', sir" to any boy of Shrewsbury School, senior or junior, that he chanced to meet on a walk'. Conversely the boys addressed him as Attewell, which – according to Cardus – was also a mark of respect, acknowledging the feudal bargain.

Cardus loved it. 'To have lived at Shrewsbury in those days and known cricket there is to have lived in a heaven down here below.' It was a pre-industrial heaven, part of the enduring rural myth that enshrined cricket as one of the abiding English verities. Attewell 'belonged to a world gone for ever . . . he spoke with a cadence almost scriptural'. By contrast his successor, the worldly Ted Wainwright, only four years younger, was a modern, urban interloper, who placed bets on horses and spent his evenings getting drunk with the school's drill-sergeant and his Sunday mornings smoking cigarettes with the older boys. Cardus himself, of course, smoked a pipe. 'I bought a tobacco jar from Pelican Snelsen, and two or three cheap briars to keep company with my Dunhill. I bought a pipe-rack. In short, I was a growing young man of the period. And there has never been a period so good for a young man to live in.'

Cricket, the microcosm

It was natural that Cardus, who was otherwise no sportsman, should love cricket. The game, at its highest level, was characterised by the control exercised by former players, frozen in the attitudes of the past. Gentlemen and players were still the official terms for amateurs and professionals. Modern organisations like the Amateur Rowing Association and the Rugby Football Union had crudely cast out people who played for money but in cricket they were part of a hierarchy. The Marylebone Cricket Club, its governing body, was, like the Jockey Club, a private club founded in the eighteenth century. Its *éminence grise*, Lord Harris, a former colonial administrator, set its autocratic tone. He was an eloquent rationaliser of social distinctions and racial pre-judice. Even more reactionary, and still captaining Yorkshire at the age of 50, was his ally, Lord Hawke, who did nothing with his life other than play cricket or pontificate about it.

There had been some shift of outlook within MCC, though not in their attitude towards the professionals on whom they depended. In the past they had been a frivolous crowd, not fully aware of the burden of leadership they carried as the game had become the emblem of British sporting values and the cornerstone of Empire. Now under Harris's influence they took their imperial responsibilities seriously. This showed in the management and leadership of Australian touring teams, which had been wrested from the clutches of, first, entrepreneurial professionals like Arthur Shrewsbury and, more recently, the irresponsible 'shamateur' A. C. Maclaren.[36] Harris and Hawke also had a potential successor, both as touring captain and later as administrator waiting in the wings. P. F. Warner, of colonial governing stock, had all the right attitudes and made the right noises, and even though he was a prolific journalist, he was discretion personified. That was what mattered in cricket.

The county structure, which was its glory, had been consolidated by the early railways, and nothing much had changed ever since. Its hours of play, the length of games and its precarious finances were determined by the wishes and social prejudices of county members, mostly retired or belonging to the leisured liberal professions. Their subscriptions, though beyond the working-class purse, were no more than a guinea or two. Yet despite the growing importance of gate-money in the face of competition from league cricket in the north and midlands the views of those who paid at the turnstiles was little considered. What chiefly drew the crowds was success and cricketers, above all, were supposed to care more about the game than winning or losing. It was marginally more acceptable that the undiscriminating masses liked to see rapid scoring, because it was the gentlemen who, according to the mythology, were best able to provide it, whilst the professionals whose livelihood was at stake were more prudently preoccupied with their averages.

The golden age of the amateur was not yet over. Mr F. R. Foster, the founder of Warwickshire's fortunes, scored 305 in four hours twenty minutes in 1914. And there were still some characters even amongst the professionals. George Gunn, the Nottinghamshire batsman, was quite unpredictable. *Wisden* records that in the match against Yorkshire in June 1913, in the first innings he was at the wicket six hours for his 132, but in the second 'he scored 109 out of 129 by most dazzling cricket'. He made such variations not only to suit the state of the game, but according to how he felt, and would sometimes make a quick half-century and join Mrs Gunn in a deck-chair in the sun rather than improve his average. Another Nottinghamshire professional produced the most astonishing feat of all, on 20 May 1911. Ted Alletson was a mediocre player who found it hard to keep his place in the team. On this occasion with his side almost beaten by an innings, Alletson, after a shaky start scored 48 in the fifty minutes before lunch, and then in the afternoon crashed the bowling about for another 142 in forty minutes.

It was his only achievement, and sadly but characteristically, there was only a handful of spectators there to see it. Hours of play apart, it took a special kind of temperament to enjoy watching cricket. County cricket, in which inconclusiveness was endemic, was much more read about than watched. Yet its custodians guarded it with supercilious disdain for its detractors and fierce determination not to have it changed. The editor of *Wisden*, S. H. Pardon, who took its sobriquet, 'The Cricketer's Bible', very seriously, was scornful of the distinguished Australian F. R. Spofforth's suggestion, after the disastrous season of 1911, that to enliven matters two runs be awarded to the fielding side for every maiden over bowled. 'Never, I should think has such an absurd proposition been put forward by a first-rate expert . . . Cricket does not stand in need of alterations. When played in the proper spirit . . . the game is as good as ever it was. It must not be tampered with to please people who think that it can have the concentrated excitement of an hour-and-a-half's football.'[37]

In 1914, at a dinner given by MCC to mark the centenary of their Lord's ground, Lord Hawke dismissed any suggestion that cricket was losing popularity. It was true that twenty years before cricket had not had to face the rivalry of golf and lawn tennis, 'but twenty years ago there were only eight first-class counties, whereas there are now sixteen. This showed that the national game was progressing and still enjoyed a fair share of public support.'[38] In fact some of the 16 got markedly more of it than others. The richer counties naturally saw no need to subsidise the weaker ones, which consequently existed in a state of genteel poverty. A small share of Test match takings could help to ease the pain but the majority lived on the edge of extinction. *The Times* had greeted the season with apprehension: 'Unfortunately there does not seem to be the same "county spirit" as there used to be. Perhaps it is owing to the fact that people have to work more strenuously than they did 20 years ago.' Yet all was not lost. 'Cricket as a game can never die while we have our public schools and universities. It will be the national game for many years because the men who have played it and supported it will wish their sons to do the same.'[39]

These same men and their sons were the pillars of MCC and the counties. It was taken for granted that county captains must be gentlemen – technically speaking. This stemmed from a belief in the indefinable something conferred by a public school education, and was rationalised by arguing that professional captains would be unable and unwilling to exercise the necessary authority over their fellow-workers. Some of the appointments were risible.

Yorkshire was by far the leading county. But when Lord Hawke retired in 1910 their illustrious professionals were led first by Sir Everard Radcliffe who had a derisory batting average and took 2 wickets at a cost of 67 each, and then by Sir Archibald White who batted at number 10 and did not bowl.

Even when amateur captains were effective players the public school spirit did not always shine through strongly. The Essex captain, J. W. H. T. Douglas, the 1908 Olympic middleweight boxing champion, was as combative on the field as in the ring. He is reputed to have got the job because his father Johnny Douglas, ABA pioneer and NSC stalwart, held the mortgage on the Leyton ground. As a county captain, a more gentlemanly contemporary declared, Douglas was 'not only bad but brutal, almost incredible in his ruthlessness'; he 'entirely ruined Hipkin as a player by bullying him' and told two others who were off sick, 'I don't care if you suffer the pangs of hell while you are unfit to turn out for the county.'[40] He became an England captain nevertheless, filling in for the stricken P. F. Warner on the Australian tour of 1911–12, winning the series but falling short on the social graces – 'I can't make a speech, but I will box any man in the room three rounds' – and led the team to triumph again in 1913–14 against South Africa.

Warner himself in his customary book about the tour was more concerned with its spiritual benefits: 'Cricket has become more than a game. It is an institution, a passion, one might say a religion . . . And in these days when cricket has become the interest of the whole Empire, whither should the Empire turn for guidance but to the club which has grown up with the game, which has fostered it, and which has endeavoured to preserve its best traditions? And it is the wish of every true cricketer that the MCC should so continue to conduct its affairs that it may always remain not only the trustee but the mother of cricket.'[41] The 'white man's burden' was carried to the extent of receiving an Indian team led and financed by the Maharajah of Patiala in 1911 and sending an undistinguished MCC party to the West Indies in 1912–13 but the favoured nation was racially-segregated South Africa. England toured there in 1909–10 and Australia went the following winter. In 1912 came a Triangular Tournament between England Australia and South Africa. This was the brainchild of the financier and politician Sir Abe Bailey whose hospitality also cheered the MCC tourists of 1913–14. The Imperial Cricket Conference set up between the three countries to organise the 1912 tournament stayed in being as the body controlling international cricket and was not enlarged until 1926.[42]

MCC were equally self-congratulatory and self-deluding over their domestic policies. Lord Hawke had drawn applause at the Lord's centenary dinner when he declared cricket 'the true democracy'. The few professionals invited – men like Jack Hobbs and George Hirst, who for all their distinction knew their place – no doubt regarded their very presence at such a gathering as confirmation of his point. One who was not present was Sidney Barnes, the greatest bowler of his day, who had taken himself back to league cricket. This was no revolutionary anarchical protest but a hard economic decision: his basic concern was to secure regular year-round employment. Even after he left the first-class county scene his genius was such that MCC, in a spirit of enlightened self-interest, had continued to call on him for Test matches. With F. R. Foster, who could bowl as well as bat, Barnes was largely responsible for England's regaining the Ashes in 1911–12. He was a considerable force in the Triangular Tournament with Australia and South Africa in 1912, and the following winter went on MCC's tour of South Africa. But there he showed himself deplorably lacking in the feudal spirit. He was unplayable – until in the Final Test he announced himself 'unavailable' when the financial sponsorship he had been promised failed to materialise. What could you do with a fellow like that? It was simply not playing the game.

Notes

1 Even this excluded 33% of men in England and Wales, 40% in Scotland and 50% in Ireland, a rough measure of the relative prosperity of the mass of people in the three parts of the realm – and, of course, it excluded 100% of women everywhere.
2 The word 'English' was used indiscriminately by almost all until comparatively recently, to refer to British, and even Irish, people as well as the English specifically. This reflected centuries of English domination and was usually, when so applied, intended either neutrally and unreflectingly or to confer a compliment on the non-English British.
3 O. Morehead, *Dictionary of National Biography*, 1931–40.
4 ibid.
5 H. Nicolson, *Diaries and Letters*, London, 1966, p. 53.
6 D. Cannadine, *The Decline and Fall of the British Aristocracy*, London, 1992, p. 369.
7 S. Duncan and G. Thorne, *The Complete Wildfowler*, London, 1911, p. 17.
8 J. Lowerson, *Sport and the English Middle Classes*, Manchester, 1993, pp. 40–1.
9 ibid., p. 51.
10 In the event Lipton's new boat *Shamrock IV* was caught in mid-Atlantic by the outbreak of war.
11 Lowerson, *Middle Classes*, pp. 51–2, is a succinct account of the expansion of the sport amongst the middle classes.
12 *Yachting Monthly*, 75th Birthday issue, June 1981, p. 1253.
13 E. Phillips, 'Angling as a Sport for Ladies', *Baily's Magazine*, July. 1906, quoted by Lowerson, *Middle Classes*, p. 210.
14 J. Lowerson, 'Brothers of the Angle' in J. A. Mangan (ed.), *Pleasure, Profit and Proselytism*, London, 1988, p. 119. It is worth noting, however, that Homer's Greeks at Patroclus' funeral games competed for highly utilitarian prizes, such as cooking pots, lumps of iron – and women (whose value was measured in terms of livestock).
15 *D.N.B.*, loc. cit.
16 Duke of Windsor, *Family Album*, London, 1960, p. 61.
17 ibid., p. 62.

18 Windsor, *Album*, p. 63.
19 S. Sassoon, *Memoirs of a Fox-hunting Man*, London, 1928: for the Edwardian period see D. Birley, *Land of Sport and Glory*, Manchester, 1995 pp. 189–90.
20 Sassoon, *Memoirs*, pp. 241–2. The Packlestone was the real-life Atherstone, many of whose leading members also appear under pseudonyms: for example Mrs Oakfield was Mrs Inge whose father, Mr Oakley, had been Master for 20 years and Captain Hinnycraft was Captain Harry Townshend, for many years Hunt Secretary.
21 *The Lancet*, 4 April 1914, quoted in K. E. McCrone, *Sport and the Physical Emancipation of English Women*, London, 1988, p. 201.
22 Sassoon, *Memoirs*, pp. 248–260.
23 See *Baily's Hunting Directory*, 1914–15, for an account of the progress made.
24 P. Willett in M. Seth-Smith et al., *The History of Steeplechasing*, London, 1966, p. 73.
25 In 1931, shortly after his return, he won the Grand National again. Coulthwaite, a Lancashire man, was an unusual trainer: he had never sat on a horse in his life but had started out as an athletics coach.
26 Miss Davison was still living at that time.
27 The full text of the telegram, together with an account of the episode by M. Seth-Smith, *A Classic Connection*, London, 1983, is given in *The Turf*, ed. J. Hislop and D. Swannell, London, 1990, pp. 226–9.
28 D. Laird, *Royal Ascot*, London, 1976, p. 180.
29 It had, in fact, as Kipling pointed out, been the Dominions who had saved the Old Country's skin in the Boer War – 'ye fawned on the Younger Nations for the men who could shoot and ride!' *The Islanders*, 1902.
30 Quoted in R. Shannon, *The Crisis of Imperialism, 1865–1915*, St Albans, 1976, p. 408.
31 For the phenomenon see A. J. Morris, *The Scaremongers*, London, 1984.
32 See the revealing table in Lowerson, *Middle Classes*, p. 7.
33 R. K. Ensor, *England 1870–1914*, Oxford, 1936, p. 445.
34 Quoted in P. Thompson, *The Edwardians*, St Albans, 1977, p. 256.
35 N. Cardus, *Autobiography*, London, 1955 edn., p. 54 et seq.
36 The transition is described in the two earlier volumes in this series, D. Birley, *Sport and the Making of Britain*, Manchester, 1993, esp. Chapter Fifteen, and *Land of Sport and Glory*, pp. 16–23, 260–3.
37 *Wisden*, 1912, extract in B. Green, *Wisden Anthology (1900–1940)*, London, 1980, p. 427.
38 ibid., pp. 281–2.
39 F. B. Wilson, 4 May 1914, reprinted in M. Williams (ed.), *Double Century*, London, 1985, pp. 184–5.
40 Sir Home Gordon, *Background of Cricket*, London, 1939, pp. 172–3.
41 P. F. Warner, *England v Australia*, London, 1912, pp. 17–19.
42 India, the West Indies and New Zealand were all admitted in 1926. The ICC lasted longer than the Empire itself. When its name was changed to the International Cricket Conference in 1965 it signified that the end had come, even for cricketers.

CHAPTER TWO

Before the deluge

The notion of playing the game was inextricably linked, in establishment minds, with the preservation of gentlemanly standards. In cricket the connection was implied by the convention of amateur captaincy. Other sports made the point explicitly by excluding professionals from competition. The most fastidious were the rowing men who rejected them even as coaches.

Old sports and the New World

The élitism of amateur rowing in Britain stemmed from its honoured place in the oldest public schools. At Eton, which was the foremost, the 'wet bobs' outranked the cricketing 'dry bobs'. The pre-eminence of the Royal Regatta at Henley-on-Thames was based on the support of the leading public schools and of Oxford and Cambridge, where rowing was the most admired athletic activity in an age of athleticism. This powerful tradition explained the Amateur Rowing Association's ruthless translation of the old term, gentleman, into the modern one, amateur, with the aid of regulations that kept out artisans as well as professionals, just to be on the safe side. Despite protests from the rabble-rousing press and pleas from woolly-minded idealists the ARA had stood firm behind the line of duty. The rival NARA, with its marginally more liberal views, was resolutely kept at arm's length.

Few foreign associations could satisfy Henley's exacting standards of purity – certainly not the Americans – and the International Olympic Committee was regarded with grave suspicion. When the Games had been held in England in 1908,[1] the ARA had been at hand to make sure the barricades were properly manned, but there was no telling what might happen when the regatta was held abroad. British rowing had suffered one or two dents to its pride recently, mostly at the hands of colonials, and there were those who thought the Olympics best left alone.[2] The ARA's hostility had been stirred up again early in 1912 by the talk in the press of getting up a public subscription to help fund the British team for the forthcoming Games at Stockholm. It was an additional annoyance that much of the talk came from the most prominent British representative on the IOC, the chauvinistic T. A. (later Sir Theodore) Cook, a Radley and Oxford oarsman. Cook, who was a journalist,[3] saw no reason why amateurism could not be reconciled with public or even commercial sponsorship, provided the money was put to the general good, not that of individual athletes. Incensed by such dangerous talk the ARA had felt obliged to issue a statement condemning 'the efforts . . . being made in other branches of athletics to raise funds by public subscription for the expenses and training of competitors' and making clear that any such dabbling with professionalism would be contrary to ARA rules.[4]

It was a matter of honour that the ARA should compete, however, and virtue was rewarded by the triumph in the eights of Leander, the élite Oxbridge club that represented Britain, with New College, Oxford, second. They did not mind that a German crew beat Thames RC in the coxed fours – the eights were what mattered. The only other rowing competition at Stockholm provided an easy victory for the British sculler William Kinnear, but this branch of the sport was even less regarded. It had never had the social cachet of team rowing and in the past had proved a source of gambling and skulduggery. Professional oarsmen, furthermore, had found an outlet for their talents in sculling, which had always had a distinct, if limited, appeal to the public, especially those who liked a bet. This was the heyday of the suave and accomplished Ernest Barry, 'world' champion and hero of many battles against Australian counterparts and local rivals. Barry and his kind were kept out of amateur rowing not just as performers but also as coaches. Consequently they were obliged to take their talents abroad where the corrupting effect of the professional was not so greatly feared.

After Stockholm, to the ARA's chagrin, the British Olympic Committee, at Cook's instigation, called for an immediate start at raising the £100,000 it reckoned would be needed to sustain an effective British team at the next Games, scheduled for 1916 in Berlin. The ARA, who had already informed the IOC that it could not 'bind itself to send crews to compete at the next or any further Olympics', felt obliged to repeat its earlier warning about the moral dangers of raising funds by public subscription. In the heated debate that followed Cook found some support, including that of Sir Arthur Conan Doyle, but a prominent member of the 1908 Olympic eight, Guy Nickalls, and the secretary of the ARA, R. C. Lehmann, indicated that their own preference would be to have nothing more to do with the Olympic movement.[5]

It did not help when in 1913 the Fédération Internationale des Sociétés d'Avirons, the self-styled international body that the ARA ignored, told the IOC that it the regarded the NARA as 'the only *bona fide* English organisation whose laws were compatible with theirs'.[6] The ARA felt no obligation to bother with these obscure international regattas. Everyone knew that their own were in a class by themselves. When Leander took the Henley Grand in 1913 it was a demonstration of the greatest club in the world winning the greatest competition. They were in for a shock the following year when a Harvard University eight gave Independence Day an extra fillip. A mock-obituary appeared in *The Times*: 'In loving memory of British Rowing, which passed away at Henley on Saturday July 4th. Deeply lamented by many sorrowing followers.'[7]

American track and field athletes had been putting it across the British since Victorian times. The London Games of 1908 had led to intense bad feeling as a result.[8] And the Amateur Athletic Association, striving to achieve respectability in its hopelessly divided and socially-mixed empire, shared the ARA's suspicion of the Olympic movement, which had clearly become a springboard for aspiring professionals.[9] The fundamental difference between the British approach and that of the Americans was explained in 1912 by Philip Noel-Baker, President of the Cambridge University Athletic Club: 'The American athlete specialises in one or two events; before any race of great importance he devotes most of his time to his training; he has a coach – often a professional.'[10]

This was entirely contrary to the conventional British outlook which favoured the all-rounder and found over-specialisation vulgar and somewhat freakish. For specialised training and professional coaching of that sort you had to go to the harriers clubs, which were manifestly not for gentlemen. (The South African winner of the London Olympics had been tuned up for the task by Sam Mussabini at the Regent Street Polytechnic, the great liberator of the lower middle classes, which not only supported the ideals of the NARA in rowing, but ran a thriving Harriers athletics club.) And the ARA set no store by field events, in which specialised coaching was essential. The Amateur Field Events Association, founded in 1910, had Sir Arthur Conan Doyle as its President and the fanatical F. A. M. Webster as its driving force, but it made little headway.

Another transatlantic characteristic noted by Noel-Baker was that the American athlete was backed by 'an organization . . . managed by paid organizers . . . supported by a reasonable amount of money'. He regarded this as dangerous: money might be the basis of horse-racing or cricket, but the result was to turn sport into a commercial enterprise. Noel-Baker, unlike many fervent amateurs, was no hypocrite, but an unusually starry-eyed idealist, who still had hopes for the Olympic ideal. Other devotees, notably T. A. Cook, wanted the best possible team for the forthcoming games in Stockholm, and thought public subscription the best way of getting it. The AAA, though torn, took its lead from the ARA. As a result there was a depleted and somewhat dispirited British entry, sustained by little money and very mixed ideals.

The two extremes in the AAA camp were exemplified by the only two gold medals won on the track. Mussabini and the Polytechnic had produced the two greatest sprinters of the time, Vic D'Arcy and Willie Applegarth, and both were members of the British team that won the sprint relay. The other gold medallist, Arnold Strode-Jackson, who won the mile, was the archetypal gentleman amateur. He was an Oxford man who had taken up athletics on the advice of his uncle, Clement Jackson, co-founder of the AAA, in preference to the stern routines of rowing. His attitude to training was casual – he preferred golf, country walks and massage – and, again on uncle's advice, 'invariably had a glass of Guinness for lunch and a nice glass of Burgundy for dinner'.[11]

Philip Noel-Baker, in sixth place behind Strode-Jackson, evinced a characteristic more talked about than seen, for he actually did love sport more for the joy of competing than merely winning. This fortified him against the dismal outcome. What the highly-organised Americans did not win – which was very little – obscure Scandinavians did. So far from being depressed, Noel-Baker was captivated by what he saw as the long-delayed efflorescence of the true Olympian spirit. It was 'an enchantment', an experience that convinced him of the need to work for international peace. 'We went to Stockholm', he wrote, 'as British athletes. We came home Olympians, disciples of the leader, Coubertin, with a new vision which I never lost.' Whereas the incidents of 1908 had been seized upon by the 'vultures of the chauvinist press', Stockholm produced nothing 'to allow disloyal critics to pretend that quarrels had occurred . . . The endemic hostility which for twenty years had been a festering sore was temporarily silenced.'[12] The emotion that mixed his metaphors no doubt also clouded his recollection. Amongst the milder chauvinistic reactions was that of The Times which saw the British performance as not only a failure, but an inglorious one, adding, 'and [we] have failed not because we lack first-class material . . . but because of our hopelessly incompetent management and lack of organisation'.[13]

Stockholm, Noel-Baker afterwards reckoned, 'gave a golden glamour to the Games in the eyes of all men in every land'.[14] The gold was more important than the glamour to those with their way to make in the world. In 1914, Willie Applegarth, by then at his peak, turned professional. There were other disadvantages from fanning the flames of international competition. After Stockholm the IOC ruled that henceforth only nationally-sponsored competitors could enter. This had some undesirable consequences, as we shall see. It also had domestic implications. Great Britain was allowed only one team not four. An International Amateur Athletics Federation was founded in 1912 on the same basis and the AAA, which affiliated to it in 1914 (and was thus no longer the premier rule-making body) retained a domination in British team selection that was to lead to future disharmony.

The British had no chance to compensate for their miseries on the Stockholm track in the indigenous team games like hockey and rugby that they had staged in London. One, boxing, which Britain had pioneered as an amateur sport, was not even permitted under Swedish law. The fervour of the ABA was undiminished, for it was making good progress at home. It was expanding steadily, with competition at every level, graduated according to weight and age, taking in more and more working-class clubs and boxers, but taking good care to protect them from contamination by professionalism. They were in little danger. The world of the pros was one apart, with different, more demanding rules that added a technical barrier to the social one. It was a rare event for an amateur to make the change and even rarer for one to make a success of it.[15]

The ladder of opportunity in the professional game was quite a different one from that of the ABA, often beginning in fairground booths or back street halls. At its pinnacle was the fashionable National Sporting Club, presided over by the Earl of Lonsdale, smoking huge cigars, expansive in white tie and tails. The aficionados, intensely grateful for Lonsdale's efforts to legalise professional boxing in its gloved, Queensberry rules reincarnation, adored him as much as the populace – a gallery to which he shamelessly played. By this time the NSC's purses rarely attracted the best heavyweights, especially the Americans, and the two outstanding performers, both outright winners of the coveted Lonsdale belt, were little men. The flyweight, 'Peerless Jim' Driscoll, of Welsh–Irish Catholic ancestry and Cardiff dockland upbringing, was a natural stylist with the courage of a lion and fiercely British – just what the crowds loved. He had fought a 'no-decision' contest with the world champion in the United States but could never get the Americans to chance their arms at the NSC. The cool and calculating lightweight Freddie Welsh, son of a Pontypridd auctioneer, was a different animal. A physical culture fanatic, he was given to wearing sombreros and long black coats and even to reading books – not at all the stereotype of the Celtic battler. Born Thomas, he had changed his name to establish his ethnic credentials, but he was soon evincing American leanings – and an accent to match. He knew, however, that the States was no place for foreigners to win titles and after failing to get the champion into the ring in Canada was biding his time back home.[16]

But it was the heavyweights who commanded most attention – and most money. Some optimists still had high hopes of the stylish former Bombardier, Billy Wells. Film cameras, the latest novelty, added to the excitement in January 1911, when Wells was the 20–1 favourite to beat 'Gunner' Moir, a crude fellow who spoilt the evening for Wells's fans – many of them ladies – by knocking him out in three rounds. Nevertheless three months later Wells managed to stay on his feet long enough to knock out the British champion, 'Iron' Hague, and a Lancashire businessman decided to put him in the ring against Jack Johnson, the formidable, black champion of the world. It was scarcely to be expected that Wells would prove to be the 'white hope' everyone was seeking. Lord Lonsdale, who along with many traditionalists objected to boxing being taken over by businessmen with no background in the sport, protested on the very cogent grounds that Wells had no chance. But the public's imagination had been caught. The purses were said to be enormous, £6,000 for the champion and £2,000 for Wells. The Empress Hall, Earl's Court, could have been filled twice over. Respectable opinion was outraged. The Free Church Council led the opposition, objecting that the spectacle would be repulsive, the more so since it was to be filmed. The LCC threatened to rescind the Empress Hall's entertainment licence, and finally the landlords, the Metropolitan Railway Company, got a court order and the show was cancelled.[17]

The following year Wells's backers sent him off to the States to prove his worth. Disappointment rather than surprise greeted his return after one win and two crushing defeats: 'Gunboat' Smith, having been outboxed for five minutes, flattened him in the sixth. But Wells's fans adored him still, and if they had to accept that he was vulnerable to forthright transatlantic tactics, he was still the best man in England. No-one even remotely considered the possibility that he would be obliged to bow the knee to a Frenchman. It seemed likely to be a mere exhibition match when at the Brussels Exhibition of 1913 he fought an unknown youngster, much smaller than himself, Georges Carpentier. Wells appeared to have won by a knockout in the first round, but the referee, presumably wanting to give the crowd a little more entertainment, stayed his hand. So, alas, did the gentlemanly Wells, allowing Carpentier time to recover. A member of the NSC offered, at this point, £1,000 to £3 on Wells, but found no takers. Then in the third round the Frenchman worked his way inside Wells's classical guard and pummelled him in the stomach, softening him up appreciably; and in the fourth he knocked him out.

This was not only a setback for Wells but a great blow to British pride, and everyone felt sure that he would redeem the national honour in the return match at the NSC a few weeks later. Tickets were eagerly sought. Five-guinea ring-side seats fetched 75 guineas. The purchasers did not see much for their money. Wells seemed a quivering jelly even before a blow had been struck, and it took Carpentier only 73 seconds to dispose of him. The crowd were aghast not only by their champion's defeat but by the manner of it. 'Peerless Jim' Driscoll leapt into the ring yelling 'Coward' at the stricken Bombardier before dissolving into tears of shame and rage. The day was saved by Lord Lonsdale who climbed up after Driscoll and gently led him back to his seat.

The boos turned to thunderous cheers for 'Lordy' and the bulldog spirit of old England that he exemplified.

Professional boxing still had an ambiguous legal status. Deaths in the ring had not ceased (for instance, 'Curly' Watson was killed at one of the regular promotions at the distinctly down-market Wonderland in the East End in a bout with the black West Indian, Frank English) and before the Wells–Carpentier fight a police inspector visited both boxers' dressing rooms to issue a formal warning against taking part in a contest that might lead to a charge of manslaughter. A year later a scheduled contest between Jim Driscoll and Owen Moran, the pride of Birmingham, was actually banned as likely to cause a breach of the peace. Lord Lonsdale briefed Marshall Hall, the most celebrated defence lawyer of the day, to appeal. This time the great advocate, who had fended off earlier attempts at interference, was unsuccessful, but the Crown, having won a technical victory, decided to withdraw its objections. The fight itself was a disappointing anti-climax, but it was an historic encounter nevertheless for the law made no more interventions. The spoils of victory went not to the gentlemanly NSC but to the entrepreneurs and money men. It was at the utterly commercial Olympia that the crafty Freddie Welsh made his breakthrough at last. The American champion Willie Ritchie had been lured to Britain by the prospects of the huge gate and Welsh's offer to fight for expenses only. On 7 July 1914, Welsh delighted the thousands of his fellow-countrymen who travelled up to London to see him by giving them the world championship they craved.

Less manly pleasures

Worries about Britain's waning prestige in the boxing ring were part of a wider concern. Many traditionalists were convinced that the decline in the nation's physique, and hence its capacity to defend the Empire, was due to the popularity of the sybaritic suburban recreations that had swept the country in recent years. Golf, the foremost among them, was an emblem of the stockbroker luxury that was eroding the old, virile values. It conferred none of the benefits of public school muscular Christianity – team-work, hard physical challenge, opportunities for leadership – and was manifestly useless for any of the challenges of life. Defence of Empire apart what was it doing to the country's economy? In 1910 the *Saturday Review* complained that businessmen, following the example of the government itself, were consumed by the passion for golf, and prophesied that 'the Waterloo or Trafalgar of commerce' would be lost on the nation's playing fields.[18] And there was great concern about the spread of Sunday golf. One-third of English courses openly advertised Sunday play, many of them corrupting caddies by offering employment.[19]

The Scots, who did not yet profane the Sabbath in this way, saw this as the inevitable result of Anglicisation. There had been nothing wrong with golf until the Sassenachs took it up: but in the Edwardian upsurge of enthusiasm for what had once been their game the English had substituted opulence for more characteristically Scottish virtues. There were Scottish sybarites, too, but it was undoubtedly London, the Home Counties and the south-east that had begun to set the pace, creating 'ideal' golf conditions artificially and securing exclusivity in a variety of ingenious and expensive ways.[20] The most notorious was Prince's Mitcham, whose founder Henry Mallaby-Deeley MP shamelessly used his position as chairman of the local Conservation Committee to protect it from intrusion by other users of the Common on which the course was laid. In the latest of a long series of legal battles the High Court in 1914 upheld the club's right to privileged treatment.[21] At St George's Hill, Weybridge (1912), an entrepreneurial company invested £25,000 in quest of an exclusive membership. Clubhouses were an important feature of the modern way of golf, and some imposing manorial style structures were built. Aristocrats, forced into economies by taxes, death duties and falling land prices, supplied them ready-made. In 1914 the Shirley Park Club at Croydon was based on the house and land sold to it by Lord Eldon, and the Royal Automobile Club reputedly spent £75,000 on a similar venture at Epsom.

In this stockbrokers' heaven the amateur club member reigned supreme. A decade after the Professional Golfers' Association had begun its operations the average club professional was still a species of domestic servant. At the Leeds GC in 1912 the professional, Cox, was told to be keener and pay more attention whilst giving lessons and reprimanded 'for not having kept the Ladies' Room in the Clubhouse in a clean and tidy condition (and) for smoking while talking to a Member, and was forbidden to smoke at all in the Clubhouse'.[22] And whilst some, as a result of the golf boom, were now reputed to be earning £300 a year or more, which might well exceed the remuneration of many club secretaries, this did not put them in the same social class.

Golf club secretaries were an entirely superior breed, often drawn from a public school, university or services background, who despite being paid were accorded all the privileges of the clubhouse and allowed to play in amateur competitions. For most golf professionals the biggest source of their new-found riches was likely to be the 'pro's shop', as the change from individually crafted club and ball manufacture to machine production shifted the emphasis towards retail trading. As club membership expanded, this could be highly profitable, but it could also lead to trouble for the unwary, the unadaptable or the harassed, particularly if they neglected their other duties. Such higher status as the professionals had achieved came from tournament play. A new generation was now emerging, in the aftermath of the early trail-blazing efforts of Harry Vardon, J. H. Taylor and James Braid in popularising competitive golf as a spectator sport – full-time tournament players, who lived off their winnings and the attendant endorsements of equipment, exhibitions and so forth.

No amateur had yet crossed the social divide. For gentlemen any rewards they were likely to collect were not sufficient to justify the stigma. It was much safer, and more acceptable, to enjoy the 'shamateur' profits of journalism, administration or golf architecture. Even the artisan Abe Mitchell, who made the crossing in 1913, did so partly because he felt unwelcome in the amateur ranks. He had begun his golf as a member of the Cantelupe, the artisan section of the Royal Ashdown Forest Club, where limited access to the course (but not the clubhouse) was given to working men in return for menial duties. Mitchell had been runner-up to John Ball in the Amateur Championship of 1912 but had not enjoyed the experience: 'Golf is the game of the classes in England, and . . . English amateurs consider that the artisan's place is in the professional ranks.'[23]

The Americans had so far offered no threat to the natural order of things, basically because they had not yet put their minds to mastering golf's intricacies. Their amateurs were certainly no match for such experienced 'shamateurs' as John Ball and Harold Hilton. They ruled the roost in Britain and Hilton went across to play in, and therefore win, the American Amateur in 1911. American professionals were similarly unassertive. None of them won the British Open.[24] Indeed they could not hold the US title against visiting Britishers, and no native-born American won it until Johnny McDermott in 1911.[25] A different era was dawning, for the 1914 winner was Walter Hagen, a new style of professional who was to change the face of golf in the post-war world, but meanwhile there was little to disturb the Arcadian idyll.

The sight of women playing golf no longer caused anyone great pain, either. The former British Ladies' champion May Hezlet, one of three distinguished Irish golfing sisters, commented in 1912, 'Even 20 years ago a woman walking in a London street attired in a short tweed coat and skirt, thick boots and carrying a bag of clubs, attracted much undesirable attention; but nowadays a whole team could walk down Bond Street or Regent Street, and no notice would be taken.'[26] Short, when applied to skirts, was a relative term. Cecilia Leitch, the champion of 1914, who wore one twelve inches above the ground, and preferred a hair-ribbon to a hat, was still thought slightly daring. But 'Cecil', as everyone called her, had already established herself as a strong personality as well as a powerful golfer.[27] In 1910, still only 19 and entirely self-taught, she had taken part in a challenge match to test the capacity of women golfers, beating (with a handicap) Harold Hilton himself, 'a result' which was, as the *DNB* puts it, 'as much publicised on the suffragette platform as in golfing circles.'

Sportswomen themselves were rarely politically-inclined, however, and least of all golfers. They had come into a man's world, and a deeply conservative one at that, and for the most part they appreciated that their acceptance depended on preserving high standards of decorum.[28] There were as yet few separate ladies' clubs and most women golfers were content to belong to ladies' sections of men's, restricted in their privileges (perhaps, for instance, not being allowed to play at weekends), usually in return for a lower subscription. Restriction to weekdays added to the social bias: it needed half a day to play a round of golf. Lady golfers were generally discouraged from, and tended to disapprove of, the type of competition that involved publicity and public display, and the Ladies Golfing Union was sternly amateur. This did not at first preclude journalism and Cecil Leitch wrote the first of three books, *Golfing for Girls,* in 1911 when she was still only 20, but this was as much crusading for the cause of women's golf as financial gain. Most ladies' clubs or sections had male professionals, their own or shared, but there were exceptions. The early women pros like their male counterparts, were mostly from the poorer classes. Some had served as caddies which was a humble start indeed. The best, like Mrs Gordon Robertson at Prince's Ladies club, Mitcham, and Miss Lily Freemantle who went to Sunningdale Ladies' in 1911, were from professional golfing family backgrounds. A remarkable example of the 'new woman', however, was Miss D. M. Smyth, a former lady amateur who actually turned professional, lured by the exotic possibilities of Le Touquet.

Lawn tennis had blazed the trail as an impeccably decorous sporting outlet for ladies, entirely suitable for sociable mixed play, yet also a serious female sport in which neither excessive violence nor the evils of competition need impair their essential femininity. They played it in exclusive schools and colleges, on private lawns and at suburban clubs, in county matches and in tournaments at fashionable resorts. Many of the leading exponents were daughters of clergymen and doctors, symbolising its happy blend of spiritual and physical benefit. Nor were they mere tomboyish slips of girls. The Wimbledon champion, Mrs Lambert Chambers (née Dorothea Douglass, a daughter of the manse) was well into her thirties but still playing as well as ever. And, as approving parents pointed out, Mrs Lambert Chambers's dignified demeanour and dress were as impressive as her play. Her book, *Lawn Tennis for Ladies* (1910) became the standard work for a generation.

Eastbourne was now the biggest of the numerous fashionable British tournaments, but Wimbledon remained in an exclusive class of its own. It had been sullied in recent years by association with commerce, but the All-England Club, which had made the mistake of going outside gentlemanly circles for its last secretary, had since put matters right and regained the moral high ground. Its pre-eminence had bred a certain arrogance. This was distinctly galling to the Lawn Tennis Association, founded in the 1880s to try to clip All-England's wings and vainly trying ever since. The LTA had assumed legislative responsibility for the game, but All-England retained imperious control over its premier tournament – and the profits that were now beginning to accrue. All-England's current secretary, Commander Hillyard, one of the founders of the LTA, had adjusted well to his new role.

The men's game was everywhere the main attraction to spectators and the main source of complaint about 'shamateurism': covert sponsorship by equipment manufacturers, sponsored tours, expenses and even converting prizes into cash. But foreigners were believed to be the worst (the French champion Max Decugis was suspended in 1910 for converting some of his prizes into fruit and vegetables and selling them for cash). It was in the hope of putting a stop to that sort of thing that the LTA in 1913 played a leading part in the formation of the International Lawn Tennis Federation. The ILTF had its headquarters in London and most of its administration was done by the LTA, which (with the USLTA standing aloof) left the British with most of their old power, fortified by the distinctly élitist outlook of the Europeans. All-England faced a dilemma. The 'golden age' dominated by Reggie and Laurie Doherty was over, leaving a gap inadequately filled by powerful colonials and persevering British veterans of no great charismatic appeal. But exclusiveness and the sporting values Wimbledon represented were even more powerful than chauvinism.

In the absence of the stylish Norman Brookes of Australia, who could spare little time from his career as a rising civil servant, the Wimbledon glory went to the New Zealander A. J. Wilding of Cambridge University, an occasional barrister who spent most of the time he was not playing tennis scorching round the world on his motor-cycle. Wilding, hitherto best-known as a doubles player, won the Wimbledon singles in the four years 1910–13 before losing the title to Brookes who returned to beat him in 1914. The two were a formidable pair in the Davis Cup, which was now becoming a more serious affair with a wider international membership, and they had held it since 1907 against American challenge. It was a great surprise, even with Wilding absent, when the veteran British pair J. C. Parke and C. W. Dixon won in Melbourne in 1912. It was to be the only British victory for some time and when the Americans won in 1913 pessimists who foresaw a long spell in the wilderness were to be proved correct. Even the Stockholm Olympics, regarded as a very minor affair, offered no opportunity for Union Jack waving, as the organisers inconsiderately arranged the grass-court competition at the same time as Wimbledon.

Greater success might well have improved the game's image amongst the more virile public school men, who had long since christened it 'pat-ball'; now it seemed we were not even good 'pat-ball' men. To the coarse-fibred masses it was a suburban ritual, not quite so comic as golf, but equally pretentious. Municipal and charitable efforts to extend it to wider social groups as an aspect of 'rational recreation' had been sporadic. There was, furthermore, no great evidence of enthusiasm amongst the working class to take up this toffee-nosed game. Having said all this, however, lawn tennis, within its limits, was remarkably successful. It had left croquet, its predecessor on the vicarage lawn, far behind, a tiny refuge for the nostalgic. Badminton, its erstwhile rival, had done better but had not yet been driven by the passion for competition into commercialism and the cult of the individual. The All-England championships, held at the Royal Horticultural Hall from 1910, took on greater importance, but still retained their initial parochialism. Irish championships had been held since 1902 and Scottish ones began in 1911, but an annual match between England and Ireland was as international as badminton got.

Bowls, which W. G. Grace had introduced to the Crystal Palace sports complex in preference to lawn tennis, was enjoying a modest vogue, inspired by Scottish traditions of excellence in contemplative, aiming sports. But the in-fighting that accompanied its revival had emphasised its insularity. Its missionary work was also hampered by the division between northern crown green bowlers – given to tournaments, betting and professionalism – and the purists of the south. This apart, whilst bowls was dismissed as an old man's game by the muscular Christians, its historic associations made it a convenient symbol of decline for those who saw sport as a debilitating distraction. A 1912 sermon in St Paul's Cathedral complained, 'There are people who imitate Drake in playing bowls but who are not in the least prepared to follow him in routing the Armada.'[29] It was really catching on as a women's sport, however, and there was a great influx of middle-class ladies to the clubs and recreation grounds of the suburbs.

Manly pleasures – for women

Athletically-inclined Edwardian women of the upper and middle classes had been inhibited as much by their own acceptance of ancient criteria of femininity as by overt male resistance. There were limits, of course. Respectable women might watch rugger and soccer and, more dubiously, boxing: they did not take part. But by 1910 the old controversies over cycling and rational dress had ceased to rage, they were active in field sports, yachting and bourgeois activities like golf and tennis, and they could play cricket if they wished – at the risk of little worse than fairly good-humoured banter. They could even row, for recreation almost without restriction and competitively if they did not obtrude themselves, physically or metaphorically, into the waters of Oxbridge or Henley. Provincial regattas sometimes included women's races as novelties – at Evesham in 1909 a women's coxed sculling race had a sewing machine as a prize[30] – but when Durham Amateur RC half-heartedly broached the question of starting a ladies' section with the ARA in 1913 they were discouraged from proceeding further. The few separate women's clubs like the early mildly feminist Furnivall Scullers (1896) and the humbler Cecil Ladies BC on the Lea, were in the NARA camp.

The most remarkable encroachment into manly sports was in hockey. This old rustic whackabout had already been modernised as a male, impeccably amateur alternative to football when it was taken up by late Victorian girls' public schools and Oxbridge colleges, and the women who saw its possibilities had wanted to come in under the male banner. Given the cold shoulder by the Hockey Association, they had developed their own organisation, including county, regional and home international networks, and though they had been near-paranoid about avoiding publicity, commercialism and the wrong sort of competition, they had built up an enthusiastic following that by now quite over-shadowed the men's. The support was mainly female, of course, and there were still plenty of male critics, medical and lay, who thought that hockey was particularly bad for women. It produces, wrote one in 1913, 'angularities, hardens sinews, abnormally develops certain parts of the body, causes abrasions, and at times disfigurement. It thus destroys the symmetry of mould and beauty of form, produces large feet and hard, coarse hands.'[31]

There had also been concern about the excesses of the few scantily-clad bold spirits from Madame Bergman-Osterberg's Dartford College.[32] But the All-England Women's Hockey Association, acutely aware of its responsibilities, had kept such aberrations firmly in check, and with Oxbridge and the superior London college, Royal Holloway, as its standard-bearers the game had no fears for the future. Its only problem was how to spread the gospel without forsaking its utterly pure amateurism. Before the new state grammar schools had begun to make an impact there were few outlets for even lower-middle-class girls to play; and clubs accustomed to mid-week practices in winter daylight hours were not suited to those who had to work for a living. The north, as ever, was a problem. In 1910 a Ladies' Hockey League had been started in the Oldham district of Lancashire, playing regular Saturday after-noon matches on a competitive basis. In three years it had increased to 36 teams in four divisions, enough to send ripples of alarm through the com-mittee rooms of the AEWHA. In 1914 there was even a challenge match between the League and the Lancashire County team. The County won easily, but who knew what might lie ahead?

The AEWHA also had a socially-superior rival. The esoteric, utterly masculine origins of lacrosse greatly added to its charms as an emblem of progressive and exclusive education for the modern young lady. It had been taken up by Roedean and a handful of other élite schools – Wycombe Abbey, Prior's Field and a Scottish outpost, St Leonard's. The first adult women's club, the Southern Ladies, was started in 1910 by a single-minded Old Roedeanian, Audrey Beeston: by 1912 it had 50 members and employed a professional, the Scottish connection had grown into an Edinburgh Ladies' Club, and the game was gaining ground in the physical education colleges who were producing the new-style games mistresses. The Ladies' Lacrosse Association formed that year soon had seven clubs and 70 schools and colleges in membership, and internationals were being played between England, Scotland and Wales.

Although the *Hockey Field,* the official organ of the AEWHA, at first gave sisterly coverage to lacrosse, it soon came to see it as a dangerous competitor. The social rivalry discouraged both groups from any democratic leanings they might have had, and it was the modern upstart netball, with its advantages of simplicity and economy of space, that moved to fill the gap. It quickly caught on in the 'tops' of the improved elementary school system, in the YWCA and in clubs for working-class and lower-professional young women. The Ling Association, which had adapted netball from the American original, had been formed at Dartford College, but its populist leanings received little encouragement from Madame Bergman-Osterberg. Nor did its Vice-President Margaret Stansfield, one of Madame's former assistants who had set up her own college in Bedford: acolytes ought not to start dispensing diluted forms of the true doctrine. Nevertheless the new PE mistresses bridged a gap between the utilitarian, rather earnest, lower-middle-class gymnastic tradition and the socially superior games cult.

The leavening influence of the PE mistresses was also felt in swimming. As a male activity its great antiquity had not conferred any great social status on swimming. It suffered greatly from its association with the lavatorial architecture of 'the Baths' Victorian cities had built as an adjunct to public health and the cleansing of the poor. In the public school tradition it was less a sport than a thing aspiring 'wet bobs' had to learn. This was how it had started in the Oxbridge women's colleges, but the girls had found it agreeable in its own right, and London's Royal Holloway had scored a distinct success when it acquired a private pool. Girton at Cambridge had followed and soon regular team matches had begun. Meanwhile it had chiefly progressed, like gymnastics, at a humbler level: women students at smaller London colleges and polytechnics used public pools and competed against town clubs. Medical opinion was more supportive than usual about swimming's suitability for women – only occasional warnings about causing the heart to pump too fast during immersion were heard – and unlike hockey it was thought conducive to producing curves rather than angularities. Even so it is a minor mystery why Edwardian women should have been so ready to reveal themselves in public and their menfolk so acquiescent. The fact remains that they were, and indeed that one of Britain's rare successes in the 1912 Olympics was in women's swimming.

Competitive swimming and public exposure were not at all de Coubertin's idea of feminine activities. The trouble had begun at the London Games of 1908 when an unofficial display of gymnastics, swimming and diving had so impressed the British Olympics Committee that they made favourable reference to it in their report. Then in 1910 the International Swimming Federation agreed to allow women's events in their competitions and the way was clear for the Swedish organisers to include two women's swimming events and a diving contest in the Stockholm programme. De Coubertin appears to have been taken unawares, and over-ruled. Afterwards he referred peevishly to the dangers of encouraging an 'impractical, uninteresting, unaesthetic and indecorous feminine Olympiad' and proposed a firmer policy in future: 'the Olympic Games must be reserved for men . . . We must try to achieve the following definition: the solemn and periodic exaltation of male athleticism with internationalism as a base, loyalty as a means, art for its setting, and female applause as a reward.' [33]

Unaesthetical the Stockholm swimming may have been, but there was nothing indecorous about it: the British team were accompanied by two ladies, Mesdames Holmes and Jarvis, who acted as chaperones as well as coaches. They also had in their midst Miss Daisy Curwen, holder of the world's record for the 100 metres, who was confidently expected to take the gold medal. Whether she would have done so will never be known, for she was rushed off to hospital with appendicitis after the semi-final. It seems unlikely, however, for the honour went to the quite exceptional Miss Fanny Durack of Australia, considered a good advertisement for the curve-producing qualities of swimming, who went on to smash existing world records at all distances up to one mile. Her biggest challenge had come from the Australian Olympic selectors who had only with great reluctance agreed to pay her fare. The British triumph in the women's relay – a team event – made up for the disappointment over Daisy Curwen and for the failure of the men in everything but the water polo, a rough sport that was becoming a British specialism. Team-games, after all, were what mattered.

Irish predilections

The suffragettes, meanwhile, were playing cat and mouse with the police, achieving such notoriety as to win them support from dissidents of every stripe, including both sides in the Irish struggle. 'I did not contemplate, for winning the vote,' recalled Sylvia Pankhurst, 'a mortal struggle to overthrow the existing government by force, such as was presently developed in Ireland . . . Yet with militancy springing up on every hand, it seemed we were on the eve of great social changes and contests.'[34] Even Asquith was showing the first signs of weakening. But events in Ireland were even more pressing.

The Liberals' 1911 Home Rule Bill had not gone far enough for the extreme Nationalists and much too far for the northern Protestants. The Ulstermen, demanding at the very least partition, began demonstrating, and arming themselves, seeking to convince the government that they would fight if Dublin rule were imposed. They found a leader in the Liberal Unionist Sir Edward Carson and new support in England. The government persevered but when in 1913 the Commons twice passed a new Home Rule Bill the Lords twice rejected it. A third Commons vote would have seen it through automatically under the new dispensation, but 'private armies' were now on the march both north and south and the King, worried about the Army's loyalty if Ulster were coerced (for its officer class was rich in Ulster Protestants) urged Asquith to make concessions. Even inveterate German-watchers were more worried about the situation in Ireland than what was going on in Europe. In December 1913 Kipling wrote privately to the editor of the *Morning Post*, 'You talk of the German danger. Does it occur to you that a betrayed Ulster will repeat 1688 in the shape of a direct appeal to Germany?'[35] The following March over 50 British Army officers stationed at the Curragh resigned rather than implement government policy, and anything seemed possible.[36]

In Dublin the authorities were increasingly worried about the Gaelic Athletic Association which they regarded as a front for insurrectionist activity. After many tribulations, financial and political, the GAA had been making real headway in their promulgation of native Irish sports. The number of clubs and club members continued to grow and, equally significant, so did the number of spectators. In 1912 18,000 people saw the All-Ireland Gaelic Football Final, producing a profit of £570, a record that was to be broken two weeks later when 20,000 watched the hurling Final. In 1913 changes in the rules and reduction of the size of teams to 15 in both games made them even more attractive to watch and attendances rose even higher – 25,000 for hurling and 35,000 for football. In sporting terms this, though irksome to loyalists, was still thought merely eccentric. But there was more in it than that. Though the GAA leadership had grown less actively political and more commercially-minded there was a powerful grass-roots nationalist fervour ready to be tapped by the extremists. The ban on members playing 'imported games' and on police, militiamen and soldiers joining, reintroduced in 1906, had been sponsored by the Irish Revolutionary Brigade, a strong if shadowy influence in the movement. The ban was brought back only by 46 votes to 32, but the annual attempts to have it lifted grew weaker and weaker.

Paradoxically, the formation of the militant Irish Volunteers in 1913 took many players of Gaelic games out of action for a time, and severely damaged some clubs – Derry in the north, for instance, where Gaelic football was just beginning to forge ahead of its soccer and rugby rivals. But it was a time of much marching, drilling and brandishing of weapons amongst young sportsmen of all persuasions. At a special meeting in December, 1913, the North of Ireland Rugby Club decided 'that in view of the political crisis all matches for the second half of the season . . . be cancelled so that members who are identified with the Ulster Volunteer Force and the Unionist clubs might have more leisure to devote themselves to the work of drilling and otherwise preparing themselves for eventualities'.[37] As the crisis deepened the GAA came under more and more pressure from its radical element to stand up for the cause. By 1914 one hard-liner was complaining that in the vast majority of members 'nationalist sentiment begins and ends with the mere practice of kicking a football or striking a hurling ball'[38] The Balkan eruption found the movement torn between constitutional nationalists, who saw an Anglo-German war as an opportunity for Ireland to become united as a reward for supporting the imperial cause, and the Sinn Feiners who saw it as a providential opportunity to strike at the British enemy.

Politics and religion did not entirely determine the kind of games Irish people played, especially amongst the middle classes of the more laid-back south: Rugby had its adherents in the Catholic University College Dublin as well as the Protestant Anglophile Trinity.[39] But while class divisions influenced the choice of football code in Ireland as they did in England, the Gaelic option confused the issue mightily, particularly in rural areas. Soccer, the urban 'people's game', was strongly 'northern', socially, geographically and in a religio-political sense, but it had taken root amongst Catholic workers before the GAA had got off the ground and now the fervour of its burgeoning crowds was spiced by sectarian rivalries. Both Belfast and Derry had strongly-supported 'Celtic' soccer teams. There were similar tensions behind the scenes, complicating the protracted struggle between clubs and the Belfast-based Irish FA, which like its counterparts in Great Britain had vainly tried to stem the tide of professionalism. But the other side of the coin was that where the Gaelic dimension was not a significant factor, as in the Protestant heartland of County Antrim, the Ulster bourgeoisie regarded soccer as a plebeian intruder. Thus in 1913 a nostalgic burgher recalled bygone days when 'Ballymena town could boast a good rugby team (before) the juggernaut of the Association code drove heavily over the prostrate forms of the once enthusiastic devotees of the older game'.[40] And soon afterwards the head-master of Ballymena Academy, disenchanted like so many of his counterparts on the mainland by the sordid state of soccer, switched to rugger.

Soccer: professionalism rampant

In England meanwhile a rebel Amateur Football Association had been set up by the few remaining élite soccer clubs to try to counter the increasing influence of professionalism in the FA. It did not survive, basically because amateurism as these purists envisaged it could no longer exist at the highest level. N. L. Jackson, founder of the Corinthians, who had been delighted by this latter-day show of spirit, was soon disillusioned, commenting sourly that 'unfortunately many so-called amateurs (i.e. amateur clubs) were not loyal to the movement. Evidently the evils of professionalism had demoralised some of these, particularly those composed of the type of player who only waits until he is good enough to turn professional to change his status.'[41] Like it or not, however, this was to be the usual relationship between the two groups in the future. For the Corinthians the professional game was irretrievably flawed by debased lower-class values. The introduction of the penalty kick in 1891 had seemed deeply insulting – no gentleman would deliberately commit a foul or stoop to take advantage of an opponent's lapse – and things had got steadily worse. By 1911 C. B. Fry, the archetypal Edwardian public school and Oxford amateur, was commenting that 'a curious conventional morality has grown up under which it is regarded as legitimate to play against the rules and the referee as well as the opposing team . . . on the principle that as there is a penalty for cheating it is permissible to cheat'.[42]

The main problem for the Corinthian-led AFA was the low technical stan-dard of football in the socially-elevated circles to which they appealed. Schools like Eton and Harrow might be disdainful of a game sponsored by newcomers like Rugby but they were not fervent contributors to the cause of competitive soccer, either. The FA on the other hand could point to amateurs still within the fold who could reach the top. Vivian Woodward, not from the same public school background as Fry but arguably more of a genuine amateur, was the favourite example. He played 23 times for the full England side, spent all his first-class career with League clubs and became a director of Tottenham Hotspurs when he retired. Yet he displayed the true amateur spirit, despite the 'dog-eat-dog' mores of the professional soccer world in which he played, not only in his unobtrusively purist attitude to payment and 'expenses' but in his chivalrous demeanour.[43]

The AFA struggled on for a while but in increasingly lacklustre fashion, and in 1913 they succumbed, dejectedly rejoining the FA. For the FA themselves the struggle with the rebel amateurs, on top of the bigger, long-standing one with the Football League, had added introspection to their insularity. They had given little time or thought to the emerging International Fédération (FIFA) when it appeared in 1904, and the embarrassment of losing their leading amateur clubs did not help in their dealings with the foreigners. But they were fortified by the knowledge that nowhere was there anything to match their own Cup and League competitions: 'home' internationals, particularly those between Scotland and England, were all that mattered.

League soccer had long been a 'northern' affair. In Scotland, where the leading schools had always preferred rugger, soccer was a proletarian religion, at its most passionate in Glasgow. In England the Football League championship was a struggle between a handful of clubs from the north and midlands, and even the FA Cup, which was more open, had gone to a southern team only once since 1882.[44] The southern professional clubs were still labouring under the handicap of their slow and painful breakaway from the shackles of the past, notably the intransigence of the ultra-amateur London FA.[45] London was by far the biggest centre of population in Britain. Yet of its 12 major professional teams only two, Arsenal and Chelsea, had achieved First Division status and both had periods of relegation. Chelsea, artificially and entrepreneurially created to meet spectator demand, was inherently unstable. Arsenal, with firmer working-class roots but precarious finances and an inaccessible ground, had to be rescued in 1910 by Henry Norris, a rich estate agent who set them up at Highbury in the playing fields of a former theological college. This upset not only local residents, who did not care for the exchange, but also Tottenham Hotspurs who had just won promotion from the Second Division and did not want a rival on their doorstep. In the event they managed to co-exist, but at the expense of Second Division Clapton Orient who were driven out to Leyton.

The north, by contrast, suffered mainly from its own success especially in the great conurbations. For the Liverpool proletariat soccer was an all-consuming passion, shot through with a sectarian rivalry equalled only in Glasgow. Yet it was Manchester, where rivalries were less explicable but equally intense, that commercial exploitation had its worst effects. Since the scandals of 1906, culminating in the suspension of City's Welsh international Billy Meredith for bribery and the selling of the rest of the team by auction on the instructions of the FA, the momentum had passed to United. Before long they had won both the Championship and the FA Cup – assisted by their latest signing, Billy Meredith.

Meredith had been one of the leaders of a strike, arising from the players' attempts to form a trade union to combat wage restrictions and the retain and transfer system.[46] It had eventually been settled, after a fashion, but the discontent lingered on. A new crisis arose in 1910 when the few remaining Union activists went to Court, contrary to the agreement reached with the FA, in support of a player who was in dispute with his club. The FA responded by suspending the chairman and secretary from football for life, and instructing all players to resign from the Union. A few held out, notably at Manchester United, Newcastle and Middlesborough, and for a while a new strike threat loomed. This was averted by a last minute compromise in which the Union got recognition from the FA and a committee to hear grievances. The FA and the League Management Committee also agreed a new maximum wage, up to £5 a week on a graduated scale with better talent money and benefits. The remaining point of disagreement was the cattle-market-style transfer system. The players decided to test it in the courts in 1912. It was declared legal and the Players' Union, having shot its bolt, subsided into insignificance, leaving Meredith to pursue his own personal campaign against the system in his singular fashion.

Signing Meredith was a typically smart move by United's Ernest Mangnall, the first of the now-familiar breed of soccer managers – high-profile, wheeling and dealing, and lavish with other people's money. Together he and Meredith made nonsense of the FA's attempts to regulate wages and were far too clever to be caught. Mangnall had big ideas in other ways. In 1910 when football grounds were dismal, shoddy affairs he persuaded his directors to finance a splendid new stadium at Old Trafford. With a capacity of 80,000, it was like nothing seen before. There was covered accommodation for 15,000, and the grandstand had tip-up seats and a tea-room. Prices were 6d for admission to the ground and 1s 6d and 2s for the covered stands: the best grandstand seats were 5s. The first game in the new stadium, against Liverpool, attracted 50,000 paying spectators and quite a lot who climbed in free – the biggest sporting crowd ever seen in Manchester. The following year United won the championship again but Mangnall had nearly bankrupted the club by his ambitious plans, and the directors, some of whom thought he was getting too big for his boots, were relieved when he left in 1912. He went, inevitably, to Manchester City and engineered another reversal of fortunes frustrated only by the war.[47]

Rugger: amateur ascendancy

Throughout most of the British Isles rugby football was determinedly amateur. It was a minority taste, but a socially superior one, particularly since

1895 when the English Rugby Football Union had rid itself of a group of Yorkshire and Lancashire dissidents who insisted on making 'broken-time' payments to working-class players. These uncouth northerners, it so happened, were also among the best players and the English international team suffered considerably, but the important thing to the RFU was the preservation of the spirit in which games should be played. Similarly, although there were a few aberrations in Wales and the Scottish border country no league – or cup-fervour debased the game at club level. The English County and Irish Provincial championships were the chief concessions to competition. Those who wanted the excitements of League rugby had to go to the breakaway Northern Union, which had gradually slithered, soccer-like, into professionalism.

To all right-thinking people the golden era Wales had enjoyed was alloyed by the 'commercial lines' (or as the Welsh themselves maintained, 'democratic lines') on which the game was run there. Fortunately Scotland, where soccer siphoned off the Glaswegian masses, had begun to redress the balance with a team drawing heavily on Edinburgh University, and Ireland had also struck an occasional blow for the true spirit of the game until England had at last begun to recover. An important source of this renewed English strength was in the public schools and the more aspirant amongst the new state grammar schools. And at their apex, sharing their burden of training the nation's leaders, were Oxford and Cambridge. The high standard of rugger (and of rowing and cricket) at the two universities was assisted by the admission policies of the constituent colleges, which competed with each other to recruit gifted players. There was much criticism of the American universities and their sports scholarships, which let in the underprivileged but athletic: the beneficiaries of the Oxbridge system were mainly drawn from a small circle of expensive public schools.

This was the royal road to international selection. 'The Cambridge side of 1910 was not a good one', wrote J. E. 'Jenny' Greenwood, a freshman member of it. 'The Captain . . . gave Blues to four other forwards who were members of his College, Pembroke.'[48] Despite this myopic approach that particular side included six future internationals. Oxford, however, who had six *current* internationals, won the 'Varsity match by 35 points to 3. By then Oxford had lost only twice since the turn of the century. Their domination depended heavily on what Greenwood called 'very experienced colonials' who came in as Rhodes Scholars. Rugger's imperial links were a source of great pride to its adherents – proof of the game's fine qualities, in fact – but they also provided painful evidence to support the claims of those who believed that Britain's erstwhile strength as a nation was ebbing away. The South African tourists of 1912–13, with a strong infusion of Boer talent, reinforced the point by trouncing all the home countries.

That year, under Greenwood's captaincy, Cambridge managed to stop the rot and in 1913, having graduated and left to train as an accountant, he decided to go back to university 'for a short term to play against Oxford, in order to help do something for Cambridge such as the Rhodes scholars had done for Oxford'.[49] Another seasoned Old Blue (1910–11–12), Barry Cumberlege, who 'had to go back for a term in order to try to get a degree', had meanwhile taken over as captain. Further help came from Wales, a source Cambridge were to find increasingly useful: J. M. C. 'Clem' Lewis was already an international when he went up as a freshman. (Both Oxford and Cambridge still attracted plenty of Scots of international calibre – 12 to Cambridge and 9 to Oxford in the period 1901–14 – but for various reasons, social as well as numerical, fewer Irish or Welsh.) From one source or another, the Cambridge team of 1913–14 had no fewer than 11 current or future internationals and might have had more of the latter but for the war.[50]

Despite Cambridge mutterings, not all the Oxford men were colonials. It had been Adrian Stoop of Oxford and Harlequins who had inspired the English international revival, and it was Ronald Poulton,[51] out of the same stable, who was the dazzling star of the side that dominated the championship in the four seasons before the war. Stoop, whose main interests outside rugby were faith-healing and the Territorial Army, and Poulton, a dashing winger renowned for his striking good looks and thorough sportsmanship, epitomised the qualities that would be needed if the country had to call on them in a sterner cause.[52] Another, less gracefully gifted, less bountifully endowed materially than the other two, but blessed with other admired British qualities, was Edgar Mobbs of Bedford Modern School.

Mobbs's brief international career had just ended but he became a stalwart of a club that exemplified the true rugger man's ideal – playing hard but always with enjoyment in mind, caring more about the game itself than the mere result. The Barbarians, who came together only for half a dozen matches a year, at Christmas and Easter against traditional opponents, invited players who combined high standards with a right approach to the game and a liking for attacking, open play. They had not yet become 'the most famous club in the world . . . and one of the last bastions of true amateurism in the world of sport' as their historian was able to record in 1977,[53] but they were already a by-word for sportsmanship and good fellowship. Mobbs, a centre three-quarter, was renowned for his determination. 'Built on generous lines,' as a contemporary report said of him in 1912, 'he was terribly hard to hold and did what we rarely see nowadays – handed off beautifully.'[54] He was that most admired rugger type, 'a man as popular off the field as he was fearsome on it,' and, the great ideal, 'a leader by example.'[55]

If all four nations saw rugger as a character-building force only the Welsh proclaimed its democratic virtues. 'Wales possesses in Rugby football a game . . . which is immeasurably more valuable than the popular code of other countries . . . an amateur sport of distinguished rank but . . . a discoverer of democracy which acts as participant and patron,' an admirer claimed in 1914.[56] Elsewhere enthusiasts were not so sure. Neither the Scots, supremely aware of the social gulf between the Edinburgh game and that of the border territory, nor the Irish, whom politics had not made entirely insensitive to social nuances, had concealed their disdain for some of the manifestations of Welsh democracy.[57] And if England grumbled more it was because they feared contamination. The purge of professionalism had not wholly eradicated working-class vulnerability to the temptations of 'broken-time' payments and the abyss beyond. Indeed the West Country, whence many fine players, particularly beefy forwards, were drawn for the national team, still remained a serious problem.

The commercial orientation of Welsh rugby clubs and players had sharpened under growing pressure from soccer. The number of professional soccer clubs in Wales had quadrupled between 1906 and 1910, and the West Country, which had many cultural similarities, had been similarly beset. Bristol City, already pillars of the Football League, had been Cup finalists in 1909. Bristol Rovers, Plymouth Argyle and Exeter City had all joined the Southern League. Lacking competitive counter-attraction and so losing the crowds, West Country rugby had also begun to lose its best players. Several, following long-established Welsh tradition, had signed for Rugby League clubs, particularly Rochdale and Oldham, but what chiefly troubled the RFU was the measures the leading clubs in Devon, the county champions of 1911 and 1912, appeared to be taking to keep their players at home. An investigation led to the suspension of officials of the Newton Abbot, Teignmouth, Torquay and Plymouth clubs, all of whom admitted making under-the-counter payments, and to the expulsion of several players for taking them. This may have been emotionally satisfying but it invited further danger. The Northern Union had already been seeking to take advantage of the situation – arranging an exhibition game in Plymouth in September 1910, for instance – and their missionary interest was further aroused by the RFU's purge.

Rugby: the professional side

The Northern Union were now doing well in their Lancashire and Yorkshire strongholds. By this time they had a soccer-style League structure and had adapted the player-oriented rules of the RFU to make it a more entertaining spectator sport. And they had one special advantage over the insular soccer authorities, deriving from the imperialist traditions of their former masters, the RFU – a good part of their revenue came from lucrative colonial tours, home and away, and from signing up star colonial players. Huddersfield, the most successful team of the immediate pre-war years, styled themselves 'The Empire Team of Stars and All Talents'. In it the local boy Harold Wagstaff played alongside men like Edgar Wrigley of New Zealand, the Australians A. A. Rosenfeld and T. P. Gleeson, Ben Gronow and John Rogers from Wales and Douglas Clark from Cumberland. It was a potent mixture.

Expansion beyond the northern heartland had been difficult, however. There had been high hopes of gaining a foothold in Wales, so great a source of players, but of the six clubs which had joined the Northern Union in 1907 and 1908 after action by the Welsh RFU over irregular payments, only one, Ebbw Vale, now remained. Coventry, who had also been obliged to sever their connection with the RFU in 1909 and join the Northern Union, looked like another possible bridgehead. In the aftermath of the Devon enquiry Plymouth, Torquay Teignmouth and Paignton set up Northern Union clubs and Coventry played two friendly games in the West Country in the Christmas holidays of 1912. In February, 1913 an England–Wales exhibition match at Plymouth was followed by a dinner at which the neophytes were advised to begin cautiously, restricting themselves to 'broken-time' payments only. In reply a local speaker commented bitterly, 'Broken-time payments' have been made in these parts for 30 years', adding wryly, 'I find the Northern Union the purer amateur body.'[58]

The RFU's zealous quest for purity was, in fact, causing concern to some lovers of the game even at the most impeccably amateur levels. Ronald Poulton himself, not only a public school amateur but a very rich one, must have brought furrows to a few establishment brows by his reaction to the 1912 enquiry: 'If it is the desire of the RFU committee practically to limit the game to players who learn it at Public Schools and in the Services and Universities, such a finding is reasonable. But I cannot believe such is their desire. Was not this, then, the opportunity to put the game on an immovable basis among all classes of the community? . . . such an action as the . . . Committee have taken will do much to prevent the expansion of the Rugby game.'[59] And, indeed, the principal beneficiary of the RFU's action was soccer. The Northern Union was unable to take root in the West Country, or in Wales, where Ebbw Vale folded in 1912, and the Coventry venture, with no local opponents in the West Midlands soccer-mad conurbation, ended the following year.

The Northern Union's cautionary words about the dangers of new clubs going beyond 'broken-time' payments were fully justified. To keep up with soccer clubs the Rugby League had to compete with them in recruiting and retaining players, but without their level of income. The average weekly attendance at Football League matches in 1913–14, over 23,000, exceeded that at the Rugby League Challenge Cup Final, the great showcase of the year. And, though propagandists were wont to claim high attendance at League matches, 10,000 was, in practice, thought worthy of special comment as an unusual occurrence.[60] The level of transfer fees, similarly, was not up to that of soccer, which had reached a record £1,000 with Alf Common in 1905. But sums of £400 or £500 were not unknown and even when the Northern Union, in agreement with the New Zealand and Australian authorities, imposed a two-year residential qualification on Dominion stars in 1913, the pattern had been set: the sensation of the year was the transfer of local boy Billy Batten from Hunslet to Hull for £600. Batten also got £14 a match under a new rationalised system, better suited to semi-professionals than a weekly wage as in soccer. (Northern Union players were still, in theory at least, required to have a week-day job outside the game.) Batten's pay, though spectacular, was not quite so generous as it seemed, for – again unlike soccer – it was 'no pay – no play'.

All of this gave a special flavour and an extra competitive edge to Rugby League football. Even the most successful clubs were precariously financed and the struggling majority were heavily dependent on the share of receipts they got from Cup and League finals and Test matches against Australia. It was followed intensely in its own heartlands, those parts of Yorkshire and Lancashire not addicted to soccer, but was either ignored or condemned as crude almost everywhere else in Britain. Its particular brand of commercialism, offering no security, sharpened the competitive edge on the field of play. Enforcing the rules depended more on the vigilance and strength of character of the referee than the honour code of the players. And since it was a game of fierce physical contact it too often spilled over into real violence.

Nevertheless, within its own circles it was the essence of manly sport and the source of national as well as local pride. In the close season of 1914 as the tension mounted in Europe an England touring team found themselves involved in a miniature war of their own in Australia. A crowd of 40,000 watched the first Test at Sydney, a very rough game. The second was played only two days later – on the King's birthday, a public holiday – and it was worse. Nevertheless, it had been very well attended and the series stood at one match all, so to catch the tide of popularity the Australian authorities suggested bringing the third, deciding Test forward. This appealed more to the treasurers than the players. The battered tourists were particularly unhappy about it, but the Rugby League Management Committee back at home, appealing to the spirit of Nelson, sent them a cable, 'England expects that every man will do his duty.' They responded in heroic fashion. Although reduced to ten men at one stage, they won the match, which earned the name

'Rorke's Drift' after an episode in the Zulu Wars of 1879.

Notes

1 See Derek Birley, *Land of Sport and Glory*, Manchester, 1995, p. 217.
2 Since the British success in the 1908 Olympics the Royal Club Nautique de Gand, Belgium, unfairly treated during its preparations for that event, had scored its third victory in the Grand Challenge Cup, the supreme prize at Henley, in 1909, but proper order had been restored by Magdalen College, Oxford, who took it for the next two years. Winnipeg BC won the Stewards' Cup for four-oared boats in 1910, the first time it had gone to an overseas crew. The victory of Sydney BC, in the 1912 Grand, seemed a further demonstration of colonial advance at the expense of the effete Mother Country.
3 Cook was an expert on the Turf, the author of its standard history and a future editor of *The Field*.
4 The British Rowing Almanack, 1912, p. 226, quoted by E. Halladay, *Rowing in England*, Manchester, 1990, p. 118.
5 *Almanack*, 1913, p. 257, *Badminton Magazine*, 35, 1912, *The Times*, 21 December 1912, 22 August 1913, 1 and 13 December 1913, *Granta*, 15 and 22 November 1913, *The Field*, 17 August 1913: see Halladay, *Rowing*, p. 118, and J. Lowerson, *Sport and the Middle Classes*, Manchester, 1993, p. 267.
6 NARA minutes, 21 October 1913.
7 *The Times*, 7 July 1914, quoted in C. Dodd, 'Rowing', in T. Mason (ed.), *Sport in Britain*, Cambridge, 1989, p. 276. It was, of course, an imitation of the *Sporting Life*'s 1882 mock-obituary mourning the loss of the Ashes.
8 See Birley, *Land*, pp. 224–5.
9 Harold Wilson, of Sheffield Hallamshire Harriers, beaten favourite in the mile, had turned professional, for instance.
10 Article in *Granta*, 1912, quoted by J. Crump in Mason, *Sport*, p. 52.
11 P. Lovesey, *Centenary History of the AAA*, London, 1979, p. 56.
12 P. Noel-Baker 'Stockholm, 1912', in Lord Killanin and J. Rodda (eds.), *Olympic Games*, London, 1984, p. 40.
13 *The Times*, 20 July 1912.
14 Noel-Baker, 'Stockholm', p. 41.
15 For Edwardian developments, amateur and professional, see Birley, *Land*, Chapter Eleven. It was 1911 before a former ABA champion went on to professional honours: Matt Wells, a Jewish boxer, temporarily took the title from Freddie Welsh, losing it again in 1912.
16 For insights into Welsh attitudes to boxing and boxers see D. Smith, 'A Welsh Fighting Class', in R. Holt (ed.), *Sport and the Working Class in Modern Britain*, Manchester, 1990, pp. 198–217.
17 S. Shipley, 'Boxing', in Mason (ed.), *Sport*, pp. 95–6.
18 Lowerson, *Middle Classes*, p. 275.
19 2 April 1910, quoted by Lowerson, *Middle Classes*, p. 283.
20 For this and related phenomena of the golfing boom see Birley, *Land*, Chapters Five and Ten.
21 Lowerson, *Middle Classes*, pp. 149–151
22 ibid., pp. 195–6. Lowerson, who devotes many pages to golf, offers valuable insights into members' preoccupations and gives much new information on the immediate pre-war period.
23 Article in *Golf Monthly*, October 1913, quoted in Lowerson, *Middle Classes*, p. 181.

24 Nor did any other foreigners. The victory of Arnaud Massy of France in the 1907 Open was the only foreign success before the war.

25 Professional tournaments had hitherto attracted relatively little attention in the States, and even when Francis Ouimet, a 20-year-old Boston shoe clerk, caused a sensation in 1913, beating both Harry Vardon and the current British Open Champion, Ted Ray, the chief interest was his youth and the fact that he was an amateur.

26 M. Hezlet (Mrs Ross) in H. Hutchinson (ed.), *The New Book of Golf*, London 1912, p. 267, quoted in K. E. McCrone, *Sport and the Physical Emancipation of English Women*, London, 1988, p. 175.

27 A doctor's daughter, she and her four sisters were all championship golfers. Unmarried, she gave long service in the committee rooms of golf and such new causes as the National Playing Fields Association, was a successful business woman, writer and public speaker, and also an active member of the Embroiderers' Guild.

28 See Birley, *Land*, pp. 111–13, 199.

29 One Canon Newbolt, quoted by Lowerson, *Middle Classes*, p. 283.

30 Halladay, *Rowing*, p. 154.

31 *Hockey* 13 March, 1913, quoted in McCrone, *Physical Emancipation*, p. 135.

32 For the wider significance of Madame Bergman-Osterberg, see Birley, *Land*, pp. 74, 93, 101–2.

33 *Olympic Review*, 1912.

34 S. Pankhurst, *The Suffragette Movement*, London, 1931 (1977 edn), p. 304.

35 2 December 1913, quoted in full in C. Carrington, *Rudyard Kipling*, Harmondsworth, 1970, pp. 488–9.

36 Asquith made an ambiguous pledge that kept the lid on the boiling kettle – but only just. No compromise proved acceptable to all parties and after a good deal of manoeuvring the original Bill was passed for Royal Assent, but by then the Germans had to be dealt with first.

37 *North of Ireland Cricket and Football Club Centenary Handbook*, Belfast, 1959, p. 17.

38 P. Rouse, 'A History of the GAA ban on Foreign Games: Part One, 1884–1971', *International Journal of the History of Sport*, December 1993, pp. 334–5.

39 Kevin Barry, martyred by execution in 1920, was a member of UCD Rugby Club.

40 Newspaper report of 14 November 1913, quoted by T. Greenwood, *Ballymena RFC Centenary Handbook*, Ballymena, 1987, p. 7.

41 N. L. Jackson, *Sporting Days and Sporting Ways*, London, 1932, pp. 132–3.

42 *C. B. Fry's Magazine*, 8 November 1911.

43 When Chelsea, to whom he had transferred in 1909, reached the FA Cup Final in 1914–15 Woodward got leave from the Army to watch the match. Chelsea invited him to play, but he declined, saying 'Bob Thompson has helped Chelsea get to the Final, so he should have the honour now.' C. Harvey (ed.), *Encyclopaedia of Sport*, London, 1959, p. 47.

44 Tottenham Hotspurs in 1901.

45 See Birley, *Land*, esp. pp. 37, 41, 239.

46 Meredith, bribery and corruption, the players' strike and related matters are also covered in Birley, *Land*, pp. 234–8.

47 E. Dunphy, *A Strange Kind of Glory*, London, 1991, pp. 51–3.

48 J. E. Greenwood, *A Cap for Boots*, London, 1977, p. 99.

49 ibid., p. 108.

50 See Greenwood, *Cap For Boots*, pp. 100–2, for the controversy over the Rhodes Scholarships.

51 In 1914 Poulton inherited a large fortune from his uncle (who had made his millions

in biscuits) on condition that he became Poulton-Palmer.

52 See Introduction and pp. 59–62 below.
53 N. Starmer-Smith, *The Barbarians*, London, 1977, p. 9.
54 ibid., p. 46.
55 ibid.
56 *Welsh Outlook*, February 1914, pp. 18–19, quoted by G. Williams, in J. A. Mangan (ed.), *Pleasure, Profit, Proselytism*, London, 1988, p. 141.
57 See Birley, *Land*, pp. 246 and 249.
58 Quoted in T. R. Delaney, *The Roots of Rugby League*, Keighley, 1984, p. 115.
59 ibid.
60 W. Vamplew, *Pay Up and Play the Game*, Cambridge, 1988, pp. 63–6.

CHAPTER THREE

Into battle

Britain, seeing her own imperial security and economic pre-eminence threatened by the Kaiser's ambitions, had somewhat reluctantly entered into alliance with France and Russia. Germany had an army and a navy primed for action. She also had a long-established plan: if attacked she would first neutralise France before turning east to deal with her other historic enemy, Russia. On 28 June, 1914, the Archduke Ferdinand, heir-apparent to the thrones of Austria and Hungary, was murdered by Serbian irredentists in Sarajevo. Most people in Britain, where monarchy was deeply respected and the Serbs were none too popular, sympathised with the Austrians and their desire for retribution. They thought little of it when the Kaiser promised full support to Austria for a punitive strike on Serbia. When Russia mobilised in pan-Slavonic solidarity and Germany in reply manned her western as well as her eastern front, there still seemed no reason to get involved. 'To hell with Servia!', a headline in the populist *John Bull*, fairly well summed it up. But when Germany demanded free passage through Belgium to get at France the time had come for Britain to stand by her allies.

It had all happened quickly and unexpectedly, and the shock was the greater because the declaration of war came over the August Bank Holiday weekend. Even so it was a popular decision. Jingoism was part of the British make-up and the Kaiser was the latest addition to John Bull's xenophobic demonology. Even the Labour Party, though generally pacifist, had its belligerents, such as the cricket-loving utopian Robert Blatchford, who felt so strongly about the German menace that he had taken to airing his views in Lord Northcliffe's capitalistic, rabble-rousing *Daily Mail*. So when the news broke, thousands gathered in Trafalgar Square and Whitehall, singing patriotic songs, waving Union Jacks and cheering. For Kipling, the people's laureate if not the establishment choice, it was a question of survival:

> For all we have and are,
>   For all our children's fate.

> Stand up and take the war.
> The Hun is at the gate!'[1]

But while men all over Europe were uplifted by the call of patriotic duty the British were warmed also by an altruistic glow: 'Secure behind the guns of the Grand Fleet, they were in no danger of invasion. They had gone to war for a cause – the neutrality and independence of "little Belgium".'[2] The bullying had to be stopped. This was 'a war to end war', to 'make the world safe for democracy'. It need not take long. 'There had been no war between the Great Powers since 1871. No man in the prime of life knew what war was like. All imagined that it would be an affair of great marches and great battles, quickly decided. It would be over by Christmas.'

Romantic ideals

Britain, unlike the continental powers had no tradition of compulsory military service. There seemed no need of conscription now to raise the relatively small British Expeditionary Force the government envisaged. Earl Kitchener of Khartoum, to whom Asquith entrusted the War Office, undertook the task of recruiting a New Army of volunteers. He was spectacularly successful. The rush to the colours was led by the sport-mad leisured classes, the 'flanneled fools and muddied oafs' and the huntin', shootin' and fishin' aristocracy whom Kipling had pilloried for their selfishness at the time of the Boer War. The public school men were imbued with the spirit of Newbolt. The aristocrats had something to prove; that they were not anachronistic parasites but true descendants of the warrior class. This was the moment when their sporting activities, once vocational requirements for the well-born, could prove their worth again.

Some, of course, were already defending the empire, like Lord Desborough's son the poet, Julian Grenfell, who had joined the 1st Royal Dragoons in 1910. An all-round athlete at Eton, boxing half-blue at Oxford and Henley oarsman, the war found him fretting in South Africa, but he was soon in action in France, setting 'an example of light-hearted courage . . . famous throughout the army'.[3] Others felt a resurgence of blood. Lord Dalmeny, the Earl of Rosebery's wayward heir, brilliant horseman and former Surrey cricket captain, was 32 and in some danger of running to seed, but he at once rejoined the Grenadiers.[4] The 27-year-old Rupert Brooke, a handsome cricketing and footballing aesthete from Rugby, had spent his life since leaving Cambridge writing his verses in idyllic and leisured circumstances. When war broke out he welcomed it as a clean break from the 'world grown old and cold and weary' and took a commission in the Royal Naval Division. Sixth-formers and undergraduates could not wait to get in on the action. 'Our one great fear was that the war would be over before we got there', recalled Sir Oswald Mosley.[5] Mosley, of landed Shropshire stock and a boxing and fencing champion at Winchester, was, like many of the commencing subalterns, only 18.

Kitchener's New Army had to adjust to the outlook of the old. Most British generals were cavalry men and their experience in the Boer War coloured their view of what was needed in this one. 'Horses were everywhere. No army had any mechanical transport. There were a few motor-cars in which generals and staff officers travelled when they condescended to get off their horses. The men slogged along on foot once they reached rail-head.'[6] The Royal Flying Corps, its only concession to operational modernity, was still a tiny body of specialists, mostly employed on observation duties. The cavalry orientation of the top brass also set the social tone. Siegfried Sassoon's George Sherston, having volunteered two days before the declaration of war, was in the local Yeomanry by September, taking his hunter Cockbird with him and selling him, as required, to the government for 'a perfunctory fifty pounds'. The regular officers were deeply conscious of where the uniforms of the in-coming 'temporary gentlemen' had been tailored, there was a clear hierarchy of regiments (with the cavalry supreme) and 'it was a distinct asset . . . to be able to converse convincingly about hunting'.[7]

The Empire was in the war, too, by proclamation of the Governor-Generals, and their sportsmen were quick to the colours. At the beginning of August the Australasian tennis players Norman Brookes and Tony Wilding found them- selves playing the German pair Otto Froitzheim and Oscar Kreutzer in the Davis Cup at Pittsburgh before a strongly pro-German crowd. The German players had announced their intention of dropping their racquets at once if war were declared. The President of the Pittsburgh club, who could not see the hurry, cut off the telephones, barred the press and succeeded in keeping back the news until the match was over. The German couple not only lost 5–0 but got themselves taken out of the war. They left at once for home but their boat was intercepted by a British warship which put them ashore at Gibraltar, whence they were taken to England and interned.[8] Brookes returned home to enlist, and Wilding went back to England to join the Royal Marines.

Notwithstanding the game's slightly ambivalent image it was their age not their lack of sturdy patriotism that kept many leading tennis players from wartime glory. Most did their bit. The retired champion Laurie Doherty probably hastened his death by undertaking anti-aircraft duties. And the LTA, in common with the authorities of other amateur games – rowing, athletics, hockey, lacrosse – at once abandoned competition for the duration. The universities (whose numbers were immediately halved and soon fell further) gave up their famous showpieces – the encounters at Lord's and Twickenham, and the Boat Race. The dashing miler Arnold Strode-Jackson found something he could take seriously. He was quickly in action and survived three wounds to become in 1918, aged 27, the youngest brigadier in the Army. But it was the rugger men who best exemplified the innocent enthusiasm to get into the fray.

Adrian Stoop was already in the Territorials, and when war came it was, in the *DNB*'s phrase, 'almost inevitable' that he would win the Military Cross for his gallantry. Ronald Poulton-Palmer immediately answered the nation's call, as did many Scottish, Welsh and Irish internationals. Most leading rugger men went in as officers, especially if they had been at schools with OTCs, but a few went into the ranks, like 31-year-old farmer J. A. King, of Headingley, Barbarians and England who left the harvesting to his three sisters and joined the Yorkshire Hussars. Edgar Mobbs, refused a commission on age grounds, became a sergeant and raised his own company of 250 sportsmen for the Northants. regiment By September Lieutenant Mobbs, still in training, was sending home comic postcards showing him leading his sportsmen through the German ranks knocking down their spike-helmeted leader with his cele-brated hand-off.[9] There were many examples of collective patriotic gestures, like the Keswick XV who joined up as a team. The Blackheath club passed a passionate resolution: 'It is the duty of every able-bodied man of enlistable age to offer personal war service to his king and Country, and . . . every Rugby footballer of the present day comes within the scope of Lord Kitchener's appeal.'[10]

Nine days after war broke out the RFU made a country-wide appeal. National, county and club games were cancelled for the duration and only a handful of charity matches were played, by services teams. True the Welsh Rugby Union hoped to hedge its bets. 'If only', wrote their secretary, 'every man in every First XV in Wales were to enlist, what a magnificent body there would be at the service of our country and even then there would still be plenty of players left to enable the game to be played as usual.'[11] But this was no doubt influenced by the belief that it would be over by Christmas. Similarly the All-England Women's Hockey Association, suspending all county, territorial and international matches in September 1914, hoped that individual clubs would keep together and carry out fixtures if they could. The mood did not last long as women as well as men looked for dramatic gestures of renunciation.

Professional sport presented bigger problems, as we shall see. Even cricket wavered whilst amateur committees decided the fate of their hired retainers. There were, of course, instant volunteers, like Mr A. Sharp of Leicestershire, who did not even stay for his second innings against Northamptonshire in the August Bank Holiday game before joining his regiment. Some of the great amateurs of the golden age, like Kenneth Hutchings and Reggie Spooner –

also a rugger international – quickly followed. Yet with a few exceptions the counties continued with their championship programme for another month. With the season almost over, W. G. Grace, in an open letter to the *Sportsman* on 27 August, called on all eligible cricketers to enlist at once and a few days later the remaining fixtures were abandoned. Lord Hawke, descended from an admiral but with no personal credentials as a warrior, made it clear to Yorkshire players that 'a strict condition of their continued engagement' would be participation in war-work.

Some elder statesmen set a personal example. F. S. Jackson, who had seen active service in the Boer War, turned away from business to raise and command the 2nd/4th West Yorkshire Regiment. A number of absentees from the Boer conflict also made belated amends. It was no great sacrifice for some impecunious and otherwise rather aimless amateurs to join up. Archie Maclaren and Gilbert Jessop, both in their forties, were commissioned, proved successful at recruiting and stayed in the army until forced out by ill-health. Their more purposeful contemporary, C. B. Fry, had been running the training ship *Mercury* since 1908. His friend, the Indian prince Ranjitsinjhi, demonstrated his intense loyalty to Crown and Empire by throwing the resources of his state into the war effort and, before wounding himself in a shooting accident, by service on the staff in France. MCC's flag was kept flying by the elderly Lord Harris (a Boer War veteran) as treasurer, assisted by the 'flanneled fool', P. F. Warner, who combined the role of secretary with that of captain in the Inns of Court OTC.

There had been an enormous patriotic response to Kitchener's appeal, strikingly reinforced by the famous posters which showed him pointing his finger and saying 'Your Country Needs You!' Half a million men joined up in the first month and a hundred thousand each month thereafter. Kitchener did not share the popular opinion that it would be over by Christmas, but this was thought a narrowly military viewpoint. A decisive sea battle would quickly settle it, most people thought. The government hoped so, too, but the German Fleet remained prudently in port. This kind of stalemate was frustrating. On land, it soon became clear, there was a stalemate of a different kind. No-one had bargained for the stark power of modern armaments – magazine rifles, machine guns, field artillery – as trench warfare and barbed wire became the backdrop to wholesale slaughter. Already by October 1914, the British Expeditionary Force, under the uninspiring Sir John French, had lost one-tenth of its members at Mons and Ypres. A diversionary naval-based assault on the Dardanelles, aimed at breaking the deadlock, in fact led to further stagnation on land at Gallipoli.

The troops in the trenches were heroes of an unconventional kind. If they had ideas of romantic glory they soon began to fade, to be replaced by cheerful resignation. Tommy Atkins dug in, cursing and joking. When he marched he sang, not about victory over the Germans but about girls ('Hello, Hello, Who's Your Lady Friend?') leave ('Take Me Back to Dear Old Blighty') his own morale ('Pack up Your Troubles in Your Old Kit-bag') or how far away from home he was: the favourite, 'Tipperary', a pre-war Florrie Forde pantomime number, did not require an Irish accent. Off-duty hours were for sentiment – Nat D. Ayer's immortal 'If You Were the Only Girl in the World' or the nostalgic 'There's a Long, Long Trail A-winding' and 'Keep the Home Fires Burning'.

That Christmas Eve, when the troops had hoped to be back home, they sang carols. So did the Germans, who put up little Christmas trees on their parapets. A few ventured out, burying the dead, greetings were exchanged and though the generals urged watchfulness for a surprise attack spontaneous and unspoken truces arose all along the line. Next day after religious services and Christmas dinner there were informal gatherings in No Man's Land, mostly for smoking, conversation and showing of family photographs. 'A' Company of the Lancashire Fusiliers played their opposite numbers at a sort of rough soccer with a tin can – and lost. Elsewhere soccer balls were produced for a kickabout between the shell-holes before darkness fell. It was a strange interlude which left a lasting impression on those who experienced it, without in any way diminishing the will to win when hostilities were resumed.

The patriotic fervour was most clearly expressed by the officer class, more articulate and taught at their public schools that leadership included showing men how to die. Early in 1915 Rupert Brooke published a sonnet that caught the spirit of the moment:

> If I should die, think only this of me;
> That there's some corner of a foreign field
> That is forever England.[12]

His death on 23 April gave it an added poignancy. And as Newbolt himself was being knighted for armchair services to the Admiralty the logic of his inspirational 'Play up! Play up! and play the game' began to unfold. As their Old Boys made the supreme sacrifice, the schools recalled with pride their preparation on the playing fields. A grieving master at Marlborough penned a series of tributes on the lines of

> Cricket and Hockey, Rackets, Fives,
> Aye, you were the master of them all . . .
> And now you've played your noblest game
> And now you've won your grandest Blue.[13]

On 5 May Ronald Poulton-Palmer went down to a sniper's bullet. Four days later Tony Wilding was killed when a shell hit his dug-out. Julian Grenfell's

'Into Battle' appeared in *The Times* on 25 May: on the same day his death was announced, giving poignancy to its macabre theme:

> And when the burning moment comes,
> And all things else are out of mind,
> And only Joy of Battle takes
> Him by the throat, and makes him blind . . .

and its moral

> And he is dead who will not fight,
> And who dies fighting has increase.[14]

Over the top

The war was democratic in its casualty lists if not in its conduct. As the heart-broken but stoical Kipling told those who sympathised with him on his son's death in action, his was but the case of thousands. The greatest families in the land suffered along with the rest. Soon the Earl of Rosebery was writing in his latest letter of condolence, '. . . the fountain of tears is nearly dry. One loss follows another till one is dazed.'[15] The act of common sacrifice was a tragic but very real contribution to community of purpose. The living symbol of unity was the King. The actual role of constitutional monarch was even sketchier in war than in peace-time for the political truce needed to defend the throne temporarily deprived its occupant of some of his normal functions. This was disappointing to George V, for with experience he had come to enjoy the role of referee. What was now required was outward and visible signs of kingship, and he was kept busy visiting military hospitals, pinning on decorations, inspecting naval and military institutions and munitions factories, visiting the Grand Fleet and the BEF.

He was fortunate to escape most of the extreme xenophobia that swept the country in the first months of the war, inducing invocations in the *Daily Mail* to refuse service from German or Austrian waiters and bringing about the resignation of his kinsman Prince Louis of Battenberg, the First Sea Lord because of his German origins. (Later when the noise had died down the King took the opportunity to change the family name, Saxe-Coburg Gotha, to the more resonantly British Windsor.[16]) Royal popularity had in fact been greatly increased by the Prince of Wales. Commissioned at the very outbreak of war, he had built up a reputation, within the limits imposed on him by the brass-hats responsible for his safety, for courage and the common touch, visiting the Front whenever he could and becoming a familiar sight on his green bicycle just behind the lines. The King worked ceaselessly in his own stolid way. He tried to set an example of austerity, publicly forswearing alcohol for the duration in April 1915. 'Signing the pledge' had been a mark of patriotism since Kitchener in the early weeks of the war had urged the public not to keep soldiers from their duty by treating them to drink. The concern had now extended to the munitions workers. Lloyd George declared that drink was 'doing us more damage than all the German submarines put together'[17] and his budget increased the price of beer to 4d a pint.

Despite heavy losses in three more unsuccessful battles Sir John French was now complaining not of a shortage of manpower but of munitions. The volunteers were still flooding in, faster in fact than Kitchener could properly absorb and train them, but ammunition was hard to come by. The government was already somewhat unpopular. It had introduced many restrictions stemming from the Defence of the Realm Act (known as Dora, an interfering old busybody) but was markedly less good at taking positive action. The press, with Northcliffe leading the chorus of criticism, made the most of the 'shells scandal'. Northcliffe wanted rid of both Kitchener, whose bureaucratic approach was stifling initiative, and the Liberal government, which was no more than a collection of separate departments presided over by Asquith, 'unshakeable as a rock, and like a rock, incapable of movement'.[18] When the First Sea Lord, Admiral Fisher, suddenly resigned in protest over the disastrous Dardanelles plan of the First Lord of the Admiralty, Winston Churchill, something had to give. Asquith remained but as head of a coalition government in which the key post of Minister of Munitions went to Lloyd George. The new style he brought was to have profound effects, both on the war and afterwards.

Meanwhile the likely effects of a glut of manpower and a shortage of both firepower and brainpower were not immediately obvious to enthusiastic armchair patriots. The Earl of Lonsdale, for example, saw it as his duty to out-do Kitchener in recruiting volunteers. Supplying fighting men from their fiefdoms was a traditional aristocratic response to national emergencies. Grandees like the Duke of Bedford, Lord Leconfield and Lord Ancaster offered generous inducements to their tenants, keeping jobs open, allowing dependants to live rent-free in tied cottages and paying them part-wages while their men were at the front.[19] But for Lonsdale the war was a new sporting occasion that was almost a personal challenge. The bust of his friend the Kaiser remained on his piano, but Germany was now an opponent that had to be knocked out and he issued thousands of gaudy recruiting posters asking

> Are you a man
>   or
> Are you a mouse?

Are you a man who will forever be handed down to posterity as a Gallant Patriot?

or

Are you to be handed down to posterity as a rotter and a coward?'[20]

Many deplored his crude intervention. The more sensitive remonstrated on principle: it was 'easy to recline in an armchair after a seven-course dinner and urge your dependants to fight' wrote one. The War Office objected on pragmatic grounds; 'Stop repeat stop collecting recruits' it telegraphed. But Lonsdale cared nothing for the plans of the War Office: for one thing the Director of Recruiting was his old rival the Earl of Derby.[21] ('I see Lord Derby has given a hundred acres of his park to be broken up for Food Production', he wrote to his land agent the following year, 'but that is the sort of thing he would do as he is entirely out for advertisement.'[22] Before long he was making a similar gesture himself at Lowther.) Lonsdale was temporarily diverted by an assignment dear to his heart, touring the remount depots to report on the state of the horses. But the recruits continued to pour in.

The slaughter was horrific. The battle of Loos in September, in which 50,000 British were lost compared with 20,000 Germans, saw the end of Sir John French but not of catastrophe. With Kitchener reduced to symbolic status – 'the great poster' his critics called him – the Army came under the control of generals who rejected all civilian control. The CIGS, Sir William Robertson, the first field marshal to have come up from the ranks, seemed to have acquired in the process the hide of a rhinoceros. He closed down the disastrous Gallipoli campaign, but whilst thus abandoning the prospects of attacking Germany through the back door left an army in place guarding the Suez Canal. At least this kept his men from being tossed away on the Western Front by the new commander, Sir Douglas Haig. A renowned polo-player and classical cavalry man with apparently more confidence than brains or imagination, Haig was content to support his French allies by throwing in men, whatever the cost in lives, to try to wear the Germans down. He remained in charge for the rest of the war seeking to make an opening for his cavalry: many thousands of infantrymen were lost and many thousands of horses were kept in France waiting for action that never materialised.

The subalterns went on gallantly leading their men over the top. Edgar Mobbs, Arnold Strode-Jackson and Adrian Stoop made more entries in the annals of glory. Those who survived have recorded, often passionately and movingly what it was like. The memorials of the rank-and-file were in their songs, often derived from music-hall successes, to which they put their own words. One of the cleaner parodies was about Charlie Chaplin, whom they adored. Chaplin, a young Cockney, was much criticised by superior folk for shirking in California, but for the troops he epitomised the little man, like themselves, cocking a snook at authority. But their rebellion was only verbal. The lasting image of the private soldier was 'Ol' Bill', a cartoon character admittedly created by an officer but universally popular. Bill's utterance of late 1915, in a shell-hole with muddy water up to his waist, 'Well, if you knows of a better 'ole, go to it!' became a catchphrase epitomising the phlegmatic humour that sustained the fighting spirit of Britain's first mass army.[23]

The Home Front and the classes

George Sherston, arriving in France in November 1915, had found 'the sober-coloured countryside . . . lifeless and unattractive . . . A hopeless hunting country, it looked.'[24] Back home a few were still enjoying the magnificent English scenery. Hunting lost many of its most fervent devotees to the Front but their women folk, those beyond military age and those required at home, like farmers, kept it going as best they could. Lord Lonsdale regarded it as a patriotic duty to assist this noble endeavour. When, that season, the members of the Cottesmore, short of money, fodder for the horses and meat for the hounds, swallowed their pride and their misgivings and asked him to come back as Master, he put his heart and soul – and considerable resources – into it. To critics he replied, 'What on earth are officers home from the front going to do with their time if there is no hunting for them?'[25] They could perhaps go shooting, if they hadn't enough of it already. The shooters, unlike the fox-hunters, could at least claim some relevance for their sport as an adjunct to the food supply. When the King visited Sandringham for the odd few days, we are told, he occasionally took his gun 'to shoot game which he sent to the hospitals'.[26] It must be hoped that the sick similarly benefited from the day's work of the eight guns that on 1 August 1915 despatched the record number of 2,929 grouse at Littledale and Abbeystead in Lancashire.[27]

But that was not the point. A principle was at stake. The model for throwbacks like Lonsdale was the Duke of Wellington facing Napoleon, in the days when officers certainly did not give up hunting – or going to the races or prizefights – in the intervals of battle. It was no help to fighting men if their simple pleasures were denied them; and home fires had to be kept burning. The same applied to summer sport. Yachting was out of the question of course. *Britannia* was laid up, like Lipton's *Shamrock IV*. Indeed all yacht-racing had finished, though the YRA remained in being, awaiting happier times. Lipton himself, now in his sixties, earned great kudos for putting his steam-yacht *Erin* into service, running in between Marseilles and Salonica with medical supplies until it was sunk by a German submarine. The yachtsmen, in the Navy or on coastal watch, putting their vessels and their skills to use, were having a good war, as the country remembered with gratitude that Britain was an island nation. This only left the Turf, which had to be preserved at all costs.

There was no question of the patriotism of racing men. On the contrary, given the orientation of the British Army, they were greatly to the fore. Harry Brown, for instance, went into the Household Cavalry and dozens of other steeplechase jockeys, amateur and professional, served in Yeomanry regiments. There were perhaps proportionately fewer of their diminutive counterparts on the Flat but the officer class was well represented amongst their trainers some of whom interrupted lucrative careers. Cecil Boyd-Rochfort, already 27, rushed to join the Scots Guards, and served throughout, winning the Croix de Guerre. But the older sort were anxious to keep the sport going against their return. Unfortunately for them both racehorses and race-goers were heavy users of the railways which were vital to mobilisation: principle apart, racing had to be suspended for three weeks in August 1914 because of transport difficulties. Meetings were then held at Haydock Park and Gatwick, however, and though rail problems, the billeting of troops on racecourses, and, to some extent, local opposition led to cancellations at Kempton Park, Stockton, Hurst Park, York, Derby, Ayr and Newbury there was no sign that the Jockey Club intended to give up the ghost.

Indeed in October the Jockey Club had argued strongly that racing ought to carry on, not for 'those who go racing for amusement' but for the sake of the industry that sustained British bloodstock breeding. This supply line for the cavalry, it was pointed out, was kept going by racing, which was an industry in its own right. As well as 400 jockeys and apprentices there were thousands of stablemen and racecourse employees – gatemen, groundsmen, caterers and so forth. Some had already enlisted on the understanding that their jobs would be kept open for them. Racing should continue, therefore, 'where local conditions will permit and where the feeling of the locality is not adverse to the meeting being held'.[28] National Hunt racing carried on that winter despite the departure of so many horses and riders for the Front, but the real test was whether the much less relevant, much more extensive flat-racing programme was to be mounted the following summer.

A division appeared even in the Jockey Club's ranks early in 1915 when one of its most prominent members, the Duke of Portland, withdrew his horses from the scheduled racing at Epsom and Ascot because he believed it wrong to hold meetings associated with peace-time luxury and pleasure. In the fierce debate that followed Ascot became a particular source of controversy. On 14 February the racing correspondent of *The Times* assured readers that Lord Churchill was 'already making the customary preparations'. With the situation at the Front now so much worse the editor, Geoffrey Dawson came out strongly against the idea. On 4 March a leading article argued, 'We are convinced that any attempt to hold the great popular racing festivals, such as

Epsom, and, above all Ascot, will make a deplorably bad impression on our neighbours and lead to misconception in the country. We should like to see them abandoned altogether for this year. The Ascot meeting falls on a date when the war may be at its climax. Can it be seemly to hold it when millions of men, including great numbers of our own people, will be at death-grips?'

Henry Cust, a former editor of the *Pall Mall Gazette* and now chairman of the Central Committee for Patriotic Organisations, agreed: 'When many thousands of men have given their lives for their country, and while many more tens of thousands are following their high example, and will be dying and suffering while the crowds cheer and lunch at Epsom, it is merely monstrous to celebrate the Great National Festival and Ascot, etc., with all their gay traditions and associations.'[29] Lord Dunraven, Irish peer, upholder of British honour in the America's Cup and a bloodstock expert, was withering: 'Ascot is a glorified garden-party with racing thrown in. It can be bracketed with Court Balls and functions of that character, and as these are postponed during the war there seems no reason why Ascot should be retained.'[30] Henry Knollys, a retired colonel, asked. 'Is it unreasonable to hope that in 1915 the upper classes of men and women will forbear from assembling in their tens of thousands . . . at Ascot, peacocking in their plumes and prattling their puerilities?'[31] The vicar of Sunningdale offered a local view: 'The Fourth Berkshire Regiment is expected to go to the Front. If racing takes place at Ascot, everyone will be spending money or making money or rushing about. But for months our interests have been much more wholesome. Golf and football have been nearly discarded . . . Why should we be thrown back into just the same rush for excitement and money as we had last year?'[32] And in a second leader on 13 March *The Times* summed up the mounting opposition, quoting a peer who asked whether it was decent 'to persevere in our two great yearly "bean-feasts" against a background of awful tragedy and amid a vale of tears'.

Against all this the Jockey Club's supporters advanced the claims of history and morale. The former Prime Minister and Derby winner Lord Rosebery, whilst typically professing to wish to remain 'remote from controversy', appealed to precedent – 'Once before our country has been engaged in a "life and death" struggle at least as strenuous and desperate as this' – recalling that the Ascot Gold Cup had been run eight days before Wellington met Napoleon at Quatre Bras. 'Our ancestors', he averred, 'were no less chivalrous and humane than ourselves.'[33] The Hon. Frederick Lambton asked why racing was being singled out for censure: he pointed out that there were 34 theatrical advertisements in that day's *Times*. His brother-in-law, Sir Hedworth Meux, a non-combatant admiral, observing that 'The best horses in the world and the prettiest women are to be seen on the Royal Heath', thought it too soon to be talking of cancellation as the war might be over before the summer. More relevantly others argued that many soldiers themselves were keen on racing. *The Times* racing correspondent reported on the significant amount of khaki on view at Gatwick. Lord Hamilton of Dalzell recalled the delight of the troops in South Africa in 1900 when the C-in-C had sent a signal announcing that the Prince of Wales's Diamond Jubilee had won the Derby. Most cogently of all, a wounded officer wrote from hospital to tell the 'amiable and generally non-warlike faddists' to 'curse if you must' at the betting, drink, bookies, jockeys and trainers, 'but please don't put the curses in our mouths'.[34]

The Jockey Club had a stormy meeting on 16 March, but after the recriminations a compromise was proposed. Ascot should be held but the social side should be curtailed – no Royal Enclosure or luncheon tents – and there should be no special trains. Even this modest austerity was too much for the Ascot Stewards who insisted on the Royal Enclosure being kept at an increased charge. As late as the beginning of May preparations for the June meeting were still going on. With the casualty lists mounting and public feeling running high, and with alarmists questioning the wisdom of gathering crowds when there might be Zeppelins overhead,[35] the government was under pressure to take some action. But action was not its strong point, and the Jockey Club was a most influential body (with not only friends but members in high places). The Postmaster-General announced that to conserve manpower telegraphic facilities would be withdrawn – but that was all.

What finally impelled action was further controversy about the effect on the railways. The Railway Executive, though ruling out cheap excursions, told the Ascot Stewards they would put on special trains if they could. In early May, as protests mounted, *The Times* put out another leader: 'It is the business of the country to see that the movements of its fighting men are not inconvenienced or obstructed by the rush of race-course crowds . . . Racing still presents its saddening contrasts to the patriotism of those who have devoted themselves to the service of the country.' Parliamentary questions grew in volume and on 19 May the President of the Board of Trade at last intervened, asking the Jockey Club to consider suspending all racing so as not to congest the railways. This was too much to ask, but the Club offered a bargain. It would reluctantly abandon Ascot and curtail the programme if a few races could be held in order to protect the bloodstock industry.

The compromise agreed was that Ascot and most other courses would close but that Newmarket, the centre of the racing industry – and the headquarters of the Jockey Club – would stage five additional meetings, with two more at Newbury, another racing town. As a result Epsom and Doncaster as well as Ascot were closed, but the Derby, the Oaks and the St Leger transferred to Newmarket, which throughout the war years staged them as well as its own traditional classics, the One Thousand and Two Thousand Guineas.[36] The change naturally made Newmarket more popular than ever: the seven races held there on 15 June 1915, attracted 214 runners. It, and the Turf in general, also became more exclusive than ever because with fewer opportunities only the best horses could hope to win races and so justify the cost of being kept in training. The chief sufferers (apart from the bookmakers who had to look elsewhere for subject matter) were the authorities of racecourses put on the suspended list since they had to continue to meet overheads. Amongst the reported sacrifices was that of the Epsom authorities who sold most of their impressive stock of wines and spirits to make ends meet.[37]

Another sport available to returning officers in most parts of the country was golf. It managed to avoid a tremendous public outcry because with major amateur and all professional competition stopped it did not attract spectators and because it took its remaining pleasures in discreet seclusion. There were local difficulties. In Ireland playing golf in war-time took on unpatriotic overtones of self-indulgence in the loyalist circles where it was chiefly played. By 12 September 1914 the *Irish Field* was reporting that the Royal Dublin Club had already lost 18 members dead, wounded or missing. Many of them were regular soldiers, but everywhere there were plenty of volunteers. In October it was reported that 10 Royal Dublin caddies had joined up: soon a professional golfers' corps was raised jocularly known as 'the niblick brigade'. Royal Dublin's course was made into rifle ranges early in September 1914. However other, more fortunate clubs escaped and continued with varying degrees of sheepishness for the duration.[38]

In England divisions were less dramatically exposed but clearly some golfers were more patriotic than others. Cyril Tolley, a future amateur champion, was a major in the Tank corps, winning the MC at Cambrai before being taken prisoner. Another, Roger Wethered, got to France a few weeks before the end. Seaside clubs sometimes found themselves forced into making a contribution to the war effort by their strategic importance. The Bridlington course was in part made over to defence works and the County Agricultural Committee took the rest. Blackpool's course was requisitioned by the military. There were examples of voluntary sacrifice, like the St George's Hill club which handed over its clubhouse to the Red Cross for use as a hospital. But there were some notable non-contributors. N. L. Jackson, bitterly regretting that he had lost the chance to sell his shares in the elite Stoke Poges club before the war made them a liability, managed to make the best of a bad job. 'The normal course of life', he wrote afterwards, 'was completely suspended [there] as elsewhere, for the duration of the war, but that is not to say that the club stood still.' It had given shelter for a while to some wealthy Belgian refugees and it was 'a welcome retreat to a large number of British officers home on leave'. These last 'were practically the only players on the course, except on Saturday afternoons and Sundays, when many of the members who were labouring hard at their businesses or on war work managed to get down for some fresh air. On weekdays our caddies were mostly men unfit for service, but at the week-ends we used to have quite a lot of munition workers offering their services in this capacity, glad to obtain some exercise and a little pocket-money into the bargain.'[39]

The Home Front and the masses

Working-class sport flourished only if it had the protection of those in high places. Boxing was another traditional sport that successfully evoked echoes of the Napoleonic Wars. It no longer had anything like the same status, but, considering that it had for some years teetered on the brink of illegality, it did pretty well. Amateur competition closed down completely, with the important exception of the services, where it flourished, but the professional side prospered, thanks to the support of such as the Earl of Lonsdale and, just as important nowadays, its interest to money men and gamblers and the uninterrupted activity in neutral America. Freddie Welsh had returned home in triumph after his title win, proclaiming his great pride in South Wales – but had immediately gone to the USA, and subsequently declared himself an American citizen. This brought sardonic comment from the Welsh press but did not affect his popular support. South Wales had its share of British patriots, of course, but the war did not eliminate the age-old Celtic passions and religious differences that marked them off from the English. These apart, its industrial ups-and-downs had given it a special character in which boxing was important both as a virility symbol in the 'mountain fighter' tradition and as a way a man with talent could rise above his surroundings. When Freddie Welsh departed, the hopes of the community rested on the flyweight Jimmy Wilde, 22 years old, a graduate of the coal-face and the boxing booths.[40]

Wilde became British champion in November 1914, by beating the Londoner Joe Symonds, but lost the title two months later to an even tougher, and much rougher product of the booths, the Scot Tancy Lee. Both fights were watched by people of fashion as well as groundlings, but were greeted by a chorus of middle-class disapproval. Not all professional boxers were scrimshankers as their critics suggested. The British welterweight champion, Johnny Basham, for instance, who took the title from Johnny Summers in December 1914, after a thrilling contest at the NSC, was soon in the Army, becoming a sergeant in the Royal Welch Fusiliers. But boxing had always been offensive to middle-class opinion and it was particularly objectionable that such degrading public spectacles should continue in war-time. Yet in

London's East End to see 'Kid' Lewis in action offered not only respite from the gloomy war news but assurance of the nation's invincible fighting spirit. Born in a Jewish ghetto Ted Lewis had had his first fight as a child, boxing for a sixpenny purse, had become a full-time professional at 13 and British featherweight champion at 16. In August 1915, an 18-year-old veteran, he took the welterweight title from the American Jack Britton. They were to have many re-matches on both sides of the Atlantic. Similarly when, in November 1915, Joe Symonds beat Tancy Lee, Jimmy Wilde's fans confidently looked forward to a return contest and the NSC to a continued supply of entertainment.

Boxing caused relatively little interruption to the war effort. Professional soccer kept a much great number of players and spectators away from their duty. The soccer authorities felt obliged to carry on with their programme. Unlike cricket their season was just about to begin and players' contracts had already been signed. This apart soccer, in their eyes, was no luxury for the privileged few, like racing, nor a time-consuming, six days a week exhibition for the leisured classes, like cricket, but an hour-and a half's concentrated weekend excitement that refreshed the worker for the next week's toil. At the end of September 1914 the Football League was stoutly defending its competition as, inter alia, 'of national service in counteracting any tendency to panic and monomania'.[41] Even the FA, which had some claims to gentlemanly standards, was displaying the pusillanimous subservience to 'the professional element' that N. L. Jackson so deplored, and was apparently chiefly concerned with the 50% drop in attendance at League matches and its effect on club finances. The FA minutes recorded the fear that 'if club receipts were stopped and players' contract liabilities remained, it would mean the bankruptcy of many clubs'.[42]

Public criticism had been muted at first, but as the BEF went into action even moderates were roused to anger. On 7 November 1914, the historian and former Oxford rowing man A. F. Pollard wrote to *The Times* about it: 'Some of us who are debarred from by age or other disqualification feel shy of urging on others a duty to which we are not ourselves liable. But we can now feel no compunction in saying what we think of causes which act as deterrents to duty, and we view with indignation and alarm the persistence of Association Football Clubs in doing their best for the enemy.' There was nothing wrong with playing football – on the contrary – and a man might be doing his duty in other fields than at the Front, but there was 'no excuse for diverting from the front thousands of athletes in order to feast the eyes of inactive spectators who are either unfit to fight or unfit to be fought for'. A club that employed a professional player was 'bribing a needed recruit to refrain from enlistment'.

This touched a raw nerve at the FA, which pointed out that many soccer players had been amongst the first to join up. There had been several meetings with the Under-Secretary at the War Office and the FA had been advised that although the full programme of peace-time was 'not in accord with public sentiment or with the cruel realities of war' the difficulty could be met by merely ending Cup ties and international matches and carrying on with League fixtures. They had asked the clubs 'to place their grounds at the disposal of the War Office on days other than match days, for use as Drill grounds' and to permit prominent public figures to address the crowds, urging players and spectators to enlist. This, of course, solved the problem of players' contracts and the clubs responded enthusiastically.[43]

Leading footballers were indeed encouraged to volunteer publicly and crowds invited to serve along with their favourites. A typical poster, under the somewhat infelicitous heading,

> Do you want to be a Chelsea Die-hard?

went on

> If so,
> Join the 17th Battalion
> Middlesex Regiment
> 'The Old Die-Hards'
> And follow the lead given
> by your Favourite Football Players.[44]

Nevertheless, in the days after Professor Pollard's letter *The Times* made depressing reading for the FA. A headline read 'One recruit at Arsenal match'. Another report told of the negative response to an emotional appeal from Colonel Burns MP, who had lost his own son in the first few weeks of the war. An editorial on 23 November compared soccer's patriotic response unfavourably with that of cricket, rugby union and rowing and called the effects of the recruiting campaign 'grievously disappointing'. As a letter from a correspondent on 25 November illustrated, the old hostility to soccer's particular brand of professionalism was never far below the surface: 'British sports and British games have done our race a service which other nations have emulated too late and freely acknowledge on the field to-day. Except, however, in this one solitary instance of professional football, they have long since fallen into their proper places as a pastime and a training, not a business or a trade.' On 28 November the FA managed to get an article printed giving its own view and claiming that over 100,000 recruits had already come in by way of football clubs. But it was losing the argument hands down.

The readership of *The Times* was highly influential but restricted. There was a world beyond the establishment and beyond the capital. The *Athletic News*, a

Manchester publication that had championed professional soccer and was convinced, despite one or two disappointments, of the value of its social contribution, took strong exception to the class bias behind the pressure to end the League programme. On 7 December it declared 'The whole agitation is nothing less than an attempt by the classes to stop the recreation on one day a week of the masses . . . What do they care for the poor man's sport? The poor are giving their lives for this country in thousands . . . There are those who could bear arms, but have to stay at home and work for the Army's requirements and the country's needs. These should, according to a small clique of virulent snobs, be deprived of the one distraction they have had for over thirty years.' This did not answer the question of the scrimshanking professional. A Footballers' Battalion was formed in December 1914, and before long soccer apologists were claiming that nearly half the professionals were now serving their country, that many of the rest were married and so forth. Nevertheless, the Colonel of the Battalion was soon complaining to the FA that only 122 out of 1,800 League professionals had joined him, and that in many cases directors and managers of clubs had done their best to discourage players from enlisting.[45]

Much of the criticism of professional soccer was undoubtedly pre-war snobbery decked in patriotic uniform, but there was more to the agitation than class. Some of the most righteous indignation was moral. The Revd Spencer H. Elliott saw gambling as the enemy as well as Germans, and himself as the people's friend: 'The war found us with forty thousand bookmakers in our country with an annual turnover of at least eighty millions. The law did not touch them. Football coupons flooded the country, offering odds that were utterly unfair, and working men, women, lads, and even girls emptied their pockets into those of anonymous scoundrels.'[46] And class did not come into the minds of the bearers of sandwich boards which once had carried religious messages to sporting crowds but now asked them, 'Are you forgetting that there is a war on?' Frederick Charrington, who gave up a brewing fortune to fight for temperance and Christianity, was a particular enemy of war-time sport. Anxiety over crowds offering inviting targets to the Kaiser's Zeppelins and aeroplanes was another classless concern. In mid-October 1915, the worst raids so far, there had been 199 casualties. The middle classes certainly did not feel themselves exempt from public scrutiny. When in the spring of 1915 the editor of *Wisden* asked the Surrey secretary whether he would be putting up the nets for the members to practise in he replied wistfully, 'The nets will be up but I don't expect our fellows will use them much. They will be afraid of being jeered at by the men in tram-cars.'[47] And during the periodic rumours of invasion hard tennis courts, the emblem of prosperity, were suspect as gun emplacements ready for use by the Germans, Wimbledon was given over to the military and even golf links were subject to requisition.

Even as the argument raged the question of League soccer was becoming academic, because of the fall in attendances, which had now become serious. While MPs discussed punitive measures (such as charging double railway fares for civilian soccer supporters or a swingeing entertainments tax) the public decided the issue for themselves. Soccer's defenders argued that the empty terraces were themselves proof of the game's loyal contribution to the cause. Where else had the crowds gone but, with the players, to the Front? The fact remained that they had gone. Were it not for the players' contracts which lasted until the end of the season the Football League would have readily ended the programme by the end of the year. But however low the attendances, the clubs had to collect some money if they were to pay the players' wages. The agony continued as public opinion hardened, with that first Christmas come and gone and the casualty lists mounting. The superior London papers began to stop publishing reports of League matches, giving only the scores. Attendances went on falling, more and more players joined up and travel became more difficult. By April 1915, with contracts due for renewal the League had had enough. In announcing the decision to cancel the following season's programme they expressed the hope 'that every eligible young man will find in the service of the nation a higher call than in playing football'.

The traditional end to the season, the FA Cup Final, was still to be played. When Sheffield United beat Chelsea at Old Trafford, Manchester, on 24 April Lord Derby, presenting the trophy, told the teams 'You have played with one another and against one another for the Cup; play with one another for England now.' The *Sheffield Daily Telegraph* called United's victory a disgrace to the city: there was no civic reception.[48] But 2,000 fans had met the returning Sheffield team at the station. Whatever the middle-class critics thought of their professional heroes, they remained heroes to the working people. Neither the steelworkers, miners and munition workers nor the men at the Front thought any the less of them. Soccer itself was something special and if there were any emblems of the British sporting spirit amongst the Tommies in the trenches, the football was high amongst them. In the autumn of 1915 the men of the 1st Battalion, 18th London Regiment went into battle at Loos with a football at their feet.

Similarly back home, it was inconceivable that soccer would end entirely, or that it would cease to be played competitively and watched by at least some supporters. In Scotland, though the Scottish FA withheld their Cup for the duration, the League programme continued unchanged (with Celtic dominant). The professionals were officially paid £2 a week during the war and were expected to have another job. One famous Celtic player, Patsy

Gallagher, was fined by a munitions tribunal for absenteeism and later briefly suspended by the Scottish Football League.[49] In Ireland there were soccer heroes like Captain James Wilton, afterwards knighted and an IFA President, who joined the 36th Ulster Division and was badly wounded at the Somme. But the clubs struggled on and all the main Cup and League competitions continued.[50] In England, too, many League clubs, however impoverished and depleted in playing strength, deemed it their duty to stay in existence. The FA and the Football League forbade all remuneration, and, instead of the national leagues, authorised regional competitions that would not interfere with the conduct of the war.[51] Some gave up at that point rather than play what amounted to local, amateur 'friendlies', but most carried on – and some evaded the regulations.

'The north', soccer's heartland, where much of heavy industry and munitions work was, attracted some men in search of 'reserved occupations' and profitable sporting sidelines to the indignation of respectable citizens. But most players just wanted something to do with their spare time like the golfers of Stoke Poges or the fox-hunters of the Cottesmore. This was certainly true of the Northern Union rugby men. They had been caught on the wrong foot by the unexpected outbreak of war and the triumphant tourists returned from Australia to face a distinct change of mood. As with soccer there was pressure to close down the Rugby League programme at once and the Union's secretary agreed that 'saving king and Country [was] more important than winning medals on the football field'. The League Management Committee, believing that 'watching the game (was) a valuable aid to morale, both for service men on leave and for munition workers', felt it their duty to carry on, but the crowds, never great, were even smaller now and they dwindled further as the casualty lists lengthened. Respectable public opinion strongly disapproved, and the season petered out dismally, ending on a sour note: the Challenge Cup Final, played before a modest crowd, almost did not take place at all because the St Helen's players went on strike for more money just before the kick-off. In June 1915, announcing the end of the Rugby League for the duration, the Management Committee admitted frankly that it could not afford to pay the players. The Northern Union was not just the League clubs, of course, and game continued semi-officially in its old county sections. The Yorkshire clubs agreed to pay the players half a crown (12½p) 'tea-money' and the Lancashire clubs followed suit. Some clubs went to the wall, including Runcorn, one of the founder members: others barely stayed alive. Oldham, Broughton Rangers and Wigan sold their now useless grandstands.

Some things were imperishable, such as the gambling habit. Hence professional athletics, like racing and boxing, flourished whilst football went by the board. The Northern Union clubs, eyes always open for avenues of diversification, had long been active in 'pedestrianism', which was a useful second string for many professional footballers, rugby as well as soccer and very popular in the north. Willie Applegarth's first professional engagement, in November, 1914, against the Australian Jack Donaldson, was sponsored for £300 by Broughton Rangers. Applegarth never appeared at Powderhall, Edinburgh, the main 'pedestrian' centre, not because of any war-time restrictions, but because the promoters refused to pay him appearance money. Powderhall was nevertheless thriving with weekly pedestrian and dog-racing meetings. At the New Year Gala, 1915, more than 23,000 spectators attended, despite heavy rain and sleet. Donaldson was the main attraction. When he and Applegarth met again on 10 April at Salford RFCs ground the small attendance presumably reflected hostility to the Northern Union and shortly afterwards the Victoria Grounds, Newcastle, drew a record crowd for their £100 Christmas handicap. It was a similar story at most of the places on the pedestrian circuit: only Pontypridd of the established centres had to close.[52] No doubt it helped war-production.

Notes

1 R. Kipling, 'For all we have and are', 1914 in *Definitive Verse of Rudyard Kipling*, London, 1940.
2 A. J. P. Taylor, *The First World War*, Harmondsworth, 1966, p. 22.
3 *DNB*. Lord Desborough, 'Willy' Grenfell, was himself a great sportsman, both of the field sports and games variety, and Chairman of innumerable sporting bodies, including the British Olympic Committee that organised the London Games of 1908.
4 Dalmeny was to be mentioned in despatches and to win the MC, the French Legion of Honour and the DSO. However after being wounded he chose to join General Allenby's HQ rather than go back to his regiment and ended the war in Palestine, safe and sound. His decision was criticised in some bellicose armchair circles. Later unfavourable comparisons were drawn between him and his younger brother Neil, who was killed in 1917, not least by Rosebery who was inconsolable. For Dalmeny's youthful achievements and indiscretions see Derek Birley, *Land of Sport and Glory*, Manchester, 1994, pp. 191–3.
5 O. Mosley, *My Life*, London, 1968, p. 44.
6 Taylor, *First World War*, pp. 23–4.
7 S. Sassoon, *Memoirs of a Fox-hunting Man*, London, 1928, p. 300. The Yeomanry was better than the infantry. In the ranks were 'two or three bank clerks, several farmers and small tradesmen's sons' and a professional steeplechase jockey as well as Sherston himself and a local MP's son.
8 For a fuller account see E. C. Pelter, *Kings of the Court*, New York, 1963 and *The Davis Cup*, New York, 1969. See also G. Hillyard, *Forty Years of First-Class Tennis*, London, 1924, pp. 15–16 for the sequel to the internment.
9 U. A. Titley and R. McWhirter, *Centenary History of the Rugby Football Union*, London, 1970, biographies section. The company, which reached 400 in the end, attracted many rugger players, including the captains of Devon County and Bedford, nine of the East Midlands XV and apparently the whole of the Long Buckley village side. See also N. Starmer-Smith, *The Barbarians*, London, 1977, p. 50,

for a reproduction of the post-card.

10 Starmer-Smith, *Barbarians*, p. 49.

11 G. Williams in T. Mason (ed.), *Sport in Britain*, Cambridge, 1989, p. 323.

12 R. Brooke, 'The Soldier', in *1914 and Other Poems*, reprinted in countless anthologies including R. Church and M. Bozman (eds.), *Poems of Our Time, 1900–1940*, London, 1945, p. 96.

13 Poems by John Bain in *The Marlburian*, 1915, quoted in full in J. A. Mangan, *Athleticism in the Victorian and Edwardian Public School*, Cambridge, 1981, the standard work on this theme.

14 *Poems of Our Time*, p. 94.

15 Quoted in D. Cannadine, *The Decline and Fall of the British Aristocracy*, London, 1992, p. 75 in a chapter entitled 'The Embattled Elite', which gives a spirited if irreverent account of the effects of the war on the privileged classes. Rosebery was himself bereaved in 1917: see note 8 above.

16 In June 1917, by a declaration covering all the royal princes. At the same time the Battenbergs became Mountbattens.

17 *The Times*, 1 March 1915.

18 A. J. P. Taylor, *English History, 1914–45*, Oxford, 1965, p. 14.

19 Cannadine, *Decline*, p. 72.

20 D. Sutherland, *The Yellow Earl*, London, 1965, p. 183.

21 Lord Derby became Secretary of State for War in December 1916. The Derby Scheme in which men of military age attested their willingness to serve, was a prelude to conscription. Single men were supposed to be called up first from the list of volunteers but in order to make this workable compulsion was needed.

22 Sutherland, *Yellow Earl*, pp. 187–8.

23 See Taylor, *English History*, pp. 61-2.

24 Sassoon, *Memoirs*, p. 298.

25 Sutherland, *Yellow Earl*, p. 89.

26 E. Cundell, *DNB*.

27 E. Parker, *Shooting Weekend Book*, London, 1952, p. 151.

28 *Bloodstock Breeders' Review*, quoted by D. Laird, *Royal Ascot*, London, 1976, pp. 181–8, on which this account of the Ascot controversy is based.

29 Laird, *Royal Ascot*, p. 182.

30 ibid.

31 ibid., p. 183.

32 ibid.

33 ibid., pp. 183–4.

34 ibid., pp. 184–5.

35 The philosopher Frederic Harrison, for instance, had written to *The Times* about it.

36 The Grand National. for a variety of reasons, could no longer be held at Liverpool after 1915, but a version, known first as the Racecourse Association Chase and then the War National, was held at Gatwick in 1916–17 and 1918.

37 See W. Vamplew, *The Turf: A Social and Economic History*, London, 1976, for this and other tit-bits.

38 W. H. Gibson, *Early Irish Golf*, Naas, 1988, p. 87.

39 N. L. Jackson, *Sporting Days, Sporting Ways*, London, 1932, p. 257.

40 For the significance of boxing for South Wales, see D. Smith, 'Focal Heroes: a Welsh Fighting Class' in R. Holt (ed.), *Sport and the Working Class in Modern Britain*, Manchester, 1990, pp. 198–216.

41 Circular dated 30 September 1914, quoted in A. J. Arnold, 'Leeds City and the Great War', *IJHS*, May 1990, p. 112.

42 ibid.
43 ibid., p. 113.
44 J. Walvin, *The People's Game*, London, 1975, p. 89.
45 S. Inglis, *League Football and the Men Who Made it*, London, 1988, p. 95.
46 Society for the Propagation of Christian Knowledge pamphlet, 1915, quoted by A. Marwick, *The Deluge*, London, 1973, p. 50. This is a valuable study of the home front in the 1914–1 war.
47 'Notes by the Editor', *Wisden 1917*: reprinted in B. Green, *Wisden Anthology 1900–1940*, London, 1980, p. 438.
48 Walvin, *People's Game*, p. 90.
49 T. Mason (ed.), *Sport in Britain*, Cambridge, 1989, p. 183.
50 M. Brodie, *100 Years of Irish Football*, Belfast, 1980, p. 12.
51 July 1915. In October 1916, after compulsory enlistment had been introduced, the FA brought in detailed regulations specifying allowable expenses and specified that club books could be called in for inspection at any time, Arnold, 'Leeds City', p. 113.
52 See Birley, *Sport and the Making of Britain*, Manchester, 1993, pp. 278–9 and *Land of Sport and Glory*, Manchester, 1994, pp. 62–5, 223, for the earlier background. For a full account of professional athletics from Victorian times see D. A. Jamieson, *Powderhall Grounds and Pedestrianism*, Edinburgh, 1945.

CHAPTER FOUR

Uphill struggle

The British had not been alone in expecting that it would soon be over. The German Olympic Committee did not regard the outbreak of war as any reason to withdraw its application to hold the 1916 Games in Berlin. Nor did de Coubertin, who had remained very keen on the idea for many months, resisting the calls of the British delegate, Theodore Cook, for the removal of the Germans from various committees. De Coubertin's refusal to consider prudential alternatives, like neutral America or Scandinavia, had lost him many friends in both France and Britain. 'I admire Pierre, who is deceiving himself and seeking to salvage the remnants of his work', commented one of his relations.[1] By the end of 1915 even de Coubertin was in despair. So far from being over, the war was expanding.

That May, after much bargaining, Italy had entered the arena. This brought few of the advantages the Allies had hoped for. The backdoor route to Berlin remained locked. The Italian Army was badly-equipped, her Navy was unreliable, and in general she was a heavy burden economically. It was a particular nuisance that she had to be supplied with British coal, which was already in great demand to meet the deficiencies of the captured French mines. On the Eastern Front the Russians, shattered by the only decisive breakthrough of the war, had lost three-quarters of a million men in prisoners alone and been forced back 300 miles before the Austrians and Germans had come to the end of their supply lines and been forced to halt. In the west the stalemate continued – even more bloodily. The Dardanelles débâcle had severely dented British confidence.

The war effort

Morale was still, by and large, surprisingly high, but fewer volunteers worried that the war might be over before they got into it. Whilst the generals put amateur heroics into perspective by their professional miscalculations and the admirals awaited their chance to settle it once and for all, the politicians had to keep the country going. The government, in fact, was showing unaccustomed activity, most evident in the vigorous efforts of Lloyd George to harness industry to the war effort. His approach, which owed nothing to the public school ethos, was to offer a mixture of cash, cajolery and compulsion that profoundly influenced not only the conduct of the war but the nature of post-war society. The new Ministry disbursed in its time some £2 billion and set up 218 large factories and 20,000 small ones. Its basic method – meeting manufacturers' production costs and allowing them 'a reasonable profit' – was inflationary and bred a contingent of war profiteers, many of them afterwards grateful political supporters of Lloyd George. But it worked.

Other ministries were less enthusiastic about intervention. When the idiosyncratic Colonel Hall-Walker decided to give up his stud and training stables he offered the government his bloodstock for nothing if it would take the two establishments off his hands. The Cabinet was well aware of the importance of bloodstock for military purposes but, as Hall-Walker put it, the offer 'met with some difficulties in departmental etiquette'. These were not resolved until the eve of the projected sale when the Ministry of Agriculture won the concession. The two establishments cost £65,625. But though the price worried some tax-payers others were more concerned with principle. Private breeders, whose value to the national economy had been recognised by the decision to allow racing to continue, were more than a little upset at the prospect of subsidised competition. They were also highly sceptical of the government's ability to run a stud successfully. Nevertheless, the *Bloodstock Breeders' Review* of January 1916, took a charitable and optimistic line: 'We feel sure that if the stud is skilfully managed with a single eye to the purpose it has to serve, is not hampered by restrictions of the red tape order to which governments are partial, and is generously endowed with funds, it has a great and beneficial future.' When it was announced that the Earl of Lonsdale, not hitherto famous in racing circles but strongly opposed to bureaucracy, was to lease the stable and the yearlings there were sighs of relief.

Meanwhile Lloyd George was having trouble with the Munitions of War Act which sought to control the movement of workers and to impose national criteria on local wage settlements. Workers in key industries were already bound by an agreement between the government and national trade union leaders not to go on strike and to discontinue restrictive practices during the emergency, but this was better observed in some places than others. The miners had declined to participate and the engineers needed a special agreement. As well as lacking sympathy with the capitalist war-mongers many local leaders suspected that the government was using the emergency as an excuse for 'dilution' by unskilled labour and consequent erosion of wage levels. Fearing betrayal by their own leadership, shop stewards, especially on the Celtic fringes, took up the running themselves. Lloyd George quickly learned the lesson that the carrot worked better than the stick for British workers. Wage incentives and a shorter basic working week with abundant overtime were measures first introduced in munitions factories that spread to industry generally.

But the climate for coercion was improving. Press attention had shifted from the shells scandal to the shirkers, allegedly 650,000 of them, who were fit to serve their country but were manifestly not doing so. Some who held back were engaged on civilian war work. At first such men had been issued with badges to protect them from crusading ladies who presented white feathers to young men not in uniform. In August 1915 a National Register was compiled: everyone, male and female, between 15 and 65 had to give details of their age and occupation, and badges became harder to come by. The government denied any intention of introducing conscription, to which the unions were firmly opposed, of which Liberals were apprehensive and which even some Tories felt would undermine the distinctively British way of going to war.[2] Nevertheless, something had to be done; fair play was just as important as freedom. The Derby scheme (under which every man had to attest his willingness to serve if required but exemption could be granted for cogent national or personal reasons) appeared at first to be the answer. But this well-intentioned exercise soon ran aground. Less than half the men of military age on the National Register came forward to attest and there were over 700,000 requests for exemption. In any event the whole thing was undermined because the government had promised that no married man would be drafted before all the single ones had been called up. In this dilemma, which some thought had been cunningly contrived, the government, in order to redeem their pledge to the married, had to apply compulsion to the single. In January, 1916, against the overwhelming opposition of the TUC, conscription was brought in for all unmarried men. By May, as the situation at the Front deteriorated, the married men had to follow.

With General Haig holding his horses and awaiting a proper supply of properly trained men, the French commander General Joffre was taking the strain. While his troops, with great loss of life, were trying to hold off the Germans at Verdun, the British racing authorities, aware of their strategic importance, used the spring of 1916 to negotiate an extended programme of racing for the summer. (They were allowed no provision in the north, where most of the munitions factories were, and an entertainments tax was introduced, but meetings were promised at Gatwick, Lingfield and Windsor as well as Newmarket and Newbury.) Meanwhile 78 divisions were poured in to Verdun's defence between February and the end of June. There were compensations. Colonel P. C. Trevor, afterwards the *Daily Telegraph*'s rugger correspondent, was finally convinced by this dogged resistance that the French now had the determination to make something of their international rugby team.[3]

Conscription did not bring everyone into the war effort. Neville Cardus was still at Shrewsbury. When the Headmaster's secretary 'rushed to the colours, like thousands of other idealists', Cardus took his place. He felt it to be a sacrifice: 'I gave up hours of my cricket regretfully, and when I heard the crack of the bat on June days outside the Headmaster's study . . . I felt sorry for myself.'[4] He was soon even sorrier. The Headmaster left to go to Eton and invited Cardus to follow him if he could get clearance from the military authorities. When he tried to get an early examination and thus an early clearance, he was told to wait his turn and so missed the job. 'Even now, a quarter of a century later,' he recalled, 'it is hard to bear the memory of the disillusionment . . . I suffered.'[5] He drifted into casual labour before finding his true métier on the *Manchester Guardian*. A few conscientious objectors 'got away with it', too, but not so easily. Though allowed to appeal to tribunals most were harried into service of some kind – labour camps if necessary – or imprisoned. Philip Noel-Baker, a Quaker and a pacifist, escaped the contempt usually felt for 'conchies' by joining an ambulance unit. He served bravely in Italy, winning the Mons Star for Valour in 1917 and the *croce di guerra* the following year.

Conscription could not be introduced in Ireland. Many Irishmen, of course, chose to fight voluntarily. Some 150,000 had enlisted by 1916. Others, as on the mainland, stayed at home assisting the war effort and making money out of it. Agriculture, the staple industry, flourished as never before. There was plenty of hunting for farmers as well as officers on leave. But, also as in Britain, the urban middle classes were acutely conscious of what the neighbours thought. 'By . . . 1915 it had become evident that the war was not going to be over quickly. Golf was not something to be spoken of when so many were dying on the Western front. Many clubs were beginning to feel the pinch with decreased subscriptions caused by the enthusiastic rush to enlist. On March 19th 1915 *Irish Life* published a survey . . . Upwards of 1250 Irish golfers were serving.'[6] The ethnic, political and social connotations of golf were similar to those of rugger. At the opposite pole were hurling and Gaelic football. As the GAA had grown more popular and commercially successful some of its sharper political edges had been blunted. But it was plunged into crisis in 1915 when Redmond, the Nationalist leader offered the services of the Irish Volunteers to Britain, hoping to bring about Irish unity by service alongside Ulster Volunteers.

The offer, even before its inevitable rejection by both Kitchener and the Ulstermen, infuriated Irish activists and resistance to conscription spilled over into armed rebellion. One of the victims was F. H. Browning, President of the IRFU and a senior officer of the Irish Rugby Football Corps, unarmed veterans who were ambushed returning from a route march on Easter Monday, 1916.[7] Conversely the splinter group of Irish Volunteers who seized the General Post Office included a number of GAA men. However, quite a few 'had gone over to the enemy'. Three prominent GAA leaders had made a last-minute attempt to get the ring-leaders to desist and most of its rank and file hurlers and Gaelic footballers wanted nothing to do with violent rebellion.[8] With Irish public opinion generally unsympathetic to the rebels and further alienated by their abortive attempts to secure German backing even fervent nationalists disapproved. The rebellion was quickly put down and at the subsequent government enquiry the GAA denied involvement and officially dissociated itself from the militants. But the story took another twist.

The British, outraged at this stab in the back, were in no mood for cool consideration. Martial law was introduced, its rough justice made even rougher by over-zealous implementation. Fifteen of the leaders were executed.[9] Irish opinion was polarised and the Irish Volunteers gained many more recruits. British anger was increased when it emerged that an Irish Nationalist MP had successfully moved an amendment to the Bill bringing in a new entertainments duty. His innocent objective had been to secure exemption to organisations founded 'with the object of reviving national pastimes'. Backbenchers protested vigorously that this gave special favour to the GAA, which took in men 'who are in open rebellion against this country' and was 'closed to all men who join His Majesty's Forces'.[10] It was left to the Chancellor of the Exchequer to decide and a long period of lobbying by both sides began.

Battle of the sexes: suspension of hostilities

If the war did nothing to assist resolution of the Irish question it did wonders for the other great Edwardian issue – votes for women. As soon as hostilities broke out, the leading suffragists had suspended their campaign for the duration of the emergency. The movement was torn apart by the decision of the legendary Mrs Emmeline Pankhurst to lead her Women's Social and Political Union into patriotic endeavour. As her daughter Sylvia recalled, Mrs Pankhurst 'toured the country making recruiting speeches. Her supporters handed the white feather to every young man they encountered wearing civilian dress and bobbed up at Hyde Park meetings with placards: "Intern them all."[11] But while Sylvia herself started her own left-wing, fervently pacifist movement based in the East End her mother was showing a quicker way to political favour.

The lead in women's war work was taken by the upper classes and it had nothing to do with liberation: it was, on the contrary, in the mid Victorian Florence Nightingale tradition. When the aristocracy sent their sons off to fight and turned their great houses into makeshift hospitals, their wives and daughters ran them. The Hon. Lionel Tennyson (an MCC tourist to South Africa in 1913–14) was nursed to recovery from his wounds by Lady Caernarvon and Lady Ridler whose temporary hospital he remembered as 'the best in London . . . the food exquisitely cooked and served'.[12] The more venturesome took their talents to the war zones. The dowager duchesses and other great ladies who organised hospitals or set up canteens behind the lines sometimes irritated the professionals and occasionally did more harm than good, but they got things done.[13] And there was a distinctively modern air about the Marchioness of Londonderry's Women's Legion, a quasi-military affair aimed at releasing men from civilian jobs for military service: its various training centres prepared women to work as cooks in Army camps, to drive ambulances and staff cars and to work on the land. By early 1916 Lady Londonderry had overcome civil service opposition and general male prejudice to win official recognition.

Not all the efforts of the volunteers seem to have been directed towards severely utilitarian duties. N. L. Jackson, trying to maintain Stoke Poges golf course with only one old man and a boy, had wangled himself a job in the Ministry of Agriculture, setting up markets for the supply of surplus vegetables and controlling the petrol supplied to volunteers to distribute them. When he asked the head of the Ministry's women's section 'whether she could not let (him) have six or eight of her women to help on the farm and devote a day or two each week to the golf course . . . she peremptorily refused . . ., pointing out that their women could only work for genuine production of food . . . She suggested, however, that I might try the Legion . . . and here I was more lucky, for I secured the services of a party of girls who had gone to help on a large estate in Sussex, but had been so disgusted with the accommodation offered them that they had returned the next morning.'[14] The land girls nevertheless both helped the war effort and the cause of liberation. The shorter skirts – and sometimes the trousers – they wore aroused comment, but were clearly functional.

Middle-class women were best placed to take advantage of the new opportunities of service. Those in male professions, such as medicine, ceased being curiosities and became much sought after. Others, with or without qualifications, determined to do their bit. In June 1916 the *Daily Mail* listed 'some of the new occupations for women' – everything from tram conductors and van drivers to window-cleaners and shell-makers. These, it was implied were not jobs for the proletariat to be undertaken for gain but opportunities for the better sort to serve their country.[15] A more obviously middle-class, and more permanent, breakthrough came with the 200,000 who went into government offices: the 500,000 'business girls', forerunners of the characteristically lower-middle-class shorthand-typists who gradually replaced the Dickensian male clerk. Such women were notable for their independent outlook. They went to restaurants alone or with women friends, sometimes even smoking in public.[16] A few signalled their seriousness of purpose by shortening their hair. Some, inspired by the example of the Volunteers of Ulster, got more direct action and a uniform by establishing a Women's Volunteer Reserve.

But a great many of the new jobs were also going to young women of the working class. Once the principle of compulsory military training of men had been accepted government intervention, backed by DORA and her offspring, spread to every walk of life. Industry was transformed, willy-nilly, as everything was subordinated to getting fit men to the battlefield. Dilution of skilled labour was superseded by 'substitution' which took skilled men away from their trades altogether. And by greatly exacerbating the shortage of civilian labour conscription opened the door to women: 800,000 went into munitions work and a similar number into transport jobs. Not all were interested in female suffrage, and some war-workers, especially in male enclaves like engineering, went back to the kitchen sink as soon as the emergency was over. But they had astonished traditionalists by the tasks they had proved capable of accomplishing and, like women of all classes, many acquired a taste for the kind of independence that came from having money of their own. For the younger ones, too, the experience of working together in a factory environment, often led, as it had done with their menfolk, to their joining together for sport and recreation, showing tastes and aptitudes that again surprised the conventional. Of the numerous soccer teams the best known, started in 1917 at the Dick Kerr engineering works in Preston, soon achieved a more than local celebrity.

A highly important social change precipitated by the war was the decline in domestic service which, in marked contrast to other female occupations, declined by 400,000. About half the new bus conductresses had previously been 'in service'. From such subservience and from their own household drudgery vast numbers went into industry and very few ever went back. Women's liberation still had some distance to trickle down, however. This was most evident in the ultimate struggle for control over their own bodies, which took a new turn in war-time conditions. Birth-control was not unknown before the war but artificial methods, even for men, were thought scandalous. Control seems to have been exercised mainly by the middle classes, for it was in this group, as the 1911 census had shown, that the birth-rate was falling. The discovery of Salvarsan, the first effective cure for syphilis in 1909, had also chiefly benefited the wealthier sort. The war brought the male contraceptive sheath into greater use, against venereal disease as well as pregnancy. By the end 'rubber goods' were available for furtive purchase in chemist's shops everywhere, but in the meantime the popular notions of 'live for the moment' and 'give the boys a good time' brought a 30% increase in illegitimate births. Debased cinema shows, plays and songs, unaccompanied women in public houses, the fashion for shorter skirts – all were blamed for creating an atmosphere of promiscuity. One of the casualties of the war was the chaperon, called to more urgent tasks. All young women enjoyed more freedom, but the working-class girls still had the babies.

Morale

In the second year of the war there were still fervent advocates of the Newbolt philosophy. Some were non-combatant theorists. John Astley Cooper, for instance, told the Royal Colonial Institute in 1916 that the Empire, which games had helped to build, had found its soul through participating in the game of war. 'Much mutual misunderstanding, distrust and ignorance is being cordially destroyed as the men of the British Isles and the Ocean Commonwealth fight side by side in the trenches of this greater game.'[17] But there were practitioners, too. Lieutenant-Colonel Edgar Mobbs, commanding his own regiment by April 1916, was putting the philosophy into action, earning enduring fame by punting a rugger ball in the direction of the enemy and urging his men to 'follow up' as he led them over the top.

Siegfried Sassoon, looking back through George Sherston's quizzical but compassionate eyes, noted other types of leader, among them 'a sturdy little public schoolboy who made no secret of his desire to avoid appearing in the Roll of Honour' and, by contrast, a former clerk in Somerset House who was an 'inspiration toward selfless patience' and 'took his men's discomforts very much to heart'. Sherston, who greatly admired the latter, added wryly, 'I need hardly say that he had never hunted. He could swim like a fish, but no social status was attached to that.'[18] The gulf between all types of officer and their men was wide. They were drawn together by their common plight, 'provisionally condemned to death' and hoping for a 'Blighty wound'. But the officers, especially the unmarried ones, felt a compensating release from past trivialities that made some sense at least of why they were there and 'in an emotional mood could glory in the idea of the supreme sacrifice'. Private soldiers got lectures from the fiery and ambitious Colonel on 'the offensive spirit, and the spirit of the regiment', high-flown concepts they only dimly understood. For his part Sherston, instructing his platoon in the evenings, confined himself to 'asking them easy questions from the infantry training manual . . . and reading the League Football news aloud'.[19]

Though the League itself was in abeyance its regional substitutes could thus claim to be doing their bit for the morale of the troops, directly when they came home on leave and vicariously when they were back in action. In the north, where soccer's morale-boosting properties had greatest scope, some clubs did extraordinarily well out of the war. Leeds City had been forced into liquidation in 1912 with liabilities of £15,000 compared with assets of only £84. The syndicate which took over in August 1915, untroubled by the national controversy, saw an opportunity and did not care much about how they took it. Already it had been approached by Tottenham Hotspurs' international forward 'Fanny' Walden seeking a spare-time adjunct to the job he had taken with a local motor engineering firm. Leeds's manager, Herbert Chapman, was delighted: a player like Walden, he reckoned, 'could be the making of the Leeds City team'.[20] (Spurs, on the other hand, were extremely annoyed and tried to get the FA to initiate an enquiry.) Chapman's war-efforts took him away to manage a nearby munitions factory, but he continued to operate through a deputy, and to good effect. Leeds won the Midland Section subsidiary tournament, which ended in May 1916, and declared a profit. The methods they used were to be the subject of an enquiry and a source of scandal after the war. Leeds City were unlikely to have been alone in their wickedness. Across the Pennines Billy Meredith, officially with Manchester United, played as a guest for his old ally Mangnall at Manchester City throughout the war.

War-time conditions intensified the old north–south divide. The Northern Union, lacking the resources to compete with soccer, continued to flounder, and the rugger men as they 'followed up' in the deadly game could hope to find their code purged of impurities when they returned. In Scotland, where the gallantry of the rugger men was legendary, the divide was plain to see. Glasgow Celtic won the League again demonstrating as they were repeatedly required to do, war or no war, their ethnic superiority over Rangers. Clydeside radicals apart Scotland not only offered a soccer programme, but was a favourite resort for sport-starved northern Englishmen. In 1916, a great year for professional athletics, Powderhall, in winter as well as summer, drew exceptional numbers of both spectators and competitors from both sides of the border.

The most obvious example of the war-time divide was in cricket. The county championship and representative match programme was suspended. At MCC Lord Hawke, recording his pleasure that 75% of first-class cricketers were in the services, pledged support for keeping the game going in the schools. MCC did in fact play 44 games in 1915 and a similar number in 1916 and, as a later chronicler commented, 'if their sides were often long in the tooth this could be offset by the youth of the school teams . . . for many were fighting or had been killed in Flanders at a time when they would normally have still been playing cricket for their schools.' [21] ('Of club cricket in the ordinary sense of the word, there was none', he continued, and an interesting by-product was that the schools widened the social circle of their fixture lists as they filled the gaps. From 1915 Winchester, 'who had for sixty years played only one school – Eton – now arranged matches with Charterhouse, Wellington and Bradfield' and appropriate similar sacrifices were made lower down the scale.)

The county clubs hung on as best they could against the day when normality would return. Surrey's 1915 report declared, 'The Committee are faced with many difficulties and uncertainties in the present National Crisis, and rely on the loyal support of the Members, as heavy current expenses have to be met whether cricket is played or not.' Happily for them, and for their fellow-sufferers, most saw it as their patriotic duty to continue to pay their sub-scriptions even with no cricket to watch, and as their main item of expenditure, the players' wage bill, no longer had to be met, it was easier to balance the books. Some, like Worcestershire, even managed with the aid of special appeals to make a modest profit. MCC itself was able to invest £50,000 in 5% War Loans. This, of course, was quite exceptional, and the chief consolation of even a big county club like Lancashire was that inflation reduced the real cost of debt repayment, whilst Gloucestershire could only solve their problems by selling their ground to Fry's, the chocolate people.[22] *Wisden* recorded with a mixture of pride and gloom the contribution they made in other ways. Military cricket continued 'and the county committees every-where put their grounds at the disposal of the troops'. Lord's accommodated various military units and the staff still employed there 'spent part of their time making thousands of hay-nets for horses'.[23] The pavilions at Old Trafford, Trent Bridge and Derby became hospitals and the Leicester ground housed a remount depot and a rifle range.

By contrast the situation in league cricket was buoyant. With no competition from county cricket the leagues enjoyed a boom, especially in the north and midlands. The Bradford League did particularly well. Early in the war the Saltaire Club had signed Sidney Barnes and were rewarded for their enterprise by gates of thousands. Other clubs, grasping the point, signed their own stars and soon many former county professionals were drawing the crowds and augmenting their war-time earnings. This was hardly what people expected of cricket The *Yorkshire Post* condemned it as 'out of harmony with the spirit of the times, directly opposed to the serious interests of the nation, and a melancholy response to the dominating and inexorable call.'[24] It went on nevertheless.

Nor were all the guest stars 'northern' mavericks like Barnes. Indeed even the archetypal 'southern' professional Jack Hobbs played league cricket for a time. Aged 32 when the war came and a married man with four children, Hobbs worked at first in a munitions factory before joining up in 1916. Meanwhile he scored a chanceless century against Barnes when they met in the Bradford League.[25] Barnes, who played in it throughout the war, found other batsmen less troublesome, for he took 404 wickets at an average of 5.5 runs apiece. This, however, was a measure of his strength not the Bradford League's weakness. The normal requirement limiting the number of professionals per club was relaxed during the war and Keighley had so many that some had to play in the second team. Their first, it was generally agreed, was good enough to have beaten any county side. George Gunn, Frank Woolley, Cecil Parkin, Percy Holmes and Schofield Haigh were amongst the 'whole host of . . . world-famous players' Fred Root of Worcestershire played against when he was invalided out of the army in 1916.[26]

The year 1916 was also good for boxing, which drew large crowds at the NSC as well as 'northern' venues. This was the year when Jimmy Wilde beat Joe Symonds and claimed the world flyweight championship, won his return match with Tancy Lee, got his Lonsdale belt, and confirmed his world title by beating the American 'Young Zulu' Kid. Freddie Welsh, an American now, and able to trust American referees, successfully defended his lightweight title against Ad Wolgast. Ted Lewis fought another battle with the tigerish Jack Britton. There was one disappointment for the bookmakers, however. After beginning so promisingly the year turned out badly for race-goers. Transport difficulties, and the war situation generally, led to last-minute curtailment of the programme. Happily the Jockey Club's stronghold at Newmarket remained inviolate, the classics were held as usual and the authorities, upper lips suitably stiff, began at once to negotiate something better for the following year.

Casualties, military, political and sporting

Stiff upper lips had been increasingly necessary since Easter. Soon after the Dublin rising came an event of great and depressing symbolic significance. At the end of May 1916 the Navy had its chance at last when the Germans changed their tactics from submarine warfare to surface aggression. But the battle of Jutland, though it drove the enemy back to port, brought no conclusive victory, only heavy losses and the exposure of inferior British armour and guns. (The Germans' subsequent reluctance to play this kind of naval game reduced the British Grand Fleet to watching and waiting inactivity again. A group of officers, shore-bound in Scotland for much of the war, stocked a local loch with fish and whiled away many hours with pleasure and profit).[27] The sea brought other shocks, again with unexpected outcome. Asquith had shirked the task of negotiating the implementation of Irish Home Rule – the nationalist price for co-operation – and Lloyd George took on the task. This did his reputation no harm and coincidentally got him the job of War Minister when Kitchener was lost at sea. Three days after he took office came the disaster of the Somme.

On the first day of the battle Captain W. P. Nevill of the 8th East Surreys gave each of his platoons a soccer ball, one inscribed 'The Great European Cup-tie Finals, East Surreys v Bavarians. Kick-off at zero', the other 'no referee', and offered a prize for the first to dribble one to the German lines. He did not survive to present it, nor many of them to receive it.[28] The Lonsdale battalion moved into action singing, to the tune of *John Peel*,

> D'ye ken Lord Lonsdale, that sportsman true?
> D'ye ken his charger of chestnut hue?
> D'ye ken that battalion of Cumberland blue
> Who will march to Berlin in the morning?

In fact most of them marched to their death. Of 28 officers and 800 men only 3 officers and 280 men survived.[29] One of the many casualties that August was John King, the rugger international, now a lance-corporal, who had left the Hussars for a front-line infantry regiment and was killed in action at Guillemont. In September there was a poignant symbol of the end of cricket's golden age in the death in action of Lieutenant Kenneth Hutchings, who had thrilled the crowds at pre-war county grounds. But the Somme was a graveyard for many sportsmen known and unknown. By November 1916 the British Army had lost 420,000 men and the Expeditionary Force had practically ceased to exist. There were still plenty of eager volunteers from the public schools to take the places of the junior officers who led their men so bravely from the Front and paid with their lives. But it was the final disenchantment for many who had begun the war with romantic ideals.

As the situation deteriorated the choice for the politicians lay between negotiated peace and what Churchill, languishing on the back benches, called 'war socialism'. It was Lloyd George who prevailed, by winning the support not only of Tories, who thought a little temporary dictatorship would be no bad thing, but of the Labour Party which held the key to union backing. He split the Liberal Party in the process and changed the face of British politics by pushing them into third place – for eighty years at least – but it produced a coalition that looked as though it might win the war. It was still only 'might'. Lloyd George's reconstructed War Cabinet of December 1916 was supposed to exercise greater control over the generals and admirals but they became even harder to handle, strengthened by the support of the disgruntled service ministers now excluded from the Cabinet.

Haig's policy remained unchanged – piling in thousands of infantry to hold the line while awaiting an opening for the cavalry. There was some talk of a new 'secret weapon', the tank. But no-one really took it seriously. The greatest technological invention of the war had been developed despite much travail and inter-departmental rivalry. Kitchener had dismissed it as 'a pretty mechanical toy' and it was despised on principle by most cavalrymen. Facetious boffins had christened the first prototypes 'Little Willy' and 'Big Willy' and the government encouraged people to go on treating the whole matter as a joke to preserve its secrecy. Some were surreptitiously sent to Haig in 1916 but when he used them at the Somme the surprise value was lost through mechanical deficiencies and the tank became even more of a music-hall joke.

Although their activities were still 'officially recognised by the Government as being of paramount importance in maintaining the horse supply',[30] the hunting set found it extremely hard to carry out their patriotic duties. Fodder for the horses and food (particularly oatmeal) for the hounds were increasingly scarce. In the winter of 1916–17 packs were reduced by an average of 40% and hunting was limited in scope almost everywhere for the rest of the war. There were manpower problems, too. Indeed many packs were rescued by women Masters. At the Atherstone the redoubtable Mrs Inge was a natural choice to follow her father and her late husband in the post. Captain Harry Townshend, still exercising his 'semi-benevolent tyranny' as Hunt secretary, regarded her as a 'splendid little woman'.[31] Fields were generally smaller but often 'very well sustained' by 'farmers, veterans of either sex, and children': 'the able-bodied element was almost entirely supplied by officers or yeomanry troopers on leave'.[32]

Money was not usually a major problem for those who carried on the hunts. Although 'many people suffered from increased income tax and rise in prices' subscriptions were readily paid: indeed 'in some favoured countries money was forthcoming from those who had done well financially during the war period'. The fortunate included farmers as well as industrialists, and some were getting too big for their boots. Non-hunting farmers, rich or poor, were a bigger nuisance than ever. One blessing was the departure of many gamekeepers taking their specialist skills to the trenches, but hunt servants had joined up in droves as well. It was hard to find able-bodied veterans willing to turn out at night to stop up earths. Shortage of petrol limited the use of motor vans to visit outlying countries and 'hunting special' trains were a thing of the past. The worst problem of all, though, was the food shortage. More and more hounds had to be put down as the war went on, and horses either did not get enough forage or had to make do with inferior hay and oats.[33]

In February 1917 the Germans resumed their unsporting unrestricted attacks on shipping and the Jockey Club was informed that there must be no more racing, even at Newmarket after the first spring meeting. There were still some 2,000 racehorses in training, and whilst the actual amount of fodder required to feed them might not matter much, the principle – not risking men's lives to feed racehorses – did. Even so, powerful voices were raised against the government's decision. The Thoroughbred Breeders' Association (led by Lord D'Abernon whose previous contribution to the war effort had been as chairman of the Liquor Control Board) pointed out that the price of yearlings had already dropped by 60% since the war and the total income of the industry by £7 to 8 million. To end racing would be the last straw. Amongst the Jockey Club members to rally to the cause were the Lords Jersey, Durham, Crewe, Rosebery (emerging from retirement for the occasion) and not least Lord Derby, the War Minister. Powerful outside support came from Lord Curzon, a member of the War Cabinet, and Horatio Bottomley, demagogue, patriotic fund-raiser and founding editor of *John Bull*. Not surprisingly the government gave in, agreeing to forty days' racing and leaving it to the Jockey Club to agree the venues with the War Office, Board of Trade and Ministry of Munitions. So at last the north – Manchester, Stockton and Ayr – got meetings as well as the southern courses.

Contrasts

The 'Northerners' were still enjoying their other special privileges in 1917. Glasgow Celtic won the Scottish League and Glentoran broke a sequence of Linfield successes to beat Belfast Celtic for the Irish Cup. In England Leeds City won the main Midland Section tournament, and again did extraordinarily well financially. They contemplated withdrawing the following season, concerned by the doubling of rail fares, but were prevailed upon to reconsider by the League's chairman, who felt that their departure would 'set back the Association game in Leeds for some years, and give fresh life to the rival code'.[34] They stayed and there was no relief for the Northern Union, now in desperate straits. However the game was there for those who wanted it, as was professional athletics. For the pedestrian promoters the biggest problem was the shortage of new stars, without which athletics had little appeal and less scope for a betting coup. Even the old stars were now in short supply. With Willie Applegarth in the army, Jack Donaldson and his fellow-Australian Mears were now the mainstay. Veterans came out of retirement to fill the gap and soldiers on leave, munition workers and the militarily unfit made up the numbers. But fields were thin, even for the handicap events, and there were few big matches, even at Powderhall.

In boxing most of the best action was in America, by Americans. They had, however, redeemed their reputation in Britain somewhat in April 1917 by joining the war. The cynical newsmen were not impressed when it was learned shortly afterwards that Freddie Welsh had offered to devote the receipts of his title defences to a fund for starting a sportsman's regiment. But his popular support was no less and the many Welsh fans were disappointed when a month later Benny Leonard took the lightweight crown from him. It was better news in June when 'Kid' Lewis made a successful expedition to Dayton, Ohio for a title fight with Jack Britton. Jimmy Wilde was now in the Army but continued to defend his flyweight title against all comers.

This selective treatment, encouraging the gambling habit and generally pandering to the weaknesses of the undisciplined working classes, troubled hitherto docile enthusiasts for middle-class sports. The editor of *Wisden* was particularly incensed not only by boxing matches but by the continuation of professional billiards, the latest amateur game to go commercial. Billiards spectators were denied the annual world championship, contested for the last three years by Melbourne Inman and Tom Reece, but otherwise the entertainment continued unabated. At the end of the 1917 season the editor of *Wisden*, thus provoked, flew a kite for the resumption of county cricket. 'There can be no doubt,' he wrote, 'that as regards the playing of cricket in war-time there was a great change of feeling last summer. People realised that with public boxing carried on to an extent unheard of before, and professional billiard matches played in the hottest weather there was something illogical, not to say absurd, in placing a ban on cricket.' He pointed out that cricketers – 'unlike our racing friends' – had no quarrel with authority. They had shut down their programme voluntarily and had every moral right to resume it. Recalling the squeamishness of the Surrey members two years before about the possible hostility of men on tramcars he noted how much the climate of opinion had changed. By this time people had 'come to regard the nightmare of war as a normal condition and cricket was felt to be as legitimate as any other recreation'.[35]

There was no serious question of county cricket resuming even if the logistical problems could have been solved. MCC had nailed their colours – and those of their professionals – too firmly to the mast. And there were too many reminders in *Wisden* 's own obituary columns of the cause for which sacrifices were being made. In October 1917, the death in Palestine of 'Tibby' Cotter, the Australian fast bowler, was a reminder that cricket, like war, was a great force for imperial unity: a year later Major R. O. Schwartz MC, South Africa's googly bowler, died. More poignant still for those who valued the feudal myths of the English game was the death in action, aged 36, of Sergeant Colin Blythe, the Kent and England left-arm spinner, whom Ranji had thought a better bowler than Wilfred Rhodes. As the *Wisden* tribute concluded, 'It is pleasant to know that the Kent Committee have decided to put up a suitable memorial to him.'[36] Even the rugger men had their inter-service games and a few other charity matches, however, and the cricketers now joined in. Yorkshire played four such games in 1917, and MCC gave official sanction to the notion by staging two matches at Lord's – one between the Army and the Australian Army, and one between the Army & Navy and the Australian and South African services. Over £1,000 was raised for charity, two army commanders sent goodwill telegrams and Admiral Jellicoe, commander-in-chief of the Grand Fleet and not a man for idle recreation made a personal visit to Lord's.

But in high summer the flood of casualties swelled again and ideals came under yet more strain. There was inspiration still for the schoolboys waiting their turn to serve, less now in winning medals than in heroic death. The never-to-be-forgotten emblem of what rugger stood for was the death of Edgar Mobbs, twice wounded in previous battles and finally killed in the third battle of Ypres on 28 July 1917. A total of 300,000 were to be killed in this most futile of all encounters before November when at last Haig took the shell of the village of Passchendaele. Not only men but the new tanks, at last in working order, and allowed another chance, had slithered to destruction in the mud. The contrast between the escapism at home and the filthy realities at the Front brought a new anger. Siegfried Sassoon, who had been three years in France, was well-known for his bravery and had been awarded the MC for bringing back a wounded lance-corporal under fire. Now at last he was driven beyond endurance. Convalescing in England he began to make public attacks on the conduct of the war. His poetry, differing sharply from the earlier, innocent ideals of Brooke and Grenfell, mourned

> The unreturning army that was youth;
> The legions who have suffered and are dust.[37]

In his plight, for such views were not welcomed from servicemen, however heroic, he was befriended by another wounded officer, Wilfred Owen. After his death Owen's lines –

> What passing bells for these who die like cattle?
> Only the monstrous anger of the guns
> Only the shattering rifles' rapid rattle
> Can patter out their hasty orisons

– became the slowly-recognised truth for survivors and an essential ingredient of the post-war mood.[38]

Meanwhile the carnage continued and the nation gritted its teeth. Lord

Lansdowne, a distinguished former leader of the Unionist peers whose son had been killed back in 1914 caused a sensation in November 1917, by his letter to the *Daily Telegraph* calling for a negotiated peace. It was not only defeatists who saw his point. Russia had been devastated by the German Army; in March the Tsar had been overthrown by the Bolsheviks, and some felt now was the time to do a deal with Germany and join her in combating the new menace. This sophisticated political concept had little appeal for most Britishers, however. The Germans were the enemy and must be defeated. Now the Americans were at last doing their bit the end must come soon. Most of Lansdowne's fellow aristocrats deplored his lapse: the great families continued to make sacrifice. The ordinary man, conscript or volunteer, soldiered on. Above all the public schools saw the war as an examination for which they had long been preparing and in which they were acquitting themselves well, not least in their emphasis on games. A 1917 essay by F. B. Malim expounded its theme with academic logic: 'What virtues can we reasonably suppose to be developed by games? First I should put physical courage . . . That it has been bred in the sons of England is attested by the fields of Flanders and the beaches of Gallipoli.'[39]

In November 1917 there came what proved to be a false dawn. Haig gave the Tank Corps its head at last on suitable ground and the battle of Cambrai was hailed as a famous victory. Church bells, generally silent for security reasons, rang out – for the only time in this war – to celebrate the victory. It had a sour taste for Sassoon, struggling with himself over whether to return to duty:

> The House is crammed: tier beyond tier they grin
> And cackle at the Show, while prancing ranks
> Of harlots shrill the chorus, drunk with din;
> 'We're sure the Kaiser loves our dear old Tanks!' [40]

The celebrations were premature. There were no infantry reserves, and no plans to follow up the tanks' break through. The joke had misfired again.

Ireland as usual provided the starkest contrast. The GAA, their lobbying against the entertainments tax having failed, decided not to pay it anyway. With their attention now firmly back on the sporting and commercial side of their enterprise they also resisted government proposals to curtail railway excursions for sporting occasions. In 1917 the hurling and football finals were held before appreciative crowds. Since the 'ban' was a major reason for their failure to get exemption, however, the GAA were forced, willy nilly, into overt defiance on political grounds. Their resolution in April proclaimed the 'principle of absolute refusal' and at the Annual Congress in August they determined not to pay regardless of any measures taken to recover the money. The Revenue Commissioners made several attempts to collect their dues, with no success, and by the end of the year gave up even trying.[41]

'Keep right on to the end'

1917 had been a bad year all round. America's involvement had produced little of substance. By the autumn the new revolutionary Russian government was out of the war and the Germans could look west. The Labour leadership had talks with the Soviets and the party divided over whether to join the international peace movement. At sea the German submarine and surface attacks on merchant shipping were so punishing that Lloyd George had himself to take over the Admiralty for a while to institute a convoy system. The tank episode was dispiriting after promising so much. By 1918 British fortunes appeared to have sunk in the Passchendaele mud.

All that remained for many was the hatred the Germans had engendered by their philosophy of total war. Some of the atrocity stories put out by the propaganda of the Northcliffe-led popular press were pure fabrications, but there were plenty of true examples of their not playing the game – torpedoing hospital ships, sinking unarmed neutral vessels and using flame-throwers and poison-gas, for instance. Kipling wanted revenge, however long it took:

> It was not suddenly bred,
> It will not quickly abate
> Through the chill years ahead
> When time shall count from the date
> That the English began to hate.[42]

Others fought on with a weary resolution that could include an occasional thought for the ordinary Germans caught up like themselves in events over which they had no control.

The Newbolt spirit still flickered bravely in the trenches. However many gaps appeared in the front-line the schools sent fresh young idealists to fill them. But the atmosphere was no longer quite the same when they got there. The survivors had not been enriched by the experience of trench warfare, which reduced life to basics. Nor were they impressed by the bigwigs who dictated their moves. They grew a protective coat of cynicism to help them cope. The old peace-time divisions – between the governing classes and the governed, between Liberal and Tory and between north and south – were superseded by a new one, between the Fighting Forces, those up there in the thick of the action, and the Rest. It was a temporary phenomenon (though it left its traces in the post-war world) and its basis was not social but moral. For the Fighting Forces, one survivor recalled, 'The Seven Deadly Sins . . . were venial, so long as a man was courageous and a reasonably trustworthy colleague.' The Rest, by contrast, were given to 'church-going and cultivating virtues at which the Fighting Forces mocked'.[43] The strongholds of the Rest were the schools, enforcing 'an almost monastic discipline' and exhorting the boys to "prove yourselves worthy of your brothers" '.

The sharp culture shock when the latest recruits got their chance is the theme of R. C. Sheriff's play, *Journey's End* set in the trenches in March 1918.[44] It also brings out neatly the extent and the limitations of the common British interest in sport at this critical time. The fresh young idealist Raleigh is talking to the older Osborne, a former schoolmaster who turns out to be a rugger international.

> *Osborne:* Rugger and cricket seem a long way from here.
> *Raleigh* (laughing): They do, rather.
> *Osborne:* We play a bit of soccer when we're out of the line.

Raleigh says 'Good!', clearly recognising the importance of the men's welfare. Soccer was not only what the men liked best, it was also easier to organise and to play – and less dangerous – than rugger. But these very qualities helped to set rugger apart as somehow the game for officers.

It was unfortunate that the summer game, which had a single code, did not lend itself better to meaningful improvisation, but there were at least some cricket enthusiasts in France who managed to keep their hands in during the intervals of battle. By 1918, indeed, they had things quite well organised. One of them told afterwards how it was done: 'On those rare occasions when the Division was out of the line . . . it was my job to reconnoitre the area for a field suitable for cricket, ask the farmer for permission to play, agree a rent and hire or borrow a roller.' There were plenty of players. 'The selection committee's problem was not so much who to choose but who to leave out. The universities, Eton, the counties and the big leagues were represented.' It was all very democratic. 'On the field there was one rank only – acting private.' But it was a typically cricket-like democracy. The instigator of the games was Major-General Sir Victor Couper and the only democratic incident recorded is the temerity of Captain F. H. Bateman-Champlain, a former Gloucestershire county player, who when batting with the General tells him to 'Run! Run like hell!'[45] And in his own recollections of that summer in France Major H. S. Altham lists the array of golden-age amateurs making the most of things. Cricket was played 'principally at Etaples, where the Essex player, Charles McGahey, looked after some very respectable matting wickets. I remember one afternoon match in particular which included quite a galaxy of stars, Johnny Douglas, Nigel Haig, Dick Twining, Harry Longman, Donald Knight and poor Reggie Schwarz . . . That fine batsman, Colonel H. S. Bush, motored some 100 miles from 2nd Army HQ at St Omer, hit a beautiful four and then off an equally good hit fell to a miraculous catch by Knight at cover, and motored back again.'[46]

The services were no longer confined to men. In 1917 the government had taken over the co-ordination of various para-military organisations, creating the Women's Auxiliary Army Corps. The WAACs were soon followed by the WRNS, the Women's Royal Naval Service, and, later, the Women's Royal Air Force. The female services followed the example of the men's in emphasising physical training and in encouraging, when duty allowed, sporting activities of all kinds. The WRAF is credited with a major innovation. Women had hitherto not been seen in track and field athletics. It was not the kind of ladylike recreation approved by de Coubertin and the IOC. Nor had it the prestige or provenance to commend it to the women's public schools and physical education colleges. There were annual sports days in a few schools and one or two colleges of London University: Royal Holloway College, for instance, had a challenge cup for indoor 'corridor' races, and University College's sports day, which started in 1913, had 18 events, but they were intra-mural affairs regarded by most students more as novelties than as serious competition.[47] Now in the purposeful atmosphere of the services the sights of the enthusiasts were raised. One of the popular men's events was the Inter-Services Athletics championships at Stamford Bridge. In 1918 the WRAF entered a team for a relay race [48] and the basis of post-war public competition was laid.

The last surprise

The decision in early 1918 to allow 80 days' horse-racing was less a sign of confidence in approaching victory than a safety-valve for growing dissatisfaction. The war news could hardly have been worse. There were plots and counter-plots among the generals and their supporters against Lloyd George and eventually he took personal charge of the War Office. Allied generals and politicians had their own differences and disputes: US President Harding had to over-rule US General Pershing. International operations were used as a cloak for domestic power struggles: the Allies were now numerically stronger but disunity prevented their taking advantage of it. But when in March the Germans mounted a new offensive, desperation at last forced the Allies to combine and they found a resolute leader in Marshal Foch of France. With every man needed at the front there was pressure on the railways again, and the Jockey Club not only lost the extra days' concession but was restricted to Newmarket again.

But even if they lost their race-meetings, northerners could still study form in the newspapers as most followers of the Turf had always done. And they could take extra pleasure in the successes of Steve Donoghue from Warrington, leading jockey in Ireland as well as England. Like Fred Archer before him Donoghue had the special kind of charisma that wins devoted followers – and wins them money. The bookmakers and the public still had plenty of sporting outlets. Boxing fans had less to cheer about as America's entry to the war took away many of the best performers for military service and made life difficult for promoters. But while Georges Carpentier was defending his country's honour as a brilliant and courageous pilot, Ted Lewis managed a fight or two in New York, disposing of Benny Leonard when he tried his hand at the heavier weight. In Britain the highlight of 1918 was when the game Dick Smith beat Joe Beckett over 20 rounds to regain the light heavyweight title. Serving soldiers were not allowed to fight for money, but when Jimmy Wilde took on Joe Conn in an open-air contest they fought for a purse of cut diamonds.[49]

The Northern Union had struggled on through the winter and spring, barely surviving, but soccer, as well as gaining recognition as the fighting man's game, brought greater financial reward to players and committees at home. Leeds City again won the Midland Section and went on to beat Stoke City (who by some quirk of war-time geography were Lancashire Section champions) for the 'League Championship': their financal future now seemed secure. Northerners and soccer players of course did their bit like everyone else. Leeds's neighbours, Bradford Park Avenue, less successfully financially but keeping going in anticipation of a return to the First Division, had the distinction of having produced the only professional soccer player to win the Victoria Cross.[50] And if League cricket, of which Bradford was the centre, enjoyed another good summer, there were further signs that the establishment saw their own variety as not only permissible but a valuable contribution to the war effort. MCC extended their programme of 'Exhibition' charity matches. In 1918 games were played at the Oval and at Folkestone as well as in Yorkshire and at Lord's. In one Jack Hobbs thrilled the large crowds with a great innings. And in another 'between a representative schools side and an eleven raised by Captain Warner, Lord Harris delighted everyone by batting for half an hour with relative ease when many, half his age, had been cheaply dismissed'.[51]

The usual Irish contrasts were found. From the beginning of the year the government, under the Tillage (Ireland) Racecourses and Golf Courses Act, required a minimum of 10% of available land to be put under cultivation. When golf clubs proved reluctant they got little sympathy from the local population, either for patriotic or commercial reasons: the Ennis Club, which had already fulfilled its quota, found some of its greens dug up. But some members held out for their right to recreation. At a Dublin Corporation enquiry in April the Revd J. L. Morrow stoutly defended Clontarf against 'would-be plot holders'. On 14 June *Irish Life* hit out against the kill-joys:

'Many people are still disposed to carp and criticise golfers for playing their game at a time when others are fighting at the front . . . we might as well banish bridge from our houses, chess and billiards from our club.'[52] And whilst in Britain conscription was extended to the age of 50 the GAA in April pledged itself 'to resist by any means in our power the attempted conscription of Irish manhood'.[53] This did not prevent the extremists admonishing the Council at the Annual Congress in August for having negotiated with the British over taxation and transport arrangements.

In France meanwhile the Allies achieved some degree of co-ordination and began to advance at last. Haig had finally learned about tanks, and, used in short sharp bursts they proved a war-winning weapon. The public were too wary by now for premature rejoicing and the habit of war was so ingrained that they were in no mood for half-measures. Kipling's response in October 1918, when the Americans were taking the lead in seeking a negotiated settlement, was that nothing but unconditional surrender would do:

> If we have parley with the foe
> The load our sons must bear.[54]

When peace finally came in November it took people by surprise much as the outbreak of war had done four years before.

Notes

1 Quoted by Marie-Thérèse Eyquem, 'The Founder of the Modern Games' in Lord Killanin and J. Rodda (eds.), *The Olympic Games*, London, 1984, p. 141.
2 For the conscription debate see D. Hayes, *Conscription Conflict*, London, 1949.
3 G. Williams, in T. Mason (ed.), *Sport in Britain*, Cambridge, 1989, p. 338.
4 N. Cardus, *Autobiography*, London, 1955 edn, p. 75.
5 ibid., p. 77.
6 W. H. Gibson, *Early Irish Golf*, Naas, 1988, p. 88.
7 T. West, *The Bold Collegians*, Dublin, 1991, p. 59.
8 P. Rouse, 'A History of the GAA Ban on Foreign Games: Part One, 1884–1971', *IJHS*, December 1993, pp. 353–5, quoting J. J. Walsh, *Recollections of a Rebel*, Dublin, 1967. p. 33.
9 One was spared, Eamonn de Valera, who was an American citizen.
10 *Hansard*, 3 May 1916, quoted in Rouse, 'GAA Ban'.
11 S. Pankhurst, *The Suffragette Movement*, London, 1932 (1977 edn), p. 594.
12 L. Tennyson, *From Verse to Worse*, London, 1933, p. 173.
13 See D. Cannadine, *The Decline and Fall of the British Aristocracy*, London, pp. 71–7, for a somewhat skittish account.
14 N. L. Jackson, *Sporting Days and Sporting Ways*, London, 1932, pp. 259–60.
15 A. Marwick, *The Deluge*, London, 1978, p. 87.
16 ibid., p. 92.
17 J. Astley Cooper, 'The British Imperial Spirit of Sport and the war', *United Empire*, September, 1916, p. 581, quoted in K. Moore, The Pan-Britannic Festival' in J. A. Mangan (ed.), *Pleasure, Profit and Proselytism*, London, 1988, p. 151.
18 S. Sassoon, *Memoirs of a Fox-hunting Man*, London, 1928, pp. 301–3.

19 ibid., p. 313.
20 A. J. Arnold, 'Not Playing the Game? Leeds City in the Great War' *IJHS*, May 1990, p. 114, quoting from S. Studd, *Herbert Chapman, Football Emperor*, London, 1981. Arnold's article is the basis of this account of the Leeds City episode.
21 B. Green, *Wisden Anthology (1900–1940)*, London, 1985, p. 1158.
22 See *Wisden*, 1916–1919, and for a somewhat less gloomy picture J. Williams, 'Was the First World War Beneficial to County Cricket?', *Journal of the Cricket Society*, Vol. 15, No. 2, spring 1991, pp. 27–31.
23 Green, *Wisden*.
24 *Yorkshire Post*, 17 June 1915.
25 J. Arlott, *Jack Hobbs*, London, 1981, pp. 73, 76.
26 F. Root, *A Cricket Pro's Lot*, London 1937, p. 180. He actually lists 26.
27 *Fishing Gazette*, 15 February 1919.
28 P. Parker, *The Old Lie: The Great War and the Public School Ethos*, London, 1987, quoted by T. Mason (ed.), *Sport in Britain*, Cambridge, 1989, pp. 1–2.
29 D. Sutherland, *The Yellow Earl*, London, 1965, p. 187.
30 Introduction to *Baily's Hunting Directory*, 1918–1920, London 1921.
31 Mrs Oakfield and Captain Hinnycraft in S. Sassoon *Memoirs of a Fox-hunting Man*, London, 1928. See Chapter One above.
32 *Baily's Hunting Directory*.
33 ibid.
34 Arnold, 'Not Playing the Game?'
35 Green, *Wisden*, p. 438.
36 ibid., p. 489.
37 'The Troops', in R. Church and M. Bozman (eds.), *Poems of Our Time, 1900–1940*, London, 1945, pp. 99–100.
38 'Anthem for Doomed Youth', in ibid., p. 102.
39 In A. C. Benson (ed.), *Cambridge Essays*, quoted in J. A. Mangan, *Athleticism in the Victorian and Edwardian Public Schools*, Cambridge, 1981, p. 195.
40 'Blighters'.
41 Rouse, 'GAA Ban', p. 356.
42 R. Kipling, 'When the English Began to Hate', 1917 in *Definitive Verse of Rudyard Kipling*, London, 1940.
43 R. Graves and A. Hodge, *The Long Week-end*, London, 1940 (1971 edn), p. 10.
44 First staged in 1928, starring Laurence Olivier as Stanhope. Published by Everyman, *Modern Plays*, London, 1937.
45 F. Stead, *The Cricketer*, spring annual, 1968. An extract is included, pp. 115–17, in A. Synge and L. Cooper (eds.), *Tales from Far Pavilions*, London, 1984, an anthology full of interest for students of the mythology of cricket.
46 H. S. Altham, "Cricket in Wartime', *Wisden*, 1940, in Green, *Wisden*, p. 1139.
47 K. E. McCrone, 'Emancipation or Recreation? The Development of Women's Sport at the University of London', *IJHS*, September 1990, pp. 216, 219.
48 It may have been against men. J. Crump, 'Athletics', in Mason (ed.), *Sport*, p. 62.
49 D. Batchelor, *The Big Fight*, London, 1954, p. 145.
50 Donald Bell, killed five days later by a shell splinter. A. J. Arnold, *A Game That Would Pay*, London, 1988, p. 73.
51 H. S. Altham, 'Cricket in War-time', *Wisden*, 1940, reprinted in Green, *Wisden*, pp. 1157–60.
52 Gibson, *Early Irish Golf*, Naas, 1988, pp. 80–1.
53 Rouse, 'GAA Ban', p. 357.
54 R. Kipling, 'Justice'.

CHAPTER FIVE

Peace breaks out

The United Kingdom lost over 700,000 men in the war and the Empire a further 200,000. A million-and-a-half were seriously wounded and 2.5 million would need disability pensions for ten years or more. Britain was not the worst sufferer. France, with a smaller population, lost nearly twice as many. Worldwide 13 million perished. (Even wars are relative. In the influenza epidemic that swept the world in the winter of 1918–19 27 million died. Britain, comparatively well-fed and clothed, lost 200,000. But there is cold comfort in relativism.) An extra dimension of the horror was that it fell so heavily on the young. A generation had been chopped back, and in various ways the best had been lost – the first to volunteer, the physically fittest, the more educated. About one in five of Oxbridge and public school men and of peers and their families gave their lives, a significantly greater proportion than the generally higher loss of officers than men (15.2% to 12.8%). Of the most vulnerable category of all, the junior officers (over 35% of whom died), most were public school men. For the survivors the manpower shortage gave more leverage to the trade unions, allowed fewer opportunities for women to marry and created a distinctive and influential category of maiden aunts.[1]

After describing the excitement of the crowds on Armistice Day Arnold Bennett, who had had a very comfortable war, wrote in his diary, 'Raining now. An excellent thing to dampen hysteria and Bolshevism.'[2] The revolutionary events in Russia had frightened everyone. Kipling reminded the pacifists and pleasure-seekers of the dangers:

> God rest you, peaceful gentlemen, let nothing you dismay,
> But – leave your sports a little while – the dead are borne this way![3]

The sports could not wait, of course, but troops were nevertheless sent to support the White Russian forces against the Soviets and some gave their lives in a cause for which they can have had little enthusiasm. Even those scheduled to come home were upset by demobilisation plans that gave priority to 'key' men who had often been the latest to join. There were strikes, unauthorised marches and various minor forms of mutiny, including, it was rumoured, some troops declaring themselves a 'Soviet'. It was Winston Churchill, back in the Cabinet as War Minister, who saved the day with a new 'fair play' policy of first in, first out.

One result of the delays was that not many were home in time for the general election called in December 1918. The absentees were entitled to proxy vote, but few got on to the electoral register in time. This was the least of their worries. Even at home the election generated little excitement. Lloyd George had been the main architect of victory. There seemed every reason to invite him to carry on and win the peace. Having broken the mould of party politics, he had risen above the fragments. His war-time coalition lost the support of the Labour Party but in the prevailing anti-socialist mood this was no great matter. More important was the backing of the Tories, now rampant as the nation looked for tangible spoils of victory: 'Hang the Kaiser' and 'Make Germany pay' were popular suggestions. Women had been rewarded for their war-effort by the vote, but only those over 30 to allow them extra time for maturation.

The Tories could have won virtually every seat in mainland Britain had they not agreed to allow a free run to 150 of the Lloyd George Liberals. As it was the Coalition won 473 seats, 339 of them Conservative and Unionist. The old Asquith Liberals could muster only 26 and Labour, with 59 became the official opposition. That there were fewer Irish members was because the 73 Sinn Feiners who swept the board outside Ulster refused to take their seats and set up their own assembly, the Dail, instead. This meant that the first woman MP to be elected under the 1918 Representation of the People Act, the Sinn Feiner Countess Marciewicz (née Gore-Booth), did not appear at Westminster.[4] It also helped to push the GAA finally over the edge of political neutrality. The government decreed that civil servants must in future take an oath of allegiance to the Crown and the GAA responded by resolving that any who did so would come within 'the ban'.

The troops were returning to a country with high hopes of becoming the 'land fit for heroes' of which Lloyd George spoke so fervently. They were given free unemployment insurance but most found jobs with little difficulty. Ex-officers, who were not insured, sometimes had to settle for disagreeably inferior positions, but prospects were better for wage-earners. War-time conditions had given the trade unions more clout and they had used it well.[5] The manpower shortage and the munitions drive had pushed wage levels up. Most workers had more than kept pace with the rising cost of living: by 1920 this was 75% above pre-war levels but the average wage of £150 a year had risen by 100%. Standard weekly working hours were also generally down from 55 to 48. Agriculture, the worst-paid industry, showed the biggest proportionate improvement, and the farmers had a particularly good war. Their employees, although still on a standard £120 a year (46s a week) were better off than they had ever been.

But there was no smooth transition to prosperity. Pent-up war-time dissatisfactions and inequalities, real and imagined, led to strikes and demonstrations. Most were fairly peaceful but the Clydeside engineers, who had come out in defiance of their union leaders for shorter hours, got involved in pitched battles with police. Two industries still under government war-time control caused most trouble. A threatened miners' strike was only bought off by the promise of a Royal Commission. An actual strike of railwaymen had to be settled on the strikers' terms. Meanwhile a mixture of gratitude for services rendered, electoral prudence, foresight and nervousness about latent Bolshevik tendencies produced a spate of welfare legislation. The Education Act, 1918, extended free, compulsory schooling to 14-year-olds. The Housing Act of 1919 called on local authorities to draw up plans for low-cost council houses. The Unemployment Insurance Act of 1920 provided for a contributory scheme of benefits (15s a week for up to 15 weeks a year). All were to be bedevilled by lack of money.

The war had been expensive. In both private and intergovernmental war-time transactions the British were less successful in collecting the money they were owed – notably by their Russian allies – than those from whom they borrowed, principally the United States. There had been heavy loss of shipping, bringing fears for peace-time trade. But the biggest immediate problem was the tax burden of repaying the National Debt, which had grown from £605 million to £7,089 million. The obligation to holders of War Loan clashed with the claims of social welfare and held back the programme of post-war reconstruction. The programme was hit harder still by inflation. In the first weeks of peace there was such a shortage of goods that almost anything would sell. Disposal of war-time surplus stock led to a small boom which showed every sign of becoming a big one: the world, it seemed, could be Britain's oyster. Rebellious shop stewards, starry-eyed reformers and reactionaries seeking a return to pre-war bliss all clamoured for an end to war-time restrictions. Nearly all were swept away, almost overnight – price controls, direction of industry, exports and imports. Unrestricted, the sale of gold, against which currency values were measured, brought the pound down from parity to $3.50, a decline that soon had the authorities trying to put the lid back on, without great effect. Internally, removal of controls sent prices rocketing, in turn triggering wage claims that the employers could hardly resist. The inflation of the war years continued and grew worse.

Post-war industrial conditions accelerated the pace of social change. At all levels from munitions millionaires to public school ex-officers who took jobs that brought money rather than status there was a further blurring of class distinctions. The old tax-exemption line was no longer a reliable guide to class: in 1919–20 some 7.25 million were paying income tax (now risen from 1s 3d to 6s in the pound). But if this made it harder to define precisely who were the middle classes there was no doubt that they went on expanding. The proportion of salary-earners grew from 12% of the working population to 22% between the censuses of 1911 to 1921. The professions were in greater demand as standards of living and of welfare advanced; civil servants and other bureaucrats proliferated; the growth and change of industry needed more managers; and middle-class women held on to their war-time gains better than the rank-and-file.[6]

It was the upper classes who felt themselves hardest hit. For the landowners in particular the advent of Lloyd George had been ominous even before the deluge, and he had used war-time conditions to get a tight grip, through his reforms of the Ministry of Agriculture, on land use. Rents had been deliberately held down during the emergency and in post-war reconstruction he deliberately excluded the patrician element from agricultural politics. The emphasis was now firmly on owner-occupation. One million acres were sold in 1919 and that was just the beginning. Taxation and death duties were blamed. But the pain of loss was often eased by cash: if rents were low, land values had shot up. Sometimes the blue-blooded themselves assisted the newer 'Lloyd George' type of aristocrat to live in appropriate style. When in 1919 Lord Ebury decided to sell his Moor Park mansion and estate, the purchaser was Lord Leverhulme (Bolton soap millionaire, baron, 1917, viscount 1922) who made a golf course on it and sold the rest for superior housing. So whilst the members of the old aristocracy deplored the devaluation of titles they profited from the process. Their own territory might be greatly reduced but their finances were in better shape than they had been for years.

This did not lessen their deep resentment of the social incursions of the vulgar rich or the political pretensions of the 'hard-faced men who looked as though they had done very well out of the war' who now filled Parliament.[7] Nor did it make them less nervous of Bolshevism. Was the reward for their war-time sacrifices and the loss of their sons to be overthrow by revolutionaries or mulcting by socialists? In fact the loss of the finest flower of British youth, though real enough, led to no dramatic shift of power and influence from the upper classes. The gaps were filled not by new proletarian leaders but by younger brothers and other survivors with the same social background and schooling. In that sense Britain did not change as radically as is sometimes suggested in nostalgic aristocratic memoirs. Indeed, the upper classes and public schools gained added esteem from the demonstration of leadership their sons had given. The values they went into the war to defend were not everyone's, perhaps, but they played a key part in winning it. Thus, though the share of the national wealth owned by the élite shrank by one-third and the landed classes' old feudal grip was further loosened, they had the great consolation that the populace showed no real sign of wanting to be rid of them. King George V, who declined to give refuge to his unfortunate kinsman, Czar Nicholas II, lest it stir up Bolshevik resentment in Britain, was fortunate that so much respect for the old order remained.

The reason, in part, was that Britain had been strengthened by her victory. Before the war, for all her self-image, she had been only one of several European world powers. She emerged from it supreme in Europe. France had been sorely stricken in the effort of victory. Germany was crushed and stripped of her colonies; she had devastated Russia before her own collapse. And the Empire, which had shown its worth by sharing in the sacrifice, emerged intact and seemingly stronger than ever. The mother-country had new policing responsibilities all over the globe This was all just as it should be – part of what it meant to be British – and the comforting heritage of rich and poor alike. A few radicals were dissatisfied. In January, 1919, the *New Statesman* complained that ' "shoots" are going on. Hounds are killing or drawing blanks. Estimates are being prepared for the refitting of yachts. The merits of rival designs for new motor cars are being discussed . . . (whilst) millions of people are starving in Europe.'[8] The British did not face the prospect of starvation, merely the annoyance that raging inflation had scared off the government from the complete ending of food rationing. Other widely-heard complaints were that it was impossible to get servants, that waiters were impertinent, restaurants crowded and *vin ordinaire* as much as 6 or 7s a bottle.

Getting back to normal

It was a crisis of this order that confronted the hunting set. Nevertheless their plight was still being recalled, 60 years on, in such melodramatic terms as 'after the holocaust of the First World War, when most of the best in Britain was destroyed, . . . the outlook was dismal.'[9] Things were certainly not easy. Few hounds had been bred in the war years and many older ones had been put down. Horses and hunt servants had both been scarce. And as war-time shortages ended costs mounted. *Baily's Hunting Directory* commented glumly 'It is a very sad state of affairs, and one for which the war is entirely responsible, but it is nevertheless a fact that the price of horses, of saddlery, clothes, forage, hound meal and every commodity that is used by a hunt establishment have risen at least 100 per cent, and that wages have gone up in similar fashion.'[10] Inevitably, too, the cost of subscriptions had risen. (No-one knew quite how much. It was not the sort of thing the best people talked about or the best hunts publicised.) But expense was no real deterrent, even at the height of the inflation, and soon hunts everywhere were reporting a great increase in the size of the fields.

Meanwhile at the end of the 1919 season meeting the Masters of Foxhounds Association was called upon to deal with some of the unfortunate consequences of the holocaust. The war-time prominence of farmers – and the pushiness of some of them – was an early source of peace-time discord. Farmers' packs, restricted to harriers before the war, were now setting up as fully-fledged fox-hunts, sometimes moving into the territory of their betters. Transgressing aristocrats needed more delicate handling. The MFHA had received a letter from Colonel J. Selby-Lowndes complaining that his Whaddon Chase country had been invaded during his absence at the Front by a fresh pack started by Lord Dalmeny, who seems to have found time from his own war to look to the future. The Association offered to arbitrate if both parties were willing to accept its good offices. War-time restrictions had increased tension between the MFHA and the National Hunt Committee over control of hunter 'chases. Some interfering NHC Stewards had disallowed applications for point-to-points 'on humanitarian grounds, owing to the rationing orders'. Another affront was their refusal to allow puppy-walkers to organise races. 'We can no more do without the puppy-walkers than we can without the farmers,' declared General Alderson, Master of the South Shropshire, 'and why they should be debarred from running horses, does not appear.' There was keen feeling that the NHC were getting above themselves: they should stick to the task the MFH had called upon them to perform in 1904, i.e. to 'prevent anything like fraud', and a resolution to that effect was passed unanimously.[11]

For all the difficulties the underlying tone was of mingled relief and excited anticipation. The MFHA meeting was full of praise for those who had carried the burden for so long and scarcely able to credit that a year before the sport's future had hung in the balance. The shooters, of course, had faced no such crisis. They had found it easier to snatch the odd moment of pleasure despite the shortage of gamekeepers and the diversion of ammunition to other purposes. But conservationists – those who reared birds in order to shoot them – faced a somewhat different climate after the war. In particular the pheasant-rearing production lines were reduced. 'The days have gone by', wrote one enthusiast, 'when . . . it was possible . . . (for a 'game shot') to come home at the end of a long day's shooting and be puzzled to remember a dozen of the hundreds of shots he had fired.'[12] They still found a few 'natural' targets. Of course, everything cost more but at least guns and ammunition were available again.

Fishermen, too, could get tackle again as manufacturers turned back from war-time activities: lead shot became available again on 1 January 1919.[13] The river bank had been a favourite source of solace for servicemen and civilians during the war and game anglers had found access to waters relatively easy. Now there came stories of inflated rents which war profiteers could afford but returning officers could not.[14] First in, first out caused a few problems. Of the River Wye's 15 bailiffs 3 had been killed and 3 others wounded in action: in March 1919 the conservators sought early release for the other 9 to help cope with the growing demand.[15] Coarse-fishing types had been deprived of the competitive, beer-drinking, gambling side of their sport during the emergency, save for a few local charity matches, for war relief, Red Cross and so forth. Now it began again as local rates of demobilisation and re-employment allowed. Angling journalists noted with satisfaction the contribution of their sport to the 'fair play' ethos that had won the war and the improbability that many returning fishrmen would waste time on Bolshevistic thoughts.[16] Up in Wigan crowds gathered on the banks of the Leeds and Liverpool canal to watch fishing matches for £10 or £20 a time between anglers 'supplied with two hot bricks to sit on and roasted potatoes in their pockets to keep their fingers warm'.[17]

Golf clubs grappled resolutely with the return to normality. N. L. Jackson told a harrowing tale of his efforts to restore Stoke Poges to its pre-war eminence. It was, he recalled, 'terribly hard work, for wages had increased by 100 per cent and the cost of food by about 120 per cent while we were unable to make a corresponding increase in our subscriptions. Consequently, although our membership soon reached 800 it was almost impossible to make a fair profit.'[18] The staff required for this enterprise now came to over 100. Due economies were made at the athletics sports provided for them in the summer by using prizes preserved from before the war, and the proceedings were marred only by 'the sad recollection of the poor fellows who had entered in 1914 but had since been called upon to make the great sacrifice'. With rather less humbug the *Irish Field* commented, 'it seems almost too wonderful to be true that once more we can, with a clear conscience, indulge in all the varied pleasures (and griefs) of the links. Thousands of golfers, who were not quite sure they were doing all they could for the Empire, will now feel a light heart in their game.'[19]

Recreational sport was one thing: organised competition, especially among the professional spectator sports, was harder to pick up again. The soccer authorities were already embarked on the last war-time season when the peace came. Apart from international matches Ireland was operating more or less normally by then so this was no great hardship. In Scotland the only significant deprivation was the absence of the Scottish Cup. The English

League, however, was caught on the hop. Whilst it was stuck with its regional competitions the Northern Union stole a march. Though the professional rugby authorities were unable to change to a full pre-war programme from 8 January 1919 they launched parallel Yorkshire and Lancashire League and Cup competitions. Few clubs had any money and some had lost their grandstands and even grounds, but it was agreed that 'broken-time' payments and up to 10s a match and 'tea-money' could be paid to the players. The games drew crowds of the sort that some had feared might never be seen again: 21,500 watched the Yorkshire Cup Final. The FA, meanwhile, began the work of post-war planning in December 1918, poised between hope and apprehension. They had had a mixed war and there were fences to be mended if the soldiers' enthusiasm was to be translated into permanent peace-time support. There were ugly rumours about war-time breaches of League regulations that would hardly help the game's image, and internationally there were worries about the Irish situation and about the line that should be taken with regard to Germany.

Amateur games that 'flu-ridden winter resumed as best they could. The rugger men obviously had some of the saddest stories to tell. In all 79 international players had given their lives; 30 Scots, 27 English, 13 Welsh and 9 Irish, together with countless ordinary club players. The Headingley team, who returned to find their ground intact but their two small stands sold for firewood, had more serious cause for melancholy: 47 of the 190 members who had served in the war had been lost.[20] It was, fittingly, the Army Rugby Union who took the lead, with the support of the English, Scottish and Welsh Unions, in organising an Inter-Services Tournament in March and April 1919, that was part commemoration of the war-time losses and part peace-time revival. Great Britain, with a team known as the Mother Country, and sides from Canada, Australia, New Zealand and South Africa (and from the recently-formed Royal Air Force) played 16 matches all over Britain including 6 at Twickenham. King George V presented a special Royal Trophy to the winners, New Zealand, who beat the Mother Country after a replay.

Ex-servicemen were amongst the earliest and strongest contributors to the post-war revival of sport. The many who began interrupted or belated university careers brought higher standards than ever before to Oxford and Cambridge and confirmed them in their pre-war athleticist orientation. Ex-officers were prominent also in administration and organising, either in voluntary work on committees or in the paid but gentlemanly posts that arose as clubs and national and regional organisations began to pick up the pieces, expand and elaborate. And it was the enthusiasm and interest of the regular services that helped to revive and encourage amateur sport at the highest levels. Theirs was a sporting world apart in which the strident claims of professionalism and commercialism did not obtrude. No private soldier became a major overnight because of his prowess in sport. It was also hierarchical. The cavalry tradition ensured, for instance, that the teams entered for Olympic equestrian events were all from the officer class; it was not until after the Second World War that sergeants were allowed in. Nevertheless the Inter-Services athletics tournament of 1919 is worth noting, not only for its contribution to the peace-time re-emergence of the sport but for the first public women's event of the new era, a 440 yards relay.

Despite the disappointment – it can hardly have been a surprise – of the IOC's refusal to allow women's athletics at the Antwerp Games the pioneers made significant progress. Though spurned by the embryonic Inter-University Athletics Board – London and the provincial institutions – most women's college and university clubs held sports days or more serious sports meetings, and there were the first stirrings of open competition. Northern Counties Ladies' Championships were held for the first time in 1919: the 100 yards was won by Elaine Burton, an intending schoolteacher and later Coventry's first woman MP. Amongst the men meanwhile there was no immediate indication that the sport could be rescued from the clutches of the professional circuit, gearing itself up to cash in on the post-war boom. At the 1919 AAA championships the success of harriers clubs and 'northern' men, notoriously vulnerable to commercial overtures, contrasted with the solitary Oxbridge victory – that of Cambridge's Guy Butler in the 440 yards. Overseas competitors dominated the longer races and field events, four going to Swedes and one to a Dane. The IOC meanwhile made hasty plans for the 1920 Games to be held in Antwerp in recognition of Belgium's sufferings in the war. There were not many arguments even from de Coubertin against the exclusion of the losing nations – Austria, Bulgaria, Germany, Hungary and Turkey – an ironic comment on the 'internationalism' that had so thrilled Noel-Baker, unwittingly undermined by the very ideals behind the decision at Stockholm to accept future entries only as part of national teams.

The rowing men did little to improve Olympic harmony. The ARA were exceedingly annoyed when the BOC, in line with the pre-war FISA ruling, had invited the NARA to nominate competitors for inclusion in the team for Antwerp. The NARA, they protested, was a body 'whose definition of an amateur was wider than that of the ARA and consequently wider than that required by the rules of the Olympic Regatta'.[21] Relations between the two were already strained by events earlier in the year. Oarsmen had been amongst the most patriotic of sportsmen in the war – forty two rowing Blues had given their lives, for instance – and they were amongst the first to look for a return to the good old days when it was over. Within a fortnight of the Armistice a letter to *The Times* was calling for the Henley Regatta to be staged the following June and by January 1919 a Leander Committee was looking into the possibility. After a meeting of the various rowing interests, the Committee regretfully concluded that it could not be done, but with no Boat Race possible in the still-depleted universities it seemed doubly important to make some sort of showing. In the event the Stewards were able to arrange four days of racing, though not for the traditional trophies.

The main event, and the one that attracted most of the headlines, was one for crews that had served 'in the Army, Navy or Air Force of any country which fought for the Allied cause.' This, for which George V had provided a trophy, was to be known as the King's Cup. It was unfortunate that the battle for the amateur soul of rowing was still uppermost in the minds of the Henley Stewards who refused entry to a crew of war veterans sponsored by the NARA who had declined to vouch that they did not infringe the ARA's manual worker clause. Neither the public nor George V were greatly impressed. *The Times*, in an article headed 'Gentlemen at Henley', deplored 'this pedantic regulation' and urged the ARA to change it as soon as possible.[22] Still the Peace Regatta went gaily on. The crowds saw ARA-testified crews from Oxford and Cambridge row against Australian, Canadian, New Zealand and US Army entries. The Australians won, but British honour was restored at the Allied Peace Regatta in Paris in which Cambridge beat both the Australians and New Zealanders.

The rowing establishment had no radical ideas of post-war re-construction and the need for change was seen, if at all, in moral rather than social terms. The most serious problem, the decline of metropolitan rowing, was one that remained from before the war. The introduction to a work by T. A. Cook in 1919 spoke of the Tideway clubs' 'uphill and ceaseless struggle against the forces of ease and enjoyment which had so insidiously encroached on the battle ground of British manliness'.[23] And the leading Tideway club, Thames RC sought to remedy the defect by making Steve Fairbairn their captain. Fairbairn, a wealthy Australian Cambridge Blue of the 1880s whose controversial coaching methods had rippled the Edwardian waters, was a firm believer in hard work. So was the radical Jack Beresford, a young Thames member who had gone into the Artists' Rifles straight from Bedford School, and was now on his way to becoming a sculling champion. The unorthodox rowing style Fairbairn advocated was thought pernicious in itself, like not playing with a straight bat or leading with a straight left. At Cambridge, which was totally riven by the issue, his efforts were mostly limited to coaching Jesus College crews more concerned with winning than looking English. It cannot have endeared him to traditionalists either that he was a fervent supporter of women's rowing, encouraging his acolytes at Jesus to assist with the development of the Newnham College Rowing Club. Newnham made their own historic contribution in 1919 by turning out in shorts – no doubt suitably lengthy – instead of the customary tunic.[24]

Yachtsmen, meanwhile, were as the *New Statesman* had scornfully noted taking out estimates for the refitting of their craft. The implication of opulent aloofness and indifference to the problems of the real world was resented by the emerging type of sailing man who looked for more active and less expensive forms of the sport. The casualty lists in *Yachting Monthly* had given ample evidence of their part in winning the war, in the trenches as well as at sea. The war, too, had reminded Britain that she was an island nation, enhancing the back-to-basics, get-away-from-it-all appeal of sailing. There was an influential section of the middle classes that loved the notion of 'messing about on boats' as much as the smarter set loved the social side of regattas and yacht clubs. For them it had been a long winter waiting for May and fitting out time. As the author of '*Ixia's* Peace Year Cruise' put it, 'Hadn't the conversation ever since demobilisation been on the lines of "What about finishing that little job on *Ixia* to-night? The gooseneck wants wringing and will you go round to the Marine Store and get a furlong or two of manila hemp and Havanas".'[25]

Those who *had* a boat to fit out were fortunate, for the cost of a new one was prohibitive. The price of materials had shot up: cast iron for keels was £45 a ton, for instance. This made even the smallest boats a costly proposition, especially as boat builders' quotations were no longer reliable. An estimated £450 for a 4.5 tonner could turn out at £900. One idea, no doubt with war-time collectivist ideas in mind, was for an amateur builders' co-operative, but yachtsmen were thought too individualistic for such ventures or the 'knock-down boats' for home assembly now being marketed. The tradition was against standardisation and purists looked with disdain at the new 4-ton 'tabloid' designs a mere one-sixth the size of the 57 foot 'belted earl' Edwardian economy class. Many doubted whether they were even safe. The smaller, handier boats had their advocates. 'It is far less risky to sail a 4-tonner round the coast than it is to ride a motorcycle', wrote one.[26] But the very comparison demonstrated the eccentricity of the idea. In fact the debates had more to do with prestige than with safety. The largest (big or J class 23–26.5 metre) boats still had the most glamour and it was by them that traditionalists measured the health of the sport. There was much head-shaking in 1919 at the news that the King was not to have *Britannia* refitted. Some blamed Queen Mary, others thought it showed his own lack of enthusiasm. All were agreed that it was a distressing sign of the times.

Yachtsmen were not greatly taken with the post-war industrial scene. Hired hands and domestic servants were in ludicrously short supply. Hotels were outrageously expensive. There was a call for a small cruiser/racer designed around living accommodation so that younger owners could sail to the various regattas and live on board whilst they were there. The editor of *Yachting Monthly* strongly advocated using aircraft factories, now idle, for dinghy production. He also vigorously took up the cause of the racing men, eager for the return of regular competition but frustrated by the inertia of the YRA. Yachtsmen had paid to keep it alive during the war, though it had had nothing to do: 'now there was a job of work on hand – the first for five years – they want to know what is being done . . . who runs the YRA, who for and what for?'

No such importune questionings marred the revival of the pre-war splendours of the Turf. Racing had suffered relatively little, and foreign competition had been much reduced. British trainers, notably the tough veteran Alec Taylor, had done well during the war years as had Steve Donoghue, who had been champion jockey throughout, winning two of the Newmarket Derbys. Restored to Epsom the 1919 Derby broke all records. It had been eagerly awaited since the beginning of the year and much was expected of the favourite, Sir Alec Black's The Panther, regarded by the experts as the greatest horse of the age. It managed only fourth place and the winner at 33–1 was Lord Glanely's Grand Parade. This, though depressing for the crowds, was very pleasant for his Lordship. Glanely, who had begun his working life as a shipping clerk, went on to become leading owner netting £30,514. Money was not his object, however: he had done well enough from business to be able to afford to buy his title from Lloyd George, reputedly for £100,000.

The return of Royal Ascot from war-time banishment was an even more potent symbol of normality. *The Times* summed up the situation very well. 'Reconstruction is a word capable of two interpretations. Some who desire it mean the construction of a new world, differing as widely as possible from that which existed before the war; others are anxious to find . . . the old world of 1913 revived.'[27] Lord Churchill's Ascot was obviously for the latter. Even the fashions seem to have been pre-war: there was a 'remarkable hat with ostrich feathers of brightest yellow, a cloak of Lincoln green which Maid Marion might have worn . . . a black-and white chess-board lady, a pink and white spotted lady'. *The Times* somewhat skittishly noted that there were in the stands 'plenty of redtabs which were really pretty things, and can be admired without bitterness by the demobilised'.

Another highly successful event of the London season that June was Wimbledon. The All-England Lawn Tennis Club had been so deluged with applications for tickets that a ballot had to be held. The finals were seen by 8,000 people. Gross receipts came to £9,000, nearly double those of 1914. There was not much for chauvinists to cheer about. The men's final was contested between Australians, G. L. Patterson proving too strong for the old champion, Norman Brookes. But the sensation of the tournament was a 20-year-old

French girl, Suzanne Lenglen. It was not only her defeat of Mrs Lambert Chambers, more than twice her age, that signified the start of a new era. Her style of play, with spectacular bounding leaps around the court, was like nothing ever seen before from a woman. So was her mode of dress. Her skirt came only just below the knee, she clearly wore no petticoat and, dispensing with a suspender belt, kept her stockings up with garters. Instead of a formal blouse, furthermore, she wore a sleeveless collarless vest. It was all very shocking but it was part of the new freedom that was in the air.

'Flappers' (both the expression and the phenomenon) had been around since the 1880s, but now they were in the mainstream of fashion. The war, with its relaxation of restraints and the familiarisation of short hair and calf-length skirts, was one reason, and another was the incursion of American modes and manners, themselves often derived from Parisian originals. Ragtime, having degenerated from its earlier polite phase into unsophisticated syncopation, now gave way to fully-fledged jazz. Dancing, of a dangerously libertarian new kind, had come in with it. In an article headed 'This Jazz Age' the *Daily Mail* in February 1919 declared 'People are dancing as they have never danced before in a happy rebound from the austerities of war . . . The "Tango", "Maxine" and "Boston" have gone with the "Turkey Trot" and "Bunny Hug" . . . Dancing without gloves has become the mode, because the cost . . . has risen to impossible figures, and smoking was never so common when sitting out.' The new dances required a freedom of movement that could not be achieved in whalebone corsets: 'Men won't dance with you if you're all laced up', as an American girl visitor succinctly put it.[28]

Mlle Lenglen, the first 'Jazz Age' tennis player, was thus merely reflecting a trend. The All-England Club, fortified in their belief that the game was well set up for the future began making plans for a new ground. The only small cloud over the proceedings was fear of declining national standards. The gloom was soon to be intensified as the Americans came seriously into the reckoning: meanwhile there was consolation in imperial strength. Altogether it was a bitter-sweet summer. The Australasian victory in the Davis Cup was an occasion to remember Tony Wilding and to say goodbye to his old partner, Brookes. There was melancholy, too, in the death of Laurie Doherty that August. He had not only set Wimbledon on its feet but had established the game itself as something worthy of British respect. In a long leading article *The Times* paid him a tribute that even W. G. Grace, the Great Cricketer, would have been glad to have: 'He played an English game in the spirit in which Englishmen think games should be played. He was a typical Englishman, and it is a source of legitimate pride to his countrymen that we can think him so.'[29]

The cricketers themselves had been full of apprehension about the resumption. Few had dared hope that the old county game could be restored in all its former leisurely glory. All sorts of radical proposals had been made to make it more entertaining – shortening the boundaries, penalising batting sides for failing to score, limiting the number of professionals (believed to be the source of merely functional, tedious, average-conscious play), even abolishing left-handed batsmen to save time changing the field around. Amid the despondency Lord Harris stood firm. As the editor of *Wisden* put it, 'In the darkest days of the war he expressed his conviction that when peace came back cricket would have all its old charm for the English people. Everything he said was amply justified . . . The season of 1919 proved beyond all question or dispute that cricket had lost nothing of its attraction to the public.'[30] The tangible, incontrovertible proof lay in the attendances, which, despite a 100% increase in admission charges to take account of the entertainments tax and greatly increased expenses, had virtually doubled. The result was 'excellent balance sheets' everywhere.

It was in fact the sort of boom that comes after long shortages and the success it brought concealed deep-seated problems that were to persist until the next war and beyond. First, there was a gulf between the successful counties – basically the metropolitan and the 'northern' ones – and the rest. At Lord's 7–8,000 had been thought a good gate before the war: now 20,000 was commonplace and 30,000 not unknown. The Oval similarly thrived, slightly further down market. Lancashire also did well and Yorkshire even better. The Roses match at Sheffield attracted 45,000. Second, the duration of the games cast county cricket in a mould that made it impossible for it to be prosperous or truly popular as, for instance, soccer was, as a week-in, week-out attraction. In 1919, nervousness about its appeal had led the authorities to experiment with two-day games, which was at least a step in the right direction. But the experiment was a muddled compromise in which most of the hours of a three-day game were crammed into two. A 7.30 finish was too late for all but the most ardent followers, and most people left long before the end to go home for dinner. And since matches were played in succession without a break the players were tired out long before the season's end.

Still, in the flush of enthusiasm over the increased gates, the answer seemed simple – a return to three-day games in 1920. And meanwhile the sheer nostalgic pleasure of it all left a warm glow. At Lord's the Middlesex amateurs had a fragile look that was at least familiar, and the Gentleman v Players fixture, apart from its general reminder of precious social values, produced a sensation – G. T. S. Stevens, a future Middlesex star, was selected for the Gentlemen whilst still at school. At the Oval, which also staged a Gentlemen v Players match, Jack Hobbs was still around, as good as ever, and the Surrey amateurs, led by D. J. Knight and J. N. Crawford, acquitted themselves well. But the northern counties had recovered best from the war, especially amongst the professionals. Yorkshire had a great new batsman in Herbert Sutcliffe and his partner Percy Holmes had vastly improved on his youthful pre-war standard. Lancashire had Charlie Hallows, whom they thought just as good, and if Reggie Spooner was coming to the end of his career Harry Makepeace seemed better than ever. J. T. Tyldesley (of the Worsley clan) still had a few seasons in him and R. K. was to prove the best of the four Westhoughton Tyldesleys. Bowlers were in shorter supply – with the 44-year-old Barnes, still the best of them, skulking in the Leagues – but Yorkshire's Abe Waddington showed great promise.

'Nothing in the season,' Wisden's editor reckoned, 'was more gratifying than the successful revival of the university match. When the fixture was provisionally arranged the outlook seemed very dubious, but watching the game at Lord's one might have imagined there had been no war.' The Times also caught the flavour of cricket's return and all it symbolised. Quoting approvingly E. V. Lucas's description of it as 'an intricate, vigilant and leisurely warfare' and describing in enthusiastic platitudes its universal appeal – from 'mean, dark streets' to village greens and from English public school to the far corners of the Empire – it concluded with a eulogy of all that seemed best in the game. 'It is not understood by the people of other countries, but we who understand it love it, because it is . . . fraught always with amazing possibilities. No cricket is more pleasant than country house cricket, and the Canterbury Week which began yesterday is the best of the year. Its revival is a sign that all is well with our great game.'[31]

There was one fear that beset members of the cricket establishment even as they enjoyed their triumphant return. 'The menace of the Lancashire and Yorkshire Leagues cannot be ignored', as Wisden put it. 'From what I am told leading professionals constantly receive from league clubs offers of better terms than they are getting from the counties, naturally the temptation of more money for less work is very strong.'[32] This rather missed the point that spectators loved it. At Nelson on the Lancashire border, the local paper was lyrical about a 'derby' game in early June. 'The match at Colne on Saturday was an "old-timer" in every sense of the phrase. The day could not have been more propitious. There was a bright and genial sun which radiated pleasure all-round', and so on to more tangible evidence of success – tram cars so crowded that some had to walk there and 'so much struggling on the return that many had to walk home' and a gate of £137, £20 more than the previous record'.[33] By September Colne were preparing for the visit of the East Lancashire Club by 'banking up the ground near the new refreshment tent' and selling tickets in advance. It was not on the scale of the Oval, perhaps, but this kind of thing was going on in small towns all over the north and midlands.

Football in the new era

September 1919, however, brought the event that truly signalled the return of peace, the first season of League soccer proper. The tone was set by an article in *The Times* praising soccer's contribution to victory. For the fighting men the round ball had done 'more than anything else to revive tired limbs and weary minds'. Everyone knew that 'association football was the game the soldiers and sailors love best'.[34] In this atmosphere of forget and forgive it was unfortunate that another scandal was about to come to light. By this time Leeds City's finances were in a sound state, all current liabilities had been discharged and a surplus of £2,000 nestled in the bank. They might well have gone merrily on getting rich had not a dispute over pay differentials arisen amongst the players. One of the disadvantaged 'blew the whistle', and even as the new season started a joint commission of the FA and the Football League began an enquiry. The club refused to hand over their accounts and deposited them with a local solicitor instead.[35]

These documents, unearthed many years later,[36] show that in spite of the war-time ban, Leeds City had gone on paying their players between £1 7s 6d and £2 2s a match. They had concealed this in the accounts by over-stating office staff wages, rates and printing and bill-posting costs. The FA at once suspended the club and the FL expelled them from the League. Four members of the controlling syndicate, the manager, Herbert Chapman, and his assistant were suspended *sine die*. The players were ordered to be sold. Over 30 representatives of other clubs turned up to the sale to pick over the remains and 14 of the 22 players on offer were transferred for fees of between £250 and £1,250. A professional auctioneer was appointed to sell the rest of the club's effects, including 'shower baths, billiard tables, jerseys, shirts, vests, knickers, spare goal posts, footballs, nets and boots'.[37]

All of this put *The Times*'s encomium into perspective and weakened the force of its call to the services and public schools to 'devote special attention to the training of the officers of the future in the game that their men will play'.[38] The services made some attempt in their own hierarchical way, but the public schools did not to want to know. Eton's scorn for the vulgarities of rugby was no basis for a crusade for soccer amongst the lower orders. The public schools that persevered with soccer did so for the old tribal reasons, not in sudden conversion to democratic principle. Both Evelyn Waugh and the Lancing College of 1919 were highly reactionary, but for both soccer was *the* game. The 16-year-old Waugh's aesthetic leanings and world-weary sophistication led him to contempt for the OTC and the regimentation that most sport involved, preference for rackets – or even fives, if he could use a glove – and hatred of 'the tyranny of House swimming'. He endured rather than enjoyed house trials for boxing. (Not that Waugh disapproved in principle. Boxing had a recognised place in public school life, both social and athletic, and there had always been keen interest in the prize ring. On 5 December he wrote: 'Last night Carpentier laid Beckett out in the first round. This has somewhat alleviated my financial distress.'[39]) In athletics he was relieved to be eliminated after putting up a decent performance. Yet in soccer which was even more rigorously organised and competitive, his attitude was quite different. As a player he had to put up with the indignity of being made into a 'third League' goalkeeper, principally because he had no talent for anything else, and as a spectator his strong partisan emotions needed the fortification of victory. But a cup triumph brought forth a lyrical reaction: 'We've won the footer jerry. It seems almost incredible . . . It is really too wonderful . . . the general delirium. The ecstatic joy is worth a life of serene happiness.'[40]

Where such soccer schools differed from the rugger ones was in the relationship with the adult game. When during the holidays Waugh went to see an FA Cup match between Swindon and Fulham he commented, 'The crowds were astounding. It is extraordinary the people who can pay 10s 6d for a seat.'[41] But they could and they did. 'The people's game' was now well on the way to becoming 'the national game'. It certainly was not just the English game. Even in Wales the claims of Cardiff City to recognition by the FL were more important to many than 'holier-than-thou' rugger. In Scotland war-time suspension of the middle-class pursuit had allowed soccer to take firmer root than ever. It was Rangers' turn to take the League honours and Kilmarnock and Albion Rovers, both newcomers, contested the restored Scottish Cup. The first post-war international was held in Belfast in October when Ireland held England to a 1–1 draw before a big crowd and the problems that beset the game there had nothing to with lack of popular appeal – quite the contrary. Both semi-finals in the Irish Cup, one in Belfast, one in Dublin, produced serious crowd trouble. The Dublin game led to Shelbourne's ground being closed for a time. The Belfast one went to a replay, which was held on St Patrick's Day, and when a Celtic player was sent off the crowd invaded the pitch, shots were fired, the Sinn Fein flag was unfurled and the terraces rang with republican songs.

In the restored FL championship, with its two divisions enlarged to 22 clubs each, the crowds were bigger than ever, in spite of a doubling of admission charges: the minimum was now one shilling (5p). Players' wages were substantially increased, to a maximum of £9 a week, with bonuses of £2 for a win and £1 for a draw. This was more than enough to preserve the relativities with industry. (Nevertheless it seemed an inadequate reflection of their attractive power to many players and the Players' Union promptly lost 1,600 of its 2,000 members, weakening its position in the leaner times that lay ahead.) A more significant gain in the long term was the League's formalisation of the war-time gate-sharing arrangements that had helped the poorer clubs to survive, requiring home teams to hand over 20% of the takings less costs. A rail strike threatened to disrupt the opening fixtures but the government authorised clubs to use petrol (still rationed) to get players to away destinations – including Clapton Orient's long trip to South Shields.[42]

It was a good year for the midlands – West Bromwich Albion won the League and Aston Villa the FA Cup – and in the north soccer more than held its own with the Northern Union. In the immediate post-war prosperity there was plenty of room for both. The Northern Union introduced its new two-division Rugby League and both finals drew record crowds. But it was a minority taste and a good soccer team could always make headway even in its strongholds. This was now demonstrated in Huddersfield. The soccer club had lost money every year since joining the Football League chiefly because of the success of the town's Northern Union 'Empire team of stars and all talents'. In the autumn of 1919 the soccer club negotiated a move to Leeds City's old ground, but were too far in debt already for the FL to approve. The setback seems to have stirred them up: they started winning their matches, got into the Cup Final and won promotion to the First Division. (Nor was this because the Northern Union team were slipping. On the contrary they won the Rugby League Challenge Cup and, having finished top of the League table, only lost the final play-off to Wigan by 3 points to 2.)

Soccer's wider appeal was also demonstrated by its breakthrough in the south. To the indignation of supporters of Barnsley and Wolverhampton in particular the FL had sacrificed considerations of equity to estimates of post-war potential by awarding the two extra places in the First Division to Chelsea and Arsenal. Londoners were now craving for top-class soccer. Tottenham, also aggrieved, won the Second Division to prove their point. The decision of West Ham United to break their contractual obligations to the Southern League and accept an invitation to the Second Division was significant both for Londoners – it was the first truly East End club to move into the upper echelons – and for the organisation of the game. The Southern League, seeing the writing on the wall, began negotiations with the FL for amalgamation.

All this post-war euphoria inevitably reinforced the FA's complacency and its patronising attitude to the other soccer-playing nations. There was nothing abroad to compare with the home international programme. It found a cloak for its disdainful attitude in the resentful post-war atmosphere towards the enemy. It is harder in a real war than in a sporting contest to

> meet with Triumph and Disaster
> And treat those two impostors just the same.[43]

The British had coped pretty well with disaster, but magnanimity in triumph eluded them for a time – as indeed it eluded Kipling. When the discussions about whether Germany and its allies should be allowed into the fold showed signs of going against them the FA withdrew from FIFA and the Scottish, Irish and Welsh Associations followed. Only two things spoiled an otherwise blissful vision. One was the turbulence in Ireland. The other, much more serious, was the loss of the gentlemanly amateurs. Despite pockets of Lancing-like support soccer was losing the battle in the public schools and the socially-reconstructive messages from *The Times* had little effect.

Rugby Union football, on the other hand, had greatly profited from its war-time inspirational role. Some had made the switch during the war years; Beaumont, for example, did so in 1917. Others, like Felstead, changed immediately afterwards, and dozens of private schools and aspirant grammar schools in the expanding local authority system followed. Over in Ulster whilst the soccer crowds were rioting, the 1919 rugger season was marked by the launch of Instonians, the Old Boys of the Royal Belfast Academical Institution, and rivals Old Campbellians. And the match between Ballymena Academy and the new town club meant that 'the stage was set for a revival of rugby football in Ballymena', an emblematic phenomenon, indeed.[44]

The added glamour rugger had acquired was further augmented by the presence of ex-officers in the university teams. J. E. Greenwood, that year's England captain, had gone back to Cambridge at the age of 28 for the sole purpose of playing in his fifth 'Varsity match. Oxford similarly were led by E. Loudoun-Shand, a pre-war Scottish cap, who had 'suffered fearful disabilities from war wounds, though no one who did not know him intimately was ever aware of them'.[45]

Amongst the ex-service undergraduates in the victorious Cambridge side were A. F. (later Sir Arthur) Blakiston, G. S. Conway, R. Cove-Smith and A. M. Smallwood, all of whom became distinguished internationals. Another, W. W. (later Lord) Wakefield, who had so enjoyed the Royal Naval Air Service that he stayed on, took advantage of its new training arrangements to go up to Cambridge a year later.

Not all Greenwood's England side were university men. A. T. Voyce, of Gloucester, after gallant service as an infantry captain in which one of his eyes was seriously damaged, was in the pack. And the half-back pair, probably England's greatest ever, were both regular naval officers, though with somewhat different backgrounds. W. J. A. Davies, the stand-off half, an Admiralty constructor, had begun as a dockyard apprentice before going on to RN College, Greenwich and war service in the Grand Fleet. C. A. Kershaw, his scrum half, son of Sir Lewis Kershaw, was a Dartmouth man, a submarine commander and a fencing champion who was to represent Britain in the

Antwerp Olympics. In the closely-fought international championship England could only share the title with Scotland and Wales (who also had their share of mature ex-service players) and the game had never been in better shape. Even France, steel tempered in the flames of Verdun, was now a serious contender, recording her first victory – over Ireland.

Notes

1 For a short account of the war losses see J. Stevenson, *British Society 1914–45*, Harmondsworth, 1984, pp. 93–6; A. J. P. Taylor, *English History 1914–45*, Oxford, 1965, pp. 120–2.

2 A. Bennett, *Journals*, 11 November 1918, ed. F. Swinnerton, Hardmondsworth, 1971, p. 431.

3 R. Kipling, 'Russia to the Pacifists', 1918 in *Definitive Verse of Rudyard Kipling*, London, 1940.

4 The honour went to the American, Nancy, Viscountess Astor, who became Conservative MP for Plymouth (Sutton) at a by-election in 1919.

5 For a sympathetic account of their achievements see G. D. H. Cole and R. Postgate, *The Common People*, London, 1938 (1961 edn) esp. Chapter Forty-two 'Revolution and the Dole'.

6 See A. Marwick, *The Deluge*, London, 1965, esp. Chapter Nine (II), 'The New Society', and Taylor, *English History*, pp. 121–3.

7 Stanley Baldwin's phrase, quoted by Taylor, *English History*, p. 129.

8 R. Graves and P. Hodge, *The Long Weekend*, London 1940 (1971 edn), p. 20.

9 Sir Andrew Horsburgh-Porter, in M. Seth-Smith (ed.), *The Horse*, London, 1979. p. 85.

10 Introduction, *Baily's Hunting Directory*, 1919–20.

11 Minutes of MFHA annual end-of season meeting June 1919.

12 E. Parker (ed.), *The Shooting Weekend Book*, London, 1952, p. 133.

13 J. Lowerson in T. Mason (ed.), *Sport in Britain*, Cambridge, 1989, p. 22, citing *Fishing Gazette*, 4 January 1919.

14 ibid., p. 22 (*Fishing Gazette*, 15 February, 1919).

15 ibid. (*Fishing Gazette*, 8 March 1919).

16 ibid. (*Fishing Gazette*, 16 August 1919).

17 ibid., p. 29 (*Fishing Gazette*, 15 March 1919).

18 N. L. Jackson, *Sporting Days and Sporting Ways*, London, 1932, p. 262.

19 *Irish Field*, 30 November 1918, quoted in W. H. Gibson, *Early Irish Golf*, Naas, 1988, p. 81.

20 *Headingley RUFC Centenary Handbook*, Leeds, 1979, quoted by A. J. Arnold, *A Game That Would Pay*, London, 1988, p. 69.

21 *Almanack*, 1921, p. 147, quoted in E. Halladay, *Rowing in England*, Manchester, 1990, p. 127.

22 *The Times*, 1 July 1919.

23 T. A. Cook, *Rowing at Henley*, London, 1919, p. xviii.

24 C. Dodd, *The Oxford and Cambridge Boat Race*, London, 1983, p. 55.

25 *Yachting Monthly*, 75th Birthday issue, July 1981, p. 1254.

26 Harrison Butler, loc. cit.

27 *The Times*, 18 June 1919.

28 Graves and Hodge, *Long Weekend*, pp. 34–5.

29 12 August 1919. This might have served as an epitaph for both Dohertys. Both died

young, Reggie in 1911 aged 39, Laurie in 1919 still only 43.

30 'Notes by the Editor on 1919', *Wisden*, 1920, reprinted in B. Green, *Wisden Anthology (1900–1940)*, London, 1980, pp. 516–18.

31 *The Times*, 5 August 1919.

32 *Wisden*.

33 *Nelson Leader*, 6 June 1919, quoted in J. Hill, 'League Cricket in the North and Midlands' in R. Holt (ed.), *Sport and the Working Class in Modern Britain*, Manchester, 1990, pp. 121–41.

34 *The Times*, 25 September 1919.

35 A. J. Arnold, 'Leeds City and the Great War', *IJHS*, May 1990, pp. 115–16.

36 By Arnold.

37 *Yorkshire Post*, 18 October 1919.

38 The Times, 25 September 1919.

39 M. Davie (ed.), *The Diaries of Evelyn Waugh*, London, 1976, 4 December 1919.

40 ibid., 19 February 1920.

41 ibid., 10 January 1920.

42 A. J. Arnold, *A Game That Would Pay*, London, 1988, p. 78.

43 R. Kipling, 'If', *Rewards and Fairies*, London, 1910.

44 *Ballymena RFC Centenary Handbook*, Ballymena, 1987, p. 7.

45 D. R. Gent, 'Rugby Football', in *Aldin Book of Outdoor Games*, London, 1933, p. 25.

CHAPTER SIX

Fair play (1919–29):
a different world

As well as helping to build up a rugby team Verdun had also given the French a fierce determination to get their own back on the Germans. The sentiment found strong echoes amongst the British public. Thus President Wilson's decent, schoolmasterly plans for a League of Nations were vitiated by his Allies' vengeful insistence on reparations, division of enemy colonies, destroying the old Austro-Hungarian empire and disarming the Germans.[1] Were the English motivated, as Kipling believed, by a cold hatred, slow to arouse but not easy to dispel? Moral outrage was nearer the mark. Either way it was understandable but counter-productive. So, too, the reaction to the continued Irish troubles and to the passive resistance of Gandhi and his followers in India. Both at home and abroad – whether in the frustrated disapproval of an emerging economic philosophy in which 'paying your way' no longer seemed to matter, or in the many new policing duties they undertook for the League of Nations across the Middle East – the British faced a new and baffling world that refused to sit still.

Post-War politics

The war and its financing had brought added strain to relations with the USA, and it did not help that when Sinn Fein formed the Irish Republican Army from the old Irish Volunteers in January 1919 and began a fierce liberation campaign a good deal of the funding came from American sympathisers. Putting down the IRA proved difficult. When the RIC and the regular Army could not cope Lloyd George brought in the Black and Tans, ex-service volunteers who struck back hard. Meanwhile the Government of Ireland Act (1920) offered two separate Home Rule Parliaments, north and south, linked by a council of Ireland. The Ulster Unionists accepted their own parliament but wanted no southern link: Sinn Fein refused to accept the British yoke, north or south. It suited their book, however, to respond to King George V's personal request for a truce in 1921. In the bargaining that followed Sinn Fein demanded an all-Ireland republic and were offered Dominion status for 26 of the 32 counties. The moderates signed a treaty and, though the extremists' angry reaction led to civil war, the British were able to extricate themselves and leave the new Irish Free State to it.

The chief casualty was Lloyd George. Reviled by Liberals and Labour for the Black and Tans, he was now loathed by the Conservatives for breaking the Union. He was running out of steam in domestic policies, too. When the post-war boom ended it was like the day of reckoning. Wages fell heavily in all the major industries during 1921, and there was a succession of strikes. Severe economy in public spending was needed. Some, like cuts in the armed services, were logical; some, like the elimination of government departments that had sprung up in the war, were positively welcomed. But the planned development of social services suffered badly, particularly public health and education, in which teachers' salaries were substantially reduced. The year 1922 was also bad for foreign affairs. When Lloyd George sought a deal on the cancellation of war debts, the USA, whose President Harding claimed not to know 'anything about this European stuff,'[2] was uninterested. When Lloyd George tried to arouse world opinion to prevent Turkey upsetting the post-war settlement of the Middle East he got no support abroad and not much at home.

Bonar Law emerged from retirement to lead the Conservatives out of the Coalition. His idea of letting the nation 'get on with its own work, with the minimum of interference at home and of disturbance abroad'[3] won them 345 seats in the general election. The Liberals dropped to third place, and only about half of their 117 members supported Lloyd George. Many of the recruits amongst the 145 Labour members were middle-class social reformers, like Major Clement Attlee, an Oxford man and former lecturer at the London School of Economics, but there were enough socialist firebrands from the Celtic fringes to keep alive fears of Bolshevik infiltration. The Special Irish Branch of the Metropolitan Police dropped the 'Irish' label and began Red-hunting. There was no cause for alarm. The Labour Party hastily disassociated themselves from the tiny Communist Party, elected as their leader the imposing rhetorician Ramsay MacDonald and waited for the rising tide of democracy to take its course.

They were encouraged by the Tories' disarray. Several of Lloyd George's old allies – Austen Chamberlain, Winston Churchill, Lord Birkenhead – sulkily withdrew from government. Law himself was a sick man. When he suddenly died he was succeeded almost by default by Stanley Baldwin whose main achievement as Chancellor of the Exchequer had been to conclude a most disadvantageous settlement of the American war debt with the dyspeptic Calvin Coolidge. His government achieved little except a stricter limit on public works and a housing scheme, introduced by the colourless but effective Neville Chamberlain. This offered subsidies to private contractors as well as local authorities to build houses for sale – more helpful to the lower middle than to the working class. Unemployment was now a burning issue, and Baldwin, who saw free trade as a malign influence in this respect, called an election to secure a mandate for a policy of Protection. This lost so many seats that the Tories barely scraped home and were defeated as soon as Parliament reassembled. The constitution required the King to invite the leader of the second largest party to form a government. It must have been an alarming prospect. He wrote in his diary, 'To-day 25 years ago dear Grandmama died. I wonder what she would have thought of a Labour Government!'[4] Yet as he explained to his mother, Queen Alexandra, 'They have different ideas to ours and they are all socialists, but they ought to be given a chance and ought to be treated fairly.'[5]

The experiment in fair play was brief and inconclusive. It produced no cure for unemployment and no sudden increase in government control. Public sector investment, which the Liberal economist J. M. Keynes was beginning to advocate, was thought financially unsound. Labour's most socialistic measure was a Housing Act, with subsidies for rented houses, which benefited at least the top slice of the working class. They also restored most of the momentum in education and adopted the slogan of 'Secondary education for all'. But they deeply disappointed the trades unions, the chief source of funds for the Labour Party, by threatening to use the Emergency Powers Act (a relic of the war and Lloyd Georgeism) against the wave of strikes, notably in the docks, that disrupted 1924. The unions backed off, but were considerably chagrined at MacDonald's demonstration of the Party's fitness to govern.

It was his excursions into foreign affairs, however, that undid MacDonald. He had been an opponent of the war – forced to resign from his golf club because of his views – and strongly supported the League of Nations' ideals. He now broke the stalemate in the Franco-German arguments over reparations, at the expense of the Entente Cordiale, and paved the way for reconciliation with Germany. This was too statesmanlike for many tastes. So was his complicated treaty with the Russians, who had convinced him that they could only pay their debts if they got a huge loan. And whilst Parliament was still in a flurry over this he persuaded the Attorney-General not to prosecute a communist on a minor charge and the government was defeated in a censure motion. In the ensuing election, with Baldwin renouncing Protection, the Conservatives took 419 seats against Labour's 151 and the Liberals' mere 40 and were entrenched for the next five years.

People of all classes felt more comfortable about the security of the Empire when the Tories were in power. Though more a matter of sentiment than of economics by this time, what the Empire added to the flow of cheap imported goods helped strengthen the warmth of feeling the British felt for their far-flung possessions. The British Empire Exhibition in Wembley Park in 1924 aroused great interest – the amusement park rather more than the educational events, perhaps – and the Prince of Wales in his much-publicised trips to various parts of the world was frequently called admiringly 'the salesman of Empire'. It was a strange pyramidal structure, with no planned future and most of the initiative for change was *ad hoc*. In 1926, however, the growing independence of the Dominions was recognised and their Parliaments, became, like Britain's own, subordinate only to the Crown, a largely symbolic link. Both George V himself and the die-hards now took more interest in the development of the colonies. The original aim of exploitation was not entirely dead but colonial administration, at the hands of unacademic games-playing public school boys, had long since become an end in itself. The mandates of the Middle East, despite the disillusion of romantics like Lawrence of Arabia, became another congenial mode of life for scions of the landed gentry – and protected the oil supplies. In India the old Raj continued, ignoring warning signs, which were attributed to Soviet propaganda. The empire, like cricket, was hard to explain to outsiders, but like cricket it was a game the British played.

Domestically the Tory government was assisted by trends, already under way when it came to power. The population growth had slowed, probably because of birth-control, and the trend towards smaller families, however worrying for eugenicists, was well established. Emigration was down to about half the pre-war level. The balance of population growth was also shifting away from the old industrial areas to the more southerly new ones. Better nutrition and medical know-how led to a general improvement in health. Britain had already regained her pre-war production level in spite of a general reduction in working hours and in the next five years improved it by 14%. Jobs were becoming easier to find. Prices reached twice pre-war levels, but wages about three times. The wage-earner achieved a bigger slice of the national income. There were promising new industries: motor vehicle and light engineering was already strong and electricity was being developed. The trouble came from the old industries now facing decline.

Winston Churchill had done well as Chancellor of the Exchequer, reducing income tax from 10s to 4s in the pound and restoring self-respect by taking the country back to the gold standard. The difficulty was that the high-value pound priced British exports out of the market. Baldwin thought the answer was reduced wages to make industries – particularly the older ones – more competitive. The miners, a million strong, were a key group, for the price of coal affected the whole of industry. The mining industry, a ramshackle affair kept going by government subsidy, had done unexpectedly well immediately after the war. Then, after a wage increase in the days of the Labour government, German and Polish imports flooded the market, undercutting British coal. The owners' loss of profits did not impress the workers who resisted pay cuts or longer hours. The government at first refused to renew its subsidy then relented, pending a Royal Commission Report. This bought time but bred expectations that were not fulfilled. The miners had now become the central figures in a fight for workers' rights that affected every trade unionist, and when on 1 May 1926, they were locked out the TUC were given authority to call a general strike.

It began resoundingly with sympathetic action from railway, engineering, electricity, gas and printing unions. But the government had put to good use the time it had bought. Troops were used to convoy food. Emergency transport plans based on road vehicles, driven by volunteers and entrepreneurial blacklegs, confounded the strikers. It also easily won the propaganda battle. Churchill, through a specially-produced newspaper, the *British Gazette*, waved the flag and rallied right-thinking men and women to the cause of law and order. The *Daily Mail*, printed in Paris, and flown in by air, carried headlines like 'The pistol at the nation's head'. After nine days of heroics the government offered a hint of marginally less drastic terms for settlement and when the miners refused to budge, the solidarity of the strike collapsed. The miners struggled on alone for six months until obliged to give in, accepting lower wages and longer hours, having gained nothing.

In the aftermath there was little resistance to the Trades Union Disputes Act, making sympathy strikes or attempts to coerce the government illegal. The Communist Party, which had reached a record 10,000 membership during the strike, soon fell back again. A framework was established, voluntarily, for co-operation between the two sides of industry. In 1928 production reached new heights, and the cost of living fell by 15%. A de-rating scheme also helped industry and thus made an indirect contribution to the unemployment problem. Local authority welfare services, particularly public assistance and housing, were standardised and strengthened. Peace looked secure and Britain seemed to be doing very nicely. It was a mood of euphoria that led to the decision to lower the voting age for women from 30 to 21 – the 'flapper vote'.

Dancing to new tunes

It had been a decade of liberation. In 1920 Evelyn Waugh had noted *en passant*: 'And Mr Einstein has discovered a new theory of the universe!'[6] For Christians such a theory was presumptuous; for conservative intellectuals it was disturbing. The notion of relativity, undermining orthodox Newtonian physics, was worse than that of evolution, for its message was that nothing could be assumed. Causality itself was soon to be questioned in Heisenberg's 'uncertainty principle'. Meanwhile the old system-building philosophers and metaphysicians were becoming distinctly unfashionable: the 'in' men were logical positivists like G. E. Moore, Bertrand Russell – and their pupil Ludwig Wittgenstein whose master-work *Tractatus Logicus-Philosophicus* was so eluci-datory as to be utterly incomprehensible. A slightly softer option was Karl Jaspers's existentialism, philosophy built around 'the being of the thinker'.[7] Most devastatingly, Sigmund Freud's psycho-analytical theories cast doubt on the very rationality of the reasoning process, whilst his uncovering of the power of the unconscious and its sex-drives intrigued café society and intro-duced the thoroughly modern dread of inhibition.

Popular versions of Freudian theory were often the only part of the new learning that trickled through. The rest was not only beyond the grasp of the averagely intelligent but outside the compass of intellectuals brought up on the humanities. Latin and Greek were still the hallmarks of an educated person, and to question their value was to indulge in the merest func-tionalism. The chief sign of intellectual ferment was that the great universities became once more a major source of creative writing, not all of it reactionary and much of it highly irreverent. The war had given a fillip to applied science and medicine, but the state-funded research councils did not greatly disturb the prevailing establishment assumption that serendipity was the true scientific approach. It had its points. By 1919 Ernest Rutherford was already working on nuclear theory, though with no application in view, and over the next dozen years led his Cambridge team to success in splitting the atom.

More immediately the war-time development of radio soon brought peacetime benefits, mostly commercially-inspired. Before long the wireless set became as central to British life as the garden. A less harmonious contri-bution to the rural idyll was that made by the intrusive internal combustion engine. Acceptable in a war-time tank or Sopwith Scout, in peace it brought only noise and disruption. Work-horses were still preferred to the tractor on the characteristic small British farm, and some people clung to the horse-drawn carriage and the pony and trap, but motor buses were fast becoming the standard means of transport in the pockets of countryside not already covered by the 20 million miles of railway. Only an élite 150,000 or so had owned cars before the war, but the 1919 slogan of 'motoring for the million' was soon to need upward revision. There were over a hundred independent motor manufacturers in 1920, and sales were brisk, though cars were not cheap. Morris, whose 4-seater Cowley cost over £500, sold 280 a month. Austin advertised 'cars of distinction'. The cheapest, the Ford disparagingly known as 'tin Lizzy', had high import duty and was heavily taxed. Then came the slump and Morris, who discovered that by reducing the price by £100 he sold even more, started a price war. The 1921 Austin Seven, only £165, introduced the Baby Car. All of this brought more and more townsfolk on quick, uncomprehending trips to the country looking for escape.

Others escaped by armchair. Sales of pulp fiction soared. There was little change in the basic themes – 'romance', melodrama, crime – perhaps a little more highly-coloured inside, but never as shocking as the lurid covers promised. More hard-back books offered low-brow entertainment – sometimes American as in Edgar Rice Burroughs' Tarzan series. The British master was Edgar Wallace who switched his massive output from colonial adventure to racing yarns and crime thrillers. For the more cerebral crime addict the detective puzzle story was spun out to novel length by writers like Freeman Wills Croft, H. C. Bailey and Agatha Christie. Nobody wanted to read tales about the war itself but spies and foreign agents were still popular, from the exotic William Le Queux to the stiff-upper-lipped John Buchan. The ex-officer in search of adventure was a favourite theme of ex-officers in search of an income from writing: Sapper's *Bulldog Drummond* appeared in 1920. And – another form of escapism – P. G. Wodehouse perfected the farcical world of Jeeves and Wooster, Lord Emsworth and the rest, to the infinite joy of all but the sourest social realists.

Social realism, in fact, was out of fashion even amongst highbrow writers. Yeats had always lived in a world of romantic myth and the stirring events in Ireland were, in the last resort, part of his psycho-drama, whilst the lofty theme of the expatriate Americans Ezra Pound and T. S. Eliot who shaped the next generation's poetic thought was the erosion of civilised values by materialist culture. The English Georgian poets in the mainstream hoped for 'the birth of a lyrical age' and avoided both political controversy and avant garde experimentation. Only the second interested the spiky Irish Catholic James Joyce whose prose epic *Ulysses* (1921) burst the bounds of the conventional novel not only in construction and language but in its 'stream of consciousness' exploration of sexual matters. It was banned. Virginia Woolf, a member of the English middle-class Bloomsbury group of aesthetes, was more circumspect in her own experiments and thus able to advance the feminist cause, albeit in a rather precious way. D.H. Lawrence's views on society became less coherent as a result of the war and he interwove them with aggressive sexual themes – working-class male triumph through the conquest of upper-class females – and increasingly found himself at odds with respectable opinion, not least amongst the working classes.

The universities' burst of creativity took no particular direction. Apart from lyric poetry (of which Robert Graves, an ex-officer who went to live abroad, was the best exponent) the prevailing mode was the satiric novel: Aldous Huxley's *Crome Yellow* (1924) was the first to cause a stir, Evelyn Waugh's *Vile Bodies* (1928) the funniest. Women figured strongly: the Oxford crop ranged from the mildly shocking Winifred Holtby and her friend and fellow socialist Vera Brittain to the snobbish creator of Lord Peter Wimsey, Dorothy L. Sayers.[8] And as the newspapers began to employ more graduates to write their swelling gossip columns (Charles Graves, Beverley Nichols, 'Peterborough' and 'William Hickey' were all Oxford men; Margaret Lane an Oxford woman) so undergraduate affairs and opinions were given more and more prominence. For the better-off students the post-war years were a time of high spirits, high jinks, eccentric clubs and elaborate hoaxes, duly reported in the popular press. The vogue for wide-bottomed trousers, 'Oxford bags', that began in 1924 made a permanent mark on male fashion. And if all this lacked high seriousness, that seemed an appropriate response to inflated establishment values that had got the world in such a mess.

Escapist trends helped blur the vision and dull the minds of painters and sculptors. The cosier aspects of life, the countryside and the world of horses and dogs and their quarry had always been the most profitable subjects for British artists. In the early Georgian years the Bloomsbury Group led by Clive Bell and Roger Fry had seemed to open new doors. After the war the expatriate American Wyndham Lewis, founder of the Vorticist movement, resumed his tireless propaganda for progressive causes, literary and artistic, and Jacob Epstein became even more shocking, a fashionable *enfant terrible*. But the war, either by death or trauma, had taken a heavy toll on native talent. Henry Moore slowly emerged towards future greatness, but a gap had opened up between even the best British painters and the continental masters of Cubism, Futurism, Expressionism and the like. Though some, like Stanley Spencer and Paul Nash, survived to translate the disintegrative war experience into great and recognisably British art, it was on a plateau left behind by Picasso, Matisse and the Europeans. And meanwhile the original liberating movement began to caricature itself.

The public was certainly baffled by modern art. The leading modern poet, T. S. Eliot, did not even offer the spice of a colourful private life. His cheerless theme was the emptiness of modern existence. *The Waste Land* (1922) –

> I think we are in rats' alley
> Where the dead men lost their bones

was followed three years later by 'The Hollow Men',

> Leaning together
> Headpiece filled with straw.

The solution, he appeared to be saying, lay in spiritual regeneration. A more popular approach was in the pursuit of pleasure. The 1920s brought novelty after novelty. Some, like the pogo-stick craze of 1921, imported from Paris and popularised by West End stars, and the elaborate and exotic mah-jong, which came from America a year later, were passing vogues. Others like contract bridge in 1925 – again imported from the States – became permanent fixtures. These things began as they always had done with leisured folk, but fashions in frivolity, though still set by 'society', were no longer restricted to it. The newspapers, in their constant search for circulation-boosters, saw to that. Their greatest made the transatlantic crossing in 1924. As *Punch* put it 'The allure of Epstein and Oxford trouserings has been for the few; the Crossword Puzzle captivated the general.'[9]

Psycho-analysis was an exciting but dangerous novelty, for Freudian theories seemed to give an imprimatur to sex as the key to mental health. Furthermore it was now being suggested, more or less openly, that women had sexual needs. Gratification was made easier by the new diaphragm introduced in 1919. Dr Marie Stopes, who was not even medically qualified, combined lyricism about married love with technical instruction that was equally valid outside wedlock. Prostitution increased. More shockingly, so did enthusiastic amateurism: in 1921 a Westminster preacher declared, 'Woman's rebound from conventional virtue is as daring as her attire.'[10] The divorce rate was by then four times more than before the war and the Matrimonial Causes Act, 1923, establishing sex equality as to grounds and reducing the cost by giving jurisdiction to Assize courts, again increased the number.

Smoking was a sign if not a cause of moral decline. In 1927 the average British per capita consumption of tobacco, 3.4 lb, was the highest of any nation. Consumption had more than trebled in the last 20 years, almost all of it in the form of cigarettes. Sales had been boosted by cunning advertisements suggesting that everything from peace of mind to sporting prowess could be had from cigarettes, and by gimmicks such as free picture cards. 'The cigarette held between slim fingers has become one of the symbols of female emancipation, while lighting a girl's cigarette is fast becoming a romantic cliché.'[11]

Drinking and dancing, both of which were coarsened and Americanised by gin and jazz music, were the natural preamble to promiscuity. The Shimmy, the Charleston and the Black Bottom in turn scandalised the nation. When the new music was not lascivious it was inane as in the great hit of 1924, 'Yes, We Have No Bananas!' The restricted hours permitted by the reformed licensing laws of the 1920s could be evaded by membership of a night club. Police raids were frequent, though tactfully arranged so as not to coincide with a visit from the Prince of Wales, European princelings or the American film stars who were the newest objects of admiration. Newspaper gossip columnists, if not yet themselves the arbiters of fashion, already decided those who were. 'Society' came to mean 'people worthy of a columnist's respectful attention'.[12] This secret was not lost on Noel Coward, an icon of the age.

A gifted actor, playwright, composer and lyricist, Coward provided, in plays with self-explanatory titles like *The Vortex* and *Fallen Angel*, a sharp-edged, brittle gaiety suffused with contemporary disillusion. Later as cheerfulness became smart again he offered British versions of musical comedy, otherwise largely American, and polished C. B. Cochran revues. What most theatre-goers wanted was entertainment, not experiment. Revivals of the classics did well, as did J. M. Barrie and old favourites like *Charley's Aunt*. The record-breaking *Chu Chin Chow*, whose run began during the war, lasted 5 years. Of serious plays Shaw's *Heartbreak House*, about decadent British society, and the long sermon *Back to Methuselah* failed, but *Saint Joan*, the hit of 1924, won him the Nobel Prize. In Ireland Sean O'Casey, after two masterpieces, infuriated everyone with the third, and left the scene. The cinema attracted ever-increasing numbers, even of the middle classes, as its technology improved and their prejudices gave way to the magic of Chaplin and Mary Pickford, 'the world's sweetheart'. Soon the range extended to the animated fantasy of Felix the Cat, cowboys like Tom Mix and William S. Hart, the slapstick of Buster Keaton and Fatty Arbuckle, the romantic Douglas Fairbanks and the glamorous Gloria Swanson, the child star Jackie Coogan and the dog Rin-tin-tin. Chauvinists of the stuffier sort resented the intrusion of American manners as much as the financial stranglehold Hollywood had got during the war. Before the end of the decade the irresistible Mickey Mouse had arrived, and with the coming of 'the talkies' there was the prospect of American speech drowning out native British accents.

Happily by then a strong counter-influence was in operation. The British Broadcasting Company, set up in 1923 as a private venture sponsored by wireless set manufacturers, became a public Corporation in 1927 with an independent Charter which forbade advertising. Its audience, already two million and growing, paid a 10s (50p) licence fee. Under the single-minded leadership of a young Scot, John Reith, it quickly became a dignified institution dedicated to the elevation of the public taste. The accents of its announcers, derived from those of Oxbridge, were not only Cis-Atlantic but Cis-Watford. Its main offerings were news, drama and music of the better sort.

British classical music, having recently discovered a national identity, was strongly resistant to exotic influence, especially the avant garde of Stravinsky and the like: Vaughan Williams and Gustav Holst, masters of the Elgar-elegaic mode, were the standard. Only the precocious William Walton managed to straddle the old world and the new and achieve international stature. He came to notice by his contribution to the entertainment *Façade* (1922 and 1926) presented by the Sitwells, aesthetically-inclined young aristocrats intent on reinstating pre-industrial eccentricity to confound the bourgeoisie. It was for the upper and outer end of society, too, that the new British National Opera Company (1922) and Glyndebourne concerts (1924) catered.

With public sponsorship of the arts a rarity and orchestras hard to maintain the missionary contribution of the BBC was immeasurable. And if it was slow to introduce modern works it did so better than anyone else. The BBC also encouraged light music and gradually extended its support for the syncopated kind. Dance bands, American-inspired, and offering a modified form of jazz, now operated in smart hotels from the Savoy in London to Gleneagles, and were imitated in every suburban salon, urban dance hall and village 'hop'. On the wireless, bands like those of Jack Hylton and Henry Hall had a slightly more inhibited style than the Americans, and when the BBC set up its own resident Dance Orchestra in 1928 its leader, Jack Payne, interspersed the hot stuff with jolly novelty numbers.

Changing gear

The jazz age was also the age of speed. After the war-time stimulus to technology there was optimism not only for British drivers who challenged for supremacy on land, sea and air but also for the machines in which they did it. The Anglo-Irish Etonian Henry Segrave (later Sir Henry) who had served in the Flying Corps had helped design the 2-litre Sunbeam he drove to victory in the 1923 French Grand Prix and the great beast in which he passed 200 mph for the first time in 1929. He tussled regularly for land and water speed records with (Sir) Malcolm Campbell, of Uppingham, the Flying Corps the Stock Exchange and the City, who bought or commissioned his famous series of 'Blue Birds'. These wealthy amateurs electrified the crowds at Brooklands, distracting attention from the dominance of Alfa-Romeo, Bugatti and Maserati and the advance of the German Auto-Union and Mercedes on the Grand Prix circuit. More satisfactorily, the victory of the Bentley team in the 1924 Le Mans 24-hour race led to sustained interest in sports car racing and Bentley won it every year from 1927 to 1930. Segrave met his death in 1929 in snatching the water-speed record from the American Gar Wood, who was thought unethical for driving in front of other boats to slow them down in his churned wake. The Americans, fortunately, preferred their own motor-racing competitions, but they made most of the headlines in the air, with Charles Lindbergh's transatlantic flight in 1927 and Amelia Earhart's demonstration of what women could do in 1928. The RAC King's Cup air race trophy had been presented by George V in 1922 to encourage improvements in British design but it seemed rather to breed complacency. The short-lived Schneider Trophy race for seaplanes was more productive and Flight-Lieutenant Webster's victory was celebrated with enthusiasm.

In motor-cycle racing the British were markedlysuperior, both in riders and machines. There was nothing to touch Sunbeam, Norton, AJS and Velocette, not even the German DW and BMW or Italian Gilera and Guzzi, on the road, at Brooklands or the continental Grands Prix. Many felt the Continentals' more liberal attitude to road-racing gave them undue advantage but the Tourist Trophy races on the Isle of Man (started in 1907) had grown into the most famous motorcycle event in the world and they were extended in 1923 by an amateur competition, the Manx Grand Prix. There was clearly a mass market ripe for exploitation. Before the war American enthusiasts had staged improvised races on harness-racing circuits and 'dirt-track racing' had since been successfully introduced to Australia, at agricultural shows and the like. Motorcycle clubs at Camberley and South Manchester tried it out in 1927 and early the next year a public event was staged on a specially-laid cinder track at High Beach, Essex. The 20,000 crowd showed its potential, commercial interests moved in quickly and licences were obtained for regular meetings – often floodlit for the evening – on tracks shared with other proletarian activities.[13] Northern and Southern Leagues were started and there were soon highly professional dare-devils battling it out in every urban centre in the country. Such thrills at a shilling a time were obviously not good for the populace, especially when accompanied by betting, and when the new speedway at Audenshaw near Manchester opened on a Sunday a local councillor described it as 'a second Sodom and Gomorrah.'[14]

Neither advancing technology nor debased urban values could crush the Arcadian dream. Cavalry officers, either demobilised or facing mechanisation, gave great impetus to the burgeoning suburban cult of the horse. Riding – as a social accomplishment or for sport – was never more popular and riding schools sprang up by the score. Many of their customers were girls, and young women as well as men found running them a congenial and rewarding occupation. The National Horse Association (1922) under its President, Sir Walter Gilbey, encouraged its member clubs to dedicate themselves not only to correct riding but to correct deportment – grooming of horse and rider was all-important in their well-bred competitions. Many clubs, however, were less interested in 'showing' than in show-jumping. The élite end of this Edwardian enthusiasm was a mixture of traditions – end-of-hunting-season frolicking, military eventing, largely foreign – and it had become a feature of the International Horse Show at Olympia over which the Earl of Lonsdale presided with his usual flair. But it had plenty of provincial counterparts, of varying quality, and in 1921 Lonsdale was invited to chair a meeting between Colonel

V. D. S. Williams, Major C. T. 'Taffy' Walwyn and some of the leading civilian riders. The resulting British Show Jumping Association developed a system of local and national competitions under standard rules that offered a ladder of achievement in what was still largely an amateur pursuit.

The end of the war brought a resumption of winter sports. Visitors to Mürren found Arnold Lunn, whose father had built up the resort as part of his travel agency business, ready to greet them with new attractions. Both recreationally and competitively the early lead had been taken by the British, and especially their public school men, in devising competitions in ski-ing, skating and tobogonning. Lunn, the founder of the Alpine Ski Club in his Oxford days, had injured himself mountaineering and been obliged to spend most of the war in Switzerland. In 1921 he successfully introduced the modern slalom and next year hosted a 'Varsity ski-ing match. The initiative was passing to the continentals, however. The Nordic Games at Holmkollen in Norway had already established a cult following but winter sports' reputation for professionalism and commercialism had limited their Olympic recognition to figure skating and even this was thought caddish and American.[15] But de Coubertin's retirement opened the floodgates and the first Winter Games were held at Chamonix in 1924. For all the controversy they were a great success. Norway produced not only the ski-ing champion but an 11-year-old skater, Sonja Henie, who was to become a sort of Mary Pickford on ice.

Hitherto in Britain ice-skating had been somewhat restricted socially and still had its pockets of élitism. One was the Westminster Ice Club which both the Prince of Wales and the Duke of York, following family tradition, occasionally visited. Here, too, the British Ice Hockey Association got under way again and superior teams like Princes' Club and Royal Engineers contended with teams from Oxford and Cambridge whose names paid tribute to the masters of the genre – the Canadians. This was hardly yet a spectator sport, but interest spread, and after a brave British showing in the 1928 games and the formation of a Scottish Association in 1929, there were high hopes. The main attraction of the rinks, figure skating, was given a further boost by Sonja Henie, but roller-skating remained the more accessible sport, socially and technically, and most of the bigger towns now had roller rinks.

All the better ones, however small, now had badminton clubs and if there was a shortage of suitably standardised halls in lesser places this did not greatly perturb the All-England Association which resumed its spirited encounters with Ireland in 1920 and with Scotland the following year. A Welsh Union, formed in 1928, showed promise for the future. The club, team play and a determined amateurism had always been to the fore in this high-suburban legacy of the palmy days of the British Raj. The All-England traditions did include annual championships, however, dominated after the war by the dedicated Sir George Thomas Bt, until age and superior Irishmen caught up with him. Overseas there was by the end of the decade a strong organisation in Malaysia, growing interest in Canada, and potential rivals in Denmark, where it showed signs of becoming the national game. Women were now becoming more than mere 'other halves' in mixed play and there were some gifted singles players. The best was the young Kitty McKane until she moved on to the more challenging Wimbledon scene in 1924.

Unconsidered trifles of earlier eras established themselves permanently and more seriously after the war. Table-tennis, after several previous attempts, now made the grade partly because the continental countries to which British businessmen had taken the game – notably Hungary – had kept it up and partly because it became popular in the universities. Otherwise London suburbia was the spiritual home of post-war advance. There were open championships for men and women in 1921 and the following year a national organisation was formed. It was called at first the Ping Pong Association but this was found to infringe commercial copyright, and gave way to the greater dignity of the Table Tennis Association. Shortly afterwards it achieved a masterstroke in securing its chairman the Hon. Ivor Montagu of Cambridge University, son of Lady Swaythling. In 1926 she presented a trophy for international competition and agreed that it be called the Swaythling Cup. Britain was given the honour of holding the first world championships, but the Hungarians completely dominated the male scene, and it was a great surprise when 20-year-old Fred Perry won the title in Budapest in 1929. Despite its pinnacle of fashionable support, table-tennis was far from exclusive and it had become a staple of lower middle-class youth organisations. Perry, a member of the Ealing YMCA club, was the son of a Stockport cotton worker with political ambitions. He had his own sights on higher things.

Another post-war success was squash, a soft-ball version of rackets – itself a derivative of real tennis – the game of exclusive clubs, the better regiments and the public schools. Places like the Bath, Queen's and the Royal Automobile Clubs had had squash courts since Edwardian times The first professional champion, Charles Read, was also a rackets and lawn tennis professional and the first full-time squash professional (at the Bath) was not appointed until 1912. It was a sideline for most amateurs, too, and in the early twenties squash was governed by a committee of the Tennis and Rackets Association, played on courts of varying dimensions, with balls of different consistency and different scoring systems. In 1922 the Bath Cup, between the West End club teams, was inaugurated by James Palmer-Tomkinson, an ardent propagandist. Though haphazard organisationally, it stimulated interest in serious competition. The Amateur Championship the following year let in the

Army rackets champion the Anglo-Irish Tommy Jameson, and the playing conditions were standardised soon afterwards by staging the championship at the Bath Club, home of the runner-up Palmer-Tomkinson. An American tour in the winter of 1923–4 established that the natives were not responsive to colonisation but brought the British factions closer to agreement on such matters as the hardness of the ball. The captain Sam Toyne, head of St Peter's, York, laid the foundation for future advance by arranging in 1925 the first public school match between St Peter's and his own old school, Haileybury. By 1928 the Squash Rackets Association was set up.

Like its real tennis and rackets ancestors, squash was a masculine affair and its early women players were mostly tomboys from sporting families with private courts and brothers home from their public schools. The three Cave sisters and the two Fenwicks benefited in this way and Miss Susan Noel, who became champion in 1930 was the daughter of the secretary of Queen's Club. These well-connected Amazons were welcomed by the Squash Committee from the beginning, held their first championships a year ahead of the men and became independent almost as soon as the SRA. It was all part of the surprising new world.

The female slimming craze of the later twenties had more to do with acquiring the currently approved tubular shape than with health, but it encouraged taking exercise. Amongst the various tablets, potions, vibrating machines and rollers on offer were more serious machines and PT courses: early morning 'physical jerks' helped male 'middle-aged spread' as well. Exercise became easier with the development of synthetic fibres, such as artificial silk (officially called rayon from 1927 but cunningly abbreviated to 'art. silk' on many manufacturers' labels) which lightened the burden that women in particular carried around. It also made clothes cheaper, brighter and less boringly durable, and, especially for women, less of a badge of class. Removing them in the fresh air was another innovation. The hot summer of 1928 helped to popularise sunbathing. Fashionable beachwear was a single-piece swimming suit with a small overskirt, loose fitting crêpe-de-chine beach pyjamas, and towelling-lined oilcloth jacket. Protective wide-brimmed Mexican sunhats and sun-tan oil followed in 1929.

Sun-worship was condemned as excessive, not only by the conventional and by medical opinion but by those suspicious of its German origins. Since the Locarno non-aggression pact of 1925 Germany had been inching her way towards membership of the League of Nations and finding many friends in Britain: she seemed to be turning her energies towards trade and industry. The Graf Zeppelin, the ocean liners that gained the Blue Riband of the Atlantic, the mighty Mercedes racing cars were evidence, and the old links between the upper classes of the two countries were being resumed. Yet the

Germans werre still regarded with suspicion. The nudism practised in the Weimar republic was linked with pacifism, vegetarianism and similar 'do-gooding' movements rather than war-mongering, but that made it nonetheless shocking – like the decadent cabarets of Berlin. It was altogether too much for a British public whose moral tone was reflected by Baldwin's Home Secretary, the fervently Evangelical Sir William Joynson-Hicks, renowned for his prosecution of exhibitions of nudity in painting and sculpture and his opposition to the revision of the Book of Common Prayer.

The British climate combined with native reticence to discourage the worst excesses of the Aryan sun cult, but another (much more decent and healthily athletic but still potentially anarchic) German fashion now became extremely popular – striding about the countryside with a rucksack. In its individualistic form, hiking,[16] this had been a pre-war student fashion, in America as well as Europe. In 1923 fashionable London suppliers began advertising the correct gear. The true hiker wore shorts and below-the-knee stockings with turn-down tops, but many women preferred skirts and coloured ankle-socks (over or, increasingly, instead of stockings). For men flannel trousers were more common and these, worn with open necked shirts and pullovers in a variety of relatively bright colours, now became the ordinary weekend wear of the middle classes, hikers or not.[17]

The really serious outdoor types went in for camping. In 1927, the Camping Club of Great Britain had 3,000 members, most of them solitary hikers who carried all their kit with them. Ramblers' clubs were a more sociable – and sometimes socialistic – variant, combining to gain access to privately-held amenities as well as to enjoy a common interest. Middle class in origin they varied in social composition according to location. Some clubs catered largely for the better-off, properly equipped with guide book, hiking boots, rucksack, khaki shorts and able to afford bed-and-breakfast accommodation. But in smoky cities like Manchester and Sheffield, with hills and moors invitingly near, there was a greater proportion of the unemployed and other plebeians and club names would bear resonantly radical names like the Clarion, a call to stem the tide of soul-destroying industrialisation.[18] Their quest for access inspired some local protests and political agitation. Nationally, however, any sympathy enthusiasts for public rights might arouse for their worthy cause was offset by fear of vandalism. During the first Labour administration of 1924 a Liberal MP, pointing out that the public were excluded from great tracts of Scotland, the Pennines and the Peak District, introduced a Bill seeking to allow access for recreational purposes, but it received little support. Nor did the government feel able to back a similar measure sponsored by its own idealistic Minister of Education, C. P. Trevelyan. Landowners, regarding rambling as the thin end of a Bolshevistic wedge, rejoiced at MacDonald's political wisdom.

There was, however, a growing desire to help young people combat the disadvantages of urban environments. The local authorities remained the chief providers. Liverpool, for instance, increased its cricket pitches from 50 to 79 and its tennis courts from 170 to 400 by the end of the decade, but there now came a major national initiative. The Duke of York, as President of the Industrial Welfare Society, took a personal initiative in setting up, and attending, summer camps in which public school boys and young workers were brought together. He was the natural choice to head the charitable National Playing Fields Association and launch its appeal for funds in 1925. This got the support of socialist leaders, including MacDonald and George Lansbury, and the famous dockers' leader Ben Tillett represented the TUC on its Council.[19]

Commercial enterprise concentrated on bringing a little of the country to the town. Some saw the vogue for greyhound racing, which began a few weeks after the General Strike of 1926, as a more humane replacement for hare-coursing. This medieval survival had long been opposed by crusading organisations like the Humanitarian League and the RSPCA. They had little chance of stopping it for its foremost exponents were aristocrats who staged it on their private estates. The Earl of Sefton, whose grandfather had started the celebrated Waterloo Cup on his estate at Altcar, and his neighbour the Earl of Derby were the leading figures and the ubiquitous Earl of Lonsdale was another enthusiast. Lord Dalmeny, the Rosebery heir, and his friend Lord Stanley, the Derby heir, were prominent in reviving its fortunes after the war. The proletarian version in which whippets chased rabbits was more vulnerable to both urbanisation and middle-class disapproval and was already giving way to a sanitised alternative – track races using an artificial quarry, typically a stuffed rabbit-skin, drawn along ahead of the dogs mechanically. The improvised races at 'flapping tracks'[20] in such places as Oldham and St Helens drew praise from the RSPCA. They also provided a cheap and convenient mixture of entertainment and gambling which enjoyed a boom in the early post-war years. The sporting press was full of the new attraction, and soon the *Sporting Chronicle*, a Manchester publication, was sponsoring races and predicting an even bigger future.[21]

These stirrings caught the attention of coursing addicts who saw an opening for a thoroughbred version. An attempt had been made as early as 1876 to interest a metropolitan audience in greyhound racing, using a new mechanical hare, and there had been occasional revivals, notably at Powderhall, but they had never lasted long.[22] Then in the mid-1920s came new impetus from America, where the combination of an electric hare and electric lights had helped to popularise dog-racing as an evening attraction which city-dwellers could enjoy after work. Armed with the patent for the hare a Canadian businessman, C. A. Munn, had enlisted the help of Major L. Lynne Dixson, a coursing trainer and judge, in getting something going in England and was introduced to Brigadier A. C. Critchley, another Canadian currently making a living in the cement industry. Critchley, shown photographs of an electric stadium in Oklahoma, immediately saw its possibilities as 'the poor man's racecourse', inexpensive but with a touch of style and glamour. This was the vision that inspired the group that in October, 1925 formed the Greyhound Racing Association Limited.[23]

The company was registered in Manchester and its first venture was to build a big new stadium at Belle Vue on the site of an old flapping track. Its first meeting on 24 July 1926, was something of a disappointment. Only 1,700 attended and there was a deficit of £25. But within 30 days the new company had paid off £10,000 of its £25,000 capital debt, within six months the stadium was being enlarged to hold 25,000 and within a year 1s (5p) shares were being quoted at £37 10s. 1n 1927 the original company was restructured as a Trust, with further social leavening from Lieutenant-Colonel J. C. T. Moore-Brabazon.[24] Its share issue, close on £1 million, helped to finance new tracks at White City and Harringay in London, Hall Green, Birmingham, and Marine Gardens and Powderhall, Edinburgh. Other promoters joined in and over 40 new tracks appeared in little over a year – at Wembley and elsewhere in London, but also in the provinces, and in Glasgow, Cardiff and Belfast. Dublin, in spite of its change of political status, was also receptive to the new craze which swept the Irish Free State, from Cork to Dundalk. The Dublin-owned and -trained Mick the Miller, which won the Greyhound Derby at White City in 1929, was soon as famous as Master McGrath.[25]

The social tone rapidly fell. In the next phase of expansion – there were soon over 200 tracks – many companies were run by bookmakers and their associates, publicans and tradesmen, especially in the East End of London and small towns in the industrial north. Promoters threw open their stadia to other dubious activities, notably the strident newcomer, dirt-track racing. The bookies, in their primary capacity, had swooped on dog-racing from the beginning, to the chagrin of the moralists. Such accessible dens of vice were a special danger to the young and the poor. Moderates like Joseph Compton, Labour MP for Gorton, who had welcomed the new sport at first, now saw it as a threat to working-class family life. To others of the working class it was a great opportunity. One of the bookies at the opening night at White City was a young man called William Hill, who had run away from school at 12 years of age and after starting as a farm-labourer had gone to work in a Birmingham tool factory, augmenting his income by taking bets from work-mates. The 'poor man's race course' was just the place to start up on his own, the first stage on the road to building up a vast gambling empire.

Notes

1 They were finally scuppered when the American Congress refused to ratify the Treaty of Versailles, which their own President had been the first to sign.
2 S. H. Adams, 'The Timely Death of President Harding', in I. Leighton (ed.), *The Aspirin Age*, London, 1950, p. 99.
3 A. J. P. Taylor, *English History 1914–45*, Oxford, 1965, p. 196.
4 H. Nicolson, *King George V: His Life and Reign*, London, 1952, p. 384.
5 ibid., p. 389.
6 M. Davie (ed.), *The Diaries of Evelyn Waugh*, London, 1976, 3 December 1918.
7 K. Jaspers, *The Psychology of World Views*, Paris, 1919.
8 W. Holtby, *Anderby Wold*; V. Brittain, *The Dark Tide*; D. L. Sayers, *Whose Body?*, all London, 1923.
9 *Punch*, 1 July 1925.
10 R. Graves and P. Hodge,*The Long Weekend*, London, 1940 (1971 edn), p. 109.
11 Report of the Imperial Economical Committee, 10 August 1928, cited in H. Heald (ed.), *Chronicle of Britain and Ireland*, Farnborough, 1992.
12 Graves and Hodge, *Long Weekend*, p. 62.
13 For example, cycle-racing and – especially – the new craze, the dogs.
14 *Ashton-Under-Lyne Reporter*, 12 July 1930, quoted by S. G. Jones in R. Holt (ed.), *Sport and the Working Class in Modern Britain*, Manchester, 1990, p. 75.
15 'Truth', 9 September 1908, describing the Olympic Games.
16 An old word of obscure origin, reintroduced, as an Americanism and usually in inverted commas, with the fashion.
17 The working class, for economic reasons, retained longer the concept of the 'Sunday suit' and its female equivalent, especially in church-going circles. This apart, for a boy in pre-war Britain his first pair of long trousers, proudly put on at the age of 13 or so, was a badge of manhood and the use of shorts in later life, by Boy Scouts, hikers and the like was thought suspect, especially among the working class. Oddly enough the prejudice did not apply to football though even there a decent length was required.
18 For the Clarion movement and cognate groups see S. G. Jones, *Sport, Politics and the Working Class in Modern Britain*, Manchester, 1988, pp. 26–34. For the founder of *The Clarion* see L. Thompson, *Robert Blatchford*, London, 1951.
19 Jones, *Sport, Politics*, p. 133. See also Holt (ed.), *Sport and the Working Class*, pp. 270–2.
20 By analogy with the rough country horse-race meetings operating outside Jockey club rules, which for some reason undisclosed in the *Oxford English Dictionary*, also bore this name.
21 M. Clapson, *A Bit of a Flutter: Popular Gambling and English Culture 1823–1961*, Manchester, 1992, p. 144.
22 An account of a meeting at the Welsh Harp, Hendon, which appeared in the *Sporting Chronicle*, 12 September 1876, has been reproduced in many histories of the sport, including A. Lennox, *Greyhounds: The Sporting Breed*, London, 1987.
23 There are various slightly differing accounts including Critchley's own recollections: A. C. Critchley, *Critch!*, London, 1961, quoted by Clapson, *Flutter*, E. C. Ash, *The Book of the Greyhound*, London, 1933 and J. Arlott (ed.), *The Oxford Companion to Games and Sports*, Oxford, 1976.
24 Afterwards Lord Brabazon of Tara. Anglo-Irish air and motor-racing pioneer, winter

sports and golf enthusiast who, after serving in the Flying Corps, entered Parliament in 1918.

25 The Irish dog owned by Lord Lurgan, Queen Victoria's Lord-in-Waiting, which after its Waterloo Cup victory of 1869 had been taken to meet Her Majesty. See Birley, *Sport and the Making of Britain*, Manchester, 1993, p. 268.

CHAPTER SEVEN

Fair play (1919–27):
old wine in new bottles

Over the centuries a self-perpetuating élite develops the knack of adapting to new situations. The changing world was particularly distressing to the old landed aristocracy, and a fair number, especially amongst the smaller fry, succumbed to death duties and Lloyd George taxation. But many simply sold off unproductive bits of their patrimony and invested in the City or the colonies. There was also still money to be made out of the land if you had enough of it, and there were ways round death-duties and similar annoyances. The fifth Earl of Rosebery was one of several great landowners who turned their estates into private limited companies.

Field sports and the cash nexus

The Rosebery estates, enriched by Rothschild connections, were in remarkably good shape. But after a distressing war the 75-year-old Earl was not, and in 1922 he entrusted the management of part of his empire to his son Harry, Lord Dalmeny, remarking acidly that at 40 it was high time he took on some responsibility. Since demobilisation Dalmeny had been helping to get gentlemanly sport back on its feet again. His part in the re-establishment of coursing has already been noted but he was even more prominent in the rehabilitation of polo. *The Field*'s correspondent, A. Wallis Myers, had discovered 'a perfect craze for polo amongst short-term Army officers' in America which he attributed to 'a sub-conscious desire to be British'. Whatever their motivation the Americans were now in the ascendancy. The British game had been hard hit by the war. Several of the leading players, including the great Leslie Cheape, had given their lives, and newcomers were finding it a costly business. At this critical time Dalmeny motored three times a week to Pelham Down on Salisbury Plain where a select group practised for matches against the Yankees, watched by admiring lady friends and regaled during the intervals by selections from the 4th Dragoon Guards' band.

But fox-hunting was Dalmeny's great passion and he had set his sights on the Mastership of the Whaddon Chase, near his father's estate at Mentmore. In 1919 his marriage had ended in an unpleasant and very public divorce. This had not helped him in his dispute with Colonel Selby-Lowndes, for the MFHA expected its members to observe the golden rule of keeping up appearances. The farming interests, who strongly favoured Selby-Lowndes in any case, signed a petition demanding his reinstatement and there were rumours that they intended to start their own pack if they did not get their way. The Association diplomatically urged both claimants to withdraw and in March 1920 the Whaddon Chase elected Lord Orkney. Two years later Dalmeny was given control of the Mentmore estate by his father. It had 4,500 acres, 15 farms and several hundred tenants, as well as the celebrated Rosebery stud, and it was strategically placed for the Whaddon Chase. In 1923 he bit into its territory by acquiring the adjoining Liscombe Park and resumed his bid. Lord Orkney obligingly stood down, and Dalmeny secured the election, remaining Master almost until the Second World War.[1]

The Whaddon Chase counted themselves fortunate in being able to attract one both affluent and born in the purple. The post-war hunting world was more than ever full of nouveaux-riches and Americans who knew nothing of the English way of life. *The Field* complained in 1923 that the 'last remnants of the old squirearchy', no longer able to afford the sport of their ancestors, were being elbowed out of their rightful preserves by brash 'new money' men.[2] The likes of Chester Beaty and Paul Mellon were considered barbarian interlopers. In practice the Americans were usually a good deal better than the home-grown would-be grandees, like the absurd Sir Julian Cahn, who shook the dignified Burton to its foundations. Both the Prince of Wales and the Duke of York were regular visitors to the Shires. When they rode with the Cottesmore in December, 1926, 'Whipster' of *Horse and Hound* reported 'the largest and smartest hunting assembly of fair ladies and scarlet we have seen for several seasons'. Many were thought social climbers – 'at best ignorant and at worst full of the arrogance of their new money'[3] – but this was scarcely a new phenomenon.

Farmers were a problem everywhere. Worst of all, of course, were the wretches who did not hunt, often small men concerned only to protect their crops and their fences. Much of the land sold by the impoverished aristocracy and gentry had been bought by tenants, who became even less supportive of hunts than before, sometimes trying to levy a charge for crossing their land. In 1928 Dalmeny had to bring all his social and economic clout to bear on two brothers who tried to resist the Whaddon Chase roaring over their 250 acres. But farmers who did enjoy hunting could also be a great nuisance, and now there were some who tried to take advantage of war-time concessions. The MFHA adjudication in a territorial dispute in 1920 might have been that of a medieval swanimote. A farmer's pack, formerly mere harriers, had been allowed during the war to hunt foxes in part of the country of the venerable Essex Union. Now they had claimed the right to hunt foxes in a bigger area and at any time they liked. They were told that their hunt could not be recognised, nor could it organise a point-to-point.[4] This kind of problem grew less as the twenties wore on, not because farmers were less pushy or the MFHA more democratic but because fewer and fewer farmers were able to afford to hunt. Once the war-time and post-war boom conditions ended, food prices fell, their incomes plummeted and hunting became a luxury, especially for the smaller farmers. Many still came out with provincial packs but very few could afford to hunt in the Shires and those who did risked being sneered at.

Conversely, as industrial profits soared the only escape from new money and its values was remoteness. The Brockleby in East Anglia suffered no great loss of tone, and the West Country enjoyed a certain immunity. Even there traditional family hunts had to beware against interlopers trying to cut a dash and Masters seeking quick results in building good packs. The etiquette of hound-breeding required the skills of a tight-rope walker. Breeding merely for show purposes was another breach of good form; some purists even considered the annual Peterborough Show a mixed blessing. Most were agreed, however, that the new Welsh Hound Show was a useful step forward for this backward region where too many hunts had a reputation for excessive conviviality and insufficient finesse. Scotland, although it had retained about a dozen packs, including some of rarefied provenance and great prestige such as the Eglinton and the Duke of Buccleuch's, was better regarded for its shooting.

Ireland, with more suitable terrain and a strong native horsey tradition, fared better, though it lost social cachet. Many ascendancy hunts had wilted under the attacks of the Land League and fewer plutocrats had come to the rescue when estates had been sold off under successive Land Purchase Acts. The latest 'troubles' were a nuisance for a while. Bolshevistic Sinn Feiners looked on hunting with baleful eyes. Indeed, during the early post-war months the *Irish Field* reported that the IRA had 'signified their intention of extending the stopping of hunting . . . to racing, pending the release of those members of their organisation who are at present in prison'.[5] But the war for independence had become an urban one and the IRA found killing policemen more effective than interrupting sport. And the new Free State government was highly conscious of the place the horse held in Irish affections and of its significance in the social and economic life of the country. In 1921 it took Leinster House, the headquarters of the Royal Dublin Society, as the seat of the Dáil, but paid £68,000 for it, and after a few years of uncertainty the Society could fairly claim once more that its Horse Show was as good as any in the world. On the hunting field outbreaks of violence were sporadic and localised, and serious ill-feeling confined to a few areas with specific local grievances. Otherwise Ireland was something of an oasis, relatively untouched by industrialisation and its values. American influence – including Irish-Americans returning home – was evident in some areas, with mixed results, but most packs continued, uncorrupted if socially undistinguished. And an enormous compensation was that hunting in Ireland was comparatively cheap. Apart from the general cost-of-living and tax advantages, wages of hunt servants were low and much of the country even had amateur huntsmen.

English hunts were not entirely sure about this practice. It had always had a few aristocratic devotees, and in 1920 *Baily's Directory* noted approvingly that, amongst the new young Masters, Lord Hillingdon with the Grafton, Lord Poltimore with the Dulverton and Captain Browne with Lord Portman's were to 'carry the horn' themselves. But though soon nearly half the English packs were following the trend, many were doing it for economic reasons and were depised as a result. In the opulent Shires when the hunt servants returned from the war it was a great age of professional huntsmen – Arthur Wilson and George Barber at the Quorn, George Leaf and James Welsh at the Cottesmore, Arthur Thatcher and Bert Peaker at the Fernie. Frank Freeman at the Pytchley was even compared with the Quorn's legendary Tom Firr. And one of the most famous combinations of Master and huntsman was that at the Grafton between Lord Hillingdon and Will Pope.

Subscription packs, once regarded as ruinous to the Master's authority and the hunt's prestige, were now the norm, but it was inadvisable to choose a Master for whom making up the deficit between the guarantee and the actual outlay was a matter of life and death. These guarantees fluctuated greatly, not always for economic reasons. The average of £1,100–£1,200 included some of £2,000 and a few of £500 Few hunts depended entirely on subscriptions, and not all were even prepared to disclose the amount publicly; but clearly there was a world of social difference between the Afonwy, a Welsh farmer's pack started in 1919 with an annual subscription of 10s, and the Fernie, hived off from the Quorn in 1853, which had a sliding scale starting at £35 for one day a week. Irish practices were gradually creeping in. 'Capping', at one time confined to harriers, was now climbing the social ladder. Some hunts could not quite bring themselves actually to pass the hat round and specified a minimum charge. In Ireland the custom was half a crown (12.5p) a day: some in England charged a guinea – an open invitation to the social climber.

Many of the new Masters were ex-officers and as soon as they became available quickly replaced the women: the splendid Mrs Inge at the Atherstone handed over to Major Henry Hawkins in 1920. But women continued to form a large proportion of hunt members even when the men came back, and were often a majority. A conventional male in 1926 was amazed to find young females at the Belvoir applying their lipsticks whilst hounds were drawing – though he freely admitted that they then rode very well.[6] Breeches, familiarised by land-girls, excited less ribald comment after the war but they were slow to appear at the better hunts. A leading authority in 1930 could still pronounce side-saddle as 'the safer, the smarter and the better seat'.[7] but astride was cheaper and faster and was remorselessly creeping in, especially amongst the young and better-shaped.

The war had less serious long-term effects than industrialisation and urbanisation, advancing 'at a rate which even the slump seemed hardly to slow down'.[8] Suburban sprawl, some thought, gave an unfair advantage to the fox which could adapt more easily to this terrain than pursuing horses and hounds. Yet this very adaptability and its vermin status kept the fox in good supply, whereas hares, which suffered from edibility, were much reduced in number. Hence, though harrier packs were still quite numerous in England, as cost-differentials with fox-hunting reduced, foot-beagling, which had strongholds in the universities and the better regiments, began to gain ground. In Ireland, where horse-riding was less élitist, the tradition of 'Sunday harriers' survived and Ulster, with several harriers' packs still had no fox-hunts. Ireland also retained two stag-hunts. This no longer had any social significance, for the once-royal sport, only possible in a few remote country districts, was now mainly of antiquarian interest. Stag hounds were 'unentered' in the Stud Book because of their great size.

Deer-stalking with guns was now the chief legacy of the royal sport of the middle ages. Some 50 major deer forests, over 1,200,000 acres, were still maintained in Scotland for the delectation of the lairds and their (often paying) guests. No longer requiring great athleticism, it had been further debased by the gruesome custom of mounting stag's heads as trophies.[9] Edwardian sporting etiquette had concerned the age and size of the targets.[10] Aesthetic considerations were a post-war refinement. J. G. Millais, artist son of the Pre-Raphaelite luminary, emphasised the importance of symmetry in his comparisons of ancient and modern head and antler size.[11] There was more money to be made from grouse-moors, but only at the expense of further undermining the old rural community. The new 'county' society, with its roots in London, had country houses, estates and even castles,[12] but made only occasional visits, usually in search of pleasure. Shooting brought in people who merely 'stayed for a few days, indulged their "saturnalia of slaughter" and then moved on again'.[13]

This gave new life to the historic antipathy between hunters and shooters.[14] Pheasant-rearing fields were the greatest battle-grounds but rising costs made owners of all game farms extra touchy. 'I am not going to beat about the bush as regards foxes,' wrote an otherwise circumspect gamekeeper in 1922, 'for I know that partridges and foxes do not go together'.[15] Most shooting men thought they paid enough for their sport, either directly in game preservation or indirectly in swingeing rents for grouse-moors, without having to behave nicely towards marauding foxes. They took comfort from the fact that both the Prince of Wales and the Duke of York appeared to have inherited their father's skill with the gun, for they resented the hunters' claims to a superior tradition.

These claims, in the absence of rational arguments, were of great importance to fox-hunters, but hunting, with its colour and excitement, had great intrinsic appeal for ordinary folk who had little enough of such things to cheer their lives. To this can be attributed the success of the unaristocratic John Masefield's *Reynard the Fox* (1919), evoking the atmosphere of the countryside and the thrill of the chase. Fox-hunting, its advocates were at pains to establish, gave 'fair law' to the quarry. In its own way shooting was also seeking morally higher ground. It was not only economic considerations that led the swing away from the mass destruction of easy targets. Some who had served in the trenches had lost the appetite for slaughter and others had acquired bourgeois values, like revulsion at conspicuous waste, but the sporting code itself adjusted to the changing times. There was a shift towards greater discrimination, a somewhat recherché cult of the difficult shot. Snipe-shooting was generally considered the sternest test of all. The new record – 227 snipe in a day – in December 1927, showed the extent of the advance.

Game fishermen, less affected by middle-class moralising – because their victims were cold-blooded and less appealing than furry or feathered creatures – also began to show more interest in the quality of the kill and the challenge it presented. Anglers' tales in the past had often been of less-than-heroic battles with salmon, using 22-foot rods: anything smaller was pretty daring. 'For many years,' the leading equipment firm of Hardy Brothers diplomatically put it in their 1924 catalogue, 'we have made stout single-handed rods for salmon-fishing. These rods have been much used by anglers who delight in giving the fish a fair and sporting chance, and at the same time taking as much enjoyment out of the sport as possible.' Now, however, this concept needed redefinition. Hardy Brothers commended to the discriminating a new approach using a 'dry-fly', quoting with approval, from a recently-published book,[16] the maxim, 'To kill a salmon on a light rod of 6 to 7 ounces is the highest art.' Naturally they hedged their bets – 'for general work we must retain our 14- to 17-foot rods' – but they printed enthusiastic letters from readers who had switched to lighter rods. It was a nice point, no doubt much appreciated by the fish.

Yachting: from J class to dinghy

In field sports the link between changes in the nation's sporting habits and its economic circumstances – an increasingly dominant influence – was complicated by falling land values and agricultural decline. In yachting the influence of the urban, industrial mainstream was more clearly discernible. At first, ironically, the early post-war industrial boom seemed to presage a return to the good old days. There was great excitement when the King brought out *Britannia* for the 1920 season. Other owners followed his lead and soon several highly impressive vessels were afloat again (including the 169 ton *Nyria* owned by a Mrs Workman) and there was even a new one on the stocks. Cowes that year attracted nine entries to the big class. 'It sounds incredible', wrote the editor of *Yachting Monthly*, his syntax slipping a little in his excitement, 'but it looks as though we should have the largest fleet of first-class yachts this summer than we have ever seen.'[17]

There was optimism, too, about the prospects of Sir Thomas Lipton's *Shamrock IV* in her delayed challenge for America's Cup. Lipton, sadly, was no more successful than before, except as a gallant sporting loser. Such chivalry, it was widely felt, was wasted on the New York Yacht Club who kept on changing the rules to their own advantage. Some of the subtler features of designer Charles Nicholson's unorthodox *Shamrock IV* – widely known as 'the Ugly Duckling' – had had to be jettisoned, chauvinists pointed out, whereas 'Wily Nat' Herreschoff's victorious *Resolute* was cleverly 'rule-designed'. Nicholson chiefly blamed the weather for the defeat and looked forward to designing another challenger.[18] But perhaps the main cause of the defeat was a new version of the old British weakness – the sharp division between gentlemanly owners and crew – with the introduction of an amateur helmsman as an extra layer in the strata of command.

The chosen leader, Sir William Burton, had a great reputation, but his critics afterwards suggested that his skill had been impaired by arduous war service with the Food Ministry. At any rate, *Shamrock IV* did better when Charles Nicholson took over the helm during the final race.[19] Long before this, how-ever, relations had become hopelessly strained. Burton had brought with him his own racing skipper, Captain Turner, to the chagrin of Captain Alf Diaper, who as skipper of the Lipton's earlier Shamrock *III*, had expected to inherit. During the trials Diaper's open contempt for the Burton regime had encouraged obstreperous attitudes in a crew already disgruntled – by mana-gerial insensitivity to their creature comforts, by the appearance on board of Lady Burton as timekeeper and observer, and by the visits of Nicholson, the designer, seeking last-minute improvements. When it came to the actual contest the Americans, more recognisably a team, and with the Secretary for the Navy, Charles F. Adams, at the helm, showed a spirit which turned a two-race deficit into victory by three races to two.

The insolent behaviour and mercenary outlook of British crews was regarded, by the yachting press and boat-owners great and small, as an ugly manifestation of Bolshevism. 'The wages asked in most quarters is ridiculous and the bluff of the men is detrimental to our sport', declared *Yachting Monthly*.[20] The big class yachts, the industrial equivalent of small factories, needing crews of 40 apart from personal servants, were the most vulnerable, especially when their owners lacked 'new money'. The first casualty, as the Lloyd George coalition began to feel the pinch, was the Royal Yacht which the Palace announced would not be racing in 1922. The 'squandering ministers' who had reduced the country to such a pass were widely blamed, and to serious yachtsmen *Britannia*'s absence at Cowes was as sharp a blow as 'the Geddes axe' in education.[21] By 1923 there were only three active survivors in the big class, and the prospects were bleak.

The new 23 metre class, known as International Rule, and its American equivalent, the J class, still needed a crew of 25 to 30 which effectively limited British America's Cup challenges in the future to tycoons. Aristocratic and gentlemanly circles – and the IOC – increasingly turned to the 12, 10, 8 and even 6 metre classes (which needed crews of eight, seven, five and three) a trend which further swelled the ranks of amateur helmsmen. These now included two kinds of 'hired assassin'. There were athletic owners, like Lord Forster and Sir Ralph Gore, both from long-established landed families, who owned smaller boats themselves but were available to pilot the bigger ones for other people. But there were also people who managed to get 'a deal of first-rate sailing without the expense of ownership', like Major St John Hughes – who also turned his hand to women's dress designing – and Mr Keele who steered Lady Constance Baird's 8 metre boat for several seasons.[22] The economic situation also stimulated interest in designing smaller, cheaper boats for cruising purposes. One of the most radical notions came from Harrison Butler: 'The poor man must eliminate (the cost of) labour by building his own boat.' He produced a design for a 21-footer to cost as little as £100, less than the cheapest car.[23]

In the process designers found ingenious low-cost solutions to such small boat problems as 'portable accommodation' for ladies. Fewer women were content with purely decorative roles in post-war yachting, and though they had the same reputation for unpredictability at the helm as their counterparts on the hunting field, active participation was generally welcomed, especially from wealthy owners. Mrs Workman's intrepidity was greatly admired: when a serious accident crippled her she had a special cockpit constructed next to the wheel of her highly successful *Nyria*. And in 1921 (cajoled by Charles

Nicholson to start a fashion) she became the first in Britain to risk the controversial Bermuda, or 'Marconi' rig on so big and expensive a boat.[24] At the next level the likes of Lady Burton and Lady Constance Baird were increasingly found in managerial or sponsorship roles. By 1925 Mrs Arthur Briscoe was cautiously optimistic about further developments: 'introduced carefully to modern small boat sailing, there is no reason why (women) should not make enthusiastic cruisers, and, in their particular sphere, useful members of the crew'.[25]

At Nicholson's the effect of the recession seems to have been marginal, though for a time they found themselves building fewer big racing yachts. In 1927 they were glad to design the *Viva* of 669 tons for Mr Alec Smith-Cochran, an elderly bachelor intent on cruising for his health, and a more modest 113 ton ketch for a Mr Nutman, something in the timber trade. Motor yachts were increasingly in demand and when Mr A. K. Macomber ordered his 545 ton motor yacht *Crusader* he explained that he was extremely keen on listening to the wireless and wanted to escape the interference from electric tram cars. Some wanted motor yachts simply to speed up cruising. One such was the former flying ace, T. O. M. Sopwith, who had made millions from aircraft manufacture during the war and was a noted speedboat racer. In 1926 he ordered a 340 ton motor yacht, superseded in 1929 by one of 502 tons.

Sopwith also had a growing reputation as a racing yachtsman, having progressed up the scale from the 12-metre to the biggest class. One of his friends was Herman Andreae, living proof that all colour had not drained from the world since the war. A hunting man, an expert shot and fisherman, and a ski-ing enthusiast, in 1928 he decided to move up from 19 to 23 metre class yachting, driving over to Nicholson's to discuss his plans in his new Bugatti straight-eight.[26] In the prevailing climate professional skippers had to turn their hands to anything they could get. Racing skippers had to settle for smaller and smaller boats, often with the status of mate to an amateur helmsman. George Williams was fortunate to find a post with Sopwith who had set his sights on the America's Cup, but Sopwith not only took the helm himself but had Andreae as his alternate and Sir Ralph Gore standing by. America's Cup racing, in any event, was currently at stalemate as Lipton, who had first option, vainly tried to persuade the New York YC to relax their requirement that contenders must build their boats first and challenge afterwards.

A less rarefied development was that of ocean-racing. The 605 mile Fastnet race began in 1925, informally organised and drawing only seven entries, but generating enough enthusiasm for the formation of the Ocean Racing Club and for a repeat the following year. In 1926 there was a good race, enlivened not only by brisk weather but by American entries. The success of the Fastnet was ensured when it was agreed to alternate it with the Bermuda race revived in 1923. At first the Fastnet competitors were sturdy cruising yachts but as early as 1927 a 50-tonner had been designed specially for racing purposes and this quickly became the norm. In in-shore racing, as the big class dwindled, more serious attention was focused on racing in the smaller classes. Britain played little part in Olympic yachting in the twenties but there were other promising developments at 6 metres. One was a team-race for the British–American Cup in 1921, especially appealing as it took the Americans a few years to master the technique with boats of this size. In 1922 the popular Seawanhaka races, started in 1895 for racing scows, went down to 6 metres and soon earned great sporting and even social prestige.

The most remarkable advance, however, came in racing for dinghies, already popular as learning yachts, novelties in improvised races and Corinthian specialisms. In 1923 the RYA brought in a standard 14 foot class and this was recognised internationally four years later. Actual international competition was slower to develop, but meanwhile dinghy-racing became highly fashionable at British regattas. The man of the hour was Uffa Fox, whose radical designs were highly influential and widely copied. Fox began as an apprentice boat-builder at Cowes, studying naval architecture at night school, and set up on his own after war service. In *Ariel*, his first boat, he won every race in the class at Cowes Week in 1925, and in 1928 his *Avenger*, with a hull designed for planing over the water rather than cutting through it, won 52 out of 57. A brilliant helmsman and an opinionated extrovert with a disorderly private life, Fox was to became one of the best-known figures in the world of yachting. Whatever he may have lacked in social graces he was successful, a quality that assumed greater and greater importance as the logic of commercialised sport unfolded.

Racing: the Flat

Success had always been what mattered on the Turf. It sadly eluded George V, who thereby missed the best opportunity British monarchs have to win the admiration of their subjects. In this he fell conspicuously short of his father's achievement, in spite of greater knowledge and deeper interest in the actual racing. And at Ascot, where Edward VII had been in his element, he was like a fish out of water. Queen Mary had as little time for racing as she had for yachting or shooting, and though she dutifully put in ritual appearances she was manifestly more at home watching a little lawn tennis at Wimbledon. She and the King presided stiffly over the family gatherings at Windsor Castle in Royal Ascot week, and were cordially cheered by the crowds as they drove along the course in their carriage, but Edwardian splendour was all but gone.

There was, however, always the Earl of Lonsdale. To the admiring populace Lonsdale, with his side-whiskers, 9-inch cigars and gardenia buttonhole, was 'a perfect specimen of a sporting grandee'. His belated excursion into ownership was on a limited scale. He did not breed his own but relied on leasing a few horses from the National Stud each year. This did not prevent his becoming a Jockey Club Steward in 1924 and its Senior Steward two years later. After an early triumph in the 1922 St Leger he won little else, and since he had not bet on the Turf (or cards) since 1878[27] he had to make his mark in other ways. When he drove to Ascot it was not in a dull black motor car, like the King, but in a horse-drawn wagonette in the gaudy colours he had made famous on the hunting field. To the cheering crowds his Ascot rig was 'the perfect turn-out . . . with its exactly matched chestnuts, the grooms and postillions in yellow livery with every buckle and button shining'.[28] Ascot drew crowds in plenty. Lonsdale apart, motor transport was now the norm. Cars, motorcycles and buses jammed the roads in 1920 and the following year the traffic was directed by the airship R36.

The effect of the recession was briefly evident in 1921 when *The Times*'s fashion correspondent deplored the 'innovation' of ladies wearing the same dress on more than one day of the meeting. The tone was also lowered by the sleeveless dresses of 1924 which revealed ugly vaccination marks. Equally chronogenetic was the varying skirt length, which in 1920 was only two or three inches below the knee, by 1922 had descended to just above the ankle, but in 1925 shot up to unprecedented heights and in 1926 even allowed a glimpse of knees from those young and bold enough to reveal them. It was quite a shock – but a relief to the textile industry – when long crinolines re-appeared in 1927. There were corresponding changes in the extraordinary hats, which – with variations – tended to have less and less hair to perch upon, first the shingle or bob, then in 1926 the severe 'Eton crop', before more luxuriant fashions returned. The men continued to wear their customary uniform: variations had connotations of class, not fashion. In the Royal enclosure dark morning coats, black silk hats and pepper-and-salt trousers were still the correct wear, though grey toppers and trousers were a permissible concession to gaiety.[29] However, *The Times* found the 1924 assembly 'very squash-hatty' and the following year the *Daily Telegraph* reported startling changes in the grandstand. 'Soft hats . . . outnumbered toppers and one even observed cloth caps. Moreover, one could hear discussions in tones bred in the North country and the Midlands.'[30]

Ascot, felt *The Times*, was a notable annual defeat for Puritanism: 'The dislike of other people's pleasure, which has been an active force in English life for nearly three centuries, will always become vocal at such provocation as Ascot', but it was exhilarating to see all sorts of people 'happily behaving as if amusement were a legitimate human function'.[31] The actual racing was of moderate standard. Ascot prize-money was still relatively modest. Apart from the Gold Cup (£3,690) and the Coronation Stakes (£3,600) only two other races offered more than £2,000. But its aristocratic aura, for those anxious to recapture Edwardian glamour, made up for that. The early post-war years were given distinction by Diadem, owned by Lord D'Abernon and trained by the Hon. George Lambton. Growing prestige led to higher standards. In 1926 the Gold Cup went to Solario, the previous year's St Leger winner and the following year Sir Abe Bailey's Foxlaw thrilled the crowds by holding off a strong French challenge. In 1928 a former hurdle-racer, Brown Jack, switching to the Flat, began a remarkable partnership with Steve Donoghue that gave Ascot a fame amongst the general public that all but surpassed its fashions.

Donoghue was an unlikely advertisement for aristocratic tradition for he had fallen foul of some of the pillars of the Turf. The Jockey Club controlled racing by the authoritarian methods it had used since the eighteenth century. It steadfastly restricted membership to the right sort and positions of influence to the old aristocratic families, setting its face against the 'new money' men, and looking askance at exotic newcomers like the Aga Khan, the fabulously rich Muslim leader who entered the scene in 1921. But in the actual business of racing the Jockey Club élite like everyone else were primarily interested in winning – either races or bets, with the latter usually taking precedence. In the mythology of the Turf the owner–breeders were held in special reverence as representing a finer tradition than brash newcomers intent on gain. In practice, owners, however aristocratic, sought at least to make their racing pay for itself and the most successful, like the Earls of Derby and Rosebery, consistently showed a profit. And in the pursuit of success the most powerful influence of all were the leading jockeys, often in combination with the bookmakers.

Owners, Stewards and officials might call these under-sized plebeians by their surnames and treat them as social inferiors, but they were the real Lords of the Turf, basically because of their scarcity value, which grew no less in an increasingly well-fed Britain. Donoghue was one of the most popular men in the country, and if he had not spent his money as fast as he made it he could have been among the richest. What leading jockeys earned is hard to estimate because so much of it came under the counter. But the fee – £200 for the ride, £1,000 for a win – offered to the American Frank O'Neill brought over from France to ride the 1920 Derby winner, Spion Kop compared favourably with, let us say, the £750 the average doctor earned in a year. And Donoghue got a present of £5,000 for winning the 1922 Derby for the philanthropic distiller, Lord Woolavington.

The old semi-feudal relationship between owner and rider had been challenged as long ago as 1885 by Fred Archer when he sent back Lord Portland's retainer, but Donoghue openly flouted it to fulfil his ambition of beating Archer's record of five Derby winners. By 1920 he was so sought after that a retainer could not hold him if another stable had a potential Derby winner, even if this meant 'jocking off' the regular stable jockey. He first did this in 1920, but guessed wrong. In 1921 he greatly upset Lord Derby and George Lambton by deserting them to ride Mr J. B. Joel's Humorist. This won him the race but lost him Lord Derby's retainer the following season. In 1922 he was involved in another 'jocking off' to get the ride on Captain Cuttle for Lord Woolavington. Then in 1923 he deserted his new 'master' for another winner, Papyrus. Woolavington's trainer, Fred Darling, refused to have him as stable jockey, but Donoghue made a private arrangement with another of Darling's owners to ride the 1925 winner, Manna.

Though the establishment muttered darkly about his irresponsibility Donoghue, assisted by a persuasive charm, got away with it – up to a point. He found it easy to persuade himself that his only duty was to his adoring public, and the familiar roar of 'Come on, Steve' whenever he was in a close finish showed that the public agreed. More people followed the star of a favourite jockey when placing their bets than studied the form of the horses. There were always owners and trainers willing to hire Donoghue, but his unreliability made him a freelance *de facto* and he increasingly found himself having to seek rather than be offered the best rides.

Whatever their eventual wealth and fame flat-race jockeys were quintessentially plebeian and each recruit had to start at the bottom of the pile. By contrast the stock of the trainers to whom they were apprenticed had steadily risen over the years. The great stables were run by men of considerable wealth. Trainers got 10% of any winnings, apart from the profit they made in weekly charges. Alec Taylor of Manton, who retired in 1928, left £500,000 on his death in 1943. Their enterprises were passed on like successful businesses. Taylor's went to Joe Lawson who had started with him as a stable lad; more often they were kept in the family. Racing family dynasties had grown up as much amongst the prosperous yeoman class as amongst the aristocracy. At Newmarket, for instance, there were three prominent sons of Billy Jarvis (which made them also nephews of Jimmy Ryan), four sons of Jimmy Waugh and four of Tom Leader. And there were now many more gentlemen trainers. In the post-war world, indeed, training race-horses for the idle rich was one of the better ways for ex-officers to make a living. When Tom Jennings, junior, retired his Phantom House stables were taken over by Major Vandy Beatty, brother of Admiral of the Fleet Earl Beatty, and in 1922 Captain Boyd-Rochfort bought Freemason House (from a bibulous Freemason) and set up on his own. Nearby, at Beaufort House, Harrovian Lord George Dundas, younger son of the first Marquess of Zetland, began training for his father, racing's equivalent of 'carrying the horn' in a family hunt.

By contrast the next great champion jockey, Gordon Richards, who had left school aged 13 to become a warehouse boy, had to overcome considerable parental resistance before he was allowed to give up this respectability and security to become an apprentice jockey in 1920. He served his time with Martin Hartigan – of the gentlemanly type of trainer – and continued to live in the communal bachelor quarters of his yard when he became an established rider. By 1925, with a retainer from Hartigan's friend, Captain Tommy Hogg, he became champion jockey. With a prudence his parents would have approved, however, he stayed on at the Hartigan yard, though he now slept in a separate private hut. He usually ate with the stable lads, but he had acquired a dinner-jacket which he sported when invited to dine at the Hartigans. A tubercular infection interrupted his riding career, but advanced his social development thanks to a fellow-patient who played golf and knew about wine. On his return to racing in 1927 he sometimes rode for an owner–trainer, a Mr Reid Walker, who allowed Richards to bring a friend to dinner 'in a little room near the big dining room' and would send them in a glass of port. At the end of the season, champion jockey again, Richards and his sister were taken to Switzerland with Captain Hogg and his family. (For those who worked throughout the summer, winter sports holidays were the thing and Switzerland was full of the racing fraternity. Curling was the approved activity for jockeys.) It proved something of an ordeal socially. Richards was by now, of course, a considerable public figure but when he married in 1928 he and his wife felt so insecure that they kept quiet about it and lived together in secret for some time.[32]

The insecurity was endemic. In 1919 the Jockey Club had commissioned a report on the finances of the Turf, and its author, Lord Dalzell of Hamilton, had called for urgent action to put it on a sounder footing. But the urge for reform had been overtaken by the unexpected post-war boom, which had greatly accelerated the cycle of prosperity that came from spectators, prize-money and improved standards of racing. It had also brought crowd disturbances, race-gangs, protection rackets and such adverse publicity that the Jockey Club was obliged in 1925 to set up a racecourse security agency. This added to racing's costs at the very time the post-war boom was ending, and with the expenses of course upkeep and wages creeping up again, and new attractions competing for attention, the outlook looked grim.

This was especially true of the owners who, as they saw it, provided the sport with all that the rest depended on. Capital costs apart, it cost at least £3 a week to keep a horse in training – £3 10s if you went to Alec Taylor – and a good deal more in the plusher places. Prizes might be bigger but the chances of winning one were correspondingly less, and over 60% of the prize-money came from the owners in entrance fees anyway. The breeders, course authorities, trainers, jockeys and all the other racing interests had their own tunnel-vision view of things. Even the punters felt they deserved more consideration. The only thing on which all agreed was that the bookmakers, who made vast and relatively risk-free profits from racing, should pay a good deal more towards its costs. That they paid so little was largely because the discriminatory Gaming Act of 1853, by banning off-course betting for cash, in betting shops and the like, had driven it underground.[33] As governments felt unable to tax the illicit, the legal on-course and credit variety escaped *a fortiori*. In 1926, however, Churchill hit upon the notion of a tax of 2% for on-course and 3.5% for off-course betting.

The experiment was a dismal failure and soon came to an end.[34] However, it gave the Jockey Club an opening for its own proposals. France had a state monopoly of betting and the government distributed a percentage of the profits to the racing interests and to the Ministry of Agriculture for horse-breeding. The Jockey Club saw itself as the obvious organisation to operate a similar system in Britain using machines known as totalisators to calculate the odds. The bookmakers, for their part, were strongly resistant to being replaced by machines or made into civil servants. The government shrank from direct action but promised not to oppose a Private Members Bill. The Act that eventually emerged did not give the reformers all they wanted. It legalised the Tote but not as a monopoly. Indeed the bookmakers retained important advantages. The Tote could only deal in cash and the big backers – for convenience and for fear of being robbed – dealt only in credit. The Tote odds, when they were eventually worked out, were often much less than could have been obtained by an early bet on the old system. And the British public preferred to deal with people rather than machines.

The Racecourse Betting Control Board set up to run the Tote was cumbersome and bureaucratic. It was not helped by the decline in attendances that began in the late twenties under the pressure of competition from other attractions. One way and another it was several years before it began to show a profit. But the significant thing was that it existed at all, and if it failed to revolutionise the finances of the Turf and to diminish the influence of the bookies it was the first official recognition of gambling as a legitimate source of assistance to sport. Not least it was a rebuff for the Jockey Club. For the RCBCB was given the task not only of running the Tote but of distributing its proceeds. This was the first time the Jockey Club's hegemonic assumptions had been checked, a truly chill wind of post-war change.

Racing: over the jumps

The flat-racing season ended early in November, and in National Hunt racing there was nothing of any great significance until the following March. This was a legacy of history for the sport's chief claims to social recognition (and gradual acceptance into the Jockey Club fold) had been the meetings held by fashionable fox-hunts and leading regiments. The Grand Military meeting at Sandown Park and the Household Brigade's at Hawthorn Hill were like minor Ascots and there were prestigious point-to-points and hunt-meetings. But there was also a largely professional circuit of steeplechases and hurdle races that had only marginal connections with hunting. The leading hurdle specialist of the twenties, George Duller, had learned its most important art, pacing, from riding his father's horses in harness-racing and he only once attempted the Grand National which still had some traces of steeplechasing's cross-country origins. Harry Brown (champion NH jockey in 1919, the last amateur to have the distinction) stoutly maintained that the best preparation for a Grand National prospect was a season's hunting, and came near to proving his point in 1921.[35] But both as a rider and a highly professional trainer he was well aware that 'chasing needed specialised preparation: it was just that the National, with its rugged and idiosyncratic fences, was in a category of its own.

Nobody quite knew what made a National winner, but a lot of people tried to produce one every year. The Irish tradition, which made less social distinction between National Hunt racing and the Flat, had made them the masters of Aintree in the past and the 1920 race put the troubles in perspective. The winner, Troytown, was bred and owned by Major Thomas Gerrard of County Meath, late of the 17th Lancers. It was ridden by Jack Anthony, a Welshman from one of the National Hunt versions of the flat-race family dynasties. Jack and his brothers Ivor and Owen had all begun riding their father's horses in point-to-points and local events before graduating to regular NH meetings. Ivor, a professional, had been champion jockey in 1912 and both he and Owen became highly successful trainers. Jack Anthony, who had ridden two Grand National winners before the war and been champion jockey in 1914, was still an amateur. Unlike Harry Brown he was not the Etonian, fashionable regiment type, but from the farming background that produced most NH trainers and owners. (The similarity was that either kind could be more expensive than the professionals.) The rewards for professional riders were greater after the war, and in the spirit of the new age Jack also turned professional in 1920. Ex-servicemen led the way, among them the greatest steeplechase jockey of all, F. B. Rees, four times champion rider, twice winner of the National, the Gold Cup and the Champion Hurdle in the twenties. Rees was one of two jump-jockey sons of a South Wales veterinary surgeon who had learned their trade as amateurs with the same Tenby stable as the Anthonys.

The 1923 National winner, Sergeant Murphy, was 14 years old when acquired by Mr Stephen Sandford, a wealthy American undergraduate at Cambridge, seeking a horse he himself could hunt and perhaps ride in amateur events; but he found him 'too much of a good thing', and put him into training again. Naturally he selected a Newmarket trainer, George Blackwell, who in 1903 had had the distinction of winning the Triple Crown on the Flat. It was a tribute to the prestige – and prize-money – of the National that Newmarket trainers went on to win it four times in the next six years. Fred Archer, nephew of the great jockey, won in 1925. Then in 1926 came Harvey Leader, who had trained the St Leger winner in 1920, and in 1927 and 1929 his uncle Tom, a pillar of Newmarket society. The 1927 winner was ridden by his son Ted, the previous year's champion NH jockey.

Rich patrons were rare in National Hunt racing: most owners were either people who owned one or two horses they had bred themselves and raced for sport, or gamblers interested only in the betting. Mr Sandford's success in 1923 aroused the interest of a number of his compatriots, and the 1926 winner had been bought by a Mr A. C. Schwarz at a suitably inflated price three weeks before the race. Sandford himself had meanwhile bought several other good 'chasers, but his main interest was in polo. (When told that the young man was prepared to pay £1,000 for a polo pony George V is said to have remarked, 'Goodness me! the most I ever paid was £30.') More serious Americans like the Bostwick brothers, who were also fine riders, Mr and Mrs F. Ambrose Clark and Mr J. H. Whitney, who was to become US Ambassador, helped put steeplechasing on its feet.

Steeple chasing was still far too dependent on the National. The enormous fields it drew made it not only a gruelling endurance test but one that needed a good deal of luck, especially as there were dozens of entries that were not up to it, falling themselves and getting in others' way. This meant casualties every year – the only question was how many. In 1928 when Tipperary Tim staggered home to win at 100–1 he was one of the only two horses out of 42 starters to finish. The Stewards tried to restrict the numbers in 1929 by raising the entry fee to £100, but there was a record entry of 66 and another 100–1 winner. The reason for the vast fields was obvious. The Grand National prize that year was £9,800. Only five other races in the whole season offered more than even £1,000, three of them also at Aintree – and four of the six were handicaps.

The best on offer at Cheltenham, accepted by the connoisseurs as a fairer, less freakish course, was the National Hunt Chase of £1,266. The Gold Cup, started in 1924 for 5-year-olds at level weights was an ideal contest but could muster only £670. Its first few runnings were of interest chiefly for a couple of Irish wins and for the 1927 winner Thrown In, owned and trained by Lord Stalbridge and ridden by his son a young officer in the 7th Hussars. The turning point was the advent of J. H. Whitney who had acquired Easter Hero, the principal cause of the débâcle in the 1928 National, and sent him to Cheltenham as a warm-up for the 1929 race. With F. B. Rees aboard he won by some twenty lengths, and the essential glamour had come to the Gold Cup. Easter Hero's credentials were confirmed when a fortnight later he came a gallant second in the 66-strong National in spite of carrying top weight and spreading a plate (damaging a hoof). And the Gold Cup's lustre was maintained when in 1930 he won easily again. The parallel Champion Hurdle, however, started in 1927, hung fire and the 1928 winner, Brown Jack, crossed over to the more profitable Flat.

The National Hunt season was still a patchy affair and its tone was lowered considerably by the numerous small steeplechase meetings on rustic courses at which £100 was a big prize, that were rarely well-organised and were not conspicuous for high ethical standards. Still they provided opportunities for local talent and a training ground for better things – and, as an old Etonian noviciate recalled, 'despite the acts of cheerful villainy sometimes perpetrated . . . these meetings were fun'. He remembered 'the jovial trainer of half-a-dozen indifferent horses' celebrating, in the bar one afternoon at Pershore, the ideal race: 'Four runners, two I knew weren't trying, one was my own and the fourth one I backed.'[36] Hurdling had its own well-known rackets. There was a sordid commercial element amongst the point-to-points, but Brigadier Stanley's reforming efforts had created the Bona Fide Hunt or Military Meeting, and the social status of the genre had been greatly enhanced, like so much else in the twenties, by the involvement of the Prince of Wales.

The Prince took rooms at Craven Lodge, Melton Mowbray, for use during the hunting season. He had been instructed in the arts of cross-country riding and jumping fences by Harry Brown, who evidently imbued him with so much of his own zest for competition that he came increasingly to prefer racing to the actual hunting. His races attracted great publicity, and when he fell off occasionally, the newspapers made the most of it. In 1924, when he had a bad fall in the Army point-to-point, there was a great press outcry and much subsequent public concern about the dangers the heir to the throne was incurring. Letters and articles appeared, suggesting that he should quit and Ramsay MacDonald, Prime Minister at the time, made a personal appeal. However as soon as he was recovered he was at it again and it was not until 1928 when the King became seriously ill that Edward changed his ways.

Queen Mary felt the time had come to ask him to give up race-riding and stick to hunting. This was a grave disappointment to him, not least because he was beginning to win a few races, even good ones, but he had little choice. When he quit, however, he was not content to carry on with hunting on its own: he sold his horses and gave up Craven Lodge. There are those who argue that the country might have been better served if he had not made the great sacrifice, for when he left the Shires he sought a refuge near Windsor and turned his attention to suburbanite pleasures. One was gardening, an exemplary hobby. Another, however, was the company of married women. Mrs Dudley Ward, with whom he had been deeply but discreetly in love since 1918, helped him with his house-hunting, but she had no monopoly of his time and he was on the brink of more dangerous liaisons.[37] His third interest was golf, which many saw as a sign of modern degeneracy in itself.

Golf: plus-fours and mid-calf skirts

At Charterhouse, to which the young Henry Longhurst was sent in 1922, golf was 'frowned upon as lacking in "team spirit" '. He could play only on a few days at the end of term and then 'by bicycling four miles each way to the West Surrey course at Enton'.[38] As a result of a later match against a group of Old Boys the course was put out of bounds for some time. But for all that the game was taking an insidious hold, and in the following decade Charterhouse were to be regular winners of the Halford Hewitt Cup for Old Boy teams. The team element was a distinctive feature of the latest phase of the English game which brought in many more of the new style public school amateurs. Whether the authorities liked it or not, pupil power brought school teams – Eton had one, and the new Stowe School which opened in 1926 had its own course. Oxford and Cambridge, standards raised by the influx and even more by the ex-service undergraduates like Cyril Tolley and Roger Wethered, became much more prominent. They played 12-a-side matches – 'every Saturday and most Sundays' – against some of the finest teams in the country, mostly around London.

This was the royal road to selection for the Walker Cup – the amateur competition against the Americans instituted in 1922 which the British never managed to win.[39] The Scots, who formed their own Golfing Union in 1920, offered something of a leavening but in large measure the game was dominated by the privileged. Attempts to assist the English working-class player centred largely on the efforts of the Artisan Golfers' Association, founded in 1921 by Lord Riddell and the distinguished professional and golf architect J. H. Taylor. There were only 12 such clubs with about 350 members but the numbers grew, slowly at first then more rapidly towards the end of the decade and it was a much-applauded achievement when William Sutton of West Cheshire Artisans won the Amateur Championship in 1929. The old feudal arrangement of menial service had now given way to lower fees for play at 'unsocial' hours and a few clubs like the Royal Eastbourne were encouraged to admit artisans as a pretext for allowing Sunday play. Regardless of clubs' willingness, however, artisans, especially if they made progress in the game, soon encountered the snobberies that Abe Mitchell had detected, and the concept was obsolescent.

The other attempt to broaden golf's social base was before its time. The LCC's pre-war experiment with public golf at Hainault Forest, pioneered by Taylor, had been a great success and a second course had been added. Taylor now campaigned for provision to the west of the city. His own club, Royal Mid-Surrey, was laid out in the Old Deer Park at Richmond and there was still a vast expanse lying idle. To create a public amenity in a Royal Park seemed to some an added indecency to the already scandalous principle of rate-payers subsidising golf. Taylor was able to interest the *Daily Mail* in the idea, however, and Lord Riddell chaired an influential steering committee to further the project. The final obstacle was HM Controller of Works who eventually agreed on behalf of the Crown to lease the 96 acres for the sum of £200 a year. The Royal Family thereafter gave full support to the venture: the Prince of Wales performed the opening ceremony and when it proved so popular as to require a second course, the Duke of York graced the occasion. At the same time the Office of Works marked the occasion by invoking its right to take over the project and installed its own Superintendent and fee-collector. Few councils followed London's lead – Birmingham was a notable exception – but generally neither Tory nor Labour gave it high priority for public expenditure and there were still only some 30 public courses in England in 1939.[40]

A more significant breakthrough in 1924 was the decision of the 17-year-old Henry Cotton to leave Dulwich College and become an assistant professional. The awful possibilities for the future were not immediately realised: the available prize-money was not great – the Open Champion received no more than £75 throughout the decade – and the stigma was a powerful deterrent. But it was an ill omen when in 1928 he crossed to the States, buying his own ticket and taking with him a letter of credit for £300 which he brought back intact. A young man could pick up very bad habits there. The Americans were intrinsically undesirable – and had become far too good at golf whilst others were bearing the brunt of the war. In 1920 when the veteran English professional Ted Ray had followed tradition by winning the US Open a group of Americans had sworn 'the Oath of Inverness', to enter the British Open each year until they got their revenge. Their victory in 1921 was tolerable since the winner, Jock Hutchinson, was Scottish-born. But there was no mistaking Walter Hagen's Detroit bloodlines when in 1922 he took Sandwich by storm. And he won three times more in a decade in which Americans won all but once. But that was only the half of it. On his first visit in 1920 he had outraged the members at Deal by refusing to change with the other professionals in communal squalor. Instead he drove from his luxury hotel in a vast chauffeur-driven car and emerged clad in his flashy golfing attire to lead an admiring crowd to the first tee. Denied the member's dining room for lunch at Royal St George's, Sandwich, two years later he had his manservant serve him champagne and other delicacies in his Rolls. And when he won he ostentatiously handed the prize-money to his caddy.

Hagen's assault on the citadel did not bring it crashing in ruins but it exposed the petty distinctions to ridicule and brought a slight acceleration in the process of change the war had brought. In 1920 Ted Ray's Oxhey club had commemorated his US Open victory by actually making him an honorary member and Taylor, Vardon and Braid were soon similarly honoured. The R&A, which had taken over responsibility for the Open in 1920, regularly consulted the PGA and conditions for the professionals, though still dependent on the host club's charity, gradually improved. By 1925 the old guard at Prestwick were persuaded to set aside part of the clubhouse instead of putting up a marquee. Still the establishment were not prepared for the Hagen type of professional or even the more polished version Cotton seemed to want to be. As his fame increased after his victory against the Americans in the 1929 Ryder Cup it did not suit him to spend his lunch-hours in a smoky club room full of bores and sycophants so he changed in his Mercedes and retired to his hotel. His critics thought he regarded himself as too good for the common herd. 'I believe', he recalled, 'that I was one of only about four professionals at that time to have a car at all. It was hardly "done" for a golf pro to own a car.'[41]

Another Ryder Cup prospect, Percy Alliss, was more typically subservient. His son Peter recalled him as entirely free of 'the politics of envy' with regard to his fellow professionals, and pragmatic, perhaps even sardonic, in his attitude to serving 'the toffs': 'If you smiled you might get a tip.'[42] Alliss was also unusual in being prepared to work for his old enemies. Quite a few professionals went to Europe, where they were greatly revered, but Alliss was the first to go to Germany. Twice wounded in the war, he had been an assistant at Royal Porthcawl and professional at Clyne, Swansea, before going to the Golf-und-Land Club, Wannsee, Berlin in 1926. This paid extremely well but involved serving an aristocratic class for whom 'the will to win, the will to be best, the will to dominate was all'.[43] Mrs Alliss had seen the Germans as arrogant bullies from the start and the advent of the Nazis persuaded even Alliss, the tolerant ex-serviceman, by 1931 that it was time to go home.

For all the advance of professional golf – further signified by being given its own team game, the Ryder Cup, in 1927 – it was an amateur age, not only in the clubs but in competition. The leisure still enjoyed by scores of young men of good family, expert coaching and wonderful facilities, produced many outstanding players. The leading British pair, Roger Wethered and Cyril Tolley, combined impeccable gentlemanly Oxford amateurism with standards of play equal to all but the very greatest professionals. And the outstanding player in the world, the American Robert Tyre Jones, was not only an equally impeccably amateur but the game's greatest attraction. When gate money was charged at the Open for the first time in 1926, the magnet was Bobby Jones, who duly won. Nor did gate-money create a situation in which 'expenses' became appearance money. And though amateurs still managed a few 'perks' like journalism, the slightest whiff of commercial exploitation sent flutters round the dovecote. Cyril Tolley, amateur champion in 1920 when still an undergraduate, had himself written a book, *Modern Golf*, in 1924, but in 1929 now a stockbroker and champion again, he was outraged to find that Fry's, the chocolate firm, had used a caricature of him, and his name, in a limerick in one of their advertisements. He sued for damages. When, after two years, he won his case a Law Lord dissented on the grounds that no thinking person could associate Tolley with such rubbish.[44]

The women were even more fervently purist. Cecil Leitch, champion again in 1920 and 1921, wrote two more books, *Golf* (1922) and *Golf Simplified* (1924) but then the LGU tightened the rules and she gave it up and turned her considerable talents to business outside golf. She was still front-page news, however, especially her duels with Miss Joyce Wethered, brother of Roger, an equally fastidious amateur and an even greater player. After her victory at Troon in 1925, an epic encounter she won only at the 37th hole, Miss Wethered retired for a time partly because of her marriage (she became Lady Heathcote-Amory) but partly because she disliked the stampeding crowds. She returned in 1929 to beat the American champion, Glenda Collett. By this time women golfers were not merely acceptable they were national heroines.

Amateur interests prevailed over the fears of the professionals in the controversial introduction of the steel-shafted club as it had done with the Haskell ball a generation earlier.[45] Any technological advance which made the game easier for the amateur was seen as a threat to the tournament professional and certainly threatened what remained of the old club-making trade, the repair of the old hickory shafts, frequently broken in play or anger. The PGA, which had set up its own Co-operative Association for bulk wholesaling in 1921, was stronger now, but in spite of its vigorous protests the R&A eventually followed the American lead and legalised steel shafts in 1929. The PGA's time was coming. As more and more equipment makers and newspapers sponsored competitions prize-money increased: it was a straw in the wind when the 1928 amateur champion T. P. Perkins, not even an artisan, turned professional.

In the meantime, however, as the German Rudolf Kircher observed in 1928, there was a big difference between the game in England and that of the original Scottish version. North of the border it could be called a national sport open to all classes and was still widely played on common land. In England it was basically an amusement of the rich, and the seclusion of the better clubs was an essential part of the pleasure. The Richmond Park development was a rarity and the magnificent Wentworth nearby, announcing another country estate's re-dedication in 1924, was a much more characteristic development.

Lawn tennis on the brink

In the other great suburban sport lawn tennis, as in golf, the British were greatly concerned at the inability of their men to fend off international challenge. Not only the Americans and Australians but the French were now markedly better and it was they who regularly contested the Davis Cup. Furthermore, unlike golf, the women did little better. In 1920 all five Wimbledon titles had gone overseas and ten years later all five were contested solely by overseas players. In 1927 the last eight in the men's singles were all foreigners. It was possible to rationalise the situation in a rather flattering way. After all the important thing about games was not winning but playing, and much was heard, as the All-England club celebrated its fiftieth anniversary, of the spiritual gifts it had conferred on the world. It had been a 'medium for the re-union of liberated youth' after the war. 'The athletic energies of youth, suppressed for five years, sought a natural outlet and found it in a pastime so cosmopolitan as lawn tennis', wrote Wallis Myers.[46] If coarser, more chauvinistic emotions entered the minds of spectators and newspaper readers they got short shrift at All-England. 'I can't help thinking', wrote Commander Hillyard in 1924, recalling the old days, 'that . . . players seemed more jealous of the reputation of the game, more fearful of the taint of pot-hunting'.[47]

All-England themselves were not immune from all modern vices. They were excessively interested in spectators, some thought. At their new Church Road ground, opened by the King in 1922, the 'ferro-concrete amphitheatre which assumed the dignity of the centre court housed . . . as many as 15,000'.[48] Many had thought it likely to be a white elephant but the £140,000 it cost turned out a prudent investment. The profits, however, even to the club, were considerably reduced by the generous share of tickets the members awarded themselves, making the modest annual subscription an even better bargain. Very little found its way to the LTA to be ploughed back into the game. The All-England vision was restricted to the 'liberated youth' who could afford to play.

Tournaments offered, in theory at least, a competitive ladder of opportunity up which anyone could aspire to climb. There were certainly plenty of them throughout the summer, rising to 50 or so in July and even more in August, but they competed or even clashed with each other except for a few traditional fixtures and the constraints of commercial prudence. It was for the county organisations and the leading clubs to arrange matches and bring on young players, a system obviously weighted heavily in favour of the better areas and the club-joining classes. The number of clubs had increased rapidly since the war – from about 1,000 to over 1,600 in 1925 and nearly 2,500 by the end of the decade; but this had lowered the game's tone by bringing in many more players from the proliferating lower-middle classes without altering its social outlook or greatly raising the standard of play. Rudolf Kircher offered a somewhat unflattering phylogenetic explanation of the phenomenon.

The English, Kircher reckoned, had a natural affinity with lawn tennis. For one thing it was a test of nerve: a tennis player had to ignore his mistakes – and those of the umpire – and the national character was well suited to this. Unfortunately the virtue could also be a vice, for it could lead to complacency 'There are hundreds of tennis players who without the slightest self-deception play badly and enjoy it.' This was not necessarily a bad thing: 'Without this happy optimism the rapid spread of the game since the war would not have been possible.' But it had its limitations. The vice was encouraged because many of the new clubs had wretched courts and players whose dress fell 'considerably short of English standards': this struck a vulgar note and was not conducive to raising standards. Hence the top English players came from a very narrow social band. Furthermore it was only a section of this group who took an interest in tennis. The best public schools, preoccupied with team-games, were not disposed to invest in expensive courts. The universities had only recently, and partially, taken it up with any enthusiasm. If an English champion were to arise it would only be after radical changes in the system, providing access to the top; or, more likely, he would be the son of a coach or a 'quondam ball-boy'.[49]

Unlike golf there was no Open championship. Professionals were fellows like Charles Read who had become an assistant at Queen's Club in 1902, when he was 13, and had been there more or less ever since. Their championships, basically contests between the coaches of the exclusive clubs, attracted relatively little interest and it was the amateurs who drew the crowds. Everyone wanted to see Susanne Lenglen, who, back at Wimbledon in 1920, further added to her contribution to female liberation by her bobbed hair, covered not by a hat but her celebrated bandeau of brightly-coloured silk chiffon. The fashion quickly spread, on and off the tennis court, as did appropriately modified versions of her skirt length and its substructure. There were brief interludes for chauvinistic admiration of Kitty McKane, who won in 1924 and, with Lenglen *hors de combat*, in 1926,[50] but then came the great American, Helen Wills, the new 'Queen of the Centre Court'.

The previous incumbent had offended the Queen of England in 1926, taking exception to her own schedule being rearranged inconveniently (and somewhat peremptorily) by Commander Hillyard, merely in order to fit in with Her Majesty's.[51] This led to some booing – not a feature of Wimbledon – and naturally caused a great scandal in the press. The incident marred the otherwise splendid atmosphere of the Jubilee tournament, graced not only by visits from the King and Queen but by the appearance (first round only) of the Duke of York in the men's doubles. It confirmed the dubious reputation of the French. In fact, the French authorities had had a great deal of trouble with Mlle Lenglen themselves, with not only her displays of temperament and off-hand attitude but her defiance of the proprieties with regard to expenses, gifts from fashion houses and so forth. All the same it was a surprise when she went overtly professional, joining Charles C. Pyle's experimental series of matches and exhibitions in the States, reputedly with £100,000 to lessen the disgrace.

The venture was a nine-day wonder. Pyle was unable to induce the established male stars, W. T. Tilden and W. M. Johnston, to take the plunge. Tilden continued for a time irritating the USLTA by cashing in on his celebrity with 'fuzzy bear' sweaters, exclusive interviews and other infringements of the code (as well as by his homosexuality) before setting up his own circus. The Wimbledon stage was given over to the French quartet Borotra, 'the bounding Basque', Lacoste, Cochet and Brugnon, and the search for a British contender grew more desperate. By the end of the decade there were two in the wings. The first, H. W. 'Bunny' Austin, the Cambridge University captain in 1928, was out of the top drawer. The other, Fred Perry was a rather different type, self-confessedly brash and attracted to tennis because he admired the handsome cars the players seemed to own. He was far from Kircher's 'quondam ball-boy' – his father, now a Labour MP, had staked him for a year whilst he gave up his £4 a week job with Spalding's to play tennis full-time. All the same he was 'very conscious that (he) was regarded as being from the wrong side of the tracks'.[52]

Notes

1 K. Young, *Harry, Lord Rosebery*, London, 1974; *Baily's Hunting Directory*, 1921.
2 D. Cannadine, *The Decline and Fall of the British Aristocracy*, London, 1992, p. 368.
3 R. Longrigg, *The History of Fox-hunting*, London, 1975, p. 199.
4 Minutes of MFHA meeting, June 1920.
5 *Irish Field*, February, 1919.
6 'Sabretache' (A. E. Barrow), quoted by Longrigg, in *Fox-hunting*, p. 209.
7 Sir C. Frederick, 'Manners and Customs', Lonsdale Library, *Foxhunting*, London,

1930.

8 Longrigg, *Fox-hunting*, p. 202.

9 See Derek Birley, *Sport and the Making of Britain*, Manchester, 1993, p. 296.

10 See Derek Birley, *Land of Sport and Glory*, Manchester, 1994, pp. 125, 183.

11 J. G. Millais, *Deer and Deer-Stalking*, London, 1913.

12 The most notorious case was William Randolph Hearst who bought St Donat's Castle in Wales, but there were many more, transatlantic and otherwise.

13 Cannadine, *Decline*, p. 366.

14 See Birley, *Sport*, pp. 175, 233, 295; *Land*, p. 120.

15 W. Hepgrave, *The Management of a Partridge Beat*, London, 1922, quoted in E. Parker (ed.), *The Shooting Weekend Book*, London, 1952, p. 127.

16 E. R. Hewitt, *Secrets of the Salmon*, London, 1923.

17 H. Reiach, quoted by J. D. Sleightholme, '1906–1981', *Yachting Monthly'*, June 1981, p. 1254.

18 J. Nicholson, *Great Days in Yachting*, Lymington, 1970, pp. 156, 159; J. A. Cuddon, *The Macmillan Dictionary of Sport and Games*, London, 1980, p. 845.

19 Nicholson, *Great Days*, p. 162.

20 Sleightholme, '1906–1981', p. 1254.

21 Sir Eric Geddes was the Chairman of the Committee on Government Expenditure which cut back the social services.

22 Nicholson, *Great Days*, pp. 125–8.

23 Sleightholme, '1906–1981', p. 162.

24 Nicholson, *Great Days*, p. 148. The American Bermuda rig, as an alternative to the traditional 'gaff' four-sided mainsail, was triangular and very tall requiring a high mast resembling a wireless mast. It had been tried before the war in Britain on 6-metre boats.

25 Sleightholme, '1906–1981', p. 1255.

26 Nicholson, *Great Days*, passim.

27 See Birley, *Sport*, p. 302.

28 *DNB*.

29 In 1922 Selfridges was offering morning coats and waistcoats for 7 guineas, trousers from 30s to 47s 6d, silk hats for 45s and white canvas spats for 7s 6d.

30 D. Laird, *Royal Ascot*, London, 1976, pp. 189 ff.

31 *The Times*, 14 June 1925.

32 G. Richards, *My Story*, London, 1955.

33 See K. Chesney, *The Victorian Underground*, Harmondsworth, 1982, W. Vamplew, *The Turf: Social and Economic History*, London, 1976, and, for a useful summary and bibliography, M. Clapson, *A Bit of a Flutter: Popular Gambling and English Culture 1823–1961*, Manchester, 1992, esp. Chapter Two, pp. 14–43.

34 The bookmakers objected to acting as tax-collectors, even staging a strike at one point. The government was obliged to retreat, reducing the tax to 1% and 2% in 1928, and the following year the Labour government dropped it altogether.

35 He fell at the second last fence, breaking his collar-bone, but remounted to finish second.

36 R. Mortimer in M. Seth-Smith et al., *The History of Steeplechasing*, London, 1966, p. 107.

37 F. Donaldson, *Edward VIII*, London (1976 edn), pp. 57–60.

38 H. Longhurst, *Only on Sundays*, London, 1964, pp. 2–3. See also *It Was Good While It Lasted*, London, 1940.

39 Their first victory was in 1947.

40 G. Cousins, *Golf in Britain*, London, 1975, Chapter Twenty-six.

41 Longhurst, *Only on Sunday*, p. 194.
42 P. Alliss, *Autobiography*, London, 1981, p. 21.
43 ibid., p. 17.
44   The caddy to Tolley said Oh Sir!
        Good shot, Sir, that ball see it go, Sir!
        My word how it flies.
        Like a cartet of Fry's
        They're handy, they're good and priced low, Sir!

   See G. Cousins, *Golf*, for the episode.
45 See Birley, *Land*, pp. 196–7.
46 A. W. Myers, *Fifty Years of Wimbledon*, AELTC, London, 1926, p. 63.
47 G. W. Hillyard, *Forty Years of First Class Tennis*, London, 1924, p. 254.
48 Myers, *Fifty Years*, p. 70.
49 R. Kircher, *Fair Play*, London, 1928, p. 68.
50 As Mrs L. A. Godfree. The British ladies also managed to win the Wightman Cup, introduced in 1923, in 1924, 1925 and 1928.
51 Both Wallis Myers' official record and Commander Hillyard's memoirs were written before Miss Lenglen disgraced herself. For an account of what happened see L. Tingay, *100 Years of Wimbledon*, AELTC, London, 1977, the official history, and the racy G. Robyns, *Wimbledon: The Hidden Drama*, Newton Abbot, 1973.
52 F. Perry, *An Autobiography*, London, 1984, p. 19.

CHAPTER EIGHT

Fair play (1919–29):
football, cricket and caste

The peculiar British caste system that Perry was confronting operated by unwritten rules that changed if there was any danger of outsiders learning them. Birth and wealth could play their part, but most important of all was the mysterious quality known as breeding. The school one went to was therefore of critical importance. The social gap between private education and the state elementary system, church or local authority, was enormous. In between, in lower-middle-class territory, were secondary schools provided or subsidised by the state. They charged modest fees but, as a condition of subsidy, had to offer at least 25% of their places free to children from elementary schools. Many of their pupils still left school at the age of 14 but after the war a growing number stayed on to take School Certificate at 15 or 16 and a few, mostly boys, went on to universities, particularly the new provincial ones. Some 1,500 scholarships were offered by the local authorities and from 1920 200 State Scholarships were added and slowly increased each year.

The Hadow Report of 1926 recommended that all pupils should go to secondary school at age 11 – some to fee-paying grammar schools with 'free places' for scholarship winners, a few to technical schools and the rest to new senior schools. This found all-party support, especially as implementation would depend largely on local discretion and local funds. Progress with the new schools was both slow and patchy, but many existing grammar schools did well out of the arrangement which helped them offer a diluted version of the public school ethos at low cost. The snobbier private schools resisted the lure of state subsidy and tried to make the climb to public school status by taking in boarders, starting OTCs and similar devices. All laid great emphasis on games. The philosophy of the muscular Christians still held sway. The value of games in building and governing the Empire had never been questioned, and they had recently demonstrated their power to provide the leadership and team spirit that wins wars. Now in peace-time there was fresh need of them. The old imperialist J. E. C. Welldon, once Headmaster of Harrow and now Dean of Durham, deploring strikes as a way of settling industrial questions, told the Labour Party how important it was 'that all persons who take part in public life . . . learn the lesson of "playing the game". It is a lesson which has been regularly taught on the playing fields of our public schools.'[1]

As the admiring German Rudolf Kircher saw it: 'Sport and play in England are not merely exercise for mind and body, but aim at making the individual a useful member of a unified whole, and such a unity of state and society is only possible if "Fair Play" is observed.'[2] This perhaps assumed a dirigisme and an enthusiasm for regimentation that were alien to the British. It certainly under-estimated their awareness of the significance of games as indicators of caste. The 1918 Education Act, recognising the need to get the masses into better shape, both literally and metaphorically, had authorised local authorities to provide camps, playing fields, swimming baths and other 'facilities for social and physical training'. But money had been scarce and few state schools had facilities of their own; certainly none to match the private sector. This apart they had to cope with the tradition of 'drill'-dominated elementary school curricula. The modern concept of physical education had as yet little currency, especially for boys. Whereas there were six women's PE colleges there were none at all for men. 'Physical jerks' had very low status in the public schools and better grammar schools. Games were taught by men with degrees in academic subjects but who had been games players themselves, preferably Blues: drill sergeants took care of whatever gymnastics were thought proper.

In one sense things were better in girls' education since their specialist colleges were producing teachers who were games mistresses as well as teachers of gymnastics and dance, a balanced philosophy that was better able to cross the line between state and private sectors. Amongst the enthusiastic successors of the élitist Madame Bergman-Osterberg the missionary spirit was strong. But it was a long time before it spread as far as the elementary schools. There was, in any event, even less scope for physical recreation in the girls' elementary schools than in the boys', where the 'drill' was leavened by sporting competition in innumerable leagues and cups, particularly in soccer and cricket. And at the top end of the social spectrum schools like Roedean, which went in for lacrosse and cricket as well as hockey, had created a parallel to the virility cult, deliberately modelled on the boys' public schools.

In these the hierarchies and snobberies were intensified as the school system expanded. An American study in 1926 found the social nuances of sport in British schools and universities perplexing, but offered a few guidelines. Setting aside the loftiest category of about 20 who preferred to call themselves 'rowing schools', 50 of the leading public schools played rugger compared with 25 who played soccer. The trend was most marked in boarding schools. In day public schools masters who had themselves been at boarding schools tended to prefer rugger but their influence was offset by home and other environmental factors: similarly most local authority secondary schools played soccer.[3]

Amateur apotheosis

Kircher believed rugger the severest test for fair play, for it meant conducting 'an apparently savage and reckless fight for the ball with the strictest self-control'. He doubted whether international contests in soccer, 'the game of the masses', made for 'mutual peace and understanding' but thought rugger a better prospect because the 'cultured Englishman can carry off a national defeat without any obvious resentment . . . [and] has become accustomed to share his honours . . . with other nations'.[4] In the post-war world rugger's imperial dimension had ensured all four home countries plenty of practice in losing. The first of the joint teams afterwards known as the British Lions did badly on its 1924 tour of South Africa, losing 9 games, including 3 of the 4 internationals (they drew the other). And the following winter the touring New Zealand All-Blacks swept the board, winning all 30 matches with a points record of 721 for, 112 against. There was no question of the Welsh redeeming British honour this time. The French also struck a few shrewd blows. They soon proved capable of beating not only the Irish (who had troubles off the field for a few years) but also the Scots; and they gave nasty shocks to England in 1926–7 and Wales the following year. Soon ugly rumours were circulating about the amateur purity of French rugby.

The domestic game had never been so popular. A crowd of 43,000 watched the Calcutta Cup at Twickenham in 1924, and the following year a new stand and extensions to terraces and enclosures made room for 13,000 more. The Scots' new Murrayfield stadium had a capacity of 80,000. And the big rugger matches were not mere spectacles, they were social occasions. The King enjoyed his visits to Twickenham for élite events like the Hospitals Cup as well as the internationals. The Middlesex 7-a-side competition, dominated by Harlequins, was a glittering addition to the social calendar in 1926. And the 'Varsity match was not to be missed. The teams of all four home countries were studded with 'Varsity men. England, who had most of them, won the Triple crown four times in the decade. The RFU had its greatest ever expansion with 231 new senior clubs affiliating in 1920–9 (compared with an average of 41 in the previous two decades), yet the England side had its greatest number of public school men.[5]

In this rarefied atmosphere the standards of enthusiasm expected from devotees reached unprecedented heights: this was no mere game but a Holy Grail. When in 1923 the RFU and Rugby School celebrated the centenary of its (imaginary) origins with a high-powered exhibition match the England captain, W. W. Wakefield, a Sedbergh man, grumbled afterwards that 'though the teams took the match in the right spirit, the Rugby boys who were watching were disappointingly apathetic. They seemed blasé.'[6] To others this restraint seemed highly desirable, a mark of superiority over soccer crowds. 'The rugby game,' noted Kircher, 'draws quite a different class of people, more select and self-controlled.'[7] He also thought they were superior intellectually: 'Rugger is more complicated and requires keener observation.'

But however well-bred the Twickenham crowds, the game's complexities often eluded both them and the players. Referees, reflecting their school-masterly origins, sought to administer justice not law, and pundits urged caution lest the game 'degenerate into a competition between the law-maker and the law-breaker'.[8] Spectators had not traditionally been to the forefront of rugger men's minds, and purists were not at all sure about the game's first experience of the 'full glare of publicity'.[9] The elder statesman of Scottish rugger, J. Aikman Smith, deeply deplored the decision by England and Wales to number the players' shirts for the Twickenham game of 1927. When asked why Scotland did not do the same he replied, 'Our men are no' cattle.'[10] Technology accelerated the descent into commercialism. The England–Wales match was broadcast live by the BBC. The commentator was H.B.T. 'Teddy' Wakelam of Marlborough, Cambridge and Harlequins, who sat opposite a written notice, 'Don't swear.' He had learned the job by describing a game to a specially-imported blind man. Sighted listeners were assisted by a numbered plan of the field and occasional interpolations by the producer – "Square four, etc.' – to tell them where play was taking place.[11]

The social values of rugger had become even more resolutely middle class as a result of the very different war-time experience of the two football codes. The division was particularly marked in Scotland. The context was one in which Scottish politics was becoming concerned more with class and economics than the traditional pigeon-holes of ethnicity and religion. The Church of Scotland was gradually resolving its differences with the United Free Churches, and the Education Act of 1918 was making generous provision for Catholics. Most people were satisfied with the amount of nationalist recognition given by such things as the distinctive legal and education systems. So the extremist radical parties – and the Liberals – lost ground and the struggle became more and more like that in England between 'haves' and 'have nots'.[12]

Across the border the Rugby League was a constant temptation to the occasional northern artisan awarded a cap: in 1925 Jim Brough the young Cumbrian fisherman who played full-back against the All-Blacks cashed in on his fame by joining the Leeds RL club. But in Scotland soccer had siphoned off the urban proletariat of Clydeside and the industrial and mining outposts in the east, and the Edinburgh, public school, Former Pupils and 'Varsity type dominated the rugger scene. Oxford in 1923 and 1924 could field a three-quarterline entirely composed of Scottish internationals – G. P. S. Macpherson, Ian Smith, A. C. Wallace and G. G. Aitken. Even the socially-mixed border clubs like Langholm, Kelso, Hawick, Galashiels and Melrose had been saved from the worst consequences of gate-money and league competition by their relative isolation from urban influences. Nevertheless the Scotland team, forwards as well as backs, tended to be alumni of the better Edinburgh and Glasgow schools. The border clubs' claims to recognition were not helped by their greater vulnerability to variations in the economic climate. Langholm was hit badly, for instance, by its dependence on the ailing textile trade in the late twenties. But their main problem was in being too far from Edinburgh, spiritually as well as geographically.

The élitism of Rugby in Ireland was increased not only by its growing social separation from soccer but by the political changes, which encouraged the spread of Gaelic games. At the same time the Free State government's scheme of things included Trinity College, Dublin, an establishment emblem whose influence was highly important in the survival of rugby. There had been no doubt of Trinity's allegiance during the war – nearly 3,000 Trinity men had volunteered and 454 had been killed, many of them rugger players. Nor was its desire for sporting and social links with Oxbridge diminished in any way by the post-war Anglo-Irish troubles. Indeed, at a time of financial stringency DUCAC, its Central Athletics Committee, though unable to subsidise a Hockey Club tour of Cork, found the money for a trip to Oxford and Cambridge. Yet, curiously enough, the basis of its post-war strength in rugby was an influx of South African Boers, some of them Rhodes scholars, who came to the medical school in preference to Oxford or Cambridge to avoid conscription. The Trinity side felt the benefit of their presence for four years after the war during which they were the dominant force in Irish rugby.[13] Linking across the border with Queen's, Belfast, also with a big medical school and strengthened generally by the war, Trinity was a vital element in preserving a single Irish RFU. Ireland played home international matches alternately in Belfast and Dublin, not very well at first but capturing perhaps better than anyone the 'spirit of the game' that rugger men so revered. Irish teams inevitably had a preponderance of the professional classes and a generous share of medical men. The economic depression, which hit first the shipbuilding and then the linen industry in the north of Ireland and debilitated the agriculurally-oriented south, had little effect on rugby clubs.

Rugger's finest achievements everywhere, in war or peace, rising above economic considerations or politics as necessary, stemmed, it seemed, from middle-class values. The proposition was painful to contemplate in Wales, which had taken pride in the democratic nature of its national game, as the national side suffered a string of embarrassing defeats. In 1929 Rowe Harding, one of Cambridge University's Welsh internationals, referred to 'the apparent decline in Welsh club Rugby', adding, 'I say "apparent" . . . because I think . . . that English Rugby has advanced whilst Welsh Rugby has stood still.'[14] (Sticking to methods that had proved successful in the past the Welsh had been slow to adopt the new back-row-forward play and tactical kicking by the half-backs, for instance.) This could have been avoided, he believed, by picking 'players with Welsh qualifications who have had the benefit of assimilating the new theories in England' but they had been 'consistently ignored by the Welsh selectors who have preferred players from the native clubs'. Later Welsh analysts, more sympathetic to this selectorial bias, have emphasised the other side of the picture. Wales felt the full force of the collapse of traditional industries after the war-time boom, and this impacted directly on rugby. The Welsh RFU's own takings from internationals were halved during the twenties and they were 'besieged by requests for help from clubs desperately trying to keep afloat. Cross Keys, Ebbw Vale, Pontypool, Blaenavon and Pontypridd sought financial assistance during 1926–7 in the aftermath of the crippling coal stoppage of 1926.' Several clubs closed down completely as the pits laid off thousands of men. At Ebbw Vale despite reduced admission charges gate receipts dwindled almost to nothing when steel-making stopped in 1929, putting 10,000 out of work.[15]

This was socially a very confusing time for Wales. Many of the old anti-English-establishment grievances had been removed (and with them much of the raison d'être of the Liberal Party) as Welsh politics, as in Scotland, lost its distinctively ethnic and religious edges and gave way to the English class-based industrially-dominated tussle. The disestablishment of the Church of Wales in 1920 was the culmination of a series of reforms that had removed drink, religion and landlordism from the centre of the political stage. More than one-quarter of the land had changed hands as the great estates were split up and sold. 'In effect the Welsh had been granted a large measure of "Home Rule" under the aegis of a Welsh-speaking, temperance-minded, non-conformist middle class, with which power and status now resided.'[16] It seems doubtful, however, if this was quite the middle class Rowe Harding had in mind when he criticised the administration of Welsh Rugby as lacking the patronage of 'the leading citizens of our towns . . . men of social standing and business ability' and called for those committee men 'not fitted either by education or experience' to be 'supplanted by men of better social standing and with a better grasp of affairs'.[17]

Whilst these wider issues awaited resolution the situation on the rugby field was being saved by the Glamorgan constabulary and kindred organisations whose recruitment had been greatly assisted by the recession. In 1926 three-quarters of the Welsh pack were policemen. Many civilian players took themselves off: some to jobs in the West Country or the Midlands, reviving the fortunes of clubs like Torquay and Coventry (and eventually forcing a dramatic change in the Welsh RFU's policy over picking exiles); some to the old magnet, the Rugby League. The exodus began in 1921 when Wigan signed Cardiff's 17-year-old full back, Jim Sullivan. He was an immediate attraction and became one of the League's greatest players. By 1927–8 there were enough Welsh stars in the League to form an international side capable of challenging England, including Rees and Evans, the half-back pair who helped Swinton equal Huddersfield's feat of winning all four cups. Conversely, the recession meant that the Rugby League was no more successful in gaining a foothold in Wales than it had ever been. Pontypridd's attempt to start a club in 1926 was an utter failure.

In its north country heartland professional rugby had handled the challenge of soccer well in the boom years. After a lucrative tour of Australia and New Zealand in the summer of 1920 – 34,000 saw the 'Test match' at Auckland – there were big crowds everywhere at home in 1920–1, and the following season when the Australians toured Britain the three Tests had average gates of 25,000. In the 1924–5 tour of Australia the first Test alone brought in £45,000. All of this helped the domestic competition. In 1922 30,000 watched Wigan beat Oldham in the championship play-off, and the League declared a profit on the season of £15,000. In 1924 a record 41,831 saw Wigan win the Cup (again against Oldham) with record receipts of £3,714. Wigan were the pacemakers. This small town between the two great soccer conurbations of Liverpool and Manchester had two Rugby League teams, though the lesser one, Wigan Highfield, composed largely of local miners, had a precarious existence and took on various guises over the years. The senior club had the Huddersfield secret of mixing local and exotic talent: their early post-war side had two South African Rugby Union stars as well as Sullivan in the backs.

It was Wigan, too, in 1927, in the keener competitive atmosphere that came with recession, who proposed that the League drop the residential qualification for overseas players. (Australian tours had been suspended for a while and New Zealand were no longer financially significant, home or away.) The League agreed – despite the protests of the Australians – and they came in their dozens at just the right time. There was no room for expansion, however. As well as Pontypridd Carlisle came and went, lasting only two months in 1928. The big clubs that could afford to speculate prospered but many small ones foundered, sustained only by hand-outs from the Rugby League's profits on tours and cup competitions. The constant vision of expanding southwards remained, however, and it was even more attractive as the south-east's relatively prosperity became more marked. No doubt this influenced the Rugby

League's bold decision to stage the 1929 Cup Final at Wembley. The gamble paid off, in that 41,500 paid £5,600 to see Wigan beat Dewsbury, but most of them were trippers from the north, the beginning of an annual ritual that afforded much amusement to the sophisticates of the capital, but encouraged none of them to add a northern idiosyncrasy to their range of leisure pursuits.

Wembley wizardry

Wembley Stadium was the wonder of the age. It was built by a syndicate, at the staggering cost of £750,000, as part of the Empire Exhibition held in the vicinity in 1924, but only after the syndicate had concluded a 21-year agreement with the FA to hold the Cup Final there. The first turf was cut by the Duke of York in January 1922, and work was completed four days before it was required for the match between Bolton Wanderers and West Ham United in April 1923. Its capacity, 127,OOO, seemed enormous, but the unusually warm weather, curiosity to see the new stadium and the presence – still a rarity – of a London club in the final brought upwards of 200,000 eager to get in. Advance tickets had been sold only for seats in the stands and the great mass was expected to pay at the turnstiles, a time-consuming formality many by-passed. Barriers were broken down and by the time the King arrived some 10,000 had invaded the pitch. His Majesty's arrival and the dutiful singing of the national anthem that followed had a calming effect, but it still took police and officials forty minutes to clear enough space for the game to start.

In the aftermath various interpretations were put on what took place. Some saw it as the inevitable result of drink and the immoderate working-class passion for a sordid professional game. The Labour MP Jack Jones suggested inadequate and discriminatory policing: 'They can turn out 900 strong for a Royal wedding, but when it comes to the *people's* amusement there is, of course, a difference.'[18] A Scottish colleague repaid old ethnic scores by the witty suggestion that the authorities should consider transferring the event to Glasgow in order that it may be properly conducted.[19] The general, and rather romantic, impression that has survived is of an over-exuberant minority, restrained by general good sense and by the patient work of a handful of police, notably Constable George Storey, on a white horse, gently persuading people back to the terraces.

For the West Ham fans neither the disturbance nor even Bolton's victory could spoil their pleasure at their team's achievement, for it was part of the fulfilment of a dream. The team, promoted to the First Division only that season, was no more local than any making its way in the League could hope to be, but it had not acquired the cosmopolitan sheen of the likes of Tottenham or Chelsea: it could not afford to, with support drawn from an area with a high proportion of trades – dockers, carpenters, fitters – whose wages were tumbling in the recession. But the manager and trainer were both locals who had been with the club since 1900. Their selling of the West Ham-born star, Syd Puddefoot – to a Scottish club, Falkirk, of all things – for a record £5.000, had been highly unpopular, but in retrospect became an extra source of pride, an example of the obstacles an East End club had to overcome. The great Cup run and subsequent relative prosperity were to give the management an undeserved reputation for foresight in preferring to bring on young players. Meanwhile on the Sunday after the match, supporters and players attended a local Congregational church to hear a sermon on the theme that the essential things in soccer were the essential things in life – discipline, unselfishness and team spirit. 'Team spirit had saved the country in the dark days of war and would bring them through the peace which seemed even more difficult than the war.'[20]

The mysterious allegiance of League soccer fans to their teams was as tribal as that of rugger men but both more impassioned and less palpable. It depended essentially on a craving for success and recognition. Hence the honour of a nondescript part of London or Birmingham, composed mainly of rows of unbeautiful houses, was defended by a group of paid players, gathered haphazard from anywhere, putting it across a rival group of mercenaries. It is hard to imagine an Etonian, say, getting much pleasure from an Old Etonians' victory assisted by three of four Harrovians and a couple of Wykehamists hired for the purpose. But League soccer clubs took over a ground and gave it an identity, and their teams' performances conferred lustre on the surrounding town seemingly by osmosis. Other kinds of allegiance, such as national, sectarian or ethnic, had to be adjusted accordingly.

It was harder for Scottish club fans to adjust their allegiances to accommodate English players than the other way round. Poor Syd Puddefoot, for instance, confided to the *Evening Standard* his disgust at his reception in Falkirk. His team-mates were unco-operative: 'Frequently I have stood half an hour without kicking the ball.' The local press were hypercritical: 'It's a bit discouraging after a game like this to read that "the £5,000 Englishman wasn't worth five shillings to his side" '. But the spectators were the most upsetting: 'You may find it difficult to believe but twice this season I have leapt over the railings after spectators who have called me names no man could endure . . . My offence, so far as I can see, is an English accent.'[21] The flow of players in the other direction, reflecting the greater prosperity of the game and of society in England, was much greater and taken more for granted by the English. In 1926 the *Athletic News* was commenting, 'In little more than a season ten fully-fledged internationals, two inter-League players . . . and a number of inter-national trialists have passed into English football.'[22] Over 70 Scots of this calibre had crossed the border since the war, amid mounting resentment at the English and growing controversy about whether the 'Anglos' should be picked for the national side. There was more of this in the committee rooms and the newspapers than on the terraces, though. All would have dropped the Anglos like a shot if they could have been sure of Scotland winning without them, but few wanted to give England the extra satisfaction of beating teams depleted by English gold and there were fierce disputes between the Scottish FA and the Football League about the reluctance of English clubs to release Scottish players for Saturday internationals.

Irish soccer was disturbed by politics much more than rugger was. Serious trouble began after the Dublin club Shelbourne had defied the Belfast-based Irish FA's instruction to travel north for a replay in the charged atmosphere of 1921. When the IFA insisted, all the Southern clubs withdrew from its jurisdiction. Unlike rugger there was no Trinity-led cross-border bonding of the middle classes, and in 1922 the Free State formed its own association.[23] It was not recognised by the British Associations and Northern Ireland's FA continued to use the term 'Ireland' for its teams. In 1923, after much wrangling, the new Southern association was given Dominion status, grudgingly agreed to call itself Eire and made its first international appearance in the 1924 Olympics. For the British Associations 'international' still myopically tended to mean 'between the four home countries'. European encounters remained casual and infrequent and more distant ones non-existent. They did not rejoin FIFA until 1924, and then began a protracted argument about the definition of amateurism that led to their withdrawal again in 1928.

Kircher, whose study tried to indicate a path along which Germany could follow Britain as 'a nation of sportsmen', thoroughly supported their stand. He was not impressed by the events of the previous 'sixty or eighty years during which England, with a vastly increased population, applied capitalistic mass-production to an essentially individualistic activity, and allowed professionalism to overshadow amateur performance'. He noted approvingly that 'the tendency seems to be on the wane and amateurism is coming into its own again'.[24] Another 60-odd years later the phenomenon may seem like the last kick of a dying mule, but there was still a bit of life left in it. Even the quintessentially professional world of soccer retained a top layer of amateur government, its values strengthened by the war, yet ready to take advantage of the romanticisation of 'the people's game' and eager to make its realities conform to its powerful new mythology. Though the pre-war talk of spectatorship and its effect on the national physique had tended to brand soccer as a principal enemy, this in fact was the team game most people played. Britain had won the war and the soccer fans had played their part in it. All that was needed was a re-assertion of the old amateur ideal.

While the fans flocked back to watch the hirelings the FA lost no opportunity to emphasise that only a very tiny proportion of soccer clubs employed even a single professional. And though a handful of schools might have taken up rugger there were thousands, including many new ones, playing soccer. There had been over 15,000 clubs and 250,000 players even before the war and the numbers had more than doubled by the end of the twenties. But if the 6,000 professionals were only about 1% of the total many of the rest would not have qualified as amateur by strict ARA or even AAA definition. Such refinements were unimportant to almost all of them. If a man did not play full-time it mattered little whether he received a pound or two for his services or in 'tea-money' as was customary in works or colliery teams. By the same token true gentlemen amateurs were in exceedingly short supply, especially at the highest levels. This was of great concern both to the soccer-playing schools, seeking adult outlets comparable to those the rugger men enjoyed, and to the FA, seeking social tone.

The Corinthians, once the flagship, were foundering. Slow to get over the failure of the AFA, they were badly in need of a new role. Few people understood (or, understanding, were impressed by) their refusal to take part in the FA Cup, and they found it harder and harder to recruit new players of the right calibre and social outlook. Their greatest player of modern times, Max Woosnam, a Cambridge man of impeccable credentials, had left them to play for Chelsea and Manchester United, with whom he achieved full international honours in 1922. The writing on the wall was becoming clear, but they had been too long working out what it meant. When they decided to enter the Cup in 1922 the FA, in acknowledgement of their former glory, traditional aversion from pre-season training and remaining social value, allowed them to delay entry until the third round. They took over the old Crystal Palace ground and for a while were a great attraction. They had average gates of 30,000 for their Cup-ties, with a record 60,000 for a game against Millwall. But they were unable to produce results to match the expectations and the support dwindled away.

Another facet of the FA's amateurism was its ready acceptance of the traditional gentlemanly duty of safeguarding the spiritual and moral welfare of the lower orders. The tide of religion was receding in Britain, but it left pools of conventional behaviour behind, and one of them was Sunday observance – always a doctrine that fell hardest on those who could find least time for recreation during the week. The FA allowed no Sunday play and when the LCC proposed to permit football matches in its parks in 1922 reminded them of this and the proposal was withdrawn. (The LCC at the same time extended the ban to organised cricket and hockey matches and in egalitarian spirit forbade those playing golf and lawn tennis to employ 'caddies or scouts . . . respectively'.[25]) Similarly the FA was assiduous in trying to rid the game of gambling. A pre-war FA commission, observing that 'scarcely a mill or factory or workshop' did not harbour agents for football pools, had concluded that they were a serious menace to the game, and a Parliamentary Bill to purge them was only postponed by the war. In 1920, with the support of the Football League, the FA lobbied for a new Bill, but its pleasure at the apparently successful outcome did not last long. The government, as in racing, drew a (largely social) distinction between ready money and credit transactions. Under the Ready Money Football Act of 1920 credit betting therefore remained legal, and the clarification of the law in fact stimulated the emergence of the great modern football pools empires.

No-one paid much attention to the puny beginnings of the Liverpool firm of Littlewood's (1922, capital £150) started by a telegraph clerk John Moores and two partners. It was a postal business in which odds were worked out afterwards – adding to the thrill – and accounts were settled in arrears to satisfy the law. The firm was in debt at the end of 1923–4 and it was two years before receipts exceeded £2,000, but thereafter the enterprise took off, and was followed by numerous imitators.[26] The FA did its best to stop them and though receiving no help from the law continued the fight by making sure that players and officials were not tainted and by sternly forbidding clubs to conduct lotteries for fund-raising purposes. This was of doubtful benefit to the game, but it did wonders for the reputation of the assiduous guardians of soccer respectability at the FA. The knighting of J. C. Clegg in 1927 was the first in a series of accolades; the opening of Wembley was a further step back up the social ladder. As one perceptive journalist put it, 'In the beginning the Cup Final was an assembly of amateur players and public schools people. Then, as the provinces challenged and professionalism arrived, democracy entered the arena. Now Wembley, with its grand parade and VIPs and high-priced seats, has re-introduced the social touch of the early days at the Oval.'[27]

The Football League were also anxious to seek respectability. They were equally opposed to gambling and stern in their condemnation of corruption. As they threw out Leeds City, the President, John McKenna, had said, 'We will have no nonsense. The football stables must be cleansed.'[28] They proved better at window dressing than stable-cleansing. But with many new clubs trying to get in the League no longer wished to be seen as brash aggressive provincials, constantly at odds with the gentlemen of the FA. They took a further step from northern sectarianism in 1920, admitting Cardiff City into the Second Division and translating the rest of the Southern League into a new Third Division. This brought in three more Welsh clubs, Swansea, Newport and Merthyr but left some English clubs with at least equal claims fretting in the Midland and North Eastern Leagues. The Football League's response to the complaints was to create a parallel Third Division (North) of equal size. Not surprisingly, since the top two Divisions were predominantly already northern, this meant scraping the barrel and eight of those who came in subsequently dropped out again. Nevertheless the arrangement remained in force for 36 years, saving greatly on travelling expenses.

The creation of the Third Division (South) at least ensured some southern honours in an otherwise barren decade. The First Division champions in the twenties were Burnley, Liverpool (2), Huddersfield (3), Newcastle, Everton and Sheffield Wednesday (2); the Second Division went to Birmingham, Nottingham Forest, Notts. County, Leeds United, Leicester, Sheffield Wednesday, Middlesborough (2), Manchester City and Blackpool. The most notable northern success was that of Huddersfield. This was a town in which employment was severely affected by the slump in wool prices after the early post-war boom, and which was historically addicted to Rugby League. The RL team faltered slightly and was now over-shadowed by a soccer team built from nothing. The builder was Herbert Chapman, who persuaded the authorities to lift his ban in 1920. Buying players shrewdly and thriftily he created a team that won the FA Cup in 1922 and the League Championship three years in a row from 1923–4 to 1925–6.

The FA Cup was more open than the League, but of the 20 finalists only Tottenham, West Ham, Portsmouth and Arsenal (2) came from the south of England. The most remarkable interlopers were Cardiff City, who were at Wembley twice, beating Arsenal on the second occasion in 1927. These, briefly, were glory years for Welsh soccer. Cardiff reached the First Division in 1921, lost the title to Huddersfield only on goal average in 1924 and stayed up quite comfortably until 1929 when their relegation plunged Wales even further into depression, except perhaps in narrow-minded rugger circles. With Swansea reaching the Second Division in 1925 it looked as though the process of Anglicisation was to be completed by the surrender of their national game. Kircher did not even mention Welsh rugby, but he had clearly seen Cardiff's Cup final and he drew racial as well as social conclusions from his experience of soccer crowds: 'The Welsh colliers and dockers are the most excitable people in Great Britain and local patriotism runs high . . . it would be an interesting experiment to see a cup final played at Cardiff, especially if Cardiff lost to a London team, and, according to Welsh opinion unfairly.'[29]

Kircher appears only to have seen Scotsmen on golf courses, where he found them – even the working classes – compliant to English notions of good form in such things as restricting their conversation to the game itself. (He contrasted this with the habits of Lloyd George whose Welshness led him into notorious error.)[30] So we are spared his comments on the encounters between Rangers and Celtic, sharpened by religious differences and re-enacting the

Irish situation, and the provincial replicas of these tussles. That Rangers won the League eight times to Celtic's twice doubtless helped assuage the pain over the Free State's defection and avoided undue triumphalism from the Catholics. Nevertheless in 1925 the *Sporting Chronicle* suggested, without much fear of contradiction, 'Disorderliness has been the big problem of Scottish football since the war.'[31] In the English conurbations, each with a share of immigrant Celts, disorders were only less because of the greater dilution of the emotion. As Kircher saw it, soccer crowds 'show that the English are not all refined. The masses are . . . un-English enough to shout vulgarly, to be happily, drunkenly enthusiastic without definite cause.'[32]

In fact to the fans the cause was definite enough; the victory of our team over theirs. The possessive adjective was flexible enough to suit any occasion. Rangers and Celtic supporters suspended their private war annually for the encounters against England. Many paid one shilling a week to the Wembley Club over many months to save up for the away matches. For them one of the great moments in history was the 5–1 victory of the 1928 'Wembley Wizards' avenging a rare defeat at Hampden Park the previous year, an astonishing score in a usually dourly-fought contest. Interestingly, the Scottish hero, then and throughout the decade, was Alan Morton of Rangers, known variously as the 'wee blue devil' or 'the wee society man', a dapper, teetotal, university type who wore a bowler hat and carried an umbrella to away matches. Fortunately he was not an 'Anglo', or these idiosyncrasies might not have been so readily accepted, even in a genius. Middle-class loyalties like those of Morton were becoming a rarity. Three of the Wembley goals were scored by Alex Jackson of Aberdeen signed by Herbert Chapman for Huddersfield in 1925. And another 'wee man' in the line-up was Hughie Gallagher who had claims to be the greatest centre-forward in the islands, better even than England's record-breaking 'Dixie' Dean of Everton. Gallagher had transferred from Airdrie to Newcastle in 1925 for a fee of £6,500, quickly becoming the idol of Tyneside but blotting his copy-book with Scottish fans in the 1929–30 season when he refused a Scottish cap to help Newcastle fight against relegation.

The reality of professional soccer loyalties – clubs' and players' – was emphasised at the season's end when Gallagher transferred to Chelsea, quickly followed by Alex Jackson. 'Was transferred' is perhaps nearer the mark, for the retain-and-transfer system allowed players little say in the matter, although star performers could be reconciled to otherwise unpalatable moves by undercover payments beyond the authorised 'signing-on' fee. Rich clubs like Chelsea and Arsenal were clearly able to manipulate the system to their advantage, but it survived as a manifestly mutually beneficial device: it kept the poorer clubs alive through the fees they got for players they had discovered and developed, and enabled them to provide enough opposition to make the competition interesting without turning it into a lottery that destroyed the established basis of success, which was the money collected at the turnstiles. It also helped curb the bargaining power of the star players and enabled the clubs, acting in concert through the League, to enforce a maximum wage. In 1922 footballers, like most other wage-earners, took a cut in pay when the League introduced the £8 winter, £6 summer maxima that were to remain in force for the rest of the inter-war period.

Sir Henry Norris, the ambitious chairman of Arsenal, was extremely concerned at the inflationary spiralling of transfer fees, and had publicly declared his determination not to spend more than £1,000 on an individual player. The results had been disappointing and, inaugurating the trend that saw managers not players as the key to success, he had persuaded Herbert Chapman to leave Huddersfield before the third of their championship wins. There was no retain-and-transfer system for managers and Chapman's salary was reputedly £2,000 a year. Ironically the first effect was a rapid change in Arsenal's policy over players' transfers. At the League's annual meeting in 1926 they proposed a self-denying ordinance but Chapman had already begun a programme of spending that cost the club £25,000 in his first two years. Early in 1927 Chelsea's match-programme commented, 'The outcry against inflated transfer fees has been loud and long, and some of the loudest in denunciation have been the foremost in the open cheque-book rush.' Arsenal's reply was, 'If insanity is to continue in this matter, then we will be insane with the rest.' Later that year Norris was suspended for making undercover payments. He sued the FA for libel but lost his case and was replaced as chairman. Chapman continued, however. In 1928 Arsenal paid nearly £11,000 to Bolton for David Jack and in 1929 £9,000 to Preston for the Scottish international Alex James.[33] Soccer glory had come at last to the south.

Cricket and the Bolsheviks

There was no tribal division in the summer game like that between rugger and soccer. Cricket's roots were pre-industrial and its devotees included more of the middle classes (and indeed the aristocracy) and attracted fewer of the urban working class than soccer, and even fewer in Scotland, Ireland and most of Wales. This process of natural social self-selection meant that cricket-lovers were a quieter breed. After the strident vulgarities of the winter all was now dignity and decorum. It was as if some rural Dr Jekyll replaced the raffish Mr Hyde as a sporting idol as soon as the spring purgation rites of the Cup final had been performed. In fact the idea of cricket probably appealed to the average Englishman more than the actual game: it was expected of him. 'If an Englishman is asked what is the most typical national game,' wrote Kircher, 'he will not say football, but cricket. This does not mean that cricket is the most popular game . . . but [that it] is pre-eminently English.'[34] (He could be forgiven for not noticing that the Welsh had joined the county championship in 1921, for they went under the name of Glamorgan, a point that underlined his substantive argument.)

Kircher was astonished at the great crowds at Lord's for games that lasted 'no less than three whole days . . . Anyone who is neither an Englishman nor a cricketer finds this slow-motion film tedious after half-an-hour.'[35] So, in fact, did most English people. The average run of county matches drew pitifully small crowds and for most enthusiasts it was the scores and accounts in the newspapers that satisfied the appetite. Even the early broadcasters considered cricket too slow for running commentaries. Yet newspaper interest was avid, and it could extend across barriers that Kircher thought uncrossable. The Irish, he reckoned, were certainly not enthusiasts. But during the Test matches in Australia in 1924–5 a Dublin writer commented, 'I have been amazed during the past few days to discover how great is the interest taken in Ireland in cricket. Ever since the Test match began all sorts of people have been telephoning at all hours of the day asking for the latest score. They could not wait to buy a paper when they finished work. Their minds were in Dublin but their hearts were far away in Sydney.'[36]

The answer was partly that schoolboys, at all types of school, and an increasing number of girls, were brought up on the game and retained a childish interest in the doings of their counties and countries (with England as the sole focus for 'home' allegiance in Tests) long after they had ceased to be actively involved. Watchers of first-class cricket were by definition the more leisured, for the game's patterns were congealed in the pre-industrial dream-world of MCC, an exercise in institutionalised nostalgia that appealed to enough of the people that mattered to keep it alive. Fred Root, who played in the Birmingham League in 1919 and 1920 while qualifying for Worcestershire, was critical – after his retirement – of the system, which, he believed, prevented cricket from becoming a really popular game. 'League cricket has proved to me that if cricket is made attractive, it receives plenty of support from the man in the street.'[37] He cited the final of the Priestley Cup played in September on Bradford Park Avenue's ground, when the takings greatly exceeded those of neighbouring Bradford City, then (briefly) in the First Division. Across the Pennines Haslingden, champions of the Lancashire League, were fêted: 'Headed by the Borough Prize Band, the team drove through the town with the cup in a char-a-banc. About twelve private cars with searchlights and a large number of people on foot accompanied the procession.'[38]

By contrast the county championship, was 'not a competitive championship

185

at all' with unequal conditions and endless arguments about the best method of deciding it. Root would have gingered this up, with penalties for slow play and all manner of innovations, bringing in an English Cup on the lines of soccer.[39] In the Leagues the professionals were looked up to rather than down upon by the amateurs, pay was generous and collections were taken to reward good performances. The county system on the other hand was patriarchal. Wages were kept down, not as in soccer by the transfer system – Root approved of that, slave market or not – but by rigid residential qualifications. And yet, once county cricket got going again the stars left the League and returned to servitude. Root himself, badly paid and playing for a county always on the edge of extinction, was pursued by League scouts in 1927, offering him £600 for the season, but resisted the temptation. County cricket and the Test matches were the pinnacle of the game and no-one had the power, the desire or the temerity to promote an alternative.

The grip of the old order was astonishing in view of the precarious state of the county clubs' finances. All but a handful – the five or six who monopolised the championship – lived from hand-to mouth. In 1924 Essex launched a public appeal for £1,000 to save them from extinction. The same year Warwickshire, more enterprising, raised £3,500. Assisted by such schemes, and occasional cheques from wealthy members, the clubs survived, at the price of further subordination to a haphazard system of patronage redolent of the eighteenth century. Fred Root was glowing in his praise of Sir Julian Cahn who made gifts to county clubs that took his fancy – first his native Nottinghamshire, to whom he gave an up-to-date winter practice shed and other amenities, and later to Leicestershire where his hunting aspirations took him. He had two grounds of his own, one at West Bridgford, Nottingham, the other in front of his stately home, Stanford Hall near Loughborough. He had a first-class side, many of its members employed in his furniture business, and was always ready to help out Nottinghamshire by supplying a player in times of need. He played himself 'in a manner of speaking', as one of his kinder critics put it.[40]

Only four counties won the championship – Middlesex (2) Lancashire (3) Yorkshire (4) and Nottinghamshire, the surprise winners of 1929, with two fast bowlers Larwood and Voce a deadly combination. Middlesex, the winners in 1920 and 1921, still had five or six amateurs, including new men such as the precocious G. T. S. Stevens and ex-officers like F. T. Mann and Nigel Haig, but after this brave flourish the honours went north where Lancashire was now as sternly professional as Yorkshire. The success of both in attracting crowds, although their cricket lacked the bravura of the golden age, showed that winning was what mattered to the public, whatever the mythology said. Not that the professionals lacked style – it was just that they played the percentages more than the amateurs, who could afford the luxury of heroic failure. Even this was changing as 'shamateurism' became more blatant than ever. An applicant for a post with Worcestershire asked £1,000 a year for acting as secretary in return for which he would give his cricketing services free. Genuine amateurs were a rarity and good ones who could afford to play regularly almost non-existent.

For the pros, playing for a successful county meant not only the prospect of a decent wage (Yorkshire came nearest the standards of soccer) but a better chance of selection for England. Tours, growing in frequency as more countries came into the Test match arena, solved the problem of what to do in winter. Most important of all, the county he played for could greatly affect the size of benefit a player could expect after substantial service. And it was the benefit that made the cricketer's lot bearable, especially after 1921 when Jim Seymour of Kent, assisted by Lord Harris, secured exemption from paying tax on his. Roy Kilner's £4,000 in 1927 was exceptional even for Yorkshire, but their players did consistently better than those of the struggling counties. Fred Root, good enough to play three times for England, had to press Worcestershire hard for £500, paid in instalments. In 1925 when he took a record 207 wickets for the county a local newspaper raised enough money to buy him a gold watch and chain, a £100 war bond and a piece of painted porcelain. In actual wages he averaged under £300 a year. As the recession deepened the county proposed a cut of 10% – having discovered that four counties paid lower rates than Worcestershire – but this appears not to have been actually implemented.[41]

P. F. Warner, aged 47, was sufficiently recovered from the strains of the War Office to lead Middlesex to their 1920 championship, wearing his Harlequins cap to indicate his fitness to lead. Captaincy, an amateur perquisite, was worth advertising, particularly to umpires, whose livelihood depended on the collective good will of the county captains. When J. W. H. T. Douglas eventually lost the job with Essex in 1928 he reckoned it made a significant difference to both his batting and bowling averages. Warner used his diplomatic skills to consolidate his position as an MCC committee man whilst remaining cricket correspondent of the *Morning Post*. He brought Harlequins' values to his assignment as editor of the *Cricketer*, a new periodical with the reassuringly familiar philosophy announced in its first issue: 'Cricket . . . as Tom Brown has told us in the best of all school stories, is an institution and the *habeas corpus* of every boy of British birth.'[42]

Preserving this precious heritage meant defending the game against the anarchical trends apparent in society. Even the editor of *Wisden*, appalled by the mayhem caused by Warwick Armstrong's visiting Australians, had wavered in his faith: 'I cannot help thinking that if, when the fixtures were arranged in December 1920, our authorities had had any idea of the Australian strength, something in the nature of systematic preparation for the Test matches would have been decided upon.'[43] The lack of system extended to an inordinate delay in choosing a captain for the first Test. This was not, Warner assured his readers, the result of 'a brilliant Bolshevik move on the part of the players selected' to 'choose their own captain and play under him, or else loot the pavilion – any pavilion – seize the till, confiscate any portable property and burn the buildings'.[44] The selectors' belated choice, the combative Douglas, fresh from leading England to a 5–0 defeat in Australia over the winter, would have been just the man to handle any such insurrection. His team, deprived of Hobbs and Hearne through illness and injury and sorely missing the churlish Barnes, did less well against the fast bowling of Gregory and McDonald, losing the first two Tests. His replacement, the Hon. Lionel Tennyson, displaying aristocratic panache and innocence of the rules, lost another and drew the rest. England called on 30 players in the series, but it was left to the maverick Archie Maclaren, now 50, to do what he had been claiming he could do all season, and assemble a team of amateurs who could beat Armstrong's side.[45]

The *Cricketer* thus faced a scene of disarray which even Warner's bland optimism could not entirely conceal. At the season's end one of his contributors, also a Harlequins rugger man, attributed much of the blame to populism: 'too much was made of what "the crowd" thought. The crowd which so often applauds the wrong thing, and which, time after time, exhibits a complete ignorance of the laws and usages of the game.'[46] Lord Harris, now in his seventies but still not to be ignored at MCC, saw the decline as part of a general social malaise, characterised by the disregard of both footloose amateurs and insubordinate professionals for such safeguards of rectitude as the residence qualifications. The following year he wrote an article refuting charges of excessive zeal and – Heaven forfend – partisanship. (One of his interventions had been in the case of the young Hammond (W. R.) who had signed for Gloucestershire though born in Harris's fiefdom, Kent.) Having disposed in short order of these baseless accusations, Harris, under the startling heading 'EFFECTS OF BOLSHEVISM', placed the disruptive elements amongst the forces seeking to undermine civilisation: 'Bolshevism is rampant and seeks to abolish all laws and rules, and this year cricket has not escaped its attack.'[47]

The menace reasserted itself in June 1924. Cecil Parkin, the eccentric Lancashire and England spin bowler (who had once invited demolition at the hands of his captain Johnny Douglas by saying 'You bowl them in for an hour or so and then I'll bowl them *out*') had been seduced by a popular newspaper into writing an article that included criticism of the current England captain,

A. E. R. Gilligan. Warner called for an unreserved apology and looked to Lancashire for action, and when nothing happened warned Parkin that if he did not make amends 'the cricket world (would) regard him as the first cricketing Bolshevist, and (would) have none of him'.[48] Nevertheless there were regrettable signs that the cancer had spread, particularly in the north of England. The Cricketer' s correspondence columns were soon besmirched by 'A Lancastrian sextette' complaining of southern bias amongst the selectors. Worse a Balliol man not only declared Parkin's complaints justified but saw him as the victim of mistaken policies in 'the self-constituted headquarters of cricket' which preferred Gilligan to the cerebral P. G. H. Fender, captain of the more plebeian Surrey. Warner published the letter, as 'fair play' demanded, but added, 'We are pained and grieved that an Oxonian should be responsible for such biased ignorance and such wrong-headed and fantastic ideas.'[49] No-one was surprised when he turned out to be a northerner.

Lord Hawke was also at the centre of a controversy in which Warner felt compelled to intervene. Hawke's unbuttoned after-dinner utterances provided good copy for journalists but were an embarrassment to his friends. At Yorkshire's annual dinner in January, 1924, he paid tribute to the modern professional. This, though taken by a paranoid purist to be 'a slightly veiled sneer at the amateur cricketer', was doubtless intended as no more than a sneaky way of drawing attention to his own selfless devotion to the material and moral standing of his men, of which he was inordinately proud. This, at any rate, was the basis of Warner's defence: 'It is almost entirely due to him that the professional cricketer of to-day is the smart, civil excellent fellow we know him to be.'[50]

After the following year's dinner Hawke went too far in clarification, crying emotionally 'Pray Heaven no professional may ever captain England!' He had been provoked by another article by the Bolshevik Parkin suggesting that Jack Hobbs should be captain. Warner's apologia in the February 1925 issue begged a few questions: 'What no doubt Lord Hawke meant was that it will be a bad day for England when no amateur is fit to play for England.' But the real villain was Parkin 'pirouetting into the limelight' again. Warner made clear that he considered Parkin's remarks offensive, not because he was a professional but because they were 'entirely contrary to the spirit of the best of games'. On the substantive issue, though, he reminded readers that captaincy involved duties off the field as well as on and these responsibilities were 'better shouldered by an amateur than by a professional'.[51]

Poor Parkin was easily put in his place. Lancashire dispensed with his services in 1926. And the rising generation of professionals chose not to rock the boat but to catch the fair wind of prosperity that was beginning to blow for those with talent. There were more tours and Test matches as West Indies and

New Zealand joined the circle, more opportunities for overseas coaching in the winter, and in the ever-growing publicity and commercialism that surrounded the game, more endorsements of everything from equipment to tobacco and more fees for 'ghosted' articles. Hobbs himself, well into his forties, was too genuinely modest and unassuming to be other than embarrassed by those who proposed him for the England captaincy and instead set an example of unflinching loyalty that so impressed the establishment that long after, in a different age, he became the first professional to gain a knighthood. Even his new young opening partner, Herbert Sutcliffe, a very different personality serving under Yorkshire captains of staggering ineptitude, drew back from crossing the threshold when opportunity offered.

Sutcliffe had been so unmindful of the proprieties as to alter his vowel sounds. The caste system required northern professionals to appear oafish, wear thick boots and speak like music-hall turns. The mere mention of places like Wigan or Pudsey, Sutcliffe's birthplace, was a sure way to raise a laugh amongst the post-war generation of writers. Not all were university men from the south. Neville Cardus at the *Manchester Guardian*, who by 1923 was already lamenting the demise of the cricketer-artist in favour of the canny utilitarian, led the way with a blend of nostalgia and snobbery that founded a new school of cricket-writing.[52] For him the 'advent into cricket, and into the Yorkshire XI of all places, of a Herbert Sutcliffe was a sign of the times. The old order was not changing, it was going'.[53] Some of the comments from the amateurs themselves merely reproduced the fashionable regional stereotypes. Thus R. C. Robertson-Glasgow of Oxford and Somerset, 'He didn't look like Yorkshire; even less a Yorkshire Number One. Pudsey was his home, but his style was not Pudsey. He had easy off-side strokes and a disdainful hook.'[54] These were the prerogatives of gentlemen, after all. Other Oxonians were positively snide. I. A. R. Peebles, a Warner protégé, revealed Sutcliffe's real offence. 'He emerged from the First World War an officer, convinced that he could take his place in any society, and to this end took pains to acquire the accents of Mayfair and Oxford rather than the broad vowels of Pudsey. This attracted a certain amount of ridicule which might have disconcerted a lesser man, but, his mind made up, he was never to be deflected.'[55]

Sutcliffe, imitation Oxonian or not, was an inspiration to young Yorkshire cricketers like Bill Bowes: 'There was something in his walk, his carriage, that compelled attention. Here was no ordinary man . . . And professionalism was very important to him.'[56] Sutcliffe believed strongly that Hobbs should be the England captain. He himself could have been captain of Yorkshire by becoming a 'shamateur'. But he was more concerned with upholding the dignity of his profession. He believed, like any lawyer or Harley Street physician, that this included reaping its rewards, but like them saw this not in simple material terms but as seeking recognition of their art. ' "Lord Hawke lifted professional cricket from there to there",' Sutcliffe told Bowes, raising his hand from knee to shoulder level. ' "Professional cricketers lifted it to there", he continued raising his hand above his head, "and even Lord Hawke always wanted it back again".'[57] In 1928 the absurdity of its position in persisting with inferior amateur captains brought the Yorkshire committee to offer the leadership to Sutcliffe whilst allowing him to remain a professional. The offer was sent by cable when he was touring South Africa. It came from the secretary but significantly Sutcliffe replied to Lord Hawke thanking the committee for the honour but respectfully declining.[58] The Sutcliffe episode is the more remarkable in that after this excursion the Yorkshire committee re-erected the barriers, retaining amateur captains for another forty years.

The feudal spirit was generally upheld in spite of such unwelcome reminders of the real world outside cricket. Warner continued his progress along the corridors of power, becoming chairman of selectors in 1926, in spite of the view – 'in certain quarters' as he put it[59] – that this was inconsistent with his journalistic activities. His tenure was not a happy one, creating immense bad feeling on the part of A. W. Carr, whom he ditched as captain when things were going badly in the Tests, in a sanctimonious fashion that stuck in Carr's throat. MCC threw out the entire selection committee at the end of the season. Warner commented afterwards in his disingenuous way 'so far as I personally was concerned there were no hurt feelings. That we had had something of a raw deal was, however, the opinion of many.'[60]

Nevertheless he had a point. England's feat in winning back the Ashes, after 19 tests without a win (achieved with the aid of the arch-professional Wilfred Rhodes, brought back at the age of 49, and masterful batting by Hobbs and Sutcliffe) was a chauvinistic delight. And Carr's replacement as captain, the gay cavalier A. P. F. Chapman who went on to win the 1928–9 series in Australia seemed to ensure a bright future for Test cricket played in the right spirit. He was said by a fellow amateur to radiate 'a debonair quality which immediately captured the imagination'.[61] A young Australian called Bradman saw him differently: 'In my first Test match England, though leading by nearly 400, went in again and left us over 700 to attempt in our last innings with two men out of action.'[62] He stored up the memory for the future.

Notes

1 J. E. C. Welldon, *Contemporary Review*, October, 1927, quoted in J. A. Mangan, *Athleticism in the Victorian and Edwardian Public Schools*, Cambridge , 1981, p. 202.
2 R. Kircher, *Fair Play*, London, 1928, p. 4.
3 H. J. Savage, *Games and Sports in British Universities*, Carnegie Foundation, New York, 1926.
4 Kircher, *Fair Play*, pp. 71–2.

5 57% between 1922 and 1931, E. Dunning and K. Sheard, *Barbarians, Gentlemen Players*, London, 1979, pp. 236, 239.
6 U. A. Titley and R. McWhirter, *Centenary History of the Rugby Football Union*, London, 1970, p. 138.
7 Kircher, *Fair Play*, p. 71.
8 D. R. Gent, "Rugby Football', in *Aldin Book of Sports and Games*, London, 1933, p. 45.
9 *Centenary History*, pp. 143–4.
10 E. W. Swanton, *Sort of a Cricket Person*, London, 1972, p. 112, re-telling a familiar story.
11 H. B. T. Wakelam, *The Game Goes On*, London, 1936, pp. 165 ff.
12 See H. Kearney, *The British Isles*, Cambridge, 1989, Chapter Eleven.
13 T. West, *The Bold Collegians*, Dublin, 1991, pp. 64–5.
14 Quoted in Dunning and Sheard, *Barbarians*, p. 224.
15 G. Williams, 'Rugby Football' in T. Mason (ed.), *Sport in Britain*, Cambridge, 1989, p. 328.
16 Kearney, *British Isles*, p. 205.
17 Dunning and Sheard, *Barbarians*, p. 223.
18 C. P. Korr, 'A Different Kind of Success', in R. J. Holt (ed.), *Sport and the Working Classes in Modern Britain*, Manchester, 1990, p. 146.
19 S. P. Jones, *Sport, Politics and the Working Class*, Manchester, 1988, p. 60.
20 Korr, 'A Different Kind', p. 147.
21 12 April 1924, quoted by H. F. Moorhouse. 'Footballers and Working Class culture in Scotland', in Holt, *Sport and the Working Classes*, p. 182.
22 ibid., p. 183 (18 October 1926).
23 There were, of course, middle class enthusiasts. Indeed the Presidents of the rival associations were Captain (later Sir) James Wilton, severely wounded at the Somme, and Sir Henry McLaughlin, CBE, a Belfast man and a Cliftonville half-back of its gentlemanly days. But the players and clubs were now predominantly working class.
24 Kircher, *Fair Play*, pp. 3–4.
25 Jones, *Sport, Politics and Working Class*, p. 151.
26 M. Clapson, *A Bit of a Flutter: Popular Gambling and English Culture 1823–1961*, Manchester, 1992, pp. 165–7.
27 Ivan Sharpe, *40 Years in Football*, London, 1954, quoted by S. Wagg, *Football World*, Brighton, 1984, p. 25.
28 B. Butler, *The Football League*, London, 1993, p. 48.
29 ibid., p. 73.
30 Kircher, *Fair Play*, p. 75.
31 28 January 1925, quoted by Jones, *Sport, Politics*, p. 60.
32 Kircher, *Fair Play*, p. 68.
33 An interesting account from the inside is B. Joy, *Forward Arsenal*, London, 1952.
34 Kircher, *Fair Play*, p. 57.
35 ibid., p. 63.
36 *Dublin Evening Mail*, 24 December 1924.
37 F. Root, *A Cricket Pro's Lot*, London, 1937, p. 182.
38 Northern Daily Telegraph, 13 September 1920, quoted in J. Hill, 'League Cricket in the North and Midlands', in Holt, *Sport and the Working Class*, p. 134.
39 Root, *Cricket Pro*, pp. 163–74.
40 Swanton, *Cricket Person*, p. 77.
41 ibid., pp. 43–7.
42 *The Cricketer*, 30 April 1925. p. 1.

43 Quoted by P.F. Warner, *Cricket Between Two Wars*, London, 1942, p. 4.
44 *Cricketer*, 21 May 1921.
45 Its star batsman, G. A. Faulkner, was a South African.
46 E. H. D. Sewell, *Cricketer*, 17 September 1921. p. 7.
47 *Cricketer*, 19 August 1922.
48 ibid., 28 June, 12 July and 9 August 1924. See D. Birley, *The Willow Wand*, London, 1979, esp. e.g., pp. 56 and 98–100 for further discussion of the 'Bolshevik menace'.
49 ibid., 5 July 1924 and subsequent issues to 6 September 1924.
50 ibid., March 1924.
51 ibid., February 1925, in a separate signed article.
52 See Birley, *Willow Wand*, esp. Chapter Nine, 'The Magic Circle' and Chapter Thirteen, 'Cardus and the Aesthetic Fallacy'.
53 N. Cardus, *Autobiography*, p. 159.
54 R. C. Robertson-Glasgow, *Cricket Prints*, London, 1943, p. 12.
55 Extract in C. Martin-Jenkins, *Wisden Book of County Cricket*, London, 1981.
56 W. E. Bowes, *Express Deliveries*, London, 1953, p. 151.
57 ibid., p. 152.
58 See J. Marshall. *Headingley*, London, 1970 for the full story.
59 Warner, *Between Two Wars*, p. 33.
60 ibid., p. 57.
61 I. A. R. Peebles in E. W. Swanton (ed.), *Barclay's World of Cricket*, London, 1986, p. 163.
62 R. Robinson, *On Top Down Under*, Stanmore, NSW, 1976, p. 193.

CHAPTER NINE

Fair play (1919–29):
musclemen – and women

Not many people had a good word for Bolshevism. If the cricket establishment saw it as a threat to their feudal dream-world it had few adherents either amongst professional sportsmen, who thoroughly approved of the capitalist system, or amongst the workers, for whom sport was the modern opiate, replacing religion. Local branches of trades unions and other labour organisations were active in sport but for most it was an escape from politics as well as from the factory. The nearest they got to revolutionary aims was the declared hope of 'Sporticus' in the *London Citizen* that the movement would eventually produce workers' teams that would play Test matches against their Australian counterparts and be good enough to win the FA Cup.[1] The British Workers' Sports Federation, established in April 1923, sought international links in the cause of pacifism, not revolution, and sportsmen who were also Marxists were a minority within a minority.

By contrast the emergent champions of the competitive free enterprise world were fast undermining traditional, gentlemanly ideals by populist and commercial values. The American approach to sport offered just as big a threat to the old order as the Bolshevistic, and it had been around longer. There was a third danger. In central Europe idealistic politicians were seeking to rescue sport from show-business by state sponsorship. In Britain the guardians of the individual sports were united only in their hostility to all forms of government intervention. The only answer seemed to be to avoid corruption by all alien ideologies. After all the British had invented sport, had they not? There was a good deal of scope for falling between stools in this approach, particularly as the foreigners seemed so often to get better results.

Boxing, wrestling and show business

Foreign success was particularly manifest in the archetypally British noble arts. The ABA, undeterred by the intrinsic implausibility of its aim of 'civilising' violence, had created a situation in which not only was taking part

194

thought more important than winning but style more important than effectiveness. The straight left was as revered as the straight bat, but markedly less useful. Like the white vest that distinguished him from the professional the amateur's straight left was a caste-mark. In the public schools, though generally a minor sport, boxing was a respected one. Yet public school men did not often appear in open competition so most of boxing was a far from upper-class affair. In its sanitised form it had become increasingly popular as a controlled outlet for aggression, and hence a necessary preparation for the hard knocks of sterner conflict. Muscular Christians, local fitness fanatics and supporters of Lads' Clubs, including the police, regarded boxing as a valuable life science for urban youth, notoriously subject to temptations of the flesh and the devil. The services regarded it highly as a training exercise. The best amateur boxer of the decade, H. W. Mallin, was a Metropolitan policeman.

Mallin was good enough to win gold medals in both the 1920 and 1924 Olympics. This, however, was an increasingly rare occurrence as foreign standards improved. In 1928 Britain won no boxing medals at all. Member countries of the Amateur Boxing Federation, the international body, increased from 5 to 30 in the twenties. Britain supplied its first chairman, John Douglas, senior, and first secretary, Val Baker, but otherwise her interest was luke-warm. The insular approach meant that as the rest developed, Britain was left behind. This apart the main feature of British boxing was the almost complete separation of the amateurs from the professional world. Their type of boxing was no preparation for the much tougher gladiatorial circuit, and the ABA was anxious that it should not become so. Yet it was in the professional ring that all the glamour lay.

The Americans managed things better. They had a new folk-hero in Jack Dempsey and an impresario, Tex Rickard, who knew how to exploit the sport's potential. And because they made no great social distinction between amateur and professional, the one being unashamedly a stepping stone to the other, the glittering prizes were open to the more intelligent and better-educated type, like Gene Tunney, marketed as a book-reading marvel who conversed with Bernard Shaw. Just as important the American system meant that their fighters understood the obligations of professionalism. The adver-tising, publicity and showmanship brought them big purses but they gave value for money. The leading British professionals, by contrast, were offered generous terms by entrepreneurs like Major Arnold and C. B. Cochrane because of their scarcity value, but were often disappointing. The heavyweights – Joe Beckett, Frank Goddard, Phil Scott – were infinitely forgettable and there were none to replace Freddy Welsh and Ted Lewis at the lighter weights. Jack Hood was an admired stylist, but he never reached the top. Even at flyweight, unconsidered in the USA, Jimmy Wilde lost his title to the Mexican Pancho Villa in 1923.

From the central European angle, however, the British approach seemed to have many virtues. 'There is no fighter like your Nordic,' wrote Rudolf Kircher, 'but the sporting life of the people absorbs the greater part of the martial spirit and makes it innocuous.' He saw boxing, rather like rugger, as a great test of sportsmanship. There was endless opportunity for fouling both in attack and defence. Yet 'in England the sport [was] not confined to schools whose business it is to turn out the Empire's leaders. The young roughs of the East End and youngsters from the lowest classes in the country regard boxing as their most enjoyable diversion.' Whitechapel 'the famous Jewish quarter in the East End' was 'one of London's chief boxing centres'. Premierland lay 'in the maze of Whitechapel's streets, amid the rows of Sheeny shops'. Beside the ring stood a Jewish gentleman in charge of the proceedings. The room was 'packed with spectators of the lower class, most of them Jews'. The atmosphere was lively, but also very orderly. The conduct of the spectators was faultless. 'In one instance in a fight between a young Jewish champion and an English youth . . . the young Jew, in the heat of the contest, hit his opponent an ugly blow below the belt, unnoticed by the referee . . . The public uproar persisted until the referee became aware of what had happened and the Jewish confraternity were greatly incensed that the young Jew was not disqualified . . . That is how Whitechapel understands Fair Play. In fact the whole conception of Premierland is a triumph of English sport as an educational force.'[2]

The handsome tribute is not diminished, or robbed of its political significance *vis-à-vis* Hitler Fascismus, by the possibility that gambling played as big a part in securing support for the Gentile as social engineering. Certainly gambling retained its historic place in professional boxing. This did not, however, corrupt the sport as much as it did in the lusher pastures of America. In this Britain may have gained from the gentlemanly conventions of the NSC, and the gambling inhibitions of the Earl of Lonsdale. The Board of Control of 1919, dominated by NSC members and philosophy, may have erred on the side of conservatism and was manifestly out of touch with reality, but it laid a stable foundation for the British Board of Control which stuttered into being in 1929.

Whatever its limitations British boxing had left wrestling far behind. The amateur game had never risen above the regional limitations of the past. The Highland Games were colourful and well-attended. Cumberland and Westmoreland style, which had produced the pre-war Olympic champion, Stanley Bacon, still had a following: the Earl of Lonsdale was a staunch patron of the Grasmere sports. But there was no national style and the British played little part in the moves towards organised international competition that began in 1921 with the formation of the Fédération Internationale des Luttes Amateurs. The first world championships in 1912 and 22 were held in Scandinavia and in the Olympics the Finns, Estonians and Swedes were the masters in the statuesque 'Graeco-Roman' style and shared the honours in free style with the Americans and the Swiss. The British managed three bronze medals in the decade.

In sport, as distinct from show business, the advance of the amateurs was all-important. Even in its pre-war golden age the professional game had needed gimmicks and stage-managed bouts to compensate for its intrinsic lack of crowd appeal.[3] Now in a publicity-conscious age of intense competition for gate-money the law of diminishing returns began to operate. International competition had little meaning, though the Americans (who had better maintained a frontiersman tradition stimulated by the Civil War) held their own world championships. All-in wrestling offered a fantastic ballet conducted by mysterious masked wonders and the like, usually presented as a struggle between good and evil: but in amongst the gimmickry and the obvious fixes there were some genuine performers. The best of them, like Ed 'Strangler' Lewis, drew big crowds against local challengers or well-known football players.

In Britain the chief demand came from provincial towns where there was a shortage of other entertainment. The sporting press ceased to include it within their ambit. There was no shortage of performers, including ex-boxers and professional rugby players, competing for small purses. Those in most demand were not always the best wrestlers but those prepared to don outlandish costumes or assume exotic or anti-social personae. Bert Assirati, heavyweight champion from 1925, was one of Britain's best ever, but the crowds were drawn more by typecast villains like 'Dirty' Jack Pye and Norman Ansell. Contests in local Corn Exchanges and Town Halls drew full houses, including a surprising number of women. Women wrestlers, sometimes performing in mud or against men, did nothing to strengthen wrestling's claim to be a genuine sport whatever they did for feminine liberation.

Post-Arcadian rowing

It was a far cry from this plebeian wallowing to the fastidiousness of the Amateur Rowing Association, which still excluded manual workers from its competitions on principle. If its serene resumption of Edwardian attitudes in spite of clamant post-war values drew criticism from the press, what else could be expected from such an increasingly vulgar source? George V had only been to Henley once, had been bored, and after the unseemly business of the Peace Regatta never went again, but the Prince of Wales went often enough to keep it truly Royal. It was, indeed, grander than ever, reconciling celebrity with exclusivity in splendid style. Costs were mounting – £8,000 compared with £3,000 before the war – and there were obvious dangers to cashing in on its popularity. 'The old standards were gone,' its chronicler observed, 'and the new standards were not to everyone's liking. The strains of 'The Arcadians' drifting over the evening air from the deck of the *Golden Grasshopper* or the *Maid of Perth* gave way to the insistent gramophone.'[4] But the social amenities were preserved by the creation of a Stewards' Enclosure reserved for the 330 subscribers.

This did not greatly please the old guard who felt that more attention should be paid to the rowing and the needs of rowers than to cocktail parties for the fashionable. They had a point. Henley could not now claim quite so confidently that the standards of its rowing matched its social cachet. The Stewards, however, took no chances of putting it to the test by admitting foreign vulgarians with professionalised habits. This left the stage clear for theological disputation between the upholders of straight-backed, clean-bladed, stylish orthodoxy and exponents of Fairbairnian all-action, method-not-style heresy. The purists' most eloquent and dedicated advocate was G. C. Bourne, an Old Blue of the early 1880s and the leading coach at Eton and Oxford, where he was a Professor of Zoology. He designed a boat on scientific principles for Oxford and in 1925 published *A Textbook of Oarsmanship* which became the Bible of orthodoxy. Fairbairn demonstrated his theories by the successive victories of Thames RC fours in the Stewards' Cup from 1926 to 1928. But eights were what counted. The Henley Grand had been won in orthodox style until 1922, first by Magdalen College Oxford, then by Leander. Thames took it in 1923 and after Leander had asserted their massive authority three years running Thames won it twice more in succession. Leander's victory in 1929 was their last before the war. Fairbairn, after a row with the Thames Committee, had moved in 1926 to London RC which was to be the prime showcase for his methods in the thirties.

Such rude incursions did little to widen the social base of British rowing which remained utterly dependent on Oxford and Cambridge. They themselves relied heavily on a few schools – and one in particular. Of the 180 Blues awarded in the period 1920–9 Eton provided 50, Shrewsbury 23, Radley 12, Oundle and Bedford 6 each and Westminster 5. The rest went to Australians (9) Americans (5) a Dane and a light scattering from 20-odd other public schools, from riverless Harrow and Rugby to St John's, Leatherhead. Some Etonians may have been fortunate to get the nod. After 1921 they did not again win the Ladies' Plate at Henley – open to colleges as well as schools – which they had taken 21 times out of 50 before the war. Otherwise Shrewsbury and Radley managed it once each but there was no great challenge from up-and-coming neophytes.

The Boat Race, so exclusive in its competitors, was yet rowing's chief exposure to popular scrutiny. The BBC began running commentaries in 1927 but this did nothing to lessen the attendance. Its popularity mystified Kircher: 'both banks of the river are crowded for miles with thousands of spectators among whom the lower classes pre-dominate. Little can be seen of the race and before you can get a glimpse it is all over.' He could only conclude, in Freudian fashion, that it was 'another outlet for mental repression' of the sort the British managed so cunningly. The undergraduate spectator, having shaken off his inhibitions, reaching 'the final stages of hysteria' during the race, afterwards 'either [got] dead drunk, or if sober [had] a destructive fit'. The man in the street also shouted and got drunk, became 'genially vulgar' and finally fell asleep. The press 'which now [thought] for the masses [lent] its powerful support' in making the Boat Race a popular festival to which they flocked 'because it was "the thing" '.[5]

Perhaps, as at Premierland, Kircher again underestimated the British liking for a flutter: 'Nor can betting be the attraction as Cambridge always win.' Oxford's lack of success – they won only once in the decade, in 1923 – merely meant that their backers could get better odds. Their disappointing performances, despite Professor Bourne's boat and instruction, nevertheless occasioned much heart-searching especially as Oxford college crews also performed badly at Henley. This last was attributed by some to the University's preoccupation with academic matters, notably in arranging examinations at a time that interfered with preparations for Henley. A worried Leander man wrote to *The Times* about it: 'it would appear that the greatest obstacle to the recovery of Oxford rowing is the apathy of the authorities in this matter'.[6] For whatever reason neither of the universities nor any of the public schools that fed them were recording the sort of progress usual in a racing sport. The average of winning Boat Race times between 1920 and 1929 was slower than those of 1900 to 1909. The record for the Grand Challenge cup set in the 1890s was still standing in 1929. Neither Eton nor any other school equalled their 1911 time in the Ladies' Plate.

It would not have been prudent, in any discussion with the gentlemen of the ARA, to attribute this lack of progress to the absence of professional coaching. The sport had been purged of this as part of the rigid, class-based separation that characterised British rowing. Professional rowing had itself been diminished in the process and its Victorian glories had dissolved with the competition from sports better designed for spectators. The post-war boom brought back a few fleeting reminders of the past. Ernest Barry, though no longer world champion, still had a following. He won an epic sculling contest against an old rival, Harry Pearce of Australia, in 1923. A week later they stroked professional crews in a race on the Thames which aroused so much interest that the manager of the New Gallery Cinema had it filmed from a steam-launch, rushed back the results to the developing room and showed it the same night. Ernest Barry's nephew, Bert, brought back the world title to Britain in 1927 and for a few more years the Thames was again at the centre of the professional rowing world. But the old days were never to return; the prize-money was too small and counter-attractions drew the gambling money away. The Tyne, which had strong professional traditions of its own, was denied even this limited revival. There were plenty of professional or tradesmen's clubs but they competed for very small prizes, with the partial and infrequent exception of the Durham Regatta or the scullers' Christmas Handicap on the Tyne.

Because of the embargo on coaching in amateur clubs such work as the professionals got was with the scullers, more or less on the side and not enough to live on. Ernest Barry himself was obliged to sell his services abroad where more liberal conditions obtained. He was eventually to succeed 'Bossie' Phelps, leader of another distinguished waterman family as King's Bargemaster but safely distanced from amateur crews. Dan Cordery, Barry's chief pre-war rival, spent most of his life abroad, coaching at Yale and, when Germany came back into the fold, preparing her squad for the Olympic Games. The fact that British professionals were in demand overseas caused no change of policy, merely greater contempt for foreign standards of amateurism. The ARA was not simply indifferent to developments in international rowing, it positively disapproved of them. Before its reluctant participation in the 1920 Olympics it informed the BOC of its conviction 'that organised international competitions . . . at regular specific intervals and the expenditure of time and money which such competitions must necessarily entail, are entirely contrary to the true spirit of amateur sport'.[7] This conviction was reinforced by the defeat of Leander, chosen to represent Britain in the eights. Leander (happily having ample leisure at their disposal) had devoted five weeks of their holiday to preparation yet had succumbed to an American crew of naval cadets, chosen from a squad of 25, brought over in a cruiser and furnished with rowing machines, a pacing crew, 4 spare men and their own doctor, masseur, cook and domestic servants.

Events in the already suspect world of sculling brought further pain. Earlier in the summer the Henley Stewards had felt obliged to refuse entry to the American J. B. Kelly, because his club, Vesper BC, had been excluded in 1906 for suspected professionalism, adding, for the guidance of the American Rowing Association, that it was possible that Kelly himself might not qualify under ABA rules. Kelly had once been an apprentice bricklayer, and few believed the Stewards' denial that this was the reason. Kelly himself was given no explanation and drew the conclusion that, not wanting their own man to be beaten, the British had taken advantage of the old rule.[8] Full revenge had to wait until after the Second World War when his son won at Henley and his daughter became a famous film star who, as Princess Grace of Monaco, received regal treatment at the Regatta. Meanwhile, though Kelly made his point by beating Jack Beresford at the Antwerp Olympics, the ARA was merely confirmed in its suspicions of Henly's dubious claims to being a true amateur competition.

The IOC, for its part, was more than a little sympathetic to the NARA's application for recognition in 1922 and though FISA felt obliged to uphold the ARA's supremacy as the single ruling body each country was allowed, the ARA was unable to prevent a NARA club, Weybridge, taking part in the 1924 Olympics in the coxed fours, an event the ARA totally ignored. (Fortunately for the establishment Weybridge, alone of the five entries, failed to reach the final.) ARA consent to clubs' participation in the events it did acknowledge was given grudgingly, and whilst Beresford won the sculling and a Cambridge crew the coxless fours, the all-important eights went to Yale representing the USA. That the British eight, who came fourth, were from Thames RC and not Leander was some consolation. In 1925 the ARA confirmed 'that it had never been in sympathy with the Olympic Games or Olympic Regattas'.[9] In 1928 at the Amsterdam Games, when an eight from the University of California at Berkeley, coxed with demoniacal and noisy frenzy, put it across Leander, it was only the coxless four from Trinity, Cambridge that saved the day for Britain. A team from the Nottingham Club had entered the coxed fours but discovered on the day before the first race that their cox was too light. At an acrimonious meeting of its Provincial Council when the ARA was charged with failing to pass on accurate information someone sourly suggested, 'Possibly it came through lack of interest in provincial rowing.'[10]

The NARA, however, had done little to commend itself as an alternative. Whilst lacking the ARA's prestige it had been too anxious to preserve its own reputation for amateurism to become popular in any sense. Only a handful of clubs not on the Thames or the Lea had joined before the war and afterwards a number of regional associations had sprung up, generally accepting the NARA's social stance without actually affiliating. Of such clubs in the north-east the Tyne was purist, the two on the Tees uncertain and a number of clubs disappeared altogether, giving way to the unashamedly working-class professional clubs. Even on the Thames the NARA faced competition from the Tradesmen's Rowing Clubs' Association which was itself trying to live down earlier associations with professionalism. Weybridge RC were members of the TRCA and only joined the NARA as a back-door route into the Olympics.[11] In this they were aided by the dreaded Fairbairn.

Fairbairn's catalogue of seditious activities culminated in his sponsorship of the new Head of the River Race that took place on the Thames in December 1926. The race itself was a controversial notion. Fairbairn's idea was to popularise and give point to winter training – surely, the purists thought, a vulgarisation of the real point of rowing, which was not racing in front of cheering crowds but enduring galley-slavery with due solemnity overlooked by a coach on a bicycle from a bleak and otherwise deserted towpath. The new race was also a long-distance affair, open (i.e. with no qualifying standard) and therefore possibly harmful to inexperienced oarsmen; and it was a time-trial, for all the world like professional cyclists defying the law on public roads. Fairbairn had an answer to all these points. The time-trial way of coping with mass entries on a narrow river underlined his point that it was not intended to be a hard-driving win-at-all-costs affair; people could try for their own personal best times. As to distance, for those who took rowing seriously this was all-important to develop strength.

To most people's surprise the first race attracted 23 entries. It also brought full press coverage, which drew attention to another, even more controversial feature – it took place on a Sunday. The ARA immediately informed the organisers that this was 'entirely contrary to the traditions and spirit of English amateur rowing'.[12] It was indeed, particularly in circles which did not care if this excluded those sections of the population with little other leisure-time. Fairbairn and his allies perforce conformed and there were as many hopes as fears that this would prove fatal, but in fact the second race, barely three months later, drew 41 entries. All except two (from Jesus College, Cambridge, Fairbairn's old stamping ground) were Tideway crews, but what it lacked in social lustre it made up in quality and enthusiasm. The race itself never looked back and it had a marked effect on the attitude to winter training and thence on the standards of rowing.

Weybridge was one of the handful of clubs with ladies' sections. None of these was within the ambit of the ARA, which thought rowing was for gentlemen and that, whilst ladies' boating was all very well, it should not be competitive. The post-war thawing of attitudes came from bottom up and was therefore slow and uncertain. This was in part a reflection of the orthodoxy versus Fairbairnism debate: racing to win involved an apparent rejection of the claims of deportment. The ladies' college clubs at Oxford and Cambridge were largely recreational and when a Ladies' Boat Race was started in 1927 – a half-mile affair on the Isis – it was a style contest. At London University Royal Holloway, who had followed the Oxbridge line before the war, staying aloof from competition, joined in the races with their less fastidious sister colleges but not without misgivings. No-one of any consequence had been impressed by Weybridge's decision in 1919 to include a race for ladies' fours in their 1919

Regatta: Weybridge was, after all, in the TRCA which had professionals like Ernest Barry amongst its members.

NARA, anxious for respectability, was no more willing than the ARA to take the ladies' clubs emerging on the Thames into membership or to sanction their competitions. In 1923, therefore, a small group led by Mrs K. L. Summerson, captain of the emblematically-named Helen Smith RC, formed its own Women's Amateur Rowing Association. Borrowing the money to buy trophies it staged a regatta which within a few years became the centre-piece of the year for the new clubs and ladies' sections. Some of the old ones were not so sure. In 1925 the Furnivall Scullers, although supportive of the principle of such an association, decided not to affiliate to WARA because of dissatisfaction with the way it was run; specifically 'the honorary secretary was party to a professional engaging in a women's race under the association's rules'.[13] The offender was presumably a member of Weybridge, now in NARA but not yet free of their past links with tradesmen. Weybridge Ladies formed their own club in 1926, taking the precaution of including the word Amateur in its title. Of the surviving women's clubs started at this time Hounslow's Alpha Women's (1927) also called itself Amateur whilst Civil Service Ladies the same year presumably felt no further clarification was necessary. In 1927 Weybridge Ladies caused further ripples by taking part in a long-distance challenge match with the Ace Club, Barnes, now defunct. Two years later the Alpha Club joined them and the foundations of the Women's Head of the River race were laid.

Gender, class and competition

Rudolf Kircher, writing in 1928, had some reservations about 'the animal directness with which the lower classes make love among the bushes of Hampstead Heath', but otherwise thoroughly approved of 'the careless frivolity of society . . . the organised exuberance of plebeian *joie de vivre* on Derby Day or Bank holidays', which recalled 'the time when puritanism was routed'. Sport and games might provide pretexts and opportunities, but they could not be said to have 'led to sexual excitation'. The young women of Britain were 'freedom personified' yet nowhere in the world could women lead such an 'unfettered life . . . with less danger of molestation'. Gone was the 'simpering gracefulness so long associated with English tennis or archery' along with long trains and feathered hats. True there were, as everywhere else, 'female monstrosities standing mid-way between the sexes . . . "flannelled fools" capable of any extravagance', the sort of 'female lunatic' who favoured cycling, 'especially tandem and in bloomers' or went in for athletics with 'unbecoming freakishness'. But most saw 'the light and amusing side of sport', regarding it 'as a pleasure not a task imposed by heavy-handed duty'.[14]

We can only imagine what he would have thought of the immediate post-war vogue for women's soccer. It centred on the remarkable Dick Kerr's Ladies team, whose war-time feats had caught the attention of male entrepreneurs on the look-out for novelty. In 1920 they played 30 matches including 'internationals' against Scotland and France, culminating in a Boxing Day charity game before a huge crowd on Everton FC's ground at Goodison Park, Liverpool, which took over £3,000 at the gate. This sparked off an enthusiasm all over the country, and by 1921 there were some 150 clubs and an English Ladies Football Association. The fervour was not sustained, partly because war-time mores did not last, and partly because the FA, with troubles enough from male professionalism, was quick to discourage the clubs from lending their grounds to such exhibitions, which it felt had little to do with soccer proper. In withdrawing approval it declared that 'the game of football is quite unsuitable for females and should not be encouraged'.[15]

Even amongst 'suitable' sports, however, Kircher was aware of the social limits of women's liberation. As yet there was 'no sport for the millions of working-class women, and the hundreds of thousands of female employees had so far had very little'. He felt this was a matter of time: there was an 'astonishing contrast between the older and younger generations' who hardly seemed to be of the same species, and much could be expected from the great expansion of secondary schooling. The schools he visited, meanwhile, appear to have been of the superior kind: 'Cricket and hockey', he noted, 'are the principal games played at girls' schools.' In fact even at the most élite establishments, which made much of female hardihood, it is doubtful if cricket had displaced lawn tennis, which had long been favoured by physical educationists who saw grace and movement as qualities to be emphasised in female development. In the twenties, stimulated and made more modern by the publicity surrounding Susanne Lenglen, it had renewed appeal to girls. Tennis was much the most popular summer game for girls in those schools which owned or had access to courts. (Rounders was the choice for those that had not, especially in Scotland and the north of England, where Liverpool was an early centre. It had little following amongst adults, and the nearest thing to a national association was the Ling Association's Rounders Committee, but it was a rare schoolgirl who did not play rounders at some stage.)

Girls' cricket, for economic as well as physical reasons, was much more restricted. Cricket fields and pitches were highly expensive. Cricket balls were very hard on dainty female hands, and bosoms were not only vulnerable but could hamper bowling, and even batting – actions that were not easy even for boys to acquire. But the deficiencies were more cultural than biological, and cricket had a strong minority appeal especially as a summer game for hockey players. The exclusive ladies' clubs, active since Victorian times were much strengthened by enthusiastic alumnae of the better schools and colleges after the war, leading to a demand for more organised adult cricket. After a successful festival week at Malvern in 1926 a Women's Cricket Association was formed. One of the leading spirits was Marjorie Pollard, a hockey international, and its chairman was Mrs Patrick Heron-Maxwell, a former President of the AEWHA. Within a year there were 10 club and 347 individual members and this had grown to 400 clubs and 1,200 members by 1929, when the first representative match was held. This, played at Beckenham between London & District and the Rest of England, was distinguished by the hat-trick of Miss Carol Valentine. Spectators must have been pleased to see that the best male traditions were preserved; it was a draw.[16]

To say that the women were preserving the best male traditions in hockey would have been deeply insulting to both parties. What they had in common was insularity and a deep devotion to amateurism, which showed itself in matters of organisation as well as on the field of play. The men resumed after the war-time closure with a flourish. A Combined Services team was formed in 1920, which after a couple of early thrashings proved the only team capable of holding its own with the South of England, which otherwise completely out-classed the other Divisions. The Inter-Divisional matches were the only competition apart from internationals and Oxford v Cambridge. There were no nationally-sponsored leagues for the clubs, many of which arranged fixtures by social as much as sporting criteria, still less open challenge cups. If there was less well-bred activity in places like Lancashire at least there was no question of seeking to attract spectators away from soccer and no gate-money, except the modest takings at representative matches which did not attract the general public, only the club faithful.

In terms of International success 1920 was a false dawn. A Great Britain side was selected by the BOC for the Antwerp Olympics and duly trounced the other three entries, Denmark, Belgium and France. But then the IOC struck hockey from its list for Paris because it had no international governing body. This took some time to arrange and the eventual Fédération Internationale de Hockey (1924), another French creation, had to manage without the British, who were above that sort of thing. The four home countries, which each had its own Association, preferred to devote their energies to their traditional exchanges, in which Ireland, and to a lesser extent Scotland, had a few successes to record against England. Only France brought outside competition – not very well. There was imperial pleasure to be had, however, in the achievement of India, who joined the FIH in 1928 and lent a distinction to the Amsterdam Olympics that bore testimony to the beneficent influence of the British Raj. Its team, alongside the Nawab of Pataudi, a future England Test cricketer, included men with such Oriental names as Broome Penniger and Richard Allen.

British women hockey-players were equally inward-looking, but more understandably and less culpably so. Their highly-successful fight for the kind of responsible liberation Kircher admired had demanded an almost neurotic pursuit of purity and avoidance of the limelight – and, of course, the Olympics were not available to them even had they sought it. The AEWHA consisted of thoroughly well-bred ladies of the type that had secured the vote by their war-time contribution, not leaping about on the streets or chaining themselves to railings. They had shut down during the war to the extent of not collecting affiliation fees or keeping records. In 1919 they had to borrow £5 from each of the constituent Territorial Associations to prime the pump again. They were soon coping with a different problem. Only 150 clubs and schools were affiliated in 1920, but this soared to 800 by 1922 and, though the curve flattened out, another 400 had joined by 1929.

Some of their inhibitions were dissolved in the post-war atmosphere. Advertising big matches was no longer forbidden and the compensating increase in gate-money did not have the corrupting influence that had once been feared. Nor did it lead to a lowering of the tone by attracting crowds of prurient men. The AEWHA still took no chances on this, however, retaining its vigilance in matters of dress. Long skirts had everywhere given way to knee-length three-pleated tunics without noticeably adding to the salaciousness of the spectacle. Many teams even wore short-sleeved round-necked blouses and below-the-knee stockings. Such an undignified exposure of naked flesh was too much for the AEWHA which insisted on its national teams wearing ties and long black stockings.[17] This outfit, which survived until 1939, set a good example to the schoolgirls who formed the bulk of the spectators at international matches, for, with different coloured tunics and Panama hats or berets, it was the standard school uniform. Advertising revenue encouraged newspapers to provide further publicity by reporting important games and tournaments. Easter tournaments, highly popular in Ireland as well as Britain, were not commercialised affairs like those of tennis, but end-of-season frolics. Teams tended to compete under outlandish or jolly *noms de guerre*. This was partly to indicate that they were scratch teams, but it also saved parent clubs from exposure to the charge that they played hockey on Easter Sunday.[18]

Whilst far from populist the AEWHA was carried along on a tide of greater post-war enthusiasm from a widening range of schools. The upper end of the market had now been cornered by lacrosse. Men's lacrosse languished some-what after the war, shrinking to London–Manchester polarity and virtually disappearing from its Celtic fringes. By contrast the All-England Women's

Lacrosse Association, from its powerful Roedeanian roots, made steady progress in the circles where it chose to move. A Scottish Association was formed in 1920 and Irish and Welsh counterparts in 1930. Women's hockey, perforce less élitist, grew strong throughout the British Isles. The AEWHA soon had an income of £900 a year whilst remaining resolutely amateur. Many clubs retained socially superior traditions, England totally dominated the home internationals and the South the Territorial contests, and unladylike behaviour was not tolerated. It was very much a British and Irish – largely Protestant – affair. Attempts at wider international involvement were few and hampered by shortage of money. The eight members of the International Federation, started in 1927, included only four from outside the British Isles – Australia, South Africa, USA and Denmark, the only xenophones. The first President was an Englishwoman.

At home there were mild signs of social change. Marjorie Pollard, who after Kathleen Bridge (née Lidderdale) was the outstanding player of the twenties, was from Peterborough and a source of strength to Midlands hockey. In 1926, furthermore, without interrupting her international career, she became a sports journalist, writing for the *Morning Post* and the *Observer*, and later extended her net widely, becoming a renowned publicist of the game, a hitherto unheard of phenomenon. More radically, in the industrial north where alien traditions of competition were as well-established as weeds, hockey had a great working-class following. In Manchester, for instance, the Sunday Schools Union Women's Hockey League had six divisions with an average of 11 teams in each (not playing on Sunday, of course).[19] And hockey was prominent in the vast array of sports played in the employees' clubs of business houses and textiles firms and organisations like Tootal Broadhurst Lee and the Fine Cotton Spinners' Association.

There were fewer masculine connotations in netball. Basketball, though well-established amongst American men, was making slower progress in Britain. Girls' secondary schools, however, had quickly taken to netball. This was especially true of those which lacked facilities for hockey – for which reason it was disparaged by the sillier snobs – and its appeal to girls who shrank from sticks and hard balls meant that the heartier type of games mistress had reservations about it. Nevertheless it required even fewer facilities than soccer, was highly enjoyable and relatively undemanding, and it spread apace, not only as a school but an adult game. A London and Home Counties Federation was formed in 1924 to accommodate the numerous leagues already active, and they joined with the Ling Association to set up an All-England Netball Association in 1926.

Its inaugural meeting, chaired by Miss Edith Thompson the current president of the AEWHA, was held at the Tottenham Court Road YWCA. The 230 delegates included representatives of schools (both Girls' Public Day School Trust and London Girls' Secondary School Association), colleges (all types except those of Oxford and Cambridge), superior factories like Cadbury's, London Banks and the Liverpool Union of Girls' Clubs. London University and civil service clubs were soon so prominent as to merit Association status alongside the County groupings that gradually built up, first in Lancashire and then throughout the country. Organisation came more slowly in the rest of the British Isles. America, where it was called basketball, had its own rules and the two other main centres where it developed, New Zealand and Australia, also did so under slightly different rules, but it was well on the way to becoming, in one form or another, a most useful addition to the female armoury.

Swimming, meanwhile, had unobtrusively become perhaps the most important. The sport's relative lack of appeal to the British of either sex, stemming from the centuries when immersion in water was looked at askance, and its lack of status in modern times, had been gradually overcome and with the discovery of the seaside the social tide had begun to turn. The short stories of P. G. Wodehouse showed that the ability to swim was a useful accomplishment for both men and women seeking either mild flirtation or a soul mate at a fashionable watering-place. Educationally swimming instruction, firmly installed in the Board of Education's curricula with its concomitant, life-saving, was given additional purpose by the increase in sea–bathing, and was even seen to have special advantages to women since the body was 'developed symmetrically' while providing 'the woman who has allowed herself to get out of physical condition' with 'a safe and pleasant approach to land exercises which will in time reduce bulk and restore muscular tissue'.[20]

But a majority, boys as well as girls, learned to swim while at school and continued if at all by visits to local municipal baths. In public schools, a swimming pool was now the norm, in other secondary schools a mark of distinction, but there were municipal baths all over the country, and the schools were able to reserve them for their swimming sports as well as the regular weekly sessions to which they were bussed. This was usually in the summer term only, for most public baths closed in the winter when the demand slackened greatly, in face of a lingering fear of catching cold. Serious swimmers in clubs who used these baths – Manchester had 34 such in 1921 – perforce found themselves seasonally restricted, too. Most adult public baths users were working-class urbanites. The Baths at Ashton-under-Lyne, a small town on the edge of the Manchester conurbation, was 'mainly patronised by artisans' many of whom came from far afield. There was a standard charge of 6d, with concessions for children, pensioners and the unemployed. For the latter the charge could be as little as 1d but the take-up rate was poor. The number of users, however, increased steadily from 32,809 in 1921 to 94, 800 in 1930. Mixed bathing also gradually increased: by 1929 there was one day for women only and two and a half exclusively for men. In Education Committee sponsored schemes there were roughly twice as many boy swimmers as girls.[21] In the south-east and in less industrialised parts of the country public pools were scarcer, less socially-restricted and more girls and women took part.

Competitively swimming was fast growing in popularity and it had been saved from the worst excesses of commercialism by its limited spectator appeal. Things were changing, by courtesy of Hollywood. Johnny Weissmuller, the hero of the Paris and Amsterdam Olympics, was the first screen Tarzan. But the Olympics were utterly dominated by the USA, and British men won no medals after a bronze in the relay at Antwerp. At this level swimming needed more practice at unsocial hours and in cheerless conditions than most British amateurs found congenial or the purists thought consistent with the amateur spirit. They were not helped either by official medical opinion which held that the crawl was 'not so correct physiologically as the breast stroke or the back stroke.'[22] Unlike athletics, furthermore, there was little scope for tactics and a correspondingly greater obsession with times and records. It certainly lacked the moral virtues of team games.

The nearest swimmers came to conformity with the team-game ethic – not very close – was in water polo. This was a sport the British had introduced at the extraordinary Paris Games of 1900 and had somehow retained its place in spite of a fearsome reputation. Known in the nineteenth century as 'football in the water' its early strongholds, like those of League soccer, were Lancashire and Scotland and though it had spread geographically to such places as Weston-super-Mare and Plaistow – and even had a few women enthusiasts – it had achieved little in social distinction or sporting finesse to justify its claims to being thought an aquatic version of polo. Its rules (since revised) were both unclear and permissive. The victory of the joint British and Irish team at Antwerp in 1920 over the Belgians did nothing to preserve allied solidarity. The crowd attacked them after the game and they had to be smuggled away, protected by armed guards. Things went more smoothly at Paris, and the French crowd, greatly surprised by their team's victory, insisted on the Belgian losers' national anthem being played as well as their own. Nevertheless when Queen Wilhelmina of Holland expressed a desire to see one of the matches at Amsterdam in 1928 there was great anxiety lest anything unseemly should occur. In particular Philip Noel-Baker, IOC Deputy Commissioner, was given the task of seeing that no British fouls occurred. He was so successful that at a Prime Ministerial reception twenty years later one of the players greeted him with, 'Ah, you're the chap that lost us the gold medal for water polo at Amsterdam.'[23]

There was of course no women's water polo in the Olympics. Female swimmers had, however, received an unexpected accolade from de Coubertin himself after the Antwerp Games: 'they have excelled, beating their previous records'.[24] British women did somewhat better in subsequent Games than their male counterparts. Lucy Morton of Blackpool won the 200 metres breaststroke in 1924, but this was the only gold medal of the inter-war years. A much bigger influence than the Olympics on changing the prevailing British attitude that women were likely to be harmed physically and eugenically by excessive competition was the feat of a 21-year-old American, Gertrude Ederle, in 1926. There was much ribald comment when it was announced with a great deal of publicity that she intended to swim the English Channel. It had been the channel crossing of Captain Matthew Webb 51 years earlier that had given swimming its first real popularity and his feat had remained one of the great emblems of British virility.[25] The *Daily News* greeted Miss Ederle's attempt with disdain: 'Even the most uncompromising champion of the rights and capacities of women must admit that in contests of physical skill, speed and endurance they must remain forever the weaker sex.'[26] She did the crossing in seven hours less than Captain Webb and two hours faster than the male record. Several men had swum the Channel in the twenties but now it became the 'in thing' for women, and no fewer than six did it in the next two years. The craze was satirised by Noel Coward in the current C. B. Cochrane revue *This Year of Grace*, and sabotaged by a Scottish woman doctor's elaborate hoax in which from a mile out at sea she was rowed across for all but the last spectacular mile. But Miss Ederle emphasised her point by making a crossing even Captain Webb had not risked, the Straits of Gibraltar, sharks and all.[27]

Meanwhile women track and field athletes were finding it hard to persuade the IOC to let them in. De Coubertin, having praised the swimmers and tennis-players in 1920, had firmly opposed further extension. 'Should women be allowed access to all Olympic sports? No. Then why allow them to take part in some and prohibit others? Which sports practised by women should constitute therefore a spectacle suitable for the crowds that assemble for an Olympiad? We do not think one can be claimed.'[28] And if the IOC rejected women's athletics on aesthetic grounds it also lacked, in Britain, the social cachet that leadership from the superior women's colleges would have brought. Apart from the services and Northern Counties clubs the post-war impetus came from colleges outside the magic circle of Oxbridge and low down in the physical education hierarchy. At Madame Bergman-Osterberg's Dartford athletics was thought a little vulgar and Swedish gymnastics both more graceful and more feminine. Staff and students of London polytechnics with physical education departments were the driving force behind the

Kensington Athletics Club (1921) and the British end of the first women's international meeting at Monte Carlo in March 1921. The British team, sponsored by *Sporting Life,* won six of the ten events. Their captain, 27-year-old Mary Lines, wearing long tubular shorts and a smock-like vest, her long hair encased in a kerchief, won three individual events and took part in two relay victories. A 17-year-old student, Hilda Hatt, cleared 4 feet 7 inches in the high jump. Later in the year Miss Lines again starred in a match in Paris between France and Britain, with world's records in the 100 yards (11.6 seconds) and 300 yards (43.8 seconds). Next day the British and French competitors, with colleagues from Czechoslovakia, Italy, Spain and USA formed the Fédération Sportive Féminine Internationale.

In 1922 the AAA politely advised British women athletes seeking organised competition that their interests would be better served by a separate governing body. It would have been surprising had it wanted to be associated with something most of its members thought unladylike and potentially injurious to health, diminishing the enthusiasm if not the capacity for motherhood and perhaps even for s–x. The Women's AAA set up that year stimulated a number of separate female clubs of which the first, London Olympiade, captained by Mary Lines, was to dominate its early championships. Of more immediate concern to the pioneers, however, was the IOC's rejection of FSFI's application for a women's track and field programme in the next Olympics, scheduled for 1924. Only fencing was to be added to the women's events. The British were prominent in the defiant world championships held in Paris in 1922, at first boldly styled the 'Women's Olympic Games' but grudgingly altered to 'World Games' after protests from the IOC. Miss Nora Callebout joined Miss Lines (2) and Miss Hatt as gold medallists and the British took the relay.

Back home many provincial universities, with Manchester giving the lead in 1921, set up women's clubs and a Women's Inter-Varsity Athletic Board was formed in 1923. The first full-scale WAAA championships had an interesting range of events with shot, discus and javelin as well as the running and jumping. London Olympiades, for whom Mary Lines won four events including a world record 440 yards, had powerful newcomers in Eileen Edwards, 220 yards, and Edith Trickey, 880 and Sophia Elliott-Lynn (later Lady Heath) of Ireland in the javelin. Vera Palmer of Middlesex Ladies set a new 440 record of 60.8 seconds later in the season and the following year Eileen Edwards not only equalled this but set new records in the 100 (11.3) and 220 yards (26.2 seconds). The circle was now spreading beyond the metropolis, to the north and to the harriers' clubs with ladies sections. However it was London Olympiade members like Eileen Edwards, Edith Trickey and Florence Haynes, with Rose Thompson of Manor Park, who carried the flag at the second World Games at Gothenburg in 1926, and with Vera Palmer, young Phyllis Green and Muriel Gunn of Mitcham brought excellent contests and a stack of new records at home and abroad.

If the star performers mostly came from a few clubs this was from historical accident rather than social élitism. Bereft of Oxbridge lustre the WAAA was doubly anxious to distance itself from the unseemly and highly nervous of publicity and commercialism. Professionalism, however, even in its mildest forms, was no problem and the WAAA was only too anxious to expand wherever it could. But in track and field athletics as distinct from conventionally 'suitable' sports it was a question of waiting for the new generation of liberated women to make their mark. With the Medical Officers of Schools Association at its conference in 1921 rejecting the idea that athletics was bad for young girls, more schools had taken it up, and schools' athletic championships, first held in 1925, greatly encouraged the competitive side. It was a school girl, Phyllis Green, who cleared 5 feet in the high jump in that year's WAAA championships. Athletics was not the most clubbable of sports but it was relatively easy for big employers, or groups of small ones, to provide facilities and young women could be accommodated relatively easily alongside men. It also enjoyed a fair amount of press support. The *News of the World* sponsored meetings and the *Daily Mirror* presented a trophy for club competition in 1925, by which time Sophia Elliott-Lynn was fairly able to claim that women's athletics had taken 'a firm hold on the popular imagination'. In 1922 there had been 'one club and about 20 girls; we now have over 500 clubs and over 25,000 girls. Our clubs embrace all classes from university clubs to Factory Girls' Clubs.'[29]

WAAA élitism was more political than social, springing from a separatist antipathy to the AAA and all its works. Vera Searle (née Palmer), one of the stauncher feminists, explained in 1928 their strong objection 'to the mixing up of men and women in the Olympic Games or any other meeting. If this actually happened it would kill our movement, and we should be absorbed by the men as in other countries. In England, we have nothing to do with the AAA; we are entirely a separate body.'[30] Amalgamation with the AAA had been the price demanded by the IAAF for a recommendation to the IOC that women's athletics be included in the programme for the Amsterdam Games that year. And though FSFI had in 1926 nevertheless successfully negotiated a programme of eight women's events with the IOC, this had been so disappointing to the WAAA (there had been 11 in the women's own World Games) that the British declined to take part. This made better political than athletic sense. Of other nations, 290 women, more than twice the number on any previous occasion, did join in. But there were bigger things at stake.[31]

The women's performances, whilst much inferior to what AAA champions had been achieving since the start in 1868, were nevertheless a revelation, not entirely welcome to some males of lesser standard. And some of the leading men, like the Olympic star Harold Abrahams found competitive women's athletics genetically and aesthetically disturbing: 'I do not consider that women are built for really violent exercise of the kind that is the essence of competition. One has only to see them practising to realise how awkward they are on the running track.'[32] Kircher saw the force of this: 'Surely it is bad enough for men to ruin their constitutions . . . women, once they begin to take the sport seriously, may become greater fanatics than the men.' However, he was, on balance, prepared to take the risk. We did not know what kind of children would be 'born of the women who have trained and raced on the track as strenuously as their fathers'. But sport was 'a great leveller of the sexes.' Most young men viewed 'with pleasant surprise the growing possibilities of the female body in the twentieth century', an awakening that was needed.[33]

Athletics the leveller

Kircher was highly impressed by men's athletics. He found the AAA a refreshing contrast to the MCC and the All-England Lawn Tennis Club, presiding over their restricted bits of turf, literal and metaphorical. Like Ranelagh or the leading golf clubs the facilities were magnificent but denied to the millions. And though footballers could manage anywhere and rugger men seemed to prefer to play in a bog he found 'the huge concrete amphitheatre' of Wembley stadium 'one of the misfires of commercial speculation', empty most of the time and ripe for take-over by 'dog-racing and betting'. By contrast the AAA governed the athletic world 'in much the same way as the Bank of England controls the City: it dominates without ruling . . . Every self-respecting club belongs to it, regulating . . . its whole work by the Association's hard and fast laws.' In return they got 'the benefit of the Association's unlimited experience'. Any works club or Boy Scout troop for a nominal fee could get a representative from the nearest branch to attend and thus be sure of the best possible technical conditions. The representatives gave their services free (apart from out-pocket-expenses) 'with a devotion that is truly sportsmanlike'.[34]

Under this beneficent regime, Kircher felt, it was in athletics, requiring little or no equipment, that the British made best use of sport as 'a unifying force'. Though not intrinsically a team game the British instinct made athletics into one. When a man won an event people thought 'more of the club, university, county or nation' to which the man belonged than of the individual. Competitors likewise did not think solely of themselves. Team contests and events were very popular. The social cohesion was remarkable. The AAA represented 'a complete sporting community' in which it was 'quite usual to see . . . lords, clerks, workmen, and students running shoulder to shoulder in the open events'. Cross-country running in particular attracted large numbers of all classes: 'Half-naked youths in training course through London streets and garden suburbs . . . shop assistants, students or workmen.' And if the 25,000 spectators at the AAA championships seemed 'to comprise proportionately more of the lower than the upper classes' this was because the event took place in the middle of a sports season that was crowded for public schoolboys whereas for the man in the street 'Stamford Bridge' was all-important.[35]

This romanticised picture from a contemporary European angle may serve as a useful corrective to the critical impatience a modern Briton may show towards this far from progressive body. For whatever Kircher gleaned from AAA propaganda about its democratic leanings it had spent much of the time since the war in trying to regain the social ground it had lost by the waning involvement of Oxbridge athletes. It had achieved this remarkably well. At the same time, furthermore, British international involvement had greatly increased chiefly through the Olympics, which had attracted the university men into the fold and in which they had performed brilliantly. Whereas previously only a few eccentrics, and socialist visionaries like Noel-Baker, had brought Oxbridge breeding to athletics now there was a corps d'élite including no less a figure than Lord Burghley, son of the Marquess of Exeter, who had become the world's leading hurdler. On the negative side the longer races and the field events, which social convention had made the province of harriers-types and Celts, languished in esteem and standards, and coaching developed in spite of rather than because of the AAA.

This one-sided revival was signalled by the formation in 1920 of the Achilles Club for Oxbridge graduates who wanted to continue in competitive athletics after going down. These were, by definition, men who took the sport seriously, realising (for the most part) the value of training and even coaching – a new breed of gentleman athletes who both revitalised the AAA's championships and went some way towards bridging a social gap that had hitherto got wider as the sport had expanded. Achilles' first great success came when the South African Rhodes Scholar Bevil Rudd narrowly beat fellow-member Guy Butler to the gold medal in the 400 metres at the Antwerp Olympics. Rudd was not given to modern notions of rigorous training or abstinence from tobacco and alcohol, but he added greatly to the post-war spirit of reconciliation and renewal which infected even the Americans. (When one of them accidentally bumped into Rudd in the 800 metres he paused and said, 'Sorry, Bevil!'[36]) Butler, the Harrovian son of a cricket Blue, was equally sporting but much more serious, a great theorist who brought something of the dedication of the great oarsmen to the task.

In setting its face against 'broken-time' and similar incentives to working-class athletes the AAA had not only bolstered professional 'pedestrianism' but had created two kinds of amateur, each of which resented the other. The war had done something to loosen social attitudes. Oxford University began the new decade by appointing as their coach Alf Shrubb, whom the AAA had declared a professional in 1905. Cambridge's young sprinter Harold Abrahams, from a Jewish sporting family, was an admirer of the renegade Willie Applegarth, and during his brief military career had run against him in an exhibition race in 1919. And at Antwerp the Achilles man had served his Olympic apprenticeship alongside Harry Edward, the black AAA champion and Applegarth's successor in Sam Mussabini's Polytechnic Harriers stable. In the more frankly competitive post-war atmosphere there developed a greater rapport between the privileged type and the gifted artisan performer, based on mutual respect for achievement. Such reaching across the divide did not always please the administrators, who were concerned lest it breed too much regard for record-breaking, over-specialisation and coaching, the dread hallmarks of professionalism. It was all very well for Philip Noel-Baker, now on the secretariat of the League of Nations, with his head full of socialist ideals, to sacrifice his own interests at Antwerp to help the plebeian Albert Hill win the 1500 metres, but there were wider considerations. Hill, who also won the 800 metres, was a 31-year-old protégé of Mussabini who had spent three years in war service, and in 1921 he turned professional.

The BOC, which had done its best over the years to encourage the IOC to eliminate international variations in the interpretation of rules concerning such things as 'professors of sport', paid leave and 'broken-time', had raised the question of pocket-money for athletes, provoking even the patrician de Coubertin to remind colleagues that there were poor as well as rich athletes. The founder was, it seems, indulging in one of his periodic bouts of self-deception. In 1921 the spirit of post-war euphoria led him to support the highly dubious winter Olympics, remarking that over the last 25 years they had 'demonstrated a quality of amateurism, of sporting dignity, frank and pure that their total exclusion . . . would take away much of strength and value'.[37] By contrast in athletics the British delegate, R. S. de Courcy Laffan, warned of the danger of making the Games a 'nursery for professionals' and there was talk of striking from the roll of honour champions who subsequently crossed the great divide.[38]

When Hill turned professional the omens still looked good for the pedestrian circuit. In 1920 3,000 people attended the three days of Powderhall's new year programme and regular weekend handicaps were soon brought back. Clyde and Motherwell soccer clubs put on successful promotions. In the north of England Newcastle, Blackpool and Manchester all offered £100 handicaps in the early twenties. Pontypridd enjoyed a revival. Powderhall set new records, with £250 prize-money for the 1922 sprint. But thereafter the effects of recession and competition from other spectator sports began to be felt. Promoters – and their bookmaker friends – looked as before to amateur stars to bring back the crowds. And there were plenty of chances of appearance money in less avowedly professional events. The difference was that this time the leading amateurs, most of whom were Achilles men, were not so easily persuaded. Even the maverick Abrahams was too long-sighted and socially-conscious to step beyond bounds. In 1923 and 1924 his remarkable performances in the sprints and long jump meant that he was 'besieged by people concerned in all sorts of athletic meetings both great and small, who were more than anxious to have him as a draw'.[39] But Abrahams was single-mindedly concentrating on his preparation for the Paris Olympics where the opposition would include the 'fastest human on earth', Charlie Paddock of the USA. That winter Abrahams had been training three times a week with Mussabini. 'Under his guidance,' he said later, 'I managed to improve that decisive one per cent which makes all the difference between supreme success and obscurity.'[40]

In 1924 the IOC, reacting to widespread concern, expressed disapproval of athletes writing about their sport for financial gain. Abrahams was one who contravened the Olympic spirit in this way. His journalistic activities, further-more, served a double purpose. Writing as 'A Famous International Athlete' in the *Daily Express* he was severely critical of the team selection for Paris: 'H. M. Abrahams is chosen for four events, which is unfortunate. From the point of view of the Olympic Games this athlete should leave the long jump severely alone.'[41] He got himself excused the long jump and, triumphantly, became the first Briton to win the 100 metres. Achilles had more conventional champions in Paris, notably Douglas Lowe in the 800 metres, who had got a Blue for soccer at Cambridge, and the more-fancied Henry Stallard who led for most of the race despite an injured foot and drew his second string home. The supreme example of the ethical amateur undeflected by fame and glory was, however, the Scot, Eric Liddell.

Liddell was an Edinburgh divinity student who intended to follow his father as a missionary and his aim in everything he did was to make the most of the gifts God had given him and to use them to the glory of God. A sprinter with enormous talent and great courage but appalling style, he explained after-wards how he came to the conclusion that he needed coaching. An expert prodded him all over, put him through his paces and told him not to pull up so abruptly: 'Thus being thoroughly humiliated, feeling that my reputation had been dragged through the mire, and that if I didn't get into the clutches of a trainer soon, every muscle in my body would give way and I should remain a physical wreck to the end of my days – I was then in a fit condition to start an athletic career.'[42] Also a great rugger player he was capped for Scotland seven times in 1922–3 but gave up the sport to concentrate on preparing for the Olympics.

That summer Liddell recorded wonderful times in winning the AAA 100 and 220 yards and became the leading British contender. Abrahams, who had been fortunate to miss clashing with him through indisposition in 1923, must have been relieved that by 1924 Liddell had decided not to compete in the 100 metres in Paris – because the heats were to be held on a Sunday – and was concentrating on preparing for the 200 and 400 metres. This decision, taken six months before, caused Liddell increasing anguish as the Games drew near, not least because he had been criticised at home as unpatriotic, since Scotland had so few chances of Olympic medals. His bronze medal in the 200 metres, ahead of Abrahams (who had already won the 100) but behind two Americans, put great pressure on him in the 400 metres. His victory in record time was the prelude not to glittering material honours or the limelight of Westminster or AAA politics to which many of his contemporaries and successors turned, but after one more season of undemanding Scottish competition to missionary work in China for the rest of his life.[43]

If the Achilles stars' excursions into Mussabini Land caused the die-hards some concern the aims of the club itself were as elevated as those of the Corinthians on whom they modelled themselves. A principal objective was to gain recognition for athletics in the public schools, through team visits and inter-school relays, for instance, and thereafter to arrange team competitions amongst the leading clubs. The early years of men like Butler, Lowe and Lord Burghley did not expose them to much open competition. Burghley, whose specialism was the 440 yards hurdles, had no opportunity to run in it at Eton or Cambridge. Oxford and Cambridge did not take part in the activities of the Inter-Universities Athletics Board, and their only club ventures were the 'Varsity match and the joint meetings with Harvard and Yale. In 1923 F. A. M. Webster (now Captain Webster) of the Field Events Association told a British Olympic Association Commission 'We cannot find anyone in England who can teach field events.'[44]

Of the athletics scene generally, however, Captain Webster, in a series of articles about the forthcoming Olympics was optimistic: 'Until a few years ago university and service athletes took but little part in public athletic competition. To-day the Public Schools' championships, promoted by the London Athletic Club are an unqualified success, and we, following America's lead, are beginning to compose our teams of something like 80% of service and university athletes.'[45] This was a specious argument. There was no comparison between the American open high school and college system and the British 'grace and favour' pattern. Public school athletes thought themselves a superior breed. 'These men', wrote Webster, 'will not take part in the ordinary handicap meeting which has been so long the vogue in England.' One who had recently done so had told him afterwards 'that the only thing more filthy than the dressing room accommodation was the language in the tent'. He had a more valid point in seeing handicap races as themselves a bar to progress. They lacked appeal to the ordinary non-betting public since it was 'almost impossible to assess the value of the finalists' performances without wading through pages of programme and making most intricate mathematical calculations'.[46] They were also a prime source of dishonest racing. Happily there were hopeful signs, even to Webster's southern gaze. The Lancashire sprinter, W. Rangeley, he noted, tried to win all the time. Northern Counties AC were also setting a fine example in a notoriously troublesome area, and the better meetings everywhere included scratch races, relays and field events.

Webster, in fact, was not only a snob but an ambitious one, seeking to create professional opportunities for middle class 'amateurs' in athletics as in other sports. Bizarrely he claimed that 'no loss of social caste is involved when the ex-service officer or Old Blue becomes a Welfare supervisor, or professional coach in either rowing or tennis, any more than it is infra dig for a man of the same class to become a trainer of race-horses'. It was a tribute to the excitement generated by the Olympic Games that *The Cricketer* allowed him space to write articles on athletics, but his readers must have been sceptical about his hopes for the erosion of the distinction between gentlemen and players. 'Next we shall have Olympic instructors in Great Britain of the [ex-officer or Old Blue] type in the services, at the universities and at the greatest of our public schools.' The extent of his delusion was evident when he added, 'In the latter places we already have them under the style of games masters.' Games, yes, but not athletics. And he was obviously flying a rather pathetic kite by concluding, 'If you want the right type of man you must, of course, be prepared to pay him properly and his salary may well run into four figures.'[47] The real world was not like that. By 1926 the leading coach was Albert Hill who took over from Sam Mussabini at Polytechnic Harriers and helped his pupil, the British Guianan Jack London, become the next sprinting star.

In 1923 the BOC, now led by General Kentish, had again pressed the IOC about 'broken-time': in 1925 the IOC had reaffirmed its opposition and the following year restricted travelling expenses for trips abroad to 21 days a year. At the same time paid leave and subsidies to students were common practice and Britain was one of the few countries to tread a virtuous path through the tangle of regulations. Abrahams had retired after injury in 1925 (joining the committee of the AAA) but though Liddell was also gone and some of the glamour inevitably lost, the enthusiasm for amateur athletics was intense. One of the results, as more and more youngsters took it up throughout Britain trying to be the next Abrahams or Liddell and spectators showed their preference for honest amateur racing, was the decline of the professional side. By 1926, though Powderhall and Clyde FC continued, there was little else in Scotland and Powderhall could not sustain their weekly promotions. (In 1927 the new craze for greyhound racing offered a lifeline. The inaugural meeting, honoured by the presence of the Duke of Atholl, drew only 7,000, but that was more than the pedestrians could attract.) There were four athletics meetings in 1928, but the last of them attracted only 28 entries and made a loss at the gate. Two years later the Greyhound Racing Association bought the stadium, and although the New Year Handicap was retained and kept something of its old prestige the glory days were past. South of the border the bubble had completely burst and only Newcastle struggled on.

Jack London and Walter Rangeley of Salford AC – Webster's respectable northerner – were each to take a silver medal behind Percy Williams of Canada in the sprints at Amsterdam. But the real momentum behind the amateur revival in international competition was with Achilles. Guy Butler, who had won four medals in his time, showed that he was still a contender by breaking the world 300 yards record at Stamford Bridge in 1926. When he mistakenly went for the 200 metres at Amsterdam his replacement in the 400, John Rinkel, also of Achilles, surpassed himself to finish fourth. Douglas Lowe was also a great quarter-miler, but he saved himself for the 800 metres, in which his second success was greeted lyrically in the Official Report: 'To describe Lowe's victory as a wonderful effort is to employ mere words in attempt to do justice to a performance which, from whatever angle one looks upon it, is unparalleled in the history of middle-distance running.'[48] Best of all was the success of Lord Burghley in the 400 metres hurdles. He had been suspected in his early days of lacking the necessary seriousness to reach the top. He had fallen over on his first Olympic outing in 1924 and the following year Abrahams had commented in one of his columns, 'He has a great future as a hurdler if he continues to train assiduously.'[49] He had shown sufficient application in 1926 to win the AAA title and again in 1927, but that year, his last at Cambridge, he had startled everyone by his escapade in running round Trinity Great Court before the clock finished its twelve midnight chimes. But after his feat in winning the gold medal at Amsterdam his team-mates carried him off shoulder-high. It was the first time the USA had failed to win this event, and his only comment to the assembled crowd was in the true British sporting spirit: 'The Americans are awfully good losers.'[50]

The euphoria was only slightly lessened by the fact that at distances longer than half a mile none of the very few British finalists finished better than fifth or got on to the record at all in the field events. (The prodigy Pat O'Callaghan who won the hammer was Irish, and didn't count any more.) This reflected a decline since the war, emphasised by the improving Europeans, particularly Scandinavian, that now appeared. In distance running the reasons were cultural as well as social. If the Achilles men did not generally engage in anything over one mile, the national preference amongst amateurs of all classes was not for pounding monotonously round a track, especially in training, but for the thrills and spills of cross-country running. By 1927 entries for the national championships reached 400, and the England team hung on to the widening International Cross-Country Championship for most of the twenties. In Olympic terms this translated best into the steeplechase, but even here there was nothing but gallant losers, after 1920. As for field events, if one can generalise about such disparate events, they require natural and rather specialised talents for even moderate performance and the avoidance of embarrassment or physical harm, and, apart from much practice, also require the good skill training and encouragement that only an expert coach can give. There were individual exponents, proficient enough, from Achilles to Polytechnic Harriers, but without coaching to encourage young talent wherever it arose there would be no future champions.

The Soviet Union, previously too preoccupied with more immediate challenges to take much interest in sport, now began to realise its potential. As a protest against the effete élitism of the IOC, in 1928 the first Spartakiade was organised in Moscow. Over a million spectators and athletes from 42 countries came to the 12 days of sporting and gymnastic activity, inaugurated by a parade of 30,000 enthusiastic banner-waving workers. The BWSF, assisted by a grant of £400 from the Russian Government, sent 35 athletes who came back with glowing accounts of the Soviet way of life and renewed conviction that an alliance of the workers of the world was its only hope of salvation.

Notes

1 *London Citizen* (Tottenham edn), 1921 and 1922, cited in S. G. Jones, *Sport, Politics and the Working Class in Modern Britain*, Manchester, 1988, p. 75.
2 R. Kircher, *Fair Play*, London, 1928, pp. 110–13.
3 See Derek Birley, *Land of Sport and Glory*, Manchester, 1994, pp. 214–15.
4 R. D. Burnell, *Henley Royal Regatta*, Oxford, 1957, p. 107.
5 Kircher, *Fair Play*, pp. 87–9.
6 *The Times*, 6 July 1929, quoted in E. Halladay, *Rowing in England*, Manchester, 1990.
7 *British Rowing Almanack*, 1921, p. 146.
8 The full story is given in H. Cleaver, *A History of Rowing*, London, 1954.
9 *Almanack*, 1925, p. 191.
10 Halladay, *Rowing*, p. 121.
11 ibid., pp. 141–3.

12 *Almanack*, 1928, p. 191.

13 Halladay, *Rowing*, p. 154.

14 Kircher, *Fair Play*, pp. 48–51.

15 J. Williams and J. Woodhouse, 'Can Play? Will Play?', unpublished paper, University of Leicester, 1991, p. 17, quoted by J. A. Hargreaves, *Women's Sport Between the Wars: Continuities and Discontinuities*, University of Warwick, Working Papers in Sport and Society, Vol. 3, 1994–5, p. 140.

16 M. Pollard, 'Women as Cricketers', in *MCC 1837–1937*, London, 1937.

17 Schoolgirl stockings were usually black, by regulation. After the Second World War, when a little more innocence was lost, such Parisian associations were thought unsuitable and black stockings were forbidden.

18 For the period see M. Pollard, *Fifty Years of Women's Hockey*, London, 1946.

19 S. G. Jones, 'Working Class Sport', in R. Holt (ed.), *Sport and the Working Class in Modern Britain*, Manchester, 1990, p. 76.

20 *Recreation and Physical Fitness for Girls and Women*, Board of Education, London, 1937, p. 224.

21 Considerably more detail in given in D. Bowker, 'Ashton-under-Lyne Between the Wars' in Holt (ed.) *Sport and the Working Class*, pp. 76–7.

22 *Report of Chief Medical Officer to the Board of Education*, London, 1928, p. 28.

23 Lord Killanin and J. Rodda (eds.), *Olympic Games*, London, 1984, p. 41.

24 M.-T. Eyquem, 'The Founder', in Killanin and Rodda, *Olympic Games*, p. 141.

25 See Derek Birley, *Sport and the Making of Britain*, Manchester, 1993, p. 309.

26 *Daily News*, 6 August 1926, quoted in D. Wallechinsky, *The Complete Book of the Olympics*, Harmondsworth, 1988, p. 466.

27 R. Graves and P. Hodge, *The Long Weekend*, London, 1940 (1971 edn), pp. 226–7.

28 Eyquem, 'The Founder', p. 141.

29 S. Elliott-Lynn, *Athletics for Women and Girls*, London, 1925, p. ix, quoted in Hargreaves, *Women's Sport*, p. 133.

30 J. Crump, 'Athletics', in T. Mason (ed.), *Sport in Britain*, Cambridge, 1989, p. 69.

31 For an explanation of the British abstention see J. Hargreaves, 'Women and the Olympic Phenomenon', in A. Thompson and G. Whannel (eds.), *Five Ring Circus*, London, 1984, pp. 58–9.

32 M. Watman, *History of British Athletics*, London, 1972, p. 230.

33 Kircher, *Fair Play*, pp. 41–2.

34 ibid., pp. 28–9, 37–8.

35 ibid., pp. 81–4.

36 Wallechinsky, *Olymics*, p. 25.

37 Eyquem, 'The Founder', p. 142.

38 Killanin and Rodda, *Olympic Games*, p. 149.

39 F. A. M. Webster, 'The Olympic Games', *The Cricketer*, 10 May 1924.

40 Watman, *History*, p. 28.

41 ibid., pp. 26–7.

42 Quoted in D. P. Thompson, 'Eric Liddell: The Making of an Athlete and the Training of a Missionary', Eric Liddell Memorial Committee, Glasgow, 1945. Liddell had been killed in February 1945, in a Japanese prison camp.

43 For a corrective to the overblown and wildly inaccurate Hollywood film, *Chariots of Fire*, about Liddell, Abrahams, Lord Burghley et al. see Wallechinsky, *Olympics*, pp. 5, 12–13 and 18–19.

44 P. Lovesey, *Centenary History of the AAA*, London, 1979, p. 120.

45 *The Cricketer*, 9 August 1924.

46 ibid., 31 May 1924.

47 ibid., 24 May 1924.
48 Quoted in Watman, *History*, p. 64.
49 ibid., p. 157.
50 N. McWhirter, *DNB*, 1981–5.

CHAPTER TEN

Changing the rules (1929–39): systems under stress

Various reasons have been adduced for Labour's winning the 1929 election, from the imposing personality of Ramsay MacDonald to the base ingratitude of the flappers for being given the vote. Whatever the reasons it was a narrow enough victory. In a three-cornered fight Labour won more seats than the Tories but not enough for an overall majority. Nevertheless Baldwin, instead of striking an alliance with the Liberals, at once resigned. It would have been unsporting to have done otherwise, he told the King. His noble gesture also had the advantage of consigning Lloyd George to a further – and as it turned out permanent – stay in the wilderness, and installing MacDonald at the head of a Labour government powerless to introduce socialist policies. This stand-off meant that all three parties tended to agree on many issues. Health and slum clearance were the priorities, and good progress was made with sub-sidised housing for rent. Labour were greatly helped by internal divisions in the other parties. For the Liberals the chief trouble was that no-one believed in the re-conversion of their leader, Lloyd George, to Free Trade. The Tories were similarly divided by the movement for Empire Free Trade started by Lord Beaverbrook, the Canadian proprietor of the *Daily Express*, and Lord Rothermere, Northcliffe's successor at the *Daily Mail*. The notion of imperial preference had more resonance than Baldwin's 'Safety First' policy and though the United Empire Party quickly collapsed as the two moguls dis-agreed, it drove the Conservatives into politicking rather than policy-making.

Labour has an innings

Labour's slant on foreign affairs, though starry-eyed, was broadly shared by the leadership of all parties. The refusal of Soviet Russia to join the capitalist League of Nations was unfortunate but made for a quieter life, and since MacDonald was no longer fool enough to lend them money few minded his renewing diplomatic relations. The Germans' mutinous demeanour was more worrying, but perhaps they only wanted fair play: world disarmament had a nice ring to it and of major politicians only Churchill, who had wanted to 'stifle all resistance' in 1919, took an independent line.[1] MacDonald saw himself as world statesman and was only with difficulty persuaded from taking on the Foreign Office portfolio himself. Happily this went to Arthur Henderson whose straightforward and even-handed approach reinvigorated the League of Nations as well as anyone could. MacDonald bent his energies to improving relations with the Americans.

The British Empire and its overtones of outmoded glory aroused hostility in the USA, just as vulgar American wealth and brash self-confidence did in Britain. Each side envied the other but did not like to admit it. If the barriers were crumbling as communications, news, entertainment and publicity shrank the distance across the Atlantic, it was a hit-and-miss process. Few foresaw the British Empire and the USA as allies in a coming clash between capitalistic democracies and totalitarian regimes, certainly not Ramsay MacDonald. He wooed the Americans in the same spirit as he relied on the moral force of the League of Nations to supersede force of arms. He started loosening the ties of empire for similar high-minded reasons. Churchill again was the odd man out in opposition.

The new policy was not a complete success. The somewhat intangible ideals of the 1931 Statute of Westminster, envisaging a Commonwealth of nations co-operating in freedom instead of by direction, depended too much on good will. The Irish Free State used it as a loophole to escape into hostile independence. The Boers were left to their own racist devices in South Africa. India remained an intractable problem: Mahatma Gandhi was brought from prison to the conference table, but there was no meeting of minds and the federal 'solution' that emerged was unconvincing. (The problems of Britain's protectorates also defied solution. In Egypt control of the Suez Canal stood in the way of independence, and in Palestine the Balfour declaration had to contend with a resident Arab population unimpressed by the aspirations of immigrant Jews.) The policy worked best for the white Dominions. Even there the Statute had to contend with the realities of economic self-determination, but there were powerful ties of blood and sentiment to weigh in the balance.

An indication of these ties had come in 1929 when loyalists in Canada, resistant to the pressures drawing them into the American orbit, conceived the notion of the British Empire Games. Since the war athletics matches between Empire teams and the USA had been an attractive fixture, often offering some consolation for the Americans' increasing domination of the Olympics. The latter had manifestly declined in sportsmanship. Why not an imperial alternative, a friendly Games, a family affair? Bobby Robinson, a flag-waving newspaper editor in Hamilton, Ontario, was the father of the scheme, which got under way when the local Olympic Club staged a match against a team from

Oxford and Cambridge. The Oxbridge team was managed by Evan Hunter, honorary secretary of the BOC, who on his return became a central figure in a Council of Great Britain, formed to organise – and fund – teams from the four home countries for an 'Empire Olympiad' in August 1930.

The Hamiltonians, apparently untroubled by the collapse of the American Stock Market in October 1929, found that their initiative involved them in a good deal of expense. Free accommodation was offered as an inducement. Even so Australia was only persuaded to take part by a $5,000 grant towards travelling expenses, and matching sums were later sent to South Africa and New Zealand. Politics were another difficulty. India declined to participate, preferring instead to enter the Far Eastern Games in Japan. Only British Guiana and Bermuda of the black colonies sent teams. And the last to confirm acceptance was England, where the necessary £8,000 was raised only after a wireless appeal in July 1930.

The announcement that the English team would be headed by Lord Burghley made up for all the anxieties and helped ensure that the Games were both well-attended and conducted in the true British spirit of fair play. As Robinson proudly proclaimed, 'From all corners of the world, competitors have come, eager, of course, to reflect credit on their respective colonies, but proud of the blood ties that bind them in a great entity.'[2] The Governor-General, Lord Willingdon, a 'Varsity cricketer before the war, spoke of the high traditions of British sport and declared that the 'greatness of the empire is owing to the fact that every citizen has inborn in him the love of games and sports'.[3] (No doubt he intended 'him' to include 'her', but the female half of the Empire were not yet invited on to the athletics track. Women *were* allowed to swim and Joyce Cooper of the Mermaid Club won four gold medals for England.) The Empire Games were to become a permanent fixture, every four years, in the intervals of the Olympics, belatedly fulfilling John Astley Cooper's Victorian dream of a Pan-Britannic Festival.[4] They were the more successful in that the impetus had come from the Empire itself.

The rugger men were also doing their bit. A British Isles team toured New Zealand and Australia in 1930, advancing the cause of imperial solidarity by losing, in thoroughly sporting fashion, four of the five Test matches played. They completed the task in 1931–2 when each of the four home countries went down to the touring South Africans, who gave the first demonstration of what was to be known as 'power play'. The International Board did less well for what remained of the Entente Cordiale, however, for in 1931 it severed relations with the French Rugby Union and its clubs because of the 'unsatis-factory condition of the game as managed and played in France', a phrase later amplified by the explanation that their 'competitive system was responsible for breaches of amateurism and unnecessarily rough play'.[5] In a masterstroke of arrogant ineptitude the decision to withdraw was announced some weeks before the England–France game in Paris that spring. The English team was booed – a deplorable lapse of taste – as they stepped on the field, and had to endure howls of derision and delight as the Welsh referee Albert Freethy disallowed two English tries enabling the French, who slotted two infuriating drop kicks, to win by 14–13. At the dinner afterwards the English fell below Kircher standards of chivalry in defeat, with A. D. Stoop making a long-winded and self-congratulatory speech recalling past triumphs and rowdier members of the party calling for whisky instead of wine. The day was saved by the suave young captain, Carl Aarvold, a future judge and President of the LTA, who was not only gracious in defeat but fluent in French – a rare combination – but the sour taste remained and poor Freethy was never allowed to referee another international.[6]

Rugby Union football was affected only in patches by the recession. The English game had been purged in the areas where its effects were most severe. Scotland's worst-hit areas were largely given over to soccer and only the uninfluential border clubs continued to suffer as the textiles industry languished. Working-class sport in Ireland meant soccer and Gaelic games. By contrast Welsh rugby was particularly badly hit by the slump as the mines and metallurgical industries on which South Wales depended were crippled. Yet across the border in the west of England, which was doing surprisingly well industrially, the game was also thriving. Gloucestershire was the leading county and supplied a fair number of players, in amongst the Oxbridge men, to the national team. The Torquay club enjoyed a golden spell with three Welsh internationals and many other imports. It was no accident that the two most famous names in the Rugby League were Welsh – Jim Sullivan and Gus Risman.

The RL found their imperial links highly profitable during the recession. Gates in four home Tests against Australia in 1929–30 exceeded 100,000 and the three in Australia two years later drew 150,000. They also benefited by receiving the French outcasts from the world of amateur rugger. On their 1933 tour Australian and British teams staged a series of games in France and when France beat Wales in Bordeaux it gave a fillip to the continental game as well as revenue to visiting British teams. Gates were up at Wembley, too, for the Cup finals and in the championship play-offs. The weaker clubs had some difficult moments but none actually went under. Indeed in 1933 Brigadier Critchley, seeking to diversify his greyhound interests and make full use of the White City stadium, acquired the congenitally precarious second Wigan club and turned it into London Highfield. The experiment was a failure. London Highfield quickly folded, as did teams started by syndicates at Acton and Streatham shortly afterwards, but if Rugby League would not transplant, in its heartland it was stronger than ever.

Meanwhile, with vision unclouded by Wall Street and untainted by Ramsay MacDonald, MCC were pursuing their own imperial dream with tours of the West Indies in 1929–30 and South Africa in 1930–31. The home Test series in the summer of 1930, however, though highly lucrative, was otherwise disastrous. Australia regained the Ashes, Bradman destroyed the English bowling and the reputation of the beau ideal Percy Chapman was shattered. More was at stake than mere chauvinism. That winter Neville Cardus, who by then had cornered the market in nostalgia, wrote a sombre piece making a connection between the decline of English cricket and the dwindling ranks of the gentlemen.[7] In 1911, he claimed, an all-amateur XI could have been picked to represent England whereas modern teams were nearly all professional. (As it happened the MCC touring team in 1911–12 had also been nearly all professional, but he was not one to let the facts get in the way of a good story.) To the end of his days Cardus regretted the end of the 'era of the amateur when professional players such as Hirst, Hayward and Shrewsbury would raise their hats when they met their captains and say "Good morning, sir", not losing but gaining dignity by doing so'.[8] 'Our Sutcliffes and Hammonds,' he sighed, 'with their tailors obviously in Saville Row, have taken us far beyond the echo of Billy Barnes and his rough, heavy-handed company of paid cricketers of the eighties and nineties.'[9]

The game, as Cardus pointed out, had changed in other ways. In 1930 Wilfred Rhodes, aged 53, and Charles Parker, aged 48, had been the best slow bowlers, and whereas 20 years earlier every county had had a good opening pair of fast men, now there were almost none. If in the affluent later twenties a career in county cricket was no longer attractive to young men it was a particularly unrewarding prospect for bowlers having to labour away on the carefully prepared wickets designed to allow batsmen to make the big scores spectators wanted to see. The underlying problem, however, was that first-class cricket's leisurely three-day game was ill-matched to its modern neo-Darwinian ethos and in the recession the weaker counties in particular viewed the future with alarm.

The northern leagues with only one professional to pay on one day a week were better placed. Their tactics in adversity were similar to those of the Rugby League, increasing their efforts to find star players to attract the crowds. The cricket leagues had no Test matches, of course, but they were able to strike a shrewd blow at MCC nevertheless. Nelson, in the Lancashire League, showed the way. They were still remembered for their spectacular signing of the Australian fast bowler Ted Macdonald in the early twenties, but they had sunk back to obscurity and deep financial difficulty long before the Wall Street crisis. Now, in 1930, they boldly decided to try to buy themselves out of trouble. They engaged Learie Constantine, a young fast bowler and fast-scoring batsman who had come to notice the previous winter on MCC's tour of the West Indies. They paid him a handsome fee – thought to be about £750 for the season, astonishing at a time when industrial wages and even salaries were tumbling – and achieved immediate success. He became a local hero. The story is told of a Lancashire schoolmistress asking a pupil when Ramsay MacDonald had previously been Prime Minister. 'Don't know, Miss,' he said, 'but I know he were t'pro for Nelson before Connie.'

In his second spell of office MacDonald was already in deep trouble, and there was soon great frustration within the Labour Party because the Cabinet seemed fearful of pursuing socialistic logic in a collapsing capitalist system. The problems of industrial decline were fudged under Labour as they had been under the Tories. MacDonald managed to persuade Ernest Bevin, the powerful leader of the Transport and General Workers' Union and Walter Citrine, the TUC secretary, that the economic situation demanded restraint. The Minister of Labour, Margaret Bondfield, set doctrinaire principles aside in favour of pragmatism and her national insurance Bill scraped through Parliament but failed to satisfy the radicals. An education Bill to raise the school leaving age to 15 fell foul of the House of Lords, but was just as much disliked by Labour's own Roman Catholic supporters, and the minister, C. P. Trevelyan, resigned 'as much out of general disagreement at the feebleness of the government as from disappointment at the loss of his bill.'[10]

The Labour government certainly proved reluctant to antagonise the old order. The urban anti-blood sports lobby got nowhere. In 1929 the RSPCA, still ambivalent about fox-hunting, promoted a Bill to abolish stag-hunting, but even this failed dismally. Its effect indeed was to bring the various factions together. It was 'a danger signal to farseeing sportsmen', wrote Walter Case, editor of Horse and Hound, urging a united front.[11] The following year he helped found the British Field Sports Society ('I do not use the meaningless and emotive term "blood sports"') under the energetic presidency of the Duke of Beaufort. And whilst they dedicated themselves to the preservation of rural Britain in the interests of hunting, shooting, fishing, wild fowling, falconry, field trials and the rest, plebeian walkers' access to Arcadia was restricted. Libertarians like Trevelyan had particular cause for irritation. That several Private Members' Bills had foundered under the Tories was hardly surprising, but they expected better things from Labour, especially as MacDonald wrote books about walking. Yet two more Bills were shelved between 1929 and 1931, because, as the Prime Minister explained, of 'the congested state of business.'[12]

This strengthened the arm of the communist-led British Workers Sports Federation which soon included a belligerent Ramblers' Rights Association.

The BWSF's activities in a wide range of sports spurred the Labour Party into counter-measures. Early in 1930 a conference at Transport House agreed to the formation of a National Workers Sports Association (NWSA) to 'encourage, promote and control amateur sport and recreation among working class organisations' by federating sporting bodies 'under the auspices of the Trade Union Congress and the Labour Party'.[13] The politics of the BWSF were alien to the best traditions of 'genuine sport', said J. R. Clynes, the Home Secretary in 1930, explaining his refusal to grant entry visas to a Soviet miners' soccer team. He would not, he told protesters, support 'these Communist sports organisations' which would be used in strikes, pickets and 'the military training of working class youth'.[14]

Soccer was a sensitive topic at the time. The BBC's broadcast commentaries – principally by George 'By Jove!' Allison, a socially-conscious journalist who had wormed his way on to the Arsenal Board – had by their dramatised style brought the game to the firesides of thousands who never went near a football ground, and this new delight was under threat. The main opposition came from the humbler League clubs, unimpressed by the publicity value of broadcasting, who saw it as a threat to their gates. But the big row was between the BBC and the FA, who had no objection in principle but who thought it right to demand a fee. The BBC flatly refused at first and as a result the 1929 Cup Final was not broadcast. The argument had continued and shortly before the 1930 final still had not been settled. Charge and counter-charge rang through the land. The FA denied that they were haggling over money: they objected to the BBC's assumption that they not only had a right to broadcast but could tell the FA how to spend the fee. They demanded that allegations of professionalism and commercial-mindedness made in the *Radio Times* be withdrawn before discussions were resumed. The newspapers were full of indignant letters from frustrated licence-payers and anguished pleas for hospital patients and the bed-ridden, but the impasse remained. The day was saved by the intercession of the Bishop of Buckingham. Speaking at an FA luncheon before the England–Scotland match he appealed, on behalf of the public and 'especially the blind, the sick and the infirm', to the nobility and generosity of the FA and their hearts were softened. The BBC stumped up £100 and the match was saved but with no guarantees for the future.[15]

For a Labour government to ban a football match took some explaining. Rudolf Kircher had identified two classes making up most of the crowds at soccer matches – 'the lowest of the proletariat' and 'townsfolk of the lower classes . . . the people who were caps in town'.[16] These were also people who voted Labour. J. B. Priestley's escapist novel of 1929, *The Good Companions*, began with an aerial view of a 'grey-green tide', the caps of men spilling from the soccer ground of Bruddersford United. The shillings spent by these men to go to a football match could be easily proved by economists and other luminaries to be an extravagance: 'When some mills are working only half the week and others not at all a shilling is a respectable sum of money.' But a shilling spent watching "t' United" offered Conflict and Art. It 'turned you into a critic, happy in your judgement of fine points'. And the excitement, away from 'the clanking machinery of this lesser life' was an essential bond with your neighbours – a man who had missed the last home match 'had to enter social life on tip-toe in Bruddersford'. The same was true of north London, which had imported Herbert Chapman's Bruddersford magic, bringing Arsenal the Cup in 1929–30 and the League in 1930–1, and of Liverpool, where Everton came back from relegation to head them the following year; of West Bromwich and Newcastle whose Cup wins lightened the industrial gloom; of Belfast which saw a rare Irish victory over England in 1930; of Glasgow where little Motherwell intervened in the Rangers–Celtic saga; and everywhere that cloth caps were worn in town and a living was hard to make.

There was another side to it, of course. When John Thompson, the Celtic goalkeeper, died after a collision in the Rangers match in 1931, the Minister at his funeral spoke more in hope than expectation: 'Those thoughtless crowds who call themselves Celtic or Rangers followers, whom both teams disown, who cheer themselves hoarse when a member of the opposing team lies writhing in pain, if they can be brought to realise the brutal cruelty of their actions, John Thompson will not have died in vain.'[17] If they could not, soccer was not likely to improve international relations which was what it was now apparently supposed to do. The FA had become sufficiently aware of the changing climate of opinion to widen its fixture list beyond France and Belgium in 1929 but on the very first occasion had horrified the nation by losing to Spain in Madrid, hitherto believed to be given over entirely to bull-fighting. The insular preoccupations that had led to the quarrel with FIFA and kept them out of the Olympics had also led the FA to decline dismissively the invitation to take part in the first World Cup in South America in 1930. But its quest for respectability and the secretary's aspirations to knighthood now had to accommodate subtle changes in the rules of the political game. A broader view was needed, especially on European relationships, if the League of Nations was to be supported. The diplomatic path proved unexpectedly treacherous. Hatchet-burying visits to Germany and Austria in 1930 produced only draws which might please the Foreign Office but were not well received by the press. In 1931 England even lost 5–1 to the French in Paris. Happily all this skirmishing had been abroad, and normality was restored when the Spaniards were invited to Britain in 1931 and crushed 7–1 reducing their highly-paid goalkeeper Ricardo Zamora to tears. 'Dixie' Dean got his eighteenth international goal and Sir Frederick Wall his knighthood.

Labour idealists, apart from international leanings, had long been anxious to improve facilities at home for the less-favoured. There had been modest progress since the war. Apart from schools, government spending on playing fields, parks and swimming pools through local authorities had risen from some £2.5 million in 1914 to nearly £7 million in 1929. Hopes that Labour would bring a dramatic advance were quickly dashed. Even before the Wall Street upset the new Minister of Health, the intellectual Arthur Greenwood, told Philip Noel-Baker, now a back-bencher, that housing and unemployment would have to take precedence over playing fields, and the prospects scarcely improved thereafter. Only the utopian George Lansbury, Commissioner of Works, waved a small but defiant flag for recreation as part of his 'Brighter Britain' campaign. Amid a volley of protest from the ascetic he grant-aided sand-pits and boating ponds in the London parks, and most controversially a Lido on the Serpentine for mixed bathing. Was this to be the greatest achievement of the Labour government, asked an opponent in November 1930? It was certainly one of the most popular, replied Lansbury.

Swimming was in fact unique in its appeal. Women were allowed to do things in or near the water that would not have been countenanced on dry land. Not that they were libertines. On the contrary there had been little relaxation in the sexless severity of the costumes or the disciplined behaviour required in amateur competition and the press generally devoted more attention to their speed and skill than to their charms. But it is somewhat surprising to find amateur ladies in the Kent and Surrey of 1930 appearing not only in races, but as members of 'ornamental swimming and figure-floating squads' in galas, water ballets and cabarets, often alongside men. As light relief in one such venture 'Miss Coppard imitated a porpoise, and a submarine, besides waltzing in the water. Mr Wilkinson imitated a torpedo, a turtle having a sunbath, and a monkey on a stick.'[18] In water polo, too, not the politest of aquatic activities, women players had reached the stage of an inter-county match, described by the local paper in glowing terms; 'The standard of play was a revelation. If the ladies lacked the speed and strength of the throw which the men possess, they have nothing to learn in gameness and sticking to their job.'[19]

Within months of his stout defence of mixed bathing Lansbury was out of office and the Labour Party was in disarray. The Wall Street collapse had badly hit exports to the USA and the large part of the world dependent on American money who could no longer afford to buy British goods and services. In little over a year unemployment rose to 2.5 million. Steel output was halved; shipbuilding, already at half its 1920 level, fell even further; cotton exports tumbled and the demand for coal began to shrink. There were countervailing forces. Industry in America and Germany was hit even more badly and import

231

costs, of both manufactured goods and raw materials, fell as world prices tumbled. Wages in Britain remained stable for those who were in work and as the effect of lower prices took hold their real value increased. But before the balance sheet could be examined a sterling crisis demoralised the Labour leadership. Macdonald was quick to protest, 'We are not on trial; it is the system under which we live',[20] but neither he nor his senior colleagues were ready to do much about it. Only Sir Oswald Mosley, who had left the Tories over their Irish policy and was now a junior minister, spoke up for planned foreign trade, direction of industry and 'social credit' to boost expansion. Met with blank incomprehension or horrified opposition by the government, and eventually expelled by the party, he left to contemplate the inadequacies of parliamentary democracy.

The economic clouds were lifted a little in 1930 by the great cautionary guide to historians *1066 And All That*, which reaffirmed Britain's status as 'top nation'. Gloom was also dispelled in one small corner of the ship-building industry by the news that Sir Thomas Lipton was to make a further challenge for the America's Cup. The New York Yacht Club's 1929 decision that future contestants should conform to the J class of the American Universal Rule[21] put Lipton at a disadvantage since the Americans already had four from which to choose. The ill-wind blew good in the direction of Charles Nicholson, however, and he cheerfully began designing and building a new boat. He had problems with its highly complex formula and *Shamrock V* lost every race. Design faults were not the only reason. The American *Enterprise* had a crew and management team that worked together whereas Lipton's reversion to a professional skipper led to tension with the gentlemanly afterguard. Lipton's quixotic efforts were finally acknowledged by the establishment and at the age of 80 he was elected to the Royal Yacht Squadron. He had no time left to enjoy the experience nor the RYS to name him as their champion in another attempt. The economic blizzard prevented the resumption of hostilities in 1931 and he died that October.

At Ascot the hard times were chiefly marked by a temporary reduction in the number of private luncheon tents. There was no economising in the fashions, for 1930 saw the return of long skirts, signalling the end of the flapper era. The annual suspension of reality was enhanced by a characteristic 'fairy-tale legend' so beloved of the press – the veteran ex-hurdler Brown Jack and his veteran jockey Steve Donoghue won the Queen Alexandra stakes six times running from 1929 to 1934. And if Windsor Castle house-parties were austere, that was how they had been since Queen Mary took them over. The Prince of Wales, who set himself up at nearby Fort Belvedere in that year of financial stringency, held parties of his own in more modern style.

Another sign of the times was the greater interest of wealthy owners in the somewhat less expensive National Hunt side of racing, among them J. V. Rank, the flour mill tycoon, and the Hon. Dorothy Paget. Miss Paget, a daughter of Lord Queenborough and one of the American Whitneys, was a particular asset – ludicrously rich, she spent as much on betting as on the upkeep of her horses, most of which were expensive failures. Lord Glanely was another who turned to National Hunt. He had just become the first self-made man to be elected to the Jockey Club, however, so this was no time to desert the flat. But he made a determined effort to economise. He had as principal jockey the champion, Gordon Richards, and at the start of the 1930 season, when it was too late for Richards to go elsewhere, Glanely decided to reduce his retainer by over £1,000. Richards protested, but with retrenchment in the air his options were limited and he was only able to get £500 of the cut restored. Richards, with a reduced number of rides, lost his championship to Freddie Fox and when in 1931 Glanely began to quibble again he went off to become stable jockey to Fred Darling, the ruthless master of Beckhampton, and from this strategic location never looked back. His sympathies with Glanely's financial difficulties were reduced by hearing him talk of spending £40,000 on yearlings.

George V was little seen on the Turf at this time. As Commodore of the RYS he also discouraged thoughts of a new challenge for America's Cup during the national emergency and Sopwith, straining at the leash, had to be patient a little longer. Apart from his inveterate apprehension about the possibilities of Bolshevik revolution, the King was anxious to assist MacDonald, for whom he had a high regard. Government attention was consumed by the need to balance the budget, restore the bankers' confidence and save the falling pound. Abandoning the gold standard was unthinkable. Increased taxation on the scale required would be a disincentive to hard work and enterprise, and not repaying the interest on the National Debt dishonourable. Cutting expenditure seemed the best, indeed the courageous way, and somehow reducing 'the dole', which businessmen saw as a deterrent to fixing competitive wages, came to seem a virility test of fitness for responsible government.[22]

Capitalism survives: the 1932 Olympics

Labour split on the issue and MacDonald was expelled from his local Hampstead party when he accepted the King's invitation to lead a coalition government to handle the emergency. He was spared the problem of Lloyd George, who was absent ill, and neither he nor his ally Baldwin wanted the war-mongering imperialist Churchill, even in an emergency. The announcement of stern measures – cutting the dole, raising income tax to 5s in the pound and reducing all state salaries and wages – bought them a little time and £80 million of foreign credit. But trades union opposition grew fiercer, and in September 1931 culminated in 'the mutiny of Invergordon' when the Atlantic Fleet refused to put to sea.[23] The dispute was quickly settled but the episode encouraged a feeling amongst foreign holders of sterling that revolution was imminent. The gold standard had to be suspended and the value of the pound fell by nearly 30%.

The call for a general election was led by Churchill, who saw 'dropping off gold' as the road to ruin. In fact it was no more than a further step in the process begun in 1914 when paper money had replaced gold sovereigns, and to the man in the street the pound in his pocket seemed the same as it had ever been – better if he was buying imported goods. When the election did come members of the coalition were able to present themselves as national saviours and sought a 'doctor's mandate' to offer more of the same unpalatable medicine of austerity. The Labour Party, who were judged to have run away from the problem, got support only in the worst pockets of unemployment or Celtic hostility. Apart from MacDonald, his Chancellor of the Exchequer Philip Snowden (who denounced Labour's election programme as 'Bolshevism gone mad') and a handful of other collaborationists, only 52 held their seats. They provided what opposition they could, though themselves divided by the uncompromising pacifism of the leader Lansbury. As Churchill put it, MacDonald thereafter 'brooded supinely at the head of an Administration which, though nominally National, was in fact overwhelmingly Conservative. Mr Baldwin preferred the substance to the form of power and reigned placidly in the background.'[24]

One of those who broke with MacDonald and found himself in the wilderness was Sam Perry, father of Fred. He was consoled by the LTA's invitation to Paris to see his son play in the Davis Cup. Fred had made a modest breakthrough at Wimbledon in 1930, beating the Italian Count Morpurgo before succumbing to Centre Court nerves. He did well enough to be selected for a six month LTA tour of America, North and South. The LTA was less fastidious about amateurism than the All-England Club. When the USLTA proposed an open tournament that year the British supported it and it was the grandees of the ILTF who stood firm against it. The LTA was desperate to win the Davis Cup and to build up a good squad. Thus though Perry remained an amateur, his selection for the tour, as he recalled, 'relieved my father of the need for any further financial sacrifice on my behalf'.[25]

In 1931 he went on an even more lavish US tour, managing to improve his game in between nights out with Jean Harlow (financed by the MGM publicity department) and similar diversions. He became convinced that the Americans had the right approach. 'After the snobbery and class divisions of the tennis set-up and life generally in England, America in 1931 was like a breath of fresh air.'[26] The America he so much admired was still deep in economic depression and a long way from Roosevelt's New Deal.

The sports enthusiasts in the Labour party had been trying to bring middle-class games within the reach of the workers. In one of its earliest efforts the NWSA sent tennis as well as soccer teams to play Dutch and German workers in Holland. At home one of the leading NWSA tennis clubs was at Ealing, whence Perry had sprung to take on the establishment. In 1932 his father wrote proudly in the Co-operative Party journal, 'our pleasure [at his success] is shared by co-operators throughout Britain, by whom Fred is justly regarded as one of ourselves'.[27] In fact like most sportsmen Perry was completely apolitical. As the NWSA prepared to hold its 'Workers' Wimbledon' that year he was greatly upset by his visit to Berlin for the Davis Cup, not because of the presence of Hitler and his storm troopers, but because he lost. 'We never discussed politics . . . I couldn't have cared less which government was where.'[28]

There were politically-inclined sportsmen. One of Baldwin's newly-elected back-bench supporters in 1931 was Lord Burghley, who had recently left the Grenadier Guards and joined the boards of several companies. The following year he tore himself away from his Parliamentary and business responsibilities to captain the British team at the Los Angeles Olympics. The AAA had the previous year indicated its reforming intentions by electing as President the 74-year-old Lord Desborough, Willie Grenfell, the archetypal late Victorian sportsman – big game hunter, Oxford rowing Blue of 1877 and President in the twenties of the MCC, the LTA and the Amateur Fencing and Wrestling Associations. He had been chairman of the BOC in 1908 and was well-equipped to steer the AAA though the muddy waters of Olympic amateurism. In 1931 the IOC took what the British regarded as a retrograde step in authorising paid leave for competitors provided their wages were paid by the employers themselves and not reclaimed from some official body. Apart from opening the door to unscrupulous totalitarian regimes this was an invitation to the purveyors of sports scholarships. Britain, disapproving of both camps, found herself more than ever dependent on Achilles and on regular officers, who now had their own élite club, Milocarian AC.[29] It was thought a giant step when Junior AAA championships were started that year to widen the range of opportunity beyond the public schools. And to the social divisions was now added a further complication. When the Scottish AAA complained of its continued subordination to the AAA in international matters the IAAF required a British Amateur Athletics Board to be set up. As the old bodies remained in existence the result was further dispute and confusion.

If assembling a British team was difficult, especially at a time of economic crisis, staging the Games at all was thought by some a miracle, by others obscene. Certainly the venue, alongside the opulence of Hollywood, drew attention to the weaknesses of the capitalist system as 70,000 jobless flocked into the city at a rate of 1,700 a day in the hope, if not of work, of at least a meal from the soup kitchens. The BWSF sent a team to the alternative Spartakiade in Moscow, and the *Daily Worker* sent back enthusiastic reports of the event. There were no ugly blemishes on the face of Soviet society. A Dukinfield cyclist reported 'A1 social and industrial conditions and good leisure facilities' and the Glasgow delegate made it clear that he wore no rose-coloured spectacles: 'one did not need to be a class-conscious worker to feel that here was something different; happy faces, no sign of the starving children we have read about . . . Yes, this is something vastly different from the spirit we had left in England.'[30]

But the bourgeois affair at Los Angeles had also turned into a notable success. The competitors were housed cheaply and sociably in a specially built athletes' village. There were plenty of spectators and if the entries were slightly down on Amsterdam the standards were much higher. The American system of open (if not integrated) high school education and sports scholarships was seen to good advantage not least in the emergence of black athletes from poor home backgrounds. The British mixture had less success. Tom Hampson, of Achilles, who won the 800 metres, was scarcely representative of the old dashing tradition – a myopic schoolmaster so dedicated that he trained with a stop-watch in his hand. Jerry Cornes, a more convivial type just down from Oxford, came second to an Italian in the mile and Pilot Officer D. O. Finlay third in the 110 metre hurdles. The other gold medal went to Tommy Green, a 38-year-old railwayman, in the unconsidered and idiosyncratic 50,000 metres walk. The oddest example of the true-blue British spirit was Lord Burghley himself, who, finding that his American rival was to carry the flag in the opening parade, decided that he must do the same so as not to take unfair advantage, suffered in the broiling Californian sun, and could only manage fifth place.

The BOC, unimpressed by the Americanisation of the Games, urged the IOC to greater vigilance in the matter of amateurism, provoking lengthy but inconclusive debate. The rowing authorities, as ever, were the most concerned. They had been much troubled by the adverse criticism they had incurred over their treatment of the Australian Henry Pearce, son of Harry, Ernest Barry's great professional rival, who had won the sculling gold medal at the Amsterdam Olympics in 1928. Pearce had hoped, not unnaturally, that the achievement would confer eligibility to compete at Henley, but the Stewards turned him down on the grounds that he was a carpenter. The fatuity of the ruling was exposed when Pearce, unable to find work in the depression, was given a job as a whisky salesman by Lord Dewar, the Canadian distiller. This noble calling entitled him to compete at Henley, where in 1931 he won the Diamond Sculls by six lengths. It was salt in the ARA's wounds when he went on to take the gold medal at Los Angeles.[31]

The NARA meanwhile had softened its attitude only to the extent of agreeing that metropolitan policemen 'who had to use motor boats in the course of their duty did not violate their status'.[32] The depression years had remarkably little effect on the clubs in either camp. Of much greater concern to all right-thinking oarsmen than the clamour for democracy was that Oxford had not won the Boat Race since 1923. This was no mere question of vulgar partisan loyalties, but of ideological disputation about style. In 1930 the incoming Oxford President resigned after only ten days in office, after a disagreement with the coaches, but his successors fared no better, and in 1932 they imported a new coach from Cambridge, Colonel J. H. Gibbon, a ruthless fanatic, intent on proving a point. Even the new boat ordered from 'Bossie' Phelps at the President's own expense brought no improvement in Oxford's performance.

The current controversy was over the use of fixed pin rowlocks or the swivel variety, which was the latest gimmick of the Fairbairn followers. At Cambridge the university did not use swivels though its colleges were beginning to do so, so that potential Presidents were subjected to increasingly severe catechisms as to their theological soundness. The matter was complicated by the fact that the great H. A. 'Jumbo' Edwards, sent down from Oxford in 1926 for failing his exams, had returned in 1930 to try to redeem himself and had spent much of the intervening period schoolmastering (!) and rowing with London RC using swivel pins. He used them for Oxford in 1930 while the rest of the crew used fixed ones. (Edwards, who had his own private aeroplane, and had even managed to persuade the authories to let him take it up to University, was not a man to be argued with.) Los Angeles brought further confusion to the great debate. Edwards won two gold medals rowing for London RC in the coxless pairs and fours (alongside the veteran Jack Beresford). But in the all-important eights the fixed pins of Cambridge, who had stayed together as Leander to take the Henley Grand, had to take second place in the Olympics to the local University of California.

Women, as well as the American way of life, were on trial at Los Angeles. Their continued participation in track events had been fiercely debated by the IOC in 1930, with Count Baillet-Latour of Belgium arguing that they should be restricted to 'aesthetical events' like gymnastics, swimming, skating and so forth. The British women, seeing no further point in refusing the half-loaf when no bread was the likeliest alternative, swallowed their pride and sent a team, belatedly. A bronze medal in the 4×100 relay was the only tangible result. That one of the team, Nellie Halstead, came from Bury AC indicated that the WAAA's performing strength, if not that of its committees, was shifting beyond the London Olympiades circle. The versatile Halstead was stronger at 200 and 400 metres – she was the current 220 yards world record holder – but there were no women's events at these distances. It was an 18-year-old American typist, Mildred 'Babe' Didrickson, already a basketball star, who caught the headlines, with gold medals in the 100 metres hurdles and javelin and a shared world record in the high jump. The IOC was not overly impressed, especially when she lost her amateur status soon afterwards by appearing in advertisements.

Only in the swimming, where Japanese men (or rather boys) swept the board, was US supremacy seriously challenged, and this turned out in the end to be of greater political than sporting significance, demonstrating how a nation could use a focused school system to win international prestige. Japan had not yet gone fully fascist but was well into 'state familism' with imperial and militarist overtones.[33] In 1931 she took the first step towards creating an eastern bloc, quarrelling with China and occupying Manchuria. The League began the slow and feeble process of condemnation that was to lead to Japan's withdrawal. Meanwhile her team at Los Angeles, subsidised to the tune of 100,000 yen, gave a foretaste of the 'new order' and further showed the Olympic potential for international disharmony, as the IOC in its first full-scale drugs scandal investigated allegations that the Japanese team doctor administered oxygen between races. The IOC, whose main worry about Los Angeles was its commercialism, had every reason to hope that the next Games, awarded to Berlin, where the sport-conscious Weimar Republic was still intact, would be conducted on a much higher plane.

Capitalism survives: hiking, boxing and soccer

German sport, indeed, still conveyed an agreeable image of the great outdoors, sun-bathing in the intervals of tramping the countryside. In Britain, despite the dismal weather of 1931, a great fervour for hiking had seized the land. Many new clubs sprang up, especially in the north where its cheapness made it a timely vogue. The time was also ripe, the Ramblers' Rights Association felt, to make a point about access to the countryside. On 24 April 1932, it duly organised a Mass Trespass of Kinder Scout, an uncultivated moor in Derbyshire. Some 400 people joined in the rally and march, demanding open access, low fares and so forth and confronting the temporary wardens appointed to protect the property, singing revolutionary songs and exhibiting enough violence to cause six of them to be arrested. The propaganda the communists sought to gain from this was far outweighed by the adverse reaction of most of the public and press, even in the north. As the *Oldham Chronicle* observed, 'The mass trespass movement seeks to take the ramblers' kingdom of heaven by force. The wiser and better way is to gain and keep that heaven by sweet reasonableness.'[34] Most people were satisfied with the commercial way. Many expeditions were sponsored by provincial newspapers. The railways also made the most of their opportunity. That Good Friday the GWR ran a 'Hikers' Mystery Special' from Paddington to greener parts, and there were soon 'Ramblers' Harvest Moon' specials and southern 'Railway Moonlight' walks over the South Downs, all vastly popular. The LMS took Lancashire folk on slow excursions through the Yorkshire Dales and ran 'Romantic Specials' to Gretna Green, just across the Scottish Border, where the village blacksmith was supposed to have special dispensation to marry eloping couples.

Communists were still seen, especially in the upper reaches of society, as a bigger threat than fascists. Amongst the general public Hitler, lurking menacingly in the background, was not taken seriously at first because his *Mein Kampf* dream of uniting the hundred million Germans world-wide in one 'Aryan' Reich seemed simply crazy. Anti-Semitism was not unknown in Britain and to anyone even mildly right wing his antics had the enormous advantage of being anti-communist. Mussolini, who had seized control in the twenties, had so far seemed the more considerable figure – with much to commend him, furthermore. Had he not, as they said, got the railways to run on time? And had he not done a great deal for Italian sport?

One of Mussolini's admirers was the politically confused son of the idealistic Earl of Lytton, Viscount Knebworth, who had entered Parliament in support of the National Government in 1931 but was increasingly assailed by doubts about the future of capitalism.[35] His Lonsdale Library volume on boxing was a lament for a once-noble sport debased by commercial values. Knebworth blamed its particular decline in Britain largely on the amateurs. He much preferred the heroes of the old prize-ring. 'These men fought for a money prize, they fought for a living, they fought as a profession, but they fought because they loved fighting, because they gloried in the proud achievement of physical effort.' In the heyday of the Pelican Club, Wonderland and the NSC, fighters 'were amateurs at heart if they were professionals in practice'. The 'degradation of the ring' had begun with the advent of 'ill-made, ugly, unworthy men' not themselves athletes but experts in 'the subtle arts of finance and showmanship', part of the 'mad lunacy of twentieth-century sport' catering for 'huge, half-educated crowds'.[36]

There should be no more distinction, Knebworth reckoned, between amateurs and professionals than was necessary – in a physical sport – to protect the part-time performer from the full-time. In their reaction to commercialism the amateurs had retreated behind euphemistic phrases like 'the art of self-defence'. Even the word 'fight' had become taboo and knockouts were considered bad form. This was not to deny the ABA's success. 'The swing from dislike of professionalism . . . has been considerable, and the result has been that amateur boxing has flourished and attained a popularity which is little short of astounding.'[37] But he believed the gulf between the two sectors was too wide. Pernickety insistence on the letter of the law and the insinuation 'that there was something infra dig and unworthy in being a professional' had had two bad effects. First, it had created an atmosphere of 'professional amateurism which is far more objectionable than the worst abuses of professionalism themselves'. Second, it 'kept from the professional ring many promising and competent young boxers who might well have made good in the greater world'.[38] The ABA, of course, did not see it as a greater world. It was a matter of regret when the amateur lightweight champion of 1931, Jack Petersen, promptly turned professional. To the public, however, he was a new hero and a new hope. Their only disappointment was that he never quite made the grade – a fine stylist but not big enough or rough enough for life at the very top.

Despite these handicaps Petersen became British heavyweight champion the following year, but this was in a field lacking in distinction, rendered more so by a colour bar that stopped black men competing for British titles even if British-born. Thus the Manchester middleweight Len Johnson could fight the champion Len Harvey but it was not recognised as a title bout. The public were not so fastidious: Larry Gains, the black Canadian, was a great favourite in Britain and was based in Leicester when he beat Phil Scott for the British Empire title in 1931. Harvey, who beat the heavyweight Gains three years later, was Jewish. This was certainly no bar, with so many Jewish promoters around, and Harvey, perhaps the greatest English boxer between the wars, was adored far beyond his native west country or his spiritual home in the East End.

Scott, for all his inadequacies, might have become world champion, when he was fouled by the appropriately-named Jack Sharkey in an eliminator following Gene Tunney's retirement in 1929. Thereafter new promoters took over who made American boxing a business and presented it as entertainment, with the sporting element a poor third. As its control fell into the hands of financially-interested, contending groups, gambling further corrupted the sport. The unreliable Sharkey was the central figure in a brief period that saw both a German champion, Max Schmeling, a Nazi hero, and an Italian, the giant Primo Carnera, soon toppled by the Jewish Max Baer. Britain was on the fringes of all this, but her biggest-ever boxing crowd watched the negro Gains beat Carnera in an open-air contest in 1932. British boxing, if undistinguished, was relatively honest. Whatever its shortcomings the new British Board of Control was run by Stewards who were financially disinterested – a major achievement in a sport chronically bedevilled by 'fixes' and now caught up in American-style razzmatazz. But everywhere match-making was increasingly dominated by publicity value, in which human interest and good copy took precedence over purely sporting matters. Knebworth complained that the boxing news in the 'cheap press' concerned everything but the actual sport.

Nothing could quench local enthusiasms, however, particularly in the areas where there was least to cheer about economically. The British featherweight champion Nel Tarleton, a supreme stylist, was Liverpool's pride, and his temporary eclipse by Seaman Watson gladdened hearts in Newcastle. In 1930 Whitechapel briefly had its own world lightweight champion when Jack 'Kid' Berg beat 'Mushy' Callahan in a local ring but Berg soon lost it in the States. Manchester had two great little men, Johnny King at bantam weight and flyweight, and Jackie Brown, world flyweight champion for three years from 1932. And up in Glasgow a lad from the Gorbals, Benny Lynch, was finishing his apprenticeship in the booths and preparing to take on – and beat – Billy Warnock from Belfast's Shankill Road. 'There's a whole family of them', Lynch's trainer told him, 'and they're hard wee men that would face up to a lion for a bob a round.'[39]

The British dilemma as the amateurs lost their battle against the forces of commercialism also showed itself in soccer. When Scotland visited Italy in 1931 the veteran London journalist Ivan Sharpe was deeply impressed by the organisation, by the Italian play and by the 'kindly, friendly' Mussolini himself. The Italians scored three goals, all greeted deliriously. 'Each time 40,000 handkerchiefs fluttered. Like three sudden falls of snow, in golden sunshine. I turned to see Mussolini, arm upraised.' In an interview afterwards Il Duce expressed his distaste for 'ever-spreading petty commercialism' and congratulated Britain on withstanding such influences and remaining 'mistress of disinterested sport'. He told Sharpe that the fascist state helped sport in every way it could and honoured greatly its football stars, who taught the virtues of clean living. He clearly 'valued sport for sport's sake'. Sharpe wrote home, 'It is time we studied the sport of continental countries. We are too insular, too content; we are letting the world go by.'[40]

In fact whilst the FA still hankered after 'disinterested sport' to the extent of controlling the national team through an amateur and amateurish selection committee of 13 members, the reality of the English strength lay in the 'petty commercialism' of the Football League – not its Management Committee nor its clubs' directors who had their own brand of amateurishness, but the intensely professional players and their managers. Now, under pressure, the

FA began to give a little. When it went to play Italy in 1933 the team was selected and controlled by the committee as usual, but the albescent black sheep Herbert Chapman was asked to go as an unofficial adviser. They managed a draw. As for Mussolini's 'sport for sport's sake' the British were spared the spectacle of Italy's triumphant staging and winning the 1934 World Cup because again they did not enter, but they saw something of its less noble side when England played the Italians at home that year. It was called 'the Battle of Highbury' and the injuries the Italians inflicted and their generally brutal play showed they were better at winning than losing. They were scarcely true-blue amateurs either, reputedly on £150 for a win plus an Alfa-Romeo car and exemption from national service.

That the England players' match fee was only £10 did not make them amateurs but rather emphasised their status as working-class hirelings. This was good pay compared with the industrial average of £3 or so a week, and, so the FA thought, a munificent bonus on top of their £8 a week maximum in the League. As Raich Carter of Sunderland, a newcomer to the side, recalled, 'I remember some of the boys . . . trying to get more money and being informed by the FA member in charge of the team that they should be glad to play for their country for nothing.'[41] But both they and the FA were trapped in a system in which the chief money-makers were the new breed of manager exemplified by Herbert Chapman. Chapman's Arsenal were now at the height of their powers, the best club side Britain had yet produced. They were to be League champions five times in the decade and never lower than sixth, winning the FA Cup in 1930 and 1936 and reaching the final in 1932. The Prince of Wales opened their new stand that year and the Earl of Lonsdale joined the Board.

Chapman lost no opportunity for publicity, whether in persuading London Transport to call the local tube station Arsenal, or encouraging his players to play cricket (usually for Middlesex) in the summer.[42] He had seen floodlit soccer on the continent in 1930 and noted its commercial possibilities. The FA would not allow floodlit matches but Chapman installed lights over his new stand and used them for training until official opinion changed. His schemes for using a white ball in poor light, for numbered shirts and for a 45-minute visible clock were also dismissed as gimmicks at first. So were his proposals for team-talks and an organised approach for international preparation. The amateurs were not the sole obstacle to progress in this respect, however. After the visit of the Austrian team in 1932 there was much press comment about their superior tactics and the fact that they had an English coach, Jimmy Hogan of Sheffield United. But even the few clubs that did employ coaches did not entrust them with the first team, still less with tactics, and they would have been spurned by the leading players if they had been. When Everton's manager tried to introduce the concept 'Dixie' Dean told him, 'The trouble is you buggers can't play.'

Priorities and prize-money

The British predilection for pragmatism also prevailed in the management of the economy, with somewhat more satisfactory results. The measures the government took in the crisis years sprang from no discernible politico-economic theory. They reduced armaments expenditure much further than Labour would have dared to do. They stopped trying to protect the pound. They risked the wrath of investors by reducing War Loan interest rates – and found them grateful for an assured 3.5% in perilous times. They reduced bank rate to 2%. They spurned the advice of those who called for a planned economy, like J. M. Keynes, but they imposed tariffs of the kind he advocated. With a glut of cheap food available world-wide they protected British agriculture by quotas and subsidies. The simple-minded notion that imposing tariffs would reduce imports without affecting exports – because British goods were best – was made more plausible by the idea of exempting the Empire. Chamberlain's dream of fulfilling his father's old Imperial Preference scheme did not last long, but it bought time and hope. And at the critical moment the middle classes found themselves with cash to spare in a world in which their money bought more at home than abroad. Enthusiasm for financial specu-lation, especially overseas, had been blunted, so if they invested at all it was in a house. The building trade was soon thriving, always a good sign. And there was plenty of cheap food for everyone, with the possible exception of the chronically unemployed, who were fast becoming a 'special case'. The general climate of opinion was optimistic.

The newspapers and their nimble-witted advertisers skilfully fed the pre-judices and preferences of their chosen segments of the market. Very few readers wanted to read about what a difficult life it was for everyone; life was difficult enough without reading about it. And the less securely prosperous they were the more this held good. Only about half the population took a daily newspaper. The numbers were increased, somewhat expensively, by a circulation war between the *Daily Mail*, *Daily Express* and *Daily Herald*: readers were offered free insurance, household goods, sets of Dickens and ency-clopaedias, touted to the aspirant as invaluable preparation for grammar school scholarship examinations. This temporarily improved the circulation of the only Labour paper the *Daily Herald*, and permanently that of the *Express*, but politics did not sell papers. Like the populist Sunday *News of the World* and *The People*, the mass-circulation dailies dealt rather in crime, sex and 'human interest'. The young Sheffield University graduate Amy Johnson's solo flight to Australia was the great marvel of 1930, much publicised by her sponsor, the *Daily Mail*, who made the most of her romance, marriage and subsequent adventures with the handsome sophisticate Jim Mollison. Nineteen thirty-two was the year of the yo-yo and the unfrocking of the scandalous Rector of Stiffkey, who afterwards appeared in a glass case on Blackpool's Golden Mile. The Loch Ness Monster made its first non-appearance in 1933.

Many who did not read daily papers took magazines, like *Woman's Weekly* or the brighter *Woman's Own* launched in 1932, and many more took specialist sporting publications or the Saturday football final. Apart from sex, which so far had no specialist magazines, sport was by far the most discussed topic, day in, day out in 1930s Britain. After the weather, amongst men at any rate, sport came next, as a bonding ritual if nothing else. The 'working man' was not greatly interested in public affairs and the extent of his information contrasted sharply with his knowledge of sport, which was often encyclopaedic. No part of any newspaper was studied more closely than the racing form, which penurious enthusiasts read avidly in the public library. They did not want to string up the bloated capitalists whose sport this was: on the contrary they greatly admired them and were duly grateful for the chance to share in the fun.

The most significant effect of the recession had been to sharpen the keenness of racehorse owners to get some return for their investment. The RBCB responded to its plight as best it could and most of its profits went in increased prize-money. Owner–breeders like Lord Derby, who made the most profit, also did the most complaining, regarding themselves as upholders of a great tradition. Lord Derby reckoned that a horse had to win £650 in England before it covered its expenses, compared with France where thanks to a Tote monopoly only £180 was needed. 'The race-horse breeding industry is entirely dependent on racing', he warned in 1932;[43] 'Do away with racing and bloodstock is forever destroyed.' But the only purpose of the Turf's bloodstock industry was to breed racehorses, and a classic winner could command high stud fees. The fee for Lord Derby's own Hyperion, the sensation of 1933, was £400: he was to be six times leading sire, after who knows how many services rendered. Breeders of such treasures did not lightly sell them but when Solario, a mere Ascot Gold Cup winner, aged ten, changed hands in 1932 he fetched 47,000 guineas. Generally speaking the road to success was through the cheque book, but breeding was far from an exact science. The 100–6 winner of the 1932 Derby, April the Fifth, had been bought as a yearling for 200 guineas and had been passed on to Tom Walls (a West End actor–manager who trained a few horses as a healthy day-time activity) on a profit-sharing basis: after his Derby win April the Fifth's stud fee was far higher than his original purchase price.

In theory the blood stock industry was a great source of export revenue, and the Aga Khan's sales abroad were thought an unpatriotic breach of hospitality. But he seemed to have an endless supply, of horses as of money. His huge stud produced the Derby winning colts of 1935 and 1936, Bahram and Mahmoud, who surpassed even Hyperion in stud fees. The Aga Khan was the outstanding success of the decade financially if not socially, heading the list of winning owners six times between 1929 and 1937 and winning the Derby three times. Lord Derby (twice), Lord Rosebery and Lord Astor also had their years of triumph with Mr J. A. Dewar the only commoner. The prize-money itself was not negligible, though the Aga Khan's £64,898 in 1934 was exceptional.

Trainers got 10% of prize-money as well as training fees, now usually £5 a week in the top stables and £4 elsewhere. Out of this came substantial expenses, notably the wages of stable lads, perhaps on the scale of one to every two horses in the best stables.[44] There was still plenty left. Joe Lawson's £93,899 in 1931 was not to be bettered for 26 years, but he continued to do well throughout the decade. His type was becoming something of a rarity, as the latest generation of the old training families, like Darling, Jack Jarvis (trainer to Lord Rosebery) the Leaders, Nightingalls and Marshes took over. Some of these were minor public school men, like Jarvis and Frank Butters, son of an English trainer overseas, formerly private trainer to Lord Derby, who secured the patronage of the Aga Khan in 1931. By 1937 he had saddled over 500 winners and netted over £500,000 for his owners. It was well worthwhile for the newer gentlemanly breed who now flooded in. 'Atty' Persse himself was still going strong and his pupil, Cecil Boyd-Rochford was leading trainer in 1937 and 1938. Gordon Johnson Houghton went from Eton and Oxford to pupillage with Jack Colling, and Bill Dalton, rider of the 1928 Grand National winner, a Cambridge graduate, took up training in preference to his uncle's law firm in 1932.

No-one knew what the leading jockeys earned, nor much cared, for the popular unscientific approach to backing successful winners was to follow the star of these heroes. The national love of a flutter had been encouraged during the darkest hour of the depression by an alien force, the Irish Sweep, a gigantic lottery in aid of hospital funds run by a Dublin bookmaker with the support of the Free State government in the precarious financial climate of 1930 and immensely popular in Britain. Its first venture, on the Manchester November Handicap, paid out £100,000 on a 10s ticket, and the following year on the Grand National, the first prize was £354,725, and well over £1 million was paid out altogether.[45] Though a substantial amount went to the organisers it was fairly conducted and, of course, the hospitals also got a share. But the anti-gambling lobbies were joined by irate chauvinists who disliked the idea of the rebel Irish corrupting the British and pocketing the proceeds. *The Times* warned that such huge prizes would lead to bribery and its Dublin correspondent snidely remarked that cashing in on 'the world's liking for a sporting chance cannot be held to accord with Arthur Griffith's proud maxim, "Ourselves Alone" '.[46]

The Empire survives a crisis

Whilst vulgarians studied racing form for solace during the difficult years the better sort preferred the cricket scores. In 1930, at a dinner for the victorious Australian tourists, HRH the Jam Singh of Nawanagar, K. S. Ranjitsinhji, was warmly applauded when he described cricket as 'among the most powerful of the links which keep our Empire together. So long as we can maintain in that Empire the spirit of sportsmanship which cricket inculcates, so long shall we be ready, as a team, to meet and defend any adversity which the future may hold for us.'[47] A year later Lord Harris described cricket as 'more free from anything sordid, anything dishonourable, than any game in the world'.[48] Then, in January 1933, with his Lordship scarcely in his grave, the Australians outraged all right-thinking people by suggesting that a new tactic used against their cricketers was unsportsmanlike. The team responsible for the tactic was sponsored by MCC. It was managed by an Oxford man and captained by another. The allegation therefore was like suggesting that the Holy Trinity was a set of atheists.

In life Lord Harris had first had difficulty with the Australians in 1878, and clearly they were not yet entirely civilised. Of the many complicated factors in establishment disapproval of Australian cricketers, the main one was that they had imperilled the feudal mould. Their touring teams were an especial threat to the old order. Australians, complained A. W. Carr, regarded cricket as 'a business almost pure and simple – a matter of money', yet they 'were made a great fuss of, and were given privileges which are denied to our own professionals'.[49] (Privileges such as all the team changing in the same room, for instance.) Carr was, unusually, a genuine amateur, a fact which seemed to embitter him: 'I am enormously fond of hunting and the country life, but here I now am in the forties with no real job of work to do.'[50] Cricket had impoverished him, so its social distinctions mattered all the more. 'I know plenty of professionals whom I would delight to have as guests in my own home, but I am afraid I cannot say the same thing about most of the Australians I have met.'

One who shared Carr's views was D. R. Jardine, whom the selectors had appointed captain for the 1931 series against New Zealand, avowedly with an eye on the following winter's tour of Australia.[51] *The Times*, though

appreciative of Jardine's qualities, commented 'his claim has yet to be proved
. . . there are others who have played the game long, *and always as it should be
played* (my italics), who have been passed over'.[52] The Yorkshire amateur
Rockley Wilson, a master at Winchester where Jardine had *been* captain, was
more forthright: 'Well, we shall win the Ashes, but we may lose a
Dominion.'[53] The appointment was an odd one. Jardine had little experience
of captaincy at first-class level, and was not generally liked because of his
imperious manner. This did not go down well in Australia where the crowds
had not warmed to him on his previous visit in 1928–9. His silk scarf and
Harlequins cap and haughty demeanour made him God's gift to the
Australian barrackers, a fearsome bunch who were wont to cry 'Where's your
butler to carry your bat for you?' as he strode to the crease, and 'Leave our flies
alone', as he swatted them, 'They're the only friends you've got!'[54] The
antipathy was mutual. 'To take the most charitable view of the situation',
Jardine wrote, 'the behaviour of Australian crowds at its best . . . is not
naturally good . . . Here was Democracy arrogating to itself the right to
demand its full pound of flesh for which it has paid the munificent sum of a
shilling or two at the gate.'[55]

Jardine had taken against Australian cricketers as long ago as 1921, when his
chance of scoring a century for Oxford against the touring team had been
thwarted by their decision to get away early, and relationships had not
improved in the meantime. Why then was he chosen as the chalice-bearer on
the periodic mission to renew the imperial faith? The answer lay in the devious
mind of P. F. Warner, that other Harlequins cap-wearer, who had oozed his
way back to chairmanship of the selectors and was determined to prove that
he should never have been discarded. England had lost the Ashes in 1930,
suffering chiefly at the hands of Bradman, who had scored 974 of their 2,743
runs, 334 of them in a single day at Leeds. Debonair captaincy had been found
wanting and A. P. F Chapman, the dashing hero of 1928–9, was ditched. In
building up his team to regain the Ashes Warner felt that 'discipline' was vital
and that it should include 'only those men who would subordinate everything
else to cricket'.[56] In choosing Jardine as leader he created a monster that
neither he nor anyone else could control.

An important question for the selectors was 'the right type of bowlers for
Australia'. Bowlers, historically a depressed class whose function had become
that of serving up deliveries with which the batsmen could entertain the
crowds, were toiling in the new commercial age on wickets prepared to last.
The final Test of 1930, scheduled to be fought to a finish, had lasted six days.
Harold Larwood, the fastest bowler in England, expressed the philosophy of
his trade: 'Purely defensive batting reduces the speed bowler to panting
futility. That is why he must drop a few short . . . And when he does . . .

everybody knows it is a ball intended to intimidate.' His county captain, A. W. Carr, had ensured that he was not beset by inhibitions: 'I made it my business to see that he took to beer.' And Larwood was frank about its effects: 'The batsmen used to hate facing us after lunch . . . We'd . . . have a few pints. Feeling no pain when we returned we'd bet each other half a crown who would be the first to crack a batsman's ribs.'[57] The other half of the 'we' was his Nottinghamshire partner, Bill Voce, also selected for the Australia tour, who when asked by an opponent what sort of team they had brought said, 'If we don't beat you we'll knock your bloody heads off.'[58]

Short-pitched bowling was accepted as legitimate, indeed inevitable, on docile pitches. So, too, was 'leg theory' in which the bowler deliberately directed his attack towards the batsman's leg-side with fielders clustered round him waiting for a catch. What was questionable was combining the two. A. W. Carr had experimented with this in county matches, more often with Voce, a left-hander, than with Larwood, and when used with both in combination in the domestic season of 1932 it had been disconcerting rather than wholly successful. Another who used it, encouraged by an aggressive county captain,[59] was Bill Bowes of Yorkshire. On 22 August, Warner, the chairman of selectors, still writing for the *Morning Post,* told its readers, 'Bowes bowled with five men on the onside, and sent down several very short-pitched balls which repeatedly bounced head high and more. Now that is not bowling: indeed it is not cricket.' But the moralistic journalist was a pragmatic selector; next month Bowes was on the boat for Australia along with Larwood and Voce.

Batting for Surrey against Bowes, Douglas Jardine had seen beyond the temporary discomfort. He had already discussed the tactics for Australia with Voce and Larwood, and Bowes would fit in nicely. The target, literally and metaphorically, was to be Bradman. Jardine, the archetypal virility cult public school man, had seen what he perceived to be a chink in Bradman's armour: he was supposed to have flinched from Larwood fliers on a wet wicket in 1930. Could Larwood bowl leg theory, he asked? He could and did. Warner, who went as tour manager, was anxious to emphasise afterwards that he knew nothing of such clandestine plottings and was utterly opposed to what the press christened 'bodyline' but he uttered no word of criticism on the tour and made no attempt to stop Jardine.

Jardine was in fact unstoppable and must remain as the principal villain of the piece. But he was also the chosen agent, known to be ruthless, of an organised attempt to win back the Ashes, merely pressing it to the logical extreme of winning at all costs. Absence through illness saved Bradman from assault in the first Test, a placid pitch in the second and fancy footwork in the third. In this match, however, described by *Wisden* as 'probably the most unpleasant ever played', others were not so fortunate. That the actual injuries were not inflicted when 'leg theory' was being employed was an accident irrelevantly seized upon by chauvinists. The low point came when Larwood was bowling, with an orthodox field, to W. M. Woodfull, the Australian captain, with Bradman at the non-striker's end. Larwood sent a ball inches from Woodfull's head. The next struck him over the heart and he crumpled in pain. Jardine – for Bradman's benefit – said, 'Well bowled, Harold.' Woodfull recovered but was still shaky. As Larwood ran in to bowl again Jardine stopped him and ostentatiously moved the slip fielders over to the leg side. The tactic worked, in that Bradman, after ducking a couple, put up an easy catch, and eventually England won the match and the Ashes. But in every other respect it was a disaster.

When Warner, characteristically, presented himself at the Australian dressing room to enquire after Woodfull's health he replied, 'I don't want to see you, Mr Warner. There are two teams out there. One is trying to play cricket and the other is not. The game is too good to be spoilt. It's time some people got out of the game.'[60] The British public, in those pre-television days, had to rely on newspaper accounts. If they read *The Times*, which had the headline ENGLAND'S GRAND RECOVERY – CHEAP AUSTRALIAN WICKETS, they would have learned that 'Australia's comparative failure on a perfect wicket (was being) keenly discussed' and that the English bowling 'did not meet with the approval of the crowd, who made hostile demonstrations when the batsmen ducked'.[61] Two days later, after another batsman had been struck on the head, the Australian *Smith's Weekly* had some different headlines: 'IT'S NOT CRICKET' – BUT WOODFULL ALWAYS PLAYS THE GAME and BOARD OF CONTROL SHOULD STATE ITS VIEWS TO THE MCC IN ENGLAND.[62] They did, in a cable of protest that put honesty before diplomacy: 'In our opinion [bodyline] is unsportsmanlike and unless stopped at once it is likely to upset the friendly relations existing between Australia and England.' The reply was withering, 'We, Marylebone Cricket Club, deplore your cable. We deprecate your opinion that there has been unsportsmanlike play. We have fullest confidence in captain team and managers', and concluded that if relations were really as bad as was suggested they would reluctantly agree to the cancellation of the rest of the tour.

The press was full of rumours and speculation as news of the rebuff to Warner leaked out. The Melbourne weekly *Truth*, suggesting that England had 'descended to the back-lane tactics of 'If you can't bowl 'em out knock 'em out', rehearsed the views of a New South Wales judge that it could be dealt with under the criminal law.[63] Under pressure behind the scenes from the Australian government, concerned about possible effects on British conversion loans and already dismal agricultural prices, the ABC replied that cancellation was not necessary – but did not withdraw its charges. Jardine, however, had cabled MCC demanding an apology, and though the Dominions Secretary, J. H. Thomas, urged caution – not wanting to see the recently concluded imperial trade agreements imperilled – it had become a matter of honour. (Indeed his Cabinet colleague, the Secretary for War, Lord Hailsham, was the incoming President of MCC and somewhat hawkish on the matter.) MCC's reply politely indicated that resumption depended on retraction. ABC, cornered – and contemplating the possible loss of revenue – replied, 'We do not consider the sportsmanship of your team to be in question' and MCC relented.

As the fuss subsided English opinion hardened into a conviction that Australians were squealers, afraid of hard knocks and poor losers. *The Times*, which considered it would be 'utterly re-actionary . . . to tell bowlers that they must go back 50 years and start all over again in an effort to find a way of curtailing a batsman's fun', gave Jardine 'full and ungrudging credit . . . for a splendid victory' when the Ashes were won.[64] Neville Cardus suggested that a statue of Larwood be erected for ending the 'fatty degeneracy' of recent Test cricket.[65] The exchange of cables continued into the summer, however, as Australia urged action to prevent a recurrence. MCC were still unconvinced, but the fast bowlers Constantine and Martindale, who used the now fashionable attack for the touring West Indies in 1933, caused some English players to revise their views. Hammond, hit on the chin, was a notable convert. Bradman was greatly amused by the turn of events. Warner left the selectors and wrote sanctimonious articles seeing everybody's point of view but condemning bodyline. Jardine wrote an utterly unrepentant book and supplied the foreword to a ghosted one by Larwood, who had also succumbed to the temptation of supplying articles and interviews for the press. Larwood was injured for most of the season, which saved the Test selectors embarrassment as enthusiasm for bodyline began to wane.

Jardine, still greatly admired by Lord Hawke and other pillars of MCC, played the West Indies bowlers without flinching and was chosen to lead England on that winter's tour of India, where he was as uncompromising on and off the field as ever. Meanwhile, however, a joint meeting of the counties and the Board of Control for home Test matches yielded to Australian argument to the extent of declaring, in November 1933, that although 'no alteration of the law was desirable' intimidatory bowling 'would be an offence against the spirit of the game'. Whilst Warner hob-nobbed with his friend Sir Alexander Hore-Ruthven, Governor of South Australia, about the desirability of ditching Jardine before the projected next visit of the Australians next summer, and J. H. Thomas, with alcoholic sentimentality, reminded MCC of their duty to the Empire, Jardine cabled from India to say he had no intention of playing against the Australians anyway. It was by no means certain that there would be a tour in 1934. MCC had only resolved to invite the Australians by eight votes to five and they were equally uncertain whether to come. But eventually with much rumbling and grumbling on both sides assurances were given, the tour went ahead and the Empire was safe for a little longer.

Notes

1 See W. S. Churchill, *The Gathering Storm*, London, 1948 (1950 edn), esp. Chapter Three, 'Lurking Dangers'.
2 M. M. Robinson, *Hamilton Spectator*, 16 August 1930, quoted in K. Moore, 'The Warmth of Comradeship', *IJHS*, September 1989, pp. 242–250, on which this section is based.
3 Moore, 'Comradeship', p. 248.
4 See Derek Birley, *Land of Sport and Glory*, Manchester, 1994, pp. 168–9.
5 U. A. Titley and R. McWhirter, *Centenary History of the Rugby Football Union*, RFU, 1970, pp. 148–9.
6 Freethy had hitherto been admired (but thought ungentlemanly) for his stern action in sending off the All-Black Brownlie at Twickenham For an account of the 1931 dinner see E. W. Swanton, *Sort of a Cricket Person*, London, 1972, p. 110.
7 N. Cardus, *The Cricketer*, winter annual, 1931.
8 N. Cardus, *The Guardian*, 1954, reprinted in *A Fourth Innings with Cardus*, London, 1981.
9 N. Cardus, *Second Innings*, London, 1950, p. 73.
10 A. J. P. Taylor, *English History 1914–45*, Oxford, 1965, p. 280.
11 *Horse and Hound*, November 1929.
12 S. G. Jones, *Sport, Politics and the Working Class*, Manchester, 1988, p. 142.
13 ibid., p. 107.
14 ibid., p. 182.
15 G. Green, *The History of the Football Association*, London, 1953, pp. 509–11.
16 R. Kircher, *Fair Play*, London, 1928, p. 67.
17 H. F. Moorhouse, 'Footballers and working class culture in Scotland,' in R. Holt (ed.), *Sport and the Working Class in Modern Britain*, Manchester, 1990, pp. 186–7.
18 *Beckenham Advertiser*, 1930, quoted by J. A. Hargreaves, *Women's Sport Between the Wars: Continuities and Discontinuities*, University of Warwick, Working Papers in Sport and Society, Vol. 3, 1994–5, p. 129.
19 ibid.
20 Taylor, *English History*, p. 285.
21 J class yachts could be anything between 76 and 67 feet at the waterline and the formula allowed this flexibility without penalising sail area so long as displacement was increased proportionately.
22 'The dole' (a name conferred by the *Daily Mail* in 1919) was 15s a week for a single man, plus 5s for a wife and 1s for each child. It lasted – for those in benefit under the 'Lloyd George' scheme – for up to 15 weeks. Beneficiaries had to establish eligibility by turning up at the Employment Exchange every day. It did not apply to farm-workers or domestic servants.
23 The dispute was a result of the Admiralty's attempt to meet the requirement of a 10% reduction in its pay-roll by a flat-rate cut of 1s a day for all ranks.
24 Churchill, *Gathering Storm*, p. 70.
25 F. Perry, *Autobiography*, London, 1984, p. 30.

26 ibid., p. 41.

27 *Co-operative News*, 21 July, 1932, quoted by Jones, *Sport, Politics*, p. 109.

28 Perry, *Autobiography*, p. 51.

29 Called after Milo, a late sixth century Olympian athlete, said to have carried a 4-year-old heifer through the stadium and eaten it all afterwards.

30 Jones, *Sport, Politics*, p. 181.

31 D. Wallechinsky, *The Complete Book of the Olympics*, Harmondsworth, 1988, p. 276.

32 In 1927. E. Halladay, *Rowing in England*, Manchester, 1990, p. 146.

33 See I. Abe, Y. Klochara and K. Nakajina, 'Fascism, Sport and Society in Japan', *IJHS*, April, 1992, pp. 1–29.

34 14 May 1932, quoted by Jones, *Sport, Politics*, p. 143. See also, for an inside view, B. Rothman (the organiser), *The 1932 Kinder Trespass*, London, 1982, and, for a balanced survey, A. Holt, 'Hikers and Ramblers', *IJHS*, May, 1987, pp. 56–67.

35 Too young to serve in the war he deeply regretted the inroads it had brought. In an uncertain world he sought the comfort of Roman Catholicism. He was killed on duty in the Auxiliary Air Force in 1933.

36 Viscount Knebworth, *Boxing*, London, n.d. (?1933), pp. 226–9.

37 ibid., pp. 229–30.

38 ibid., p. 230.

39 J. Burrowes, *Benny*, Edinburgh, 1982 (London, 1984 edn), p. 173.

40 I. Sharpe, *Forty Years in Football*, London, 1954, quoted in S. Wagg, *The Football World*, Brighton, 1984, pp. 28–9.

41 R. Carter in E. Lanchberry (ed.), *Footballer's Progress*, London, 1950, p. 73.

42 Joe Hulme was one of a select band to become double internationals. The Compton brothers were near-misses and Ted Drake played for Hampshire.

43 Speech, quoted by T. Weston, *My Racing Life*, London, 1952.

44 For costs in the thirties, and the general background, see Capt. E. Rickman, *On and Off the Race Course*, London, 1935.

45 First prizes were soon restricted, first to £30,000, later to £50,000, but there were more of them and these were still enormous sums.

46 *The Times*, 22 and 24 November 1930.

47 ibid., 11 September 1930.

48 Letter to *The Times*, 3 February 1931.

49 A. W. Carr, *Cricket With the Lid Off*, London, 1935, p. 47.

50 ibid., p. 68.

51 See P. F. Warner, *Cricket Between Two Wars*, London, 1942, p. 102: 'Our ideas, workings and selections invariably had [Australia] in view.'

52 R. B. Vincent, *The Times*, 11 June 1931.

53 B. Stoddart, 'Cricket's Imperial Crisis', in R. Cashman and M. McKernan, *Sport in History*, Queensland, 1979, p. 132.

54 Still perhaps the best book on the series J. Fingleton's *Cricket Crisis*, London, 1946, has the authenticity of a participant, the skill of a professional writer, and the extra astringency of one not too enamoured of Bradman. See also R. Robinson, *The Wildest Tests*, London, 1972; D. Frith, *The Fast Men*, London, 1975, Chapter Eleven; D. Birley. *The Willow Wand*, London, 1978, Chapter Seven; L. Le Quesne, *The Bodyline Controversy*, London, 1983.

55 D. R. Jardine, *In Quest of the Ashes*, London, 1933, pp. 198, 209.

56 Warner, *Cricket Between Wars*, p. 106.

57 H. Larwood with K. Perkins, *The Larwood Story*, Harmondsworth, 1985, pp. 52, 46; Carr, *Cricket With the Lid Off*, p. 51.

58 Frith, *Fast Men*, p. 144.

59 A. B. Sellars, in his first season. A slightly better performer than Yorkshire's usual amateur leaders, he was an earthy disciplinarian.
60 *Larwood Story*, p. 8. There are many versions, but even Warner agreed that this was the substance.
61 *The Times*, 16 January 1933.
62 *Smith's Weekly*, 18 January, 1933; facsimile in P. Hayter (ed.), *Great Tests Recalled*, London, 1990, p. 39.
63 *Larwood Story*, pp. 158–64.
64 *The Times*, 1 and 7 February 1933.
65 *The Observer*, 12 February 1932.

CHAPTER ELEVEN

Changing the rules (1929–39): borrowed time

Whilst the bodyline drama was being enacted unemployment reached its peak. Nearly 3 million were now out of work, deprived of dignity as well as wages. The means test, introduced to ensure that expenditure on the dole was not swollen by claims from people with resources of their own to draw on, was deeply resented as a humiliating invasion of privacy. The government had other worries. When the National Socialist Party took control of Germany in January 1933 Britain was gripped by a burning desire for peace that showed itself in a spate of anti-war books and plays. There seemed a deplorable diminution of the Newbolt spirit when the Oxford Union passed its notorious resolution in February 1933, 'that this House will not fight for King and Country'. That October Hitler walked out of the Disarmament Conference as a prelude to leaving the League of Nations altogether and in a by-election at East Fulham a few days later the Labour candidate took the seat. This was construed as a vote for pacifism and frightened Baldwin out of facing the responsibilities of defence. Chamberlain, however, saw it as protest against the means test and set to work on a scheme of improvement. Meanwhile the hunger marches began, an inspiration of the communists to draw attention to the plight of the jobless by parading selected groups of them through the streets of the capital. MacDonald steadfastly refused to receive their deputations, and although the public's sympathy was aroused there was no stampede towards revolution.

Britain was not that kind of country. For one thing, though governments might come and go, above them stood the monarchy, an emblem of unity just as strong as in Victorian times and now much more accessible. George V, always assiduous in his public duties and with a palpable concern to set an example in war and peace, had grown in popularity over the years, and had recently made the first of his highly-successful Christmas broadcasts to the Empire. The Prince of Wales, for his part, was perhaps the most admired and popular man in Britain, and it was he who exemplified the nation's approach to 'the problem of the unemployed'. Early in 1932, addressing a meeting at the

Albert Hall organised by the National Council of Social Service, he had declared it 'vast and baffling if looked at in the mass, though easier to help when broken up into individual pieces', considering 'each member of the unemployed population as a single, separate personality, beset by depression, labouring under a sense of frustration and futility.' His appeal for volunteers set hundreds more helping the Council in a range of activities, from setting up Welsh Land Settlements that put unemployed families to work on farms to clubs and centres with a concern for their physical condition. The Prince kept a personal eye on this latter development, which gave it enormous cachet. Like most of his class at the time he saw communism as a bigger threat than fascism, and he became concerned that the clubs were too often 'run by the wrong sort of people'. 'People like you ought to run them', he told Mrs Dudley Ward and she duly started the first Feathers Club, called after the Prince of Wales's insignia.

There were many strands in the enthusiasm for physical fitness that was overtaking Britain. The state at first had little to do with it. Though the Ministry of Labour encouraged physical training at its instruction centres for unemployed juveniles, that was about the extent of government intervention. Unemployed adults had no great zest for keeping fit, especially those accustomed to hard manual labour, and they certainly did not like being dragooned into it, least of all by the government. The introduction of 'physical training' at the NCSS's centres for the unemployed also proved distinctly unpopular until less regimental-sounding names like 'physical recreation' were adopted, and swimming and a few games were brought in to sweeten the pill. And the camps provided by the Prince's well-intentioned volunteers had to overcome the suspicion that they might be 'labour camps'.

Nor did government initiatives play any part in the developments in physical education for men that were now belatedly beginning. They were, in any event, far from militaristic. In the public schools a progressive few were replacing the old drill-sergeants by non-military 'directors of physical education', in some cases as at the Quaker school, Leighton Park, avowedly as an alternative to OTCs, in others from educational conviction. Thus at Mill Hill the headmaster was inspired by the innovative S. F. Rous, a teacher at Watford Grammar School who later became secretary of the FA. There was still no specialist PE college for men, and the first, at Leeds in 1933, came not from government pressure but through the benefaction of the Carnegie Trust. The Board of Education allowed it to run a one-year course for teachers already qualified in other subjects.

Women took the lead in popularising recreative physical exercise as they had done in PE. The female 'keep fit movement' began in the north-east on the initiative of a Sunderland teacher impressed by developments in Denmark and Sweden and it quickly spread, notably to Lancashire where the flagging cotton trade had put many females out of work. One of the NCSS's constituents, the National Council of Girls' Clubs, took up the idea which soon became a national phenomenon. Constructive use of enforced leisure was not the only motivation. An important factor, at all economic levels than the very poor, was that better feeding brought both greater energy and excess poundage. This was more of a problem on the 'southern' side of the great divide. Mrs Bagot Stack's Women's League of Health and Beauty, started in London in 1929, caught on like a bush fire. There were regular rallies and demonstrations at the Albert Hall and in Hyde Park. They had no flavour of Hitlerite 'Strength through Joy'. Indeed the League expressly sought to further the cause of peace, and its utopian stance was exemplified by a mime in its 1933 demonstration symbolising the reconciliation of Capital and Labour.[2]

This reconciliation, sorely needed after Wall Street, was made easier by the fact that most people in Britain were now better off than before the financial crisis. The National Government had done pretty well, albeit from top down. Their crisis measures had created a better psychological climate that cheered up the City and started a modest industrial recovery. The middle classes' foray into the housing market had triggered a housing boom in which slum clearance and subsidy-assisted private building schemes also benefited. The most noticeable result was the proliferating ribbon development spreading suburbia along the highways. Annual sales of motor cars had increased even through the difficult years of 1929–31. Now they rocketed, to the especial benefit of the Midlands – Coventry, Birmingham, Oxford, Luton – and to the public danger everywhere. Motor-cycles, some with side-cars, catered for speed enthusiasts, the young and folk of modest means. With prices falling, real wages had risen by 10% since 1929. People bought furniture, household appliances and electrical equipment, sometimes assisted by the latest American device of hire-purchase, known familiarly as the 'never-never'. This reaction was not quite what the austere Chamberlain had in mind but the benefit to home industries, especially the new ones like electricity supply, plastics and man-made fabrics, was enormous. The exporting spree did not last and the rest of the world reacted predictably to British tariffs, but the initiative was not entirely lost. After the American banks failed in March 1933, President Roosevelt devalued the dollar as part of his New Deal, but by then Britain, stealthily building up gold reserves, was quietly confident.

Keeping afloat

One of the first signs of the new dawn was the renascence of the America's Cup. Sopwith had bought *Shamrock* from the Lipton estate and sailed her for two seasons, awaiting an opening in the clouds, until at the end of 1933 the King gave the signal and he felt able to set Nicholsons to work on his new boat. For once the Americans seemed to be at a disadvantage. Harold Vanderbilt, the holder, had difficulty getting a syndicate together, and as *Enterprise* no longer conformed with the regulations (which had changed yet again) he was obliged to cannibalise her to construct a new one, and to borrow a set of sails. He called the new boat *Rainbow* and the omen was good. Though the British yacht seemed a better design than the American there was no real opportunity of trying her out: *Shamrock* was the only other active British big class boat so *Endeavour*'s preparation was a tour of the annual regattas, as much a social as a competitive experience.

But Sopwith at least expected to have a well-drilled and harmonious crew at the end of it. The tour had the opposite effect: the men went on strike for more pay a week before they were due to sail for America. Not a man to give in to blackmail, Sopwith sacked them and invited volunteers from the Royal Corinthian Yacht Club. These were extremely keen and skilful small boat sailors, but obviously not ideal for J class work. Sopwith's temperament did not help relationships with his opponents either. Before the race he accused them of using an unauthorised winch and of stripping *Rainbow* down to a ludicrous extent, even removing the owner's bathtub. There was a gentleman's agreement to avoid protests during the actual racing if humanly possible. This held until the crucial fourth race, with *Endeavour* 2–1 up. In an incident at the start, with the British the more blameworthy, neither side complained, but later when Sopwith believed himself fouled again he not only protested but brought up the earlier episode. Instead of disqualifying him outright the Race Committee over-ruled his protest on a technicality, leaving him for the rest of his life convinced that he had been swindled out of the Cup, which he duly went on to lose in a cloud of rancour.

The experience merely stiffened his resolve and he continued to give a lead in yachting's notable contribution to economic recovery. Aldous Huxley had recently presented a modern nightmare in his *Brave New World*. It was a world whose inhabitants made the sign of the Model T instead of the cross, children played Centrifugal Bumblepuppy and sportsmen of the appropriate class could choose between Electro-Magnetic or Obstacle Golf at Stoke Poges. 'Strange', mused the Director of Hatcheries and Conditioning, 'to think that even in Our Ford's day most games were played without more apparatus than a ball or two and a few sticks and perhaps a bit of netting. Imagine the folly of allowing people to play elaborate games which do nothing whatever to increase consumption.'[3] In the capitalistic real world there was no need of compulsion. As a famous American designer put it, 'The modern America's Cup racer bears not the slightest resemblance to any useful craft in the world, and she does not contribute to the development of yachting as a true sport apart from the satisfaction of an illogical national vanity. But . . . they have the fascination of sin.'[4] Sopwith sold his 'old' boat to Herman Andreas and ordered a new one, *Endeavour II*, for a further attempt. Meanwhile Charles Fairey, a rival aircraft manufacturer who was Commodore of the Royal London YC, tried to usurp Sopwith's prerogative by issuing a challenge for the Cup in a slightly smaller K class boat. Whether contemptuous of such a proposal or concerned for protocol the NYYC stalled and allowed nature to take its course. Fairey was duly reminded of the unwritten custom and withdrew in confusion. A further olive branch to Sopwith and the RYS came when Gerald Lambert of the NYYC brought his boat over for the Jubilee regatta season in which *Britannia* made her final appearance and brought out many more flag-waving crowds.

Huxley's *Brave New World* implied advancing technology, but the British tradition was against too much science, especially when wedded to art. Esoteric theories abounded – the latest was Admiral Turner's metacentric shelf – but the Americans also brought tank-testing to the task, technically somewhat in advance of the Nicholson 'suck-it-and-see' approach. In the *America's* Cup of 1937 *Endeavour II* was never in the hunt with *Ranger*. Nevertheless the British were not convinced: 'Is it not time to give mathematics a rest and talk about "balance" in plain language?' asked *Yachting Monthly*, drawing the debate about the 'shelf' to a close. Added to idiosyncratic and often overbearing amateur management this pragmatism was a good recipe for continued failure, gallant or otherwise.[5] Olin Stephens's 1931 economy size (52 feet) innovation of the depression years also led to American domination of the Fastnet race and an expensive new specialism that the British caught up with only at the end of the decade.

Though yachts might be smaller, for the best people they still had to be custom-built. Nicholson's customers in the 30 feet range included the 80-year-old Sir Hercules Langrishe and J. C. T. Moore-Brabazon MP. John Nicholson, greatly daring, suggested to his father that they might go in for batch-production of a 'little cruiser-racer' of the same size. Predictably the old man thought this likely to affect the carriage trade, but relented to the extent of allowing him to build six. As John Nicholson put it these boats, whilst not for Rolls-Royce owners, were not for the Ford man either (a £100 Ford has just come on the market), 'but more for the Rover type of owner'.[6] They cost £875, complete except for bedding and cutlery. But capitalism was remorselessly democratic. For £350 David Hillyard offered a 5-ton auxiliary yacht with optional gaff or Bermuda rig and a Stuart Turner 8 hp engine, and Captain O. M. Watts of Albemarle St a 4-ton Harrison Butler design for £297 (or £77 down and the rest in easy payments).

For racing men the growing interest in one-design classes both stimulated batch-production and reduced bickering about the rules. The Lee-on-Solent Club ordered 20 18 foot boats and the 17 and 16 foot one-design classes gained in popularity. The biggest Olympic class was now the 8 metre, and Britain won a rare gold medal at the 1936 Games in the 5-man 6 metre class. The Americans were now just as good at the smaller end, however, and whilst the Seawanhaka International was keenly contested the British lost all five of the British–American Cup series in the thirties. At home Uffa Fox yielded the dinghy sailing honours to Stewart Morris, Peter Scott (the painter–naturalist) and John Winter but was an unending source of innovation challenging existing theories. There was, indeed, plenty of innovation but the faith in intuition remained.

Cheaper craft, like smaller cars, were often marketed as just the thing for ladies: Hillyards sold scores of 'smaller craft suitable for cruising women'. An article in *Yachting Monthly* was entitled 'Little Ships for the Woman Owner, what she can buy for a limit of £300.' 'Before the Great War,' it read, 'only a handful of women cared about the great sport of boat sailing, and those few were either ornamental passengers on large yachts or part of a small but enthusiastic band in the smaller one-design classes on the Solent and the Clyde.' Now they were everywhere: women sailors were 'not even a matter of passing interest'.[7] Altogether yachting was 'at last shedding its aura of complete exclusiivity'. But as 'getting away from it all' became more popular it became more difficult. Apart from the crowded yacht clubs the noise of the internal combustion engine was inescapable. The most famous boat of the day was *Bluebird* in which Sir Malcolm Campbell beat Gar Wood's world record in 1937 and took it up to 141.74 mph before the war.

Brave Old World

The encroachment of modernity was even more noticeable on the land, and the upper classes who had customarily enjoyed its pleasures saw themselves as defenders of a citadel. Politicians were sometimes insufficiently appreciative of this. 'It seems to be the great aim of successive governments to take away all that you have', complained the former Lord Dalmeny, now sixth Earl of Rosebery, in 1931.[8] In his case they were far from successful. He still had Mentmore and the stud, his estates in Scotland and houses at Newmarket and Epsom. And the Whaddon chase was doing well; by 1932 he was confidently predicting that 'hunting will last as long as anything else in this country'. In this he was secure in a powerful tradition. 'We condition the masses to hate the country', explained one of Huxley's characters. 'But simultaneously we condition them to love all country sports.'[9] The question was whether the new and dangerous forces in Britain – Bolsheviks, intellectuals, the rising lower middle classes – were to be allowed to spoil things.

'I have only now and again met hunting people,' wrote J. B. Priestley in 1934, 'and I do not understand them. Men and women whose whole lives are organised in order that they may ride in pursuit of stray foxes two or three times a week, who risk their necks for a vermin's brush . . . who spare no pains to turn themselves into twelfth-century oafs.' He had a particular disdain for the types who 'pretend to be solemnly doing their duty when in reality they are indulging and enjoying themselves.'[10] A more charitable interpretation is that they were exhibiting only the degree of hypocrisy required to fend off possible attacks from the legislators or urban moralists. The British Field Sports Society felt embattled in the struggle against 'the ignorant but violent attacks' of hostile groups, encouraged by certain 'unfortunate incidents' involving inhumane practices connected with the digging out of foxes and so forth.[11] But the attacks, 'expressing either the views of Sophists and Humanists or resentment at privilege and display', were sporadic and much milder than they were later to become. When the 4-year-old Princess Elizabeth, indicating that continued royal patronage was assured, was at covert-side to view away Frank Freeman's last fox with the Pytchley in April 1931, there was 'no breath of that strident urban dismay that greeted Princess Anne's day or two in Yorkshire in 1972'.[12]

Whatever its morality, hunting, Priestley noted, was 'taking on a new lease of life, in spite of the shortage of money'. The cash flow problem mainly showed itself in the smaller number of American MFH, which nobody minded very much. There was certainly no perceptible shortage of native 'new money'. Sir Julian Cahn was more prominent than ever at the Pytchley and Fernie, and if Nottinghamshire was somewhat poorer for his crossing the border, the second Lord Trent, managing director of the Boots empire, was an addict with a ready cheque book. Varying degrees of economy were needed. The 'lawn meet' replaced the old hunt breakfast, except for social climbers 'with unusual determination and wealth' and there were soon complaints that 'helpers with trays of drinks were being mobbed by free-loading foot-people, many locally notorious and some inimical to hunting'.[13] 'Capping' was now quite usual and 'field money', another Irish invention previously restricted to harriers in England, was introduced to Warwickshire in 1933 and gradually spread. Everywhere it became more important – and no easier – to persuade hunt members to live up to their guarantees. But despite all this fox-hunting thrived. There were 189 packs in Britain and 28 in Ireland; and fields, as Priestley intimated, were swelling. Well over half now consisted of women. Of these, even as the thirties began, half rode astride and thereafter only their own inclinations and fashion-consciousness deterred them. One of the most colourful figures was Mrs Sylvia Masters, Master of the Tipperary: 'she could blow her horn at full gallop, with a cigarette in her mouth; she was the first woman to ride 100 point-to-point winners'.[14]

Threatened legislative reform did not greatly trouble the BFSS although it was concerned at the Caledonian Power Bill which might damage fishing in the Highlands and nervous of the effects of electrifying railway lines. The chief target of the 'antis' was stag-hunting, which – since there were now only six packs in remote parts of England and little evidence that they actually killed anything – hardly seemed worth it. The in-roads of urbanisation also curtailed hare-hunting: harrier packs now numbered only 59, compared with 85 in the twenties, and 20 of these were in Ireland. Much of the harrier territory was taken over by beagle packs, which increased from 49 to 75, but relatively little killing now occurred. Like otter-hunting, which increasingly became otter-finding, much pedestrian pursuance, apart from poaching, was of a ritualistic kind, an excuse to dress up in outlandish gear. Really determined animal killers took a gun, and the deer-stalkers still had nearly a million acres for their pleasure.

Eric Parker, Eton, Oxford, naturalist, fisherman and loving chronicler of cricket and public school life, was the laureate of the shooters. With no tradition save besticide to call upon, his method was rather to indicate progress. Thus he made much of the modern preference for beauty and symmetry rather than mere size in antler-count. And in a comparison of Edwardian bird-shooters with those of the thirties he emphasised that 'the great pheasant era' when four-figure totals were daily entries in the game-books was 'a thing of the past' and 'the outlook of the shooting man . . . much more natural'. He gave a quasi-moral flavour to the comparison by indicating a shift of interest to problems 'better worth attention'. In 1905 when the *Badminton Magazine* asked the leading experts of the day to name the most difficult shot, 14 out of 15 had named pheasant. Thirty years later when *The Field* posed the same question snipe, grouse, partridge, wood pigeon, pochard, teal, golden plover and tufted duck all had their advocates and only one chose a 'high and curling pheasant'. (An old Scottish keeper, displaying the laconic wisdom that brought Sassenach tips, answered 'Weel, I'm no sure, for it a' depends.')[15]

Yet mass despatch of pheasants still had its appeal. Thus Lord Dorchester recalled with delight 'One Crowded Hour' in 1937: 'Sixty-five we have. Shall we reach 70? And by single birds we creep up to 68, 69 and hurrah! – 70 . . . I am more than satisfied, yet with the perverseness of human nature I shall never cease to speculate about what my bag might have been had I not run out of cartridges.'[16] The shooters' equivalent of the fox-hunters' pageantry, colour and equine magnificence was the love they bore towards their dogs. Parker composed lachrymose verses to a favourite young gun dog, snatched untimely from his master's side:

> So short, the life has passed. The dream remains.
> Still may I watch you with an inward eye.
> Still may I love you with unwounded heart.[17]

The shooters enjoyed remarkable freedom from censure even by the moralistic, perhaps because they were relatively inconspicuous. Continued royal patronage did their cause no harm: both the Prince of Wales and, more seriously, the Duke of York followed in father's footsteps. And they were protected, not threatened, by legislation. The vestiges of the ancient law of the forest, transmogrified by capitalism, had passed from hunting to shooting. The basic authority, the Game Act of 1831, defined game as hares, pheasants, partridge, grouse, heath or moor game, black game and bustards. The creatures which could be killed by licence, stemming from the various subsequent Agricultural Holdings and Ground Game Acts, ranged from woodcock, snipe, quail and landrail to rabbits and deer. Close seasons were specified for each feathered species under the Wild Birds Protection Act. A licence did not convey the right to enter another person's land, but conversely owners, occupiers and shooting tenants had varying degrees of exemption and protection from civil action. Privilege, over the years, had come to be more easily bought but rank still persisted. Gamekeepers of owners or occupiers had power of arrest, but those of tenants had not, and those of lords of manors had special powers. Conservation, so far as the law was concerned, was for the preservation of good sport. Agriculture was a lesser consideration, especially in the form of forestry, for it was not easy to reconcile with the sporting man's ideal terrain. As Parker put it 'the forester's aims' were 'so far-sighted, so altruistic, almost so inhuman as almost to be beyond the purview of the ordinary countryman'. In days of changing ownership of land and varying taxes only the state could sustain scientific forestry.[18]

Angling had its own hierarchies, of fish and men, and its laws and privileges were as hard to reconcile with either conservation or the rights of the citizen as the shooters'. Yet this was the least contentious element of the historic triad. Killing fish, cold-blooded, scaly and slippery, was contested only by cranks, and anglers were subjected to jokes rather than criticism. Reputedly preferring wet weather to fine, spending endless, fruitless hours on river banks, festooned with equipment and laden with solid and liquid supplies, they were the butt of much simple-minded humour. Socially, too, fishing had stronger claims to classlessness than other field sports, for although it was in fact segregated this caused little acrimony but seemingly encouraged the different categories to fiercer allegiance to their own allotted calling.

The socially-superior game-anglers were not entirely immune from the spirit of the age. There was, for instance, an annual international trout-fishing match, started at Loch Leven in 1932. But for the most part their competitive instincts were satisfied by boasting in the club bar or waspish disputes in specialist journals. 'It is odd' wrote one commentator, 'that our gentle art should engender heated discussion, recrimination, hatred and spiteful speech, but we may note that even Christians hate one another for the love of God'. In fact two distinct creeds had grown up: 'One, that the exact imitation of a natural fly is necessary for success; the other, that any attempt at imitation must be so imperfect that it does not matter what one fishes with.'[19] There were other such theological disputes and controversial new fashions, like the use of spinners, which took some of the labour out of fly-fishing. Most at least kept the manufacturers happy at times of recession, for angling, in its own quiet way was as good a stimulator of consumption as Electro-Magnetic Golf.

At the other end of the scale coarse-fishing was a principal solace to the unemployed during the recession. It had always been, particularly in its organised, competitive form, a 'northern', urban and industrial affair and this orientation had become more pronounced as, in the good times for the traditional industries during the later twenties, employees and employers alike had seen it as a valuable escape from 'the clanking machinery of this lesser life'. South Yorkshire, which had new and thriving collieries as well as the old and thriving Sheffield steelworks, was a great centre. So were Nottingham, Hull, Derby, Lincoln, Leeds and Lancashire. South of Birmingham – keen but not very successful – there were pockets like Bristol but elsewhere, including London, fashions were more purely recreational. Wigan, the hardihood of whose pleasure-seekers we noted earlier (in Chapter Five), had benefited from sponsorship by enlightened colliery-owners in the good days, and now at the depths of depression, with the unhappy record of the worst death-rate in the country, still had 1,900 serious anglers on its local canals.[20] Of club members at Worksop, near Sheffield, 90% were unemployed, walking or cycling to rivers and ponds to save money. This became a normal practice as the rail excursions that had made many clubs became scarcer.

Revival came quicker in the midlands than the north and soon the Birmingham Tramways and the Midland 'Red' bus company were organising trips and offering prizes for competition. Before long fishermen everywhere were adding to the bus and car traffic seeking out and descending on the remoter stretches of water as well as lining the canal banks. But if the centre of gravity in terms of numbers moved slightly further south, from Sheffield to Birmingham (where 22 clubs closed during the recession but 52 new ones were formed) the trophies still went north. Sheffield Hull and Lincoln were the star clubs of the National Federation of Anglers' Championships, with only the odd intervention on home waters by Loughborough on the Soar and Groves

263

and Whitnall on the Gloucester Canal. And the sole southern interloper in the individual championships, a Bristolian who neither betted nor fished on Sundays, was manifestly a freak.[21]

Changing world

In 1934 Chamberlain announced that the worst of the recession was over. He reduced income tax to 4s 6d, restored the dole cuts and half the government salary reductions. By 1935, restoring the other half, he was able to declare that the nation was 80% recovered. As A. J. P. Taylor observed, 'The claim was unduly modest. Production was ten points higher than in 1929; wage rates had fallen since then by 3%, the cost of living by 13%.'[22] But this did not tell the whole story. If there was more work available nationally, in areas dependent on moribund industries many were in desperate straits. Two-thirds of the jobless lived in the Celtic fringes and the north of England, another source of division between 'them' and 'us'. London and the south east, the most favoured area before and after the recession, had quickly recovered and was back to almost normal. The midlands and the south west, next in the scale of prosperity, had been even quicker to recover and were soon better off than in 1929. Things were much more difficult in Scotland, the north of England, and, numerically smaller but worst-hit, Wales and Northern Ireland. The situation, which reflected the changed pattern of trade and the incidence of new industries, was to remain essentially unchanged until the war.[23]

Priestley, whose sideswipe at the fox-hunters came in an account of a journey round the country in 1933, found it a confused and confusing place. There was still, for those who could afford it, the Old England of 'cathedrals and minsters and manor houses and inns, of Parson and Squire; guide book and quaint highways and by-ways . . . which at its best cannot be improved upon in this world.' But it had 'long ceased to earn its own living' and had given way to 'the industrial England of coal iron, steel, cotton, wool, railways . . . sham Gothic churches, square-faced chapels, Town Halls, Mechanics Institutes, mills, foundries, warehouses, refined watering-places, Pier Pavilions, Family and Commercial Hotels, Literary and Philosophical Societies, back-to-back houses, detached villas with monkey trees . . . slums, fried fish shops (and) public houses'. Out of this the tough and enterprising had made their piles, and their children, 'well schooled, groomed and finished', had become 'almost indistinguishable from the old inhabitants, the land-owning aristocrats'. But they 'had found a green and pleasant land and left a wilderness of dirty bricks' in which the less fortunate classes had endured 'monstrously long hours of work, miserable wages, and surroundings in which they lived like black beetles'. Now there was a new land, originating in

America and 'belonging far more to the age itself than to this particular island', a land of 'arterial and by-pass roads, of filling stations and factories that look like exhibition buildings, of giant cinemas and dance-halls and cafés, bungalows with tiny garages, cocktail bars, Woolworth's, motor coaches, wireless, hiking, factory girls looking like actresses, greyhound racing and dirt tracks, swimming pools and everything given away for cigarette coupons'.

Priestley saw much to commend it. It was essentially democratic. You needed money, but you didn't need much money to have a reasonable life. It was a land 'at last, without privilege . . . Jack and Jill are nearly as good as their masters.' The 'very modern things, like the films and wireless and sixpenny stores . . . [made] no distinction whatever between their patrons'. Here was the broad-minded socialist speaking. But there were flies in the ointment. Things were 'also cheap in the other sense of the term', often 'simply a trumpery imitation of things not very good in the original'. There was a depressing monotony and too much was 'being stamped on from the outside, probably by astute financial gentlemen, backed by the Press and their publicity services'. Here was the fastidious middle class liberal talking. Perhaps his most revealing remark was 'There is almost every luxury in this (new) world except the luxury of power or the luxury of privacy.'[24] But for the most part the working classes did not yearn for either, except perhaps within the family.

For the conditioned lower class town-dweller solitude often spelled loneliness and the countryside was something to be endured or to be filled with activity, preferably in a group. It upset Priestley that it should be so. On his journey he spent a Sunday morning in the country near his native Bradford and was dismayed to find that youthful mores had changed: 'we used to set out in twos and threes, in ordinary walking clothes, for our Sunday tramps. Now they were in gangs of either hikers or bikers, twenty or thirty of them together and all dressed for their respective parts. They almost looked German.'[25] That year the topic of hikers' dress came up in *The Times*. One correspondent bemoaned the 'spectacle of the country's youth and maidens in hideous uniforms' all in drab, potato-coloured khaki and wondered why they could not wear brighter colours. But another complained that in his district hikers wore 'disgustingly garish clothes and dressed like pirates with coloured handkerchiefs round their heads': he wanted to see them all in grey flannel. And a third took exception to their shorts 'revealing knobbly knees, fat legs and broad hips'.[26] The truth was that they seemed to the liberal middle classes out of place in the 'quaint highways and by-ways'. The bikers offended Priestley even more; his car passed 'troops of them all along the road up to Grassington' and he wondered 'exactly what pleasure they were getting from the surrounding countryside, as they never seemed to lift their heads from their handlebars, but went grimly on like racing cyclists'.

If privacy was not always valued power was thought best left to others. Priestley noted as a hopeful sign a change in the new generation that 'The young people of this new England do not play chorus in an opera in which their social superiors are the principals.'[27] There was, at least in part, a shift in working-class values towards those of the burgeoning lower middle classes who were the new, inarticulate but insistent focus of political and commercial attention. But the working classes of the old Britain were still there, helpless in the face of an economic misery in which they were increasingly isolated from the prosperous majority. The Etonian George Orwell, a practising rather than a theoretical socialist, experiencing thirties life in industrial Sheffield noted the subservience of the workers to authority: 'whereas the bourgeois goes through life expecting to get what he wants, within reason, the working man always feels himself the slave of a more or less mysterious authority.'[28] When the lower orders acted it could only be collectively, and their options were limited. The Unemployment Act of 1934, designed to take the dole out of the political arena, merely emphasised the stark regional divisions, for the new standardised rates of assistance were in many cases lower than that previously provided locally. The biggest hunger march took place in March 1935, in South Wales when thousands took to the streets in protest. But that was it. People tut-tutted but nobody really wanted to know – except the communists, grinding their blunt revolutionary axes.

Priestley was particularly severe on the American elements in the new Britain. They were certainly the dominant influence. American movies were undoubtedly the best, or so thought the four out of ten Britishers who at least once a week visited local cinemas – Odeons, Gaumonts and Regals with their distinctively palatial styles, Art Deco interiors and mighty Würlitzer organs. Chaplin's *Modern Times* of 1935 was greatly admired by intellectuals but Gary Cooper's *Mr Deeds Goes to Town* had a more agreeably escapist theme. The first native success was the Hungarian Alexander Korda whose *The Private Life of Henry VIII* introduced a wave of plush costume dramas, and showed, in the star Charles Laughton, that the British still were the best at acting, a dubious attribute. No British writer proved as screenable as Hemingway, nor in the prevailing gangster mode as good as Dashiell Hammett, though the young Graham Greene did his best; and American humour, from the Marx Brothers script-writers to the New Yorker set, was more congenial than the black comedies of Evelyn Waugh.

The Left was building up strong support amongst the intelligentsia, however. Whilst Yeats and Eliot retreated further into their own transcendental philosophies and the Georgian poets became suitably antiseptic text-book material for the new Higher School Certificate, the next generation – W. H.

Auden, Stephen Spender, C. Day Lewis – were of the left, the last a practising communist. Auden (with Christopher Isherwood, the 'camera-eye' novelist of European decadence), Eliot and Yeats all attempted to restore the poetic drama, but with something less than Shakespearean force. More accessibly, the chameleon Noel Coward who had hailed the new decade with the sophisticated *Private Lives* followed quickly by the patriotic, sentimental *Cavalcade*, now offered a series of shows, enlivened by numbers like *Mad Dogs and Englishmen* that showed the old country at its most lovably eccentric. Apart from Shaw, now in self-admiring decline, drama with serious themes was scarce: Priestley's problem plays and the early offerings of James Bridie, Scotland's first notable dramatist, were the best. Play-goers seeking enlightenment on the unemployment issue had to be satisfied with a dramatisation of Walter Greenwood's 1933 novel *Love on the Dole*. Orwell, still an obscure novelist, was trying to live down his Etonian past in Wigan, but while he conscientiously gathered material, Lancashire was winning greater fame for its singing comedians: George Formby and Gracie Fields were the big British film stars. And while the Left Book Club informed the sensitive and the Penguin and Pelican sixpenny paperbacks confounded the sceptics by their breakthrough, the Saint, Biggles and Jeeves satisfied the greater thirst for escape.

The great indoor game of the era, Monopoly, came from the USA, symbolising the general restoration of faith in capitalism, and the British version merely substituted pounds for dollars. Similarly the popular music that filled the air-waves was an antiseptic version of the American original. The greatest sales in pop records were of the strict-tempo sweetness of the very British Victor Sylvester. When Duke Ellington gave jazz concerts in London they were tricked out with confectionery trifles. The BBC were expert at the right mixture of dignity and fun. 'Horsey, horsey, don't you stop' was typical. No smut, of course, and they had problems with some of Formby's lyrics, like 'When I'm Cleaning Windows'. This greatly suited their family audience, but even they rebelled over John Reith's sedate Sunday, deserting in droves to the pirate station Radio Luxembourg, which added advertising to its impiety. Children became Ovalteenies instead of reading improving books.

The press emblematically indicated its commitment to the prevailing vogue for nonsense by engaging experts in it. The *Express*'s 'Beachcomber' was the general favourite though connoisseurs preferred the *Sunday Express*'s Nathaniel Gubbins. Horoscopes were another irrational attraction, with rival astrologers nearly as important as racing tipsters. Of these the *Daily Mail*'s 'Robin Goodfellow' (Captain Eric Rickman) had the edge, though he still had to keep working for his living. The *Mail* also had the best children's cartoon character and club leader, Teddy Tail, a mouse with a knotted extremity.

Stunts and competitions for adults included seaside holiday games like spotting Lobby Lud, reciting a formula whilst carrying the appropriate newspaper and winning a prize. A splendid opportunity for special supplements and a host of lucrative by-products came in the summer of 1935 with the Silver Jubilee of George V. As the nation paid homage, the Royal College of Needlework added to the multiplicity of souvenirs a sampler for home embroidery that testified to his virtues:

> Prince of sportsmen, brilliant shot,
> But happiest aboard his yacht.[29]

In fact the monarch was probably happier still at Newmarket, though despairing by now of success. He was handicapped by lack of money, the most important ingredient on the Turf. It was essential for hiring top jockeys. They made thousands of pounds before they started from retainers, often two or three, payments simply for being available. Gordon Richards, at the very top, could name his own price, and though he scorned the wheeling and dealing of Steve Donoghue, he did very nicely. Even the Aga Khan, for whom bargaining was part of the fun, was no match for him when he tried to secure *second* call on his services in 1935. And George V, who was seeking a successor to Joe Childs as Royal jockey at the time, was simply out of his class. He asked his racing manager Brigadier Tomkinson to approach Freddy Fox as well as Richards – 'these two are absolutely straight . . . you can't say that about all of them'. He preferred Richards, who was younger, but knew he was expensive: 'Gordon Richards might like to ride my horses, but one never knows . . . He would not have to break with Beckhampton as I really have so few . . . I should think £1,000 retainer for Richards would be right.'[30] He had miscalculated and the Aga Khan won after all.

The King's sporting interests were commemorated, at this time of growing interest in the physical well-being of the nation's youth, by the creation of the King George's Jubilee Trust, which raised substantial funds by public subscription to assist voluntary youth work. Another voluntary effort in 1935 was the Central Council of Recreative Physical Training. Dreamed up by Phyllis Colson, a former PE teacher, now an organiser, and strongly backed by the Ling Association and the National Association of Organisers of Physical Education, it was representative of all the main amateur sporting bodies. It had distinguished patrons, the King and Queen as well as the Prince of Wales, and its President was Viscount Astor. Its aims were vaguely co-ordinative, but it was cumbersome and short of funds, and it was a year before it received its first substantial grants, £1,000 each from the Jubilee Trust and the National Playing Fields Association. The government, unimpressed by unfavourable comparisons with state provision in Germany, Italy, Japan and the Soviet

Union, did very little. However, Carnegie was going well and Loughborough College now started another one year full-time teacher's course for men. It also held summer schools and in 1934 the AAA held its first-ever coaching course there. Its leader was F. A. M. Webster, who founded the grandly-named Loughborough School of Athletics, Games and Physical Education in 1936. Its ambitious three-year specialist course was not recognised by the Board of Education and did not last long.[31] But things were stirring.

Golf and glamour

The open-air and fitness craze had made exposure of limbs and throats (if not yet chests and bosoms) fairly commonplace. It was part of the changing fashion scene, male and female, in which new materials, light in texture and often bright in colour, transformed ideas of leisure-wear. But beyond this there was a significant new phase in the liberation of women that was more overtly sexual, probably initiated by the post-war surplus of females and certainly stimulated by the burgeoning publicity, advertising and entertainments industries. The most startling, if also the silliest, exhibition of this kind obliged the LGU to issue a stern injunction against 'any departure from the traditional costume of the game'. Most needed no urging. Lady Heathcote-Amery was still setting a dignified example and the new stars Enid Wilson, Diana Fishwick, Wanda Morgan and the up-and-coming Pam Barton dressed discreetly in skirts which came down to mid-calf and jumpers that kept the arms properly covered. But there had been untoward happenings in the 1934 English Women's Championship. A Miss Gloria Minoprio had appeared in trousers.

Bifurcated leg-coverings were not entirely unknown in golf. Cecil Leitch had worn voluminous, below calf-length affairs even before the war but anything intended for fashion rather than weather-protection was unthinkable. Miss Minoprio's intention, leaked to the press in advance, was clearly to attract attention and an unusually large number of male reporters awaited her arrival on the first morning. They were not disappointed. Stepping from a large yellow limousine, she revealed herself sheathed in a skin-tight costume of midnight blue, with a pair of form-hugging pants. She wore a turban and her thickly-powdered face was a dead-white mask. Sadly, her golf, handicapped by some strange self-denying ordinance that impelled her to use only one club, was not as impressive as her appearance. She played with care and precision – and in silence – but lost by 6 and 5. Henry Longhurst headed his account, 'Sic transit Gloria Monday', a joke he was able to repeat for several years until on one occasion she actually got to the second round when he substituted 'Sic transit Gloria Tuesday'. All in all Minoprio was a story for the

Tatler rather than the sporting press. Nevertheless, though not exactly a role model, she was the forerunner of a trend, and the advantages of slacks were such that by the end of the decade Longhurst could write, 'Nearly half the field in women's championships to-day turn out in trousers. But', he added wistfully, 'none of them fit like Gloria Minoprio's.'[32]

Another emergent trend was so far confined to the other side of the Atlantic. 'Babe' Didrickson, the brash young star of the Los Angeles Olympics, having tried vaudeville and various other commercial enterprises, turned to golf. She played it like a man and was stronger and better than most. In 1935, still only 21, she was lured into undertaking a professional tour playing exhibitions with Gene Sarazen (1932 winner of both the US and the British Opens) and was lost for some years to the amateur game. Since there were not enough women professionals to make up an interesting tournament this put her out of competitive golf.[33] Women professionals of any kind were still uncommon in Britain, and, though girls like Poppy Wingate, (Templenewsam, Leeds) and Meg Farquhar (Moray) became assistants to club professionals, there was no question of tournament play or exhibitions. The absence of Miss Didrickson made it easier for Pam Barton to show her paces across the Atlantic – she won the US Women's Championship in 1936 – but for the most part the gloom was unrelieved: the Curtis Cup, started in 1932, was as one-sided as its male equivalent, the Walker Cup.

Male golfers, unaffected by changing sex-balances or much else of social significance, were cutting no swathes through conventions in dress. Henry Cotton's stylish and frequently changing attire, in his regal appearances on the course or on the stage at the London Coliseum, was a partial exception born of his Americanisation. In 1933 he wrote in the *Aldin* handbook, 'Even in aristocratic old England we may play in shirt sleeves . . . and even a shirt open at the neck is permitted. It is only about eight years ago that a brother of mine was asked by a member of the committee of a well-known London club to put on a jacket as shirt sleeves were not permitted on the course, as they lowered the tone of the club. That snobbishness has gone, thanks to our Royal golfing enthusiast, HRH, the Prince of Wales, and to our American cousins . . . What looks smarter . . . than white plus fours, a sleeveless pullover and stockings to match, with coloured shoes – black or brown and white?'[34] He recommended a belt rather than braces, though admitted this was controversial.

But Cotton was a professional and to set out to look like him was to invite invidious comparison and accusations of immodesty. Professionals were now greatly admired and Cotton had a special glamour. But they were still excluded from clubrooms, a social division too many amateurs not only insisted upon but positively enjoyed. The ever-widening gulf between amateur and professional playing standards was not lessened either by the restrictions on artisans, or the snobbish attitude to the emergent performer on municipal courses. The Artisan Golfers' Association had 15,000 members by 1937 but its 172 clubs were only a tiny fraction of the 1,500 parent clubs – of which some 350 had been created since the war. Working-class encroachment was more than balanced by growing public school interest. Sixty-four Old Boys' Golfing Societies each entered five pairs every year for the Halford-Hewitt competition. There was great excitement and hope for the future when 18-year-old John Langley of Stowe School, holder of the Boys' Championship, reached the final of the English amateur in 1936, but by then much of the competitive edge had gone out of the amateur game. Though the Walker Cup was comparatively little regarded in the USA, the Americans managed to win it all but once in the decade.

At the highest level, the demise of the amateur had been signalled neatly by Bobby Jones's retirement in 1930 after his astonishing Grand Slam.[35] Unlike in lawn tennis, where the growing American professional circuit was eager to get hold of the best amateur talent, in golf there was a protectionist policy on both sides of the Atlantic. The British PGA (having in mind the T. P. Perkin affair and the growing artisan movement) put a curb on talented amateurs taking short cuts to lucrative professionalism by requiring them to spend five years qualifying before they could play in tournaments. Consequently not many adults made the switch. Only two Walker Cup players – both Scots – crossed the divide. Jack McLean, Scottish Amateur Champion 1932-3-4, changed in 1936 and Hector Thompson, the 1935 winner, in 1939. And very few public schoolboys were tempted in spite of Henry Cotton's spectacular achievements.

The PGA's rising importance was reflected by the appointment in 1933 of R. T. C. Roe, Lieutenant-Commander, RN (Retd) as its secretary. This gave the Association the necessary social confidence in its dealings with the R&A and both sides were able to relax into an agreed *modus vivendi*. The PGA sought no share in the game's governance but was dedicated to improving the prize-money. Even here there was no great conflict. Though the prize-money for the Open, funded by 'the management', increased only gradually – to £500 in total with £100 for the winner – its prestige was such and its indirect benefits to the champion so great that it mattered little. There was in any case a great increase in commercial sponsorship. Dunlop funded a new competition in 1931 and other golf ball manufacturers were quick to follow. Penfold were active throughout the thirties but the most spectacular single event was the Silver King £1,000 in 1936. Golf was fortunate enough to become part of the news-paper circulation war and in the same year the *News Chronicle* started one at £1,000 only to find itself up-staged by the *Daily Mail*'s at £2,000.

Suddenly British golfers were headline news again, not Tolley and

Wethered, but the professionals, who won the Ryder Cup in 1933; and then Henry Cotton ended a 13-year American sequence of victories in the Open in 1934. The PGA itself was in good shape, in spite of fierce internal conflict about whether the needs of the tournament gladiators or the club professional should come first. Its master-stroke of unification was the successful resistance in 1937 to the R&A's proposal to limit the number of clubs that could be used in competition. The advent of matched, steel-shafted clubs had brought a massive expansion of output: manufacturers now offered a vast range of clubs, including half-sizes. This sophistication was welcomed both by the club professionals who sold the clubs and the tournament stars who endorsed them, and it was a further step in the direction of Electro-Magnetic Golf for the average club member.

Tennis: trousers and Teutons

In lawn tennis, where tournament professionalism was still seen as a transat-lantic aberration, standards of dress were set by the ladies and gentlemen of the leading clubs. They were both conservative and albocentric. The number of clubs affiliated to the LTA had increased rapidly in the twenties and was still growing: the 1,620 clubs of 1925 almost doubled in the next decade.[36] Inevitably this led to some lowering of tone. No doubt a few of these players wore coloured clothing like recreation ground performers but as the new suburbs proliferated the degree of whiteness of the clubs was as important as the postal address and there were jokes about some being 'skimmed milk' rather then 'full cream'.

The distinguished (amateur American) writer of the tennis section of the *Aldin* handbook took candescence for granted: 'For the boy, white flannels and a shirt of flannel of the white Oxford variety, with soft collar attached, are recommended' and 'For the girl, either the one – or two piece white costume is suitable.' He also assumed that the boy's trousers would be long – 'clear of the ground or . . . turned up at the cuff', and that the girl's costume would be a skirt, pleated so as to be 'both graceful and roomy.'[37] But even the most elevated circles were not proof against the growing fashion for shorts. The first British pioneer was as notable for hardihood as sexual provocation for it was in March 1932, that a Miss G. E. Tomblin took to the courts, bare-legged when all about her were wearing (white) stockings, and exposed her knees to the elements as well as the cameras at the Chiswick Hard Court Club. The garment, if bifurcated, was respectably roomy, but it would never do for Wimbledon, people thought.

All-England's first sansculotte was in fact a man, not the socially-suspect Perry but the Cantabrigian Davis Cup player and 1932 finalist, 'Bunny' Austin.

His reasons were severely practical: he was given to cramp and in distress during a match in 1931 had cut off the bottom half of his sweat-drenched flannels. The relief was such that he wore a purpose-built pair in the US championships the following year. This caused something of a sensation, but his appearance in them at Wimbledon in 1933 along with four other players aroused only mild interest and amusement. The general effect, however, was to confirm people's impression that Austin was less virile than the long-trousered Fred Perry, who had the look almost of a cricketer – for whom virility, as had been recently demonstrated, was all-important. Shorts certainly gave Austin no advantage in the lucrative fashion endorsement business: it was Perry who was used by Simpson's of Piccadilly 'as a sort of clotheshorse to try out Daks tennis trousers'.[38]

It had been a fashion stunt that same liberationist year when the dress designer Eileen Bennett wore pale-blue shorts at a pre-Wimbledon party given by Lady Crosfield. 'They were terribly respectable and not as we know them to-day', she recalled forty years on. 'Much more like a divided skirt. Imagine how amazed I was when my photo was on the front page of all the newspapers the next day', she added disingenuously.[39] It was certainly not with an eye to the *Tatler*, however, when in 1934 the American Helen Jacobs wore shorts in actual play; and the victorious US Wightman Cup team also broke with tradition. These were near-knee-length shorts of the utmost seriousness, unglamorous white versions of the colonial administrator's khaki. Within a year or two shorts became, if not commonplace, accepted, and as skirts grew shorter and stockings were discarded ('Of recent years, especially in the United States, stockings have been discarded by the great majority of the younger players during the summer season.'[40]) shorts were preferable, ladies thought, to the display of knickers, whatever their colour.

The queenly Helen Wills Moody, eight times Wimbledon champion between 1927 and 1938, was not a shorts person (as our handbook explained she favoured 'the two-piece costume of short-sleeved middy blouse and knee-length skirt'); nor was the sturdy Betty Nuthall, first British winner of the US championship in 1930; nor the surprise British Wimbledon champion of 1934, Dorothy Round. Miss Round, indeed, was an entirely admirable character. If, unlike Perry, she could claim no working-class credentials she was not from the upper reaches of society either, but the daughter of a midlands building contractor. The family had a tennis court in the garden and she practised at first with her three brothers: then when she outgrew them she travelled – a mile walk followed by train and tram journeys – from her home in Dudley to a Birmingham club where she got much of her practice playing against men in their lunch hours. Her tennis dresses were home-made and usually cost about 12s 6d (62½p) for the material. As the press were always pointing out she was a teetotaller, a non-smoker and a Sunday School teacher. She was saved from an agonising decision in 1933, when it had been intended to play the finals on a Sunday, by a providential downpour. That year she lost to Mrs Moody, but in 1934 with the champion injured beat Miss Jacobs, shorts and all. It was unfortunate that her thunder was to be stolen by Fred Perry, the hero of the hour, the twin star – with Cotton – who restored British pride in two of the sports she had given to the world.

Though Betty Nuthall's win in the USA had been appreciated by the *cognoscenti*, it was the men's game that mattered to the general public. Britain had not won the Davis Cup since 1912 or the Wimbledon men's singles since 1909. It was an irony that the saviour was to be a man for whom patriotism meant little and whose methods were not those held dear in British sporting mythology. 'I guess I was the first Englishman to bring the American attitude to the game . . . never wanting to come second' he told a reporter. Herein lay the difference between him and the true blue Austin, who an American journalist described as 'a man who saves his top game for the time when they tell him the royal standard flies above Wimbledon, the King and Queen are in the box, and the honour of the Empire is at stake. Playing for himself, Austin is only a brilliant player; playing for England, John Bull and the dominions, he's an inspired one.'[41]

The LTA was dedicated enough to the task of regaining the Davis Cup to employ not only Dan Maskell, the All-England professional, as coach but Tom Whitaker, the Arsenal trainer, for fitness training. Perry, seeking the extra edge, went for sessions at Highbury every day when he was not actually playing. He thus further enlarged his circle of celebrity friends – film stars Bette Davis, Bebe Daniels and Ben Lyon, a Lea & Perrin's sauce heir who had transplanted a Scottish castle to Newport, Rhode Island, the Jack Hylton and Guy Lombardo bands – by adding famous soccer players, though only on the training ground. The sort of place where Perry dined, given the chance, was Sovrani's Blue Train in Piccadilly, a favourite night-spot of the Prince of Wales. In the autumn of 1933 the Prince congratulated him warmly on winning the US and Australian championships but couldn't remember whom he had beaten – Jack Crawford of Australia.

On that trip, Perry recalled, 'there was still a lot of bad feeling between the two countries engendered by the . . . bodyline cricket tour . . . In fact, one of the reasons for our tennis team being there was as a placatory gesture'.[42] He would have done better to lose, perhaps, but if was not in his nature. On his return, everyone wanted to know whether he was going to turn professional. But he was not ready yet. He now worked for Slazenger's – officially their Australian branch so that he could remain eligible for tournaments in Britain but actually under world-wide contract to them. So there was much to consider. There was no point in turning professional until the professional game had something like the spectator appeal of the amateur. So far it had signally failed to gather momentum. Henri Cochet's decision to turn in 1933 was not a success, and when the young Ellsworth Vines, the current Wimbledon champion, followed him that winter it caused a surprise that he had made the move so early.

When Perry won Wimbledon in 1934 the pressure mounted. At the Centre Court itself his reception was strangely muted. He had won in straight sets, Crawford was again the victim and as the Associated Press correspondent noted, 'Crawford received far more applause than Perry.' Some, especially in the USA, saw the reason as the All-England members' snobbish resentment at a social outsider taking the title. One committee member had said to Crawford, in Perry's hearing, 'Congratulations. This is one time the best man didn't win.' Perry himself saw the hostility as something more complex – the fact that he was too keen to win, too ruthless. It was not 'an approach generally favoured in England at the time . . . not in tennis, anyway'.[43] The general public were less inhibited – the placards had the single word 'Fred'. He had worn Daks trousers and the store Simpson's, which had prepared a *Daily Mail* mock-up with the headline 'Fred wins Wimbledon in Daks', offered him a lifetime contract of one shilling for every pair of Daks sold, but he still held out. He also turned down the latest offer from the Tilden professional circus. So Britain kept her hero and achieved her long-awaited Davis Cup win.

It was touch and go whether this would be Perry's last appearance. The USLTA again proposed an open tournament but the ILTF again refused. Perry asked permission to make an 'instructional' film but was turned down. He won Wimbledon again in 1935 from Baron Gottfried von Cramm. An American paper had the headline 'English Ace wins in straight sets from Teuton Foe', but the sporting Baron was greatly admired at the All-England. They preferred not to think about the alternative to him. The Nazis were now well in control, introducing conscription and building pocket battleships in contravention of the Treaty of Versailles. Many in high places still felt that the hand of friendship should be extended to the old enemy. Indeed the Prince of Wales that very month told the British Legion, of all organisations, that it should give a lead in this. This horrified his father, but there were ostriches within the government, too, for while the French Premier, Pierre Laval, was winning communist support for rearmament by making a treaty with Stalin, the British saw fit to conclude a naval agreement with Hitler.

British socialists and chauvinists alike were appalled. The FA at this critical hour found itself somewhat stranded in its new European policy. The German team had been invited to play a friendly international that December at White Hart Lane, Tottenham. London labour and radical movements were particularly incensed. The newly-knighted Sir Walter Citrine, secretary of the TUC, led a deputation to the Home Office calling for cancellation. The Nazis, they pointed out, now directly controlled sport through a State Commissioner who vetted the racial composition of teams and liquidated Jewish and even Catholic sporting bodies.[44] But Hitler, greatly heartened by the Prince of Wales's attitude, and seeing the prospects of an alliance against the communists, had sent his Ambassador, Von Ribbentrop, to London to make the most of the opportunity. The Home Secretary, Sir John Simon, said that cancellation was out of the question and the match went ahead. Indeed there was no popular revulsion at the idea – there was a capacity crowd of 60,000 and only six arrests outside the ground. What better way to confound a potential enemy than to demonstrate superiority on the playing field?

But of course this made winning even more important than it usually was to soccer fans. The sporting press saw it as an important test for the FA and its new secretary, S. F. Rous, the progressive schoolteacher preferred to the strongly-fancied Fred Howarth of the Football League. Without the influence of the persuasive Chapman who had died the previous year, and with Rous still feeling his way, the FA was back in the clutches of the backwoodsmen. The Honorary Treasurer, Harry Huband, a fervent supporter of amateurism, was put in charge of the team and he told reporters that he was against issuing tactical instructions to international teams. Many agreed with him – as did the players – but the *Manchester Evening News* correspondent ventured to suggest that it was 'important at least that the inside men should have some arrangement with the wing halves and the halves with the backs'. If England did not win by four or five goals 'the Selection committee rather than the players will receive and deserve severe criticism'.[45] They were no doubt fairly satisfied with the 3–0 victory, and Hitler's consolation was the formation of the Anglo-German Fellowship.

Life after bodyline

To everyone's regret the Germans did not play cricket, but if international harmony was the aim, this was just as well. It was, *Wisden* declared afterwards, 'next to impossible to regard the cricket season of 1934 as other than unpleasant'. Particularly deplorable was 'the attitude of a certain section of the press in what seemed . . . an insane desire to stir up strife'.[46] The background was the disinclination of A. W. Carr, the Nottinghamshire captain, to emasculate his attack by joining in the gentleman's agreement not to use bodyline. In June Larwood put himself beyond the pale, like Parkin ten years earlier, by a newspaper article alleging political interference to keep him and Jardine out of the Tests. The article appeared in the middle of a game against

Lancashire in which he and Voce caused several injuries. That August in a tour match, with Larwood and Carr ostensibly unfit, Voce whirled a couple of overs round the Australians' ears in poor light and after protests was himself declared unfit to continue the next day.[47] The chain of events led to Carr's losing the county captaincy and the final demise of bodyline. Bradman made 304 in the fourth Test and 244 in the fifth and Australia won the ashes.

All of this led, *Wisden* reported, to 'tittle-tattle of a mischievous character which in the long run prompted the inevitable question: "Are Test matches really worthwhile?" ' This was, we should remind ourselves, the sort of question the British always asked when any sport they had invented began to be dominated by foreigners – the Australian twang, people noticed, was like a Cockney trying to talk American. And the middle classes were particularly concerned when the foreigners were vulgarians. In cricket the question was now academic. Test matches had become an economic necessity, not only to satisfy the commercial spirit of the age but to preserve county cricket, the relic of pre-capitalistic feudalism. A commission of enquiry in 1937 revealed that the counties collectively were losing £27,000 annually. Only a share of the Test match proceeds kept the poorer counties alive.

Their failure to draw the crowds was widely attributed to the onset of cautious professionalism: 'It stands to reason', as a Cardus adherent put it, 'that cricket dominated by amateurs must be livelier than cricket in which professionals . . . set the tone.'[48] Yet the game was entirely controlled by amateurs. Fred Root, tongue loosened in retirement, blamed them for the 'slow play and unsportsmanlike tactics' that were so prevalent: 'Many times have I been ordered by my captain to bowl negatively . . . Not only in county matches, but in a Test match have I received these instructions.'[49] Jardine's control over his professionals was not confined to bowlers. He positively boasted of his influence over the batsmen: 'Sutcliffe was criticised for going slow during the second half of the innings. He was playing under instructions . . . mine and mine alone.'[50] Jardine himself was a dour performer. And to give the batting '"concrete in the middle" – a phrase which Douglas Jardine liked', as Warner waspishly put it – he preferred the dogged R. E. S. Wyatt to more flamboyant performers like the Nawab of Pataudi. Wyatt, who fortunately resembled Jardine in nothing else, took on the England captaincy in 1934. He was resolutely opposed to the new lbw law (designed to give the bowlers more chance) which obliged batsmen like himself to rely less on negative pad-play, arguing instead for bigger wickets.

County cricket, with less chauvinistic pulling power, evoked much unreflecting clamour for 'brighter cricket' and much talk of the good old amateur days, but the truth was that crowds were more interested in fierce competition and results than jolly play, especially when it was of low standard. Of Leicestershire in 1934 *Wisden* commented: 'The public demanded brighter cricket and their demands were certainly complied with, but even so the "gates" were extremely disappointing. Indeed on the occasion of Shipman's benefit the attendances were so poor that the player found himself some £60 out of pocket as a result of the match.' This misfortune was overcome by a special Sportsman's Match and the club's financial plight was alleviated by donations from well-wishers in established hand-to-mouth tradition.

The leagues had come through the recession better than the first-class game. With Constantine Nelson had quickly eliminated their overdraft, and soon the whole league benefited as rival clubs followed their lead. The Central Lancashire League also joined in. Rochdale made an offer of £1,000 to Constantine himself, staved off by a £500 loyalty bonus from Nelson. George Headley and Martindale followed Constantine from the West Indies and Amar Singh from India. Bradman received many offers. He could not be tempted, but other Australians were, like Vic Richardson and Alan Fairfax (who demonstrated A. W. Carr's point about their preferential treatment by playing for the Gentlemen in their annual fixture against the players in 1934 between professional engagements for Accrington). English professionals, even in the north, usually only turned to League cricket at the end of their careers like George Macaulay and Emmott Robinson or on their way up like Yorkshire's new discovery Hedley Verity, the hero of England's only Test victory in 1934, who had played for Middleton in the Central Lancashire League in 1930 and 1931. There were also men good enough to play county cricket but who preferred the security of a year round weekday job, like Leslie Warburton, a Lancashire bank clerk. For these men, fees of perhaps £200 or £300 a season, with the prospect of collections – averaging say £30 a time – was an attractive proposition. Fred Root, who made the switch in 1932 when he had reached the age of 40, enjoyed the change. He found the view from 'the cabinet of first class cricket' that the Lancashire League was a circus or music-hall version of the game to be 'an illusion': 'Never have I played in any kind of cricket that provides greater thrills.'[51]

Notes

1 Donaldson, *Edward VIII*, London (1976 edn), p. 134.
2 P. C. McIntosh, *Physical Education in England Since 1800*, London, 1974, pp. 233–4.
3 A. Huxley, *Brave New World*. London, 1932 (1994 edn), p. 26.
4 Charles Burgess, 1935, quoted in J. A. Cuddon, *Macmillan Dictionary of Sport and Games*, London, 1980, p. 852.
5 Connor O'Brien c. 1938 quoted by D. Sleightholme, *Yachting Monthly*, 75th Birthday Issue, June 1981, p. 1259.
6 J. Nicholson, *Great Days in Yachting*, Lymington, 1970, pp. 93–4.
7 GNFS, *Yachting Monthly*, May, 1938.

8 In a speech on receiving the Freedom of Queensferry.

9 Huxley, *Brave New World*, p. 19.

10 J. B. Priestley, *English Journey*, London, 1934, Chapter Five (Harmondsworth, 1977 edn), p. 114.

11 See, for instance, the report by Lord Middleton in *Baily's Hunting Directory*, 1938–9.

12 R. Longrigg, *The History of Foxhunting*, London, 1975, p. 199.

13 ibid., p. 210.

14 ibid., p. 212.

15 E. Parker (ed.), *The Shooting Weekend Book*, London, 1942, pp. 91–5.

16 Lord Dorchester, *Sport, Foxhunting and Shooting*, London, 1937; extract in Parker, *Shooting Weekend*, p. 289.

17 *Shooting Weekend*, p. 250.

18 ibid., pp. 112–13.

19 Article in *Journal of the Flyfishers' Club*, 1930.

20 J. Lowerson, 'Angling', in T. Mason (ed.), *Sport in Britain*, Cambridge, 1989, pp. 22–3. For death rates and their connection with poverty, see J. Stevenson, *British Society 1914–45*, Harmondsworth, 1984, p. 216.

21 Lowerson, 'Angling', p. 26, citing *Fishing Gazette*, 20 October 1938.

22 A. J. P. Taylor, *English History 1914–45*, Oxford, 1965, p. 351.

23 For regional percentages of unemployment see table in Stevenson, *British Society*, p. 271.

24 Priestley, *English Journey*, Chapter Twelve, passim.

25 ibid., p. 167.

26 R. Graves and P. Hodge, *The Long Weekend*, London, 1940 (1971 edn), p. 272.

27 Priestley, *English Journey*, pp. 326–7.

28 G. Orwell, 'The Road to Wigan Pier Diary', 7 March 1936 in *The Collected Essays, Journalism and Essays*, ed. S. Orwell and I. Angus, Harmondsworth, 1970, p. 224.

29 Graves and Hodge, *Long Weekend*, p. 313.

30 27 February 1935. See H. Nicolson, *George V: His Life and Reign*, London, 1953 and G. Richards, *My Story*, London, 1955.

31 McIntosh, *Physical Education*, pp. 238–9.

32 H. Longhurst, 'Sic transit Gloria', *It Was Good While It Lasted*, London, 1940, Chapter Eleven.

33 When she returned to the amateur game, as Mrs Zaharias, after the war, she was in a class of her own.

34 H. Cotton, 'Golf', in *Aldin Book of Sport and Games*, London, 1933, pp. 242–3.

35 The US and British Amateur and Open.

36 The highest figure was 3,220 in 1938.

37 J. H. Doeg (US champion, 1930) and A. Danzig, 'Tennis' in *Aldin Book of Outdoor Games*, London, 1933, pp. 375–6.

38 F. J. Perry, *Autobiography*, London, 1984, p. 81.

39 G. Robyns, *Wimbledon: the Hidden Drama*, Newton Abbott, 1973, p. 128.

40 Doeg, *Aldin Book*, p. 377.

41 Perry, p. 91 (Henry McLemore, 1935).

42 ibid., p. 70.

43 ibid., p. 78.

44 S. J. Jones, *Sport, Politics and the Working Class in Modern Britain*, Manchester, 1990, p. 183.

45 S. Wagg, *Football World*, Brighton, 1984, p. 29.

46 'Notes by the Editor', *Wisden*, 1935, reprinted in B. Green, *Wisden Anthology, 1900–1940*, London, 1980, pp. 1014–18.

47 See A. W. Carr, *Cricket with the Lid Off*, London, 1935, Chapter Eleven, and D. Birley, *The Willow Wand*, London, 1979, pp. 91–3.
48 J. C. Squire, Introduction to N. Cardus, *Cricket*, London, 1931.
49 F. Root, *A Cricket Pro's Lot*, London, 1937, p. 172.
50 D. R. Jardine, *In Quest of the Ashes*, London, 1933, p. 95.
51 F. Root, *A Cricket Pro's Lot*, London, 1937, p. 185.

CHAPTER TWELVE

Changing the rules (1929–39): new leaders; same game

Even Ramsay MacDonald, the great supporter of collective security, was now having serious doubts about the German threat. The new White Paper on Defence in March, 1935, concluded that it was necessary for Britain to rearm. Predictably Hitler saw this as an excuse for restoring conscription. Anxieties were set aside for a while in the modern-style mafficking of the Jubilee, after which MacDonald bowed out. He handed over the reins to Stanley Baldwin, who displayed his customary lack of resolution in deciding what direction to take. By November he had called an election to test the mood of the people. With all parties divided on the armaments issue it was a confused affair, which decided nothing. Baldwin's initial choice as Foreign Secretary was Sir Samuel Hoare who concocted the government's first significant act of policy, the Hoare–Laval Franco-British plan. This blatantly attempted to fudge the issue of sanctions against Mussolini for his breach of sportsmanship in invading Abysinnia and in the subsequent outcry Hoare lost his job. His successor, the elegant Etonian aesthete Anthony Eden, formerly the Minister for the League of Nations, withdrew the plan, putting the final nail in the coffin of collective security, and leaving a policy vacuum. There was great nervousness about Hitler's growing air strength (based on exaggerated rumours) but equal reluctance to turn motor car plants into aircraft factories and risk Britain's fragile prosperity.

George V's death in January 1936 evoked deep emotion. The passing of Rudyard Kipling as his sovereign lay dying prompted a *Daily Telegraph* reader to suggest that the King had 'sent his Trumpeter ahead': his last words were said to be, 'How is the Empire?' The country had lost its father figure. But Queen Mary remained as an enduring reminder of what he represented, and few doubted that his son, who took the style Edward VIII, was a worthy successor. It was confidently expected that he would shake up the politicians.

Edentide and amateurism

Sir Samuel Hoare, an Oxford lawn tennis Blue, was also President of the LTA, and after Fred Perry's 1935 victory over Von Cramm he had found time from pact-making to telephone him – in Hollywood – beseeching him, in the national interest, not to turn professional. (In the absence of an Anglo-German Test match at Lord's a return match between Perry and Von Cramm at Wimbledon was the next best thing.) He hinted that the LTA would find ways of showing its gratitude. Perry's father, doubtless feeling that socialist integrity was at stake, also pleaded with Fred to do his bit for Britain. The hope of LTA assistance kept him in the amateur fold over the winter. By the spring of 1936, with nothing forthcoming, he was determined to make the break but had lost a couple of titles and some marketability through staleness, injury and loss of form. When Von Cramm beat him in the French championships in May, it became vital for Perry to win his last Wimbledon. Fortunately Von Cramm had incurred a groin strain, told no-one but his masseur, who told no-one but Perry, who won again in straight sets, 6–1, 6–0, 6–0. At the season's end, with another Davis Cup and US championship under his belt, Perry made his deal. Sir Samuel Hoare sent the defector a pained message – 'Why did you do it?' – and his honorary membership of All-England was withdrawn. No doubt the same would have happened to future British winners who deserted, but, though the professional circuit was now thoroughly established and a constant lure, there were no more British champions.

The oarsmen, protected from such sordid events by their lack of commercial appeal, were free to concentrate on the burning issue of fixed or swivel pins. Oxford, theologically confused, had gone on losing, despite the frantic efforts of Colonel Gibbon, who in 1934, at his own expense, had a new boat built for them. It was completed in 72 hours – for cash and a barrel of beer – but they lost anyway. When Cambridge purity was finally eroded in 1935 and the Blue boat made the switch, their coach Peter Haig-Thomas, a man to whom 'orthodoxy was a matter of faith far transcending allegiance to his old university', took himself and two acolytes to Oxford. Oxford reverted to orthodoxy but were beaten by a distance. Pembroke, Cambridge, rubbed it in by winning the Henley Grand, and the final straw was when a Swiss crew took the fours. They were from a football club and had taught themselves to row by watching films of Pembroke and from reading Steve Fairbairn's books.

The Jubilee and the King's departure had brought a great resurgence of imperial fervour. None of this rubbed off on the Henley Stewards who refused entry to a team of Sydney policemen under the ARA 'manual labour' clause'.[1] The MCC, however, with Warner back in favour, were in a position, to redress the balance. Whilst the Government of India Act of 1935 gave Gandhi only a little of what he sought the Raj was still in place – just. A team was sent to England in 1936 under the leadership of the Maharajkumar of Vizianagram, a cricketer of the Julien Cahn variety who was given a knighthood before the Lord's Test. Warner, who completed his qualifications by offering the olive branch to Australia, got his the following year. The 1936–7 tour was led by his protégé G. O. Allen, an Etonian but Australian born, a fast bowler but a notable abstainer on the bodyline tour.

The cricket establishment was also pleased with the outcome of the new lbw law, which occasioned more concern than the Defence White Paper. After two trial seasons it became permanent and seemed to be improving things. Spectators, however, wanted not brighter cricket but competition. Yorkshire, who won the championship seven times in the decade, did so in less than dashing fashion, but had far the biggest crowds. The less populous counties fared badly, however good they were. Derbyshire, who broke into Yorkshire's near-monopoly in 1936 after two seasons near the top, just about remained solvent. Counties like Northamptonshire, Glamorgan, Worcestershire and Leicestershire, forever near the bottom, were in desperate straits. Attempts were made to enliven individual matches by adjusting the points system to put more emphasis on winning rather than avoiding defeat. But this did not alter the basic problem that very few counties had a serious chance of contending for the title. 'Had cricket not been so firmly established as our national game,' wrote Fred Root, '. . . the superiority of the few would have sounded its death-knell in any competitive sense.'[2]

Root had hesitated about joining the leagues. 'I was prejudiced by the rumours I heard . . . Those big wages were fictitious, they said: the cricket was poor; the wickets were bad. So ran the gossip of the dressing rooms.'[3] The rumours were wrong, and he spent four happy years at Todmorden. An unexpected bonus was the community involvement. On the evening he arrived net practice was in full swing and there were as many people there to cast an eye over the new acquisition as on a good day at a county match at Worcester. 'Everybody seems to be a member of their respective Lancashire League club. They would rather miss joining the Co-op than the cricket club and when bad times make money scarce their sacrifices to enable them to pay their annual subscriptions are most pitiful.' They were not totally ascetic: 'There are cricket "pools" in the summer, as there are football pools in the winter, and almost every club or "pub" runs a wonderfully interesting "sweep" on Lancashire League cricket every week.' But they were not merely bar-flies: the roller squad was cheerfully active and weeding and litter disposal meticulously done: 'Cotton manufacturers rub shoulders with their own weavers, and the 'ground staff' is democratic to a degree.'[4] His book had a mixed reception.

It must have been galling for the status-conscious 'Jenny' Greenwood, now the RFU's youngest President, when in 1936 the Duke of Kent asked by way of polite conversation, 'Do you pay your players well?'[5] It would have seemed even more depressing had he known that the Duke was shortly to succeed to the throne. For rugger men the old King had been part of a glorious era, shining with new hope as it neared its end. Cambridge University had made a missionary tour of the USA in the winter of 1934–5. K. C. Fyfe, a Scottish international member of the party, stressed afterwards that a main reason for the tour was to impress on people that 'the game was . . . meant to be enjoyed by businessmen' and did not need the 'specialisation or intensive training' the Americans brought to sport. The locals were not impressed: 'We had a hard workout . . . for an hour and a half, and went off the field feeling very fit; imagine then our consternation when we read our evening papers and discovered that we had "indulged in a gentle warming-up exercise".'[6] Nevertheless the British had learned something from their drubbing by the South Africans and when the All-Blacks came the following winter they lost to both England and Wales.

The English victory, in which the naturalised Russian Prince Alexander Obolensky scored two dazzling tries, made the better newsreel material and is still discussed with awe in Twickenham bars. But the New Zealanders had been softened up by their dramatic last-minute defeat at Cardiff Arms Park the month before. The Welsh, despite losing their hooker with a broken neck, not only recovered their form, but their national confidence. In doing so they abandoned the forlorn dream of distinctively un-Anglicised working-class purity – any hope of that had vanished in the slump – and embraced the Rowe Harding philosophy. The team that beat the New Zealanders was a mixture of 'Varsity backs – Vivian Jenkins, G. R. Rees-Jones, Wilf Wooller, Cliff Jones – and artisan forwards. It was democratic enough to preserve rugby's unique position: 'Welsh peers and labourers' and all the classes in between united 'in acclaiming and cheering the Welsh team . . . (in) a victory that probably is impossible in any other sphere', averred the *Western Mail*.[7]

The mixture was certainly more dilute elsewhere. In England D. R. Gent was expressing concern that the proliferation of Old Boy's teams might be affecting the standard of the open clubs, and in Scotland, where the Former Pupils' clubs were dominant, the resurgence of the textiles trade, busy supplying fashionable garments for the leisure industry, did not markedly increase the proportion of border club representation in the national team. In Ireland the City of Derry XV was strengthened on special occasions by players from the Royal Leicestershire Regiment stationed nearby, including the English international D. A. Kendrew, a future Major-General and Governor of Western Australia. The humbler Ballymena, who had just reached senior level, were nevertheless mostly from the town's leading school and they could call on the services of Irish international Sean Waide, an Oxford man, when he was home on vacation.[8] 'Varsity rugger was at a high level and its players dominated the international scene, which without the ostracised French was a well-balanced sporting contest with each country taking the title in turn.

More and more clubs were formed as the schools' switch from soccer began to take effect. Few of them were rich and gate-money was deplored in the highest circles: floodlit matches had been banned. The RFU itself did pretty well, though. Nearly 70,000 watched the All-Blacks game at Twickenham in January 1936, replenishing coffers already swollen enough to make a contribution of £1,000 to the King George V Jubilee Trust. In their bounty, too, they decided to respond to requests for moratoria on loans by allowing the clubs to repay at 4%, the rates the bank charged them rather than the current 5%, and the following season, when the loans totalled £40,659, decided they could afford to drop the rate to 2.5%. There was a hint of past tensions when the North v South fixture was revived, and it was discontinued 'as a result of breaches of the laws against professionalism'.[9] The menace of the Rugby League was ever-present. It continued to thrive in its northern fastness and though the London experiment had failed, its tentacles now extended to Newcastle. Happily Coventry remained inviolate. Its post-war revival had scarcely been touched by the slump: Its unemployment rate in 1934 was a mere 5.4% and its population rose from 128,000 in 1922 to 220,000 in 1939, the fastest growth in Britain. Many were immigrants seeking work and by 1937 21.5% of them were Welsh, but, as they readily found work in industry, the effect was to revive the faltering Rugby Union tradition, shoring it up against the all-pervading soccer, rather than spread the Rugby League.

Glasgow was as ever mad about soccer, but they had other addictions. 20,000 people crowded the city centre in September 1935 to welcome home Scotland's first world champion boxer. He had just beaten Jackie Brown of Manchester, knocking him down eight times before the referee stopped the fight in the second round. MacNib of the *Evening Post* was moved to poesy:

> Glasgow at last with flag unfurled
>   Sits right atop the cockeyed world.
> Our Wee Men may honk their klaxon
>   Since one of them has laid low the Saxon.

He added a cautionary note: 'Just take one tip from me old Benny and keep your head.'[10] It was no mere routine warning against swollen-headedness. The new champion was Benny Lynch, 22 years old with 84 fights behind him, a broken marriage and a serious drink problem. He got £1,000 for the title fight and when his manager from the early days could get only £300 for the next he sacked him. He lost the fight – to Jimmy Warnock in Belfast – but the blow to his pride steadied him for a while and after a string of wins over the best in Britain he was ready to take on the Americans. They as ever were more interested in the heavyweights. So were most of the British public. Everyone saw the newsreel films of James J. Braddock, 'the Cinderella man' beating Max Baer and the *cognoscenti* discussed the claims of Joe Louis and Max Schmeling. British hopes plummeted when Jack Petersen lost the national title to the South African Ben Foord in August 1936. Few outside Wales talked about Tommy Farr from Tonypandy who the previous year had lost the light-heavyweight title to Eddie Phillips. But Farr, a veteran of the fairground booths, was to surprise everyone.

Ideologies on parade

Democratic wheels turn slowly and in various directions. In November 1934, the Minister of Health had suggested at their annual dinner that the BMA might do something to alert the nation to the benefits of physical culture. It set up a committee which reported, in April 1936, the results of a survey estimating that, for instance, 84% of girls' secondary schools had no gymnasium and 72% of boys between 14 to 18 got no physical recreation, but that 750,000 amateurs played organised football under FA auspices every Saturday. It was a patchy and unsatisfactory situation, but the Board of Education knew that already. Circular 1445, which it had issued four months earlier, had called for an expansion of PE at all levels – a daily period in every elementary school, three periods a week besides swimming and games in secondary schools, more organisers and a suitable admixture of physical training and recreation in voluntary classes for adults, and more playing fields, building on the pioneering work of the NPFA. More significantly, its preamble obliquely acknowledged what the press was increasingly saying – that the Germans and Italians were way ahead in provision for the mass of the people.

They were ahead of the game in every way. In March 1936, with the League of Nations' attention focused on Mussolini's activities in Abyssinia Hitler reoccupied the Rhineland with a token force, and France and Britain were too weak, in every sense, to resist. Only the Soviet Union proposed sanctions against Germany. Instead Britain reassured France and Belgium that she would stand by them if they were attacked, a policy which had the advantage of requiring no immediate action. Meanwhile Mussolini, hampered but not deterred by economic sanctions, overran Abysinnia. With Baldwin at the helm civil servants were making what policy there was on defence. Behind the scenes new and progressive military plans were being laid and scientists beginning to make some impression on the military mind. The invention of radar was not only vital in itself but it exposed the error of over-reliance on bombing planes and spurred the growth of Fighter Command. But the new programmes were launched slowly and without real conviction.

There was no question of either France or Britain plunging into the Spanish Civil War when the League of Nation's non-intervention agreement broke down and the fascist Franco was being supported by Italy and Germany and the Republic's armed factory workers by Soviet Russia. Instead, it became a great ideological debate. Right wing aesthetes and literati generally sided with Franco. The intellectual Left found the cause they had been waiting for, suitably detached from the realities of home affairs, in this microcosmic international struggle. Some were more involved than others. With the Labour Party dithering, Orwell, the practising socialist, suffered in Catalonia. Auden wrote a poem about it. His *Spain*, 'locating the struggle not in the revolutionary effort . . . but in the moment of personal choice',[11] revealed the bourgeois sympathiser not the committed activist. Unlike Orwell, who drew an astringent moral from his disillusionment with Soviet opportunism, Auden soon took himself off to the fleshpots of America. The BWSF, thwarted in its attempt to achieve a boycott of the Berlin Olympic Games, had eagerly responded to the call for a People's Olympiad in Barcelona and 41 athletes actually travelled there, only to be frustrated by the outbreak of hostilities. The British team, whose women members 'showed fine fortitude in the circumstances', expressed solidarity with the workers, and some had to be prevented from joining in. While cynics thought the episode 'some sort of Communist Party stunt' the returning team got great publicity for the cause and many left-wing sportsmen joined the International Brigade. 'Sam Masters . . . claimed to be the first British volunteer in Spain [and] Clem Beckett, George Brown and Walter Tapsell lost their lives on Spanish soil.'[12]

Hitler saw the French stance on Spain as tolerance of a Bolshevik threat to Europe. He still had hopes of the British, however, particularly under their new king. The forthcoming Olympics were an opportunity not only to demonstrate the cultural superiority of Nazism over America's commercialised version of democracy but to win the regard and friendship of the archetypal sporting amateurs. The IOC had got over its initial horror at the Nazi appropriation of the Games, and on receiving Hitler's assurance in May 1934 that there would be no political, racial or religious bias in the selection and treatment of competitors, the British and American threat of boycott had been withdrawn.[13] As the Games approached, Britain's man on the spot, Sir Eric Phipps, who was aware of the reality behind the propaganda exercise and was unimpressed by the temporary removal of Anti-Semitic placards, apprised the government of the telling effect a last-minute boycott would have. The socialist NWSA had been pressing for withdrawal for months but a resolution put to a special meeting of the AAA was defeated by 200 votes to 8. The Jewish Harold Abrahams wrestled with his conscience but, focusing on ideals beyond the immediate, decided that the honourable course was to go and report the occasion fearlessly for the press and radio. A few progressive groups, the wayward Oxford Union, the BWSF and the liberal *Manchester Guardian* opposed British participation, but the true voice of the nation was the *Sporting Chronicle and Athletic News*: 'We will not tolerate any interference with our sport or with our sense of fair play.'[14]

The government, secure behind the tradition that in Britain sport was free from politics, saw no reason to disrupt the propagandist plans of a regime dedicated to manipulating it. Indeed the Foreign Office now saw the Games as a suitable vehicle for appeasement. Official policy had formerly been that anything concerning the Olympics was strictly a matter for the BOC and that 'the eternal bickering which goes on over them' was ample reason for the government to stay out of it.[15] However, when Japan put in a bid for the 1940 Games, the British Ambassador, in January 1936, urged support on the grounds that it might contribute to peace in the Far East, and the Foreign Secretary, Eden, commented, 'Then for heaven's sake let us encourage it. I could even run in the mile myself!'[16] It was a considerable embarrassment, therefore, when a few weeks later it was learned that the BOC had entered a rival bid, with the support of the Lord Mayor of London. The Cabinet, though agreeing that Japan's increasingly aggressive behaviour did not warrant chivalrous gestures decided nevertheless to give the BOC 'a hint' not to rock the boat. There was a good deal of 'left-hand, right-hand' in what followed and the Lord Mayor took a little persuading where his duty lay, but the BOC was compliant and the diplomats breathed again.

Meanwhile in the new spirit of Anglo-German rapprochement Sir Robert Vansittart, chief official at the Foreign Office, though avowedly anti-Nazi, accepted an invitation to the Berlin Games and urged the French Ambassador to discourage communist plans to disrupt them. In the end the Admiralty sent a warship to Kiel, not for reconnaissance purposes, but to grace the Olympic regatta. The reward was a stirring British victory in the 6-metre yachting. There was little else to shout about. There was certainly no triumph for the British amateur ideal in the rowing. Germany won five of the seven events. Leander provided the eights crew and came fourth. Fortunately for the Henley Stewards the Australian policemen did not reach the finals, but the Leander men were lucky to escape with merely verbal censure from these outraged artisans. The only British success was in the double sculls, and for this neither the ARA, still keeping the Olympics at arm's length, nor the amateur ideal could claim credit. Beresford and Southwood of Thames RC had trained for ten months in the hope of selection and in the whole time had found only one race to compete in, the Vesta RC Open – Henley had no such vulgar event – and the pair were reduced to offering to pace any crews that would make use of them. The Olympic invitation came, quite casually, from the Chairman of the ARA a mere month before the regatta. Then, in violation of the conventions, they put themselves in the hands of Eric Phelps, the professional champion, much as Abrahams had done with Mussabini in 1924, and it was this, according to Beresford, that made all the difference.[17]

For the most part the British showed themselves as the last amateurs, genuine according to their own lights but unconvincing. In boxing the straight left was no match for coarser European and even Argentinean methods The soccer team was so genuinely amateur as to be almost randomly selected: an unruly competition was won by Italy with Britain equal fifth with Germany (having a rare failure). The Germans were the supreme horsemen, not only victorious but showing that gallantry was not the prerogative of democracy: Britain took one bronze medal. German male and female gymnasts swept the board whilst the Italians evoked memories of earlier traditions in the fencing, rivalled only by the Hungarians – and German women. In these events Britain scarcely signified. In swimming neither men nor women managed better than sixth place. Germans even took a cycling gold medal from the French experts: the British came third in the team pursuit.

But it was the athletics that attracted most attention. This notorious meeting, celebrated on film, endlessly discussed and much written about,[18] was essentially a matter between the Americans, concealing the 'professionalised' orientation of the sports scholarship system beneath a cloak of concern for ethnic minorities, and the Germans, trying to make a racist point beneath a veneer of conformity to IOC expectations. In the event the main point made was that it was possible for a nation to become top Olympic dog if it sent its athletes away at public expense to special training camps for several months. The IOC expressed its concern, but it is unlikely that it would have done anything about it, particularly as it soon awarded the next Games to Japan, an announcement greeted with a three-day official celebration in Tokyo.[19] Meanwhile, while Jesse Owens was wiping the smile off Hitler's face before turning his gold medals to financial advantage and the fascistic Avery Brundage moved to power on the IOC, the British performed moderately well but below their own immodest expectations.

Their finest achievement was the gold medal in the 4×400 metres with a team that showed some social progress, with Bill Roberts of Salford alongside (in ascending order of rank) Fred Wolff of London AC, Godfrey Rampling of Milocarians and Godfrey Brown of Achilles. Their second gold was won by Harold Whitlock in the proletarian 50 kilometres walk. There was similar balance in the silver medals of Ernie Harper in the marathon, Donald Finlay in the 110 metres hurdles, improving on his Los Angeles performance as he advanced in rank in the RAF, and Godfrey Brown, part of the winning relay team, who came within a fraction of a second of winning the 400 metres. An Achilles man won the 1500 metres but he was a New Zealander, Jack Lovelock, and although Lovelock, who lived in Britain, was almost part of the family, there were many who mourned for Sidney Wooderson. Wooderson, a pale, small spectacled 21-year-old, from Blackheath Harriers and coached by Albert Hill, was an archetypal underdog, the sort of hero Priestley's new Britons could identify with. He had beaten Lovelock in the AAA championships but injured an ankle and did not advance beyond the heats.

Brundage brought no new hope for women liberationists. Later on, as President, he was to summarise his policy: 'I think women's events should be confined to those appropriate to women – swimming, tennis, figure-skating and fencing, but certainly not shot-putting.'[20] Meanwhile the restricted women's programme in Berlin had the added interest of political significance. This was often spiced by sexual innuendo. Thus the Americans not only took the 100 metres but also produced the type of Nordic beauty Hitler admired. The 6 foot Missouri farm-girl Helen Stephens afterwards claimed that he invited her away for the weekend. Happily it was months before it was discovered that a German competitor in the high jump was a hermaphrodite.[21] A German girl lost in a photo-finish in the hurdles, but to an Italian, which wasn't too bad. The world-record-breaking German team who dropped the baton in the final of the 4×100 relay let in the Americans. The British, overshadowed by all this, did moderately well. Their relay team (the veteran Olympiade Eileen Hiscox, Violet Olney, Audrey Brown, A. G. K.'s sister, and Barbara Burke of Mitcham AC) came second because of the German misfortune. The finest performance was by Dorothy Odham, a 16-year-old from Mitcham, who finished equal with a Czech and a German in the high jump but was defeated in a jump-off.

Slipshod democracy

The preservation of true amateur values was no real comfort for the British 'failure' in Berlin. In November 1936, *The Times* called for 'a great national effort to improve the physique of the nation', citing the King, Edward VIII, as an example of a truly 'fit man'.[22] The national fitness campaign pushed the plight of the workless further down the political agenda. The most poignant of all the hunger marches, from Jarrow, took place that month, but it was also the smallest. With the Communist party's attention now on Spain it was organised by the town's Labour council and MP, Ellen Wilkinson, with Conservative support. Yet despite this highly respectable backing Baldwin refused to meet the marchers: 'This is the way civil strife begins,' he told the House of Commons, 'and civil strife may not end until it is civil war.'[23] The government was even-handed in its concern, and had recently introduced a Public Order Act to crack down on Oswald Mosley and his uniformed thugs. When it came to lifting up the distressed areas it was less effective.

The most celebrated policy statement of the new monarch, 'Something must be done about unemployment', was uttered in South Wales a few days after the Jarrow march. It soon became a somewhat mocking epitaph, for he had already told the Prime Minister that he intended to marry the American divorcée Mrs Wallis Simpson, and in less than a month he was gone.[24] There were a few who indulged Edward in the vain hope that a morganatic marriage would allow him to stay on the throne, some even suggesting that, failing government consent, he should appeal directly to the country, precipitating an election at which a loyalist party would be swept into office. One who would have been favourite to lead such a party was Winston Churchill, whose exasperation with Stanley Baldwin over defence was by now intense. Had such a coup been effected he would have had some work to do convincing Edward who the foremost enemy was. One well-informed observer confided in his diary, 'The King is . . . going the dictator way, and is pro-German, against Russia and against too much slipshod democracy.'[25]

The slipshod democrats had their way, however, with Baldwin, invoking the heads of Commonwealth governments and aided by the Archbishop of Canterbury, speaking for Britain. Edward made his poignant abdication broadcast, and the nation turned back to more important matters. For Churchill and his little band of sympathisers this meant Hitler. For the left it meant unemployment. For the majority it meant sport. 'Gubby' Allen's men had just won the first Test in Australia. Benny Lynch was in training for his forthcoming match against the transatlantic world champion, 'Small' Montana. The obscure Charlton Athletic, newly-promoted from the Second Division, were now challenging Manchester City and Arsenal for leadership of the First. In loftier circles 'football' meant rugger, but was just as absorbing. At Christmas P. G. Wodehouse wrote to an old school friend, 'isn't it amazing that you and I, old buffers of fifty-five with Civilisation shortly about to crash, can worry about school football? It is really almost the only thing I do worry about.'[26]

People were aware, of course, of Neville Chamberlain's replacing Baldwin, retiring with acclamation at his finest hour, but few saw much significance in it. The new man carried an umbrella, they noticed, but that was a wise precaution and no-one wanted a reckless fellow at the helm. Yet the difference was profound, for instead of a bumbling preoccupation with party politics Chamberlain brought a considered policy to foreign affairs. Its basis was turning the other cheek. His reaction to Eamon de Valera's translation of the Irish Free State to Eire, a republic whose constitution's first article laid claim to the whole island, was to conciliate him in the hope of winning his goodwill: the Irish were treated as if they were still members of the Commonwealth, given British citizenship and, to Churchill's dismay, handed back three naval bases held by treaty. Chamberlain was similarly placatory to Hitler, being convinced that Germany could be brought to civilised behaviour through tolerance and understanding of her designs on neighbouring states. This triumph of Freudian rationalisation, which now seems mad, was widely shared – for example by the Dominions at the Imperial Conference held in 1937. The new leader of the Labour Party, Clement Attlee, was an exception, for he denounced the drift to abject appeasement of the dictators; but he was thought a mere stop-gap leader and his mild manner was mistaken for weakness.

Chamberlain, his supporters could fairly claim, had served the country well in domestic matters. The Britain he led was still, despite permeation by the various burgeoning middle groups, socially divided into 'the toffs' and the rest, and her wealth too ill-distributed, her power-structure too class-ridden to change the underlying stratification. The north had a hard core of about three-quarters of a million on the dole and Scotland one-quarter of a million. The proportion of unemployment in Northern Ireland (23.6%) and Wales (22.3%) contrasted sharply with that of London and the south-east (6.4%).[27] Two thousand tax-payers had an average income of £43,000 a year compared with the doctor or lawyer with £1,000, the bank clerk with £350, and the great mass with £250 or less.[28] Yet this was a considerable flattening of the Edwardian pyramid. Orwell's The Road to Wigan Pier (1937) wrung the withers of the compassionate, but did little to disturb the complacency of the great majority. Real wage levels had fallen only slightly with the price rises brought by world recovery and then remained stable until the war. Though investment abroad resumed import restriction was not needed. Above all, food was cheap.

Punters of the world unite

Orwell nevertheless regarded the sample household budgets printed in the newspapers, showing that it was possible to survive on a per capita expenditure of 4s a week on food, as an irrelevant sham. For him the advance of the 'new England' was a confidence trick: 'Twenty million people are underfed . . . Whole sections of the working class who have been plundered of all they really need are being compensated, in part by cheap luxuries . . . It is quite likely that fish-and-chips, art-silk stockings, tinned salmon, cut-price chocolate . . . the movies, the radio, strong tea and the football pools have between them averted revolution.' The pools were undoubtedly the greatest of these diversions to the male half of the population at this time of stress: as the Pilgrim Trust's investigators commented, 'The extent to which the interests and indeed the whole lives of so many of the Liverpool unemployed centre around the pools must be seen to be believed.' But it was a general addiction. Some 10 million people now sent in their weekly coupons, and the annual turnover reached £50 million by the end of the decade. The firms, led by Littlewoods and Vernons, provided £20,000 a week in advertising for the newspapers, and pools guides, permutation systems and professional prophets abounded. Some 30,000 people were engaged in the industry and its by-product mail-order business. The GPO's weekly sales, in postal orders and stamps, increased to the extent that subpostmasters and mistresses demanded extra cash. While the Baptist Church led the protests about the moral effect a Worthing butcher complained that his customers were buying cheap imported meat to save up for the pools. And as Orwell noted, 'Hitler's march into the Rhineland raised 'hardly a flutter of interest' but the football authorities' attempt to stop the use of the fixtures by the pools' firms 'flung all Yorkshire into a storm of fury'.[29]

For the FA, persistent opponent of all forms of gambling, the pools were a menace the game could do without, and the Football League, strongly influenced by the Methodist C. E. Sutcliffe, joined with it in recommending to the Royal Commission on Lotteries and Betting in 1933 that the pools be abolished altogether. The Commission rejected this as discriminatory and the authorities tried other means. When Sutcliffe became President of the League in 1935 the clubs were forbidden to take advertisements for the pools in their programmes and round the ground, and then attempted to stop the pools firms printing their fixture lists in which they claimed copyright. Technically they were probably right, but the pools people found it easy to circumvent this by telephoning round the clubs and, as Orwell indicated, the public were enraged by the very idea. The Football Pools Association offered to soften the blow by making an ex-gratia payment to be used for the good of the sport but the FA wanted no tainted money. A Liberal MP who tried to get the law changed in 1936 was denounced as a spoilsport by an enthusiast who wished his name was 'on the list of those killed on the roads' at the time. Both this and the 1938 Bill put forward by A. P. Herbert, MP for Oxford University, were thrown out by a House of Commons with a proper grasp of political realities.[30]

The expansion of football pool gambling did nothing to diminish the popularity of greyhound racing. The Royal Commission reported over 220 tracks in Britain: the 5.5 million attendances of 1927 had increased to 38 million by 1938. Off-course betting was illegal, as on the Turf, but the number of tracks and evening meetings made attendance much easier. The ease of access and their estimated 10% share of all gambling turnover made dog-tracks a favourite target of the anti-gambling lobbies and those whose concern it was to protect the moral well-being of the working-class young. The promoters had particularly exposed themselves to censure by illegally introducing the Tote, intended by Parliament to meet the needs of the Turf which was both socially superior and held to be in financial need. Court action by an indignant bookmaker, another aggrieved class, led to its being declared illegal in 1932. This did not stop the practice at the White City and elsewhere, nor the retaliatory banning of bookmakers, and when the High Court reversed the decision, the floodgates were open. The Betting and Lotteries Act of 1934 legalised the Tote, but tried to limit its use to twice a week. It did not succeed.

Gambling, Orwell might have noted, was the social cement behind the sports that had helped to stave off revolution in earlier, more fissile times. The chief virtue of the Tote was as a bookmaker that always paid up. On the Turf (still a favourite vehicle for punters, accounting for half the total turnover of some £500 million) it appealed to the small man since the minimum stake was 2s, and its profits grew from £10,000 in 1933 to £177,550 five years later. This was not quite the goldmine the Jockey Club had hoped for – especially since they did not control the proceeds – and it was constrained by the new Betting and Lotteries Act. The Tote had contrived an ingenious way to cash in on the vast, off-course betting market by arranging with Guardian Pari-Mutuel Ltd (later Tote Investors Ltd) to provide credit betting on an agency basis: they set up offices all over the country, with commentaries from the course on 'the London and Provincial News Agency 'blower'. The scheme had a setback when the Tote 'clubs' that offered a congenial place to sit and have a drink whilst placing a bet were declared illegal. The backstreet bookie was still in business, and yet another Parliamentary investigation had come to the conclusion that his existence was an insuperable objection to taxation. The 1934 Act, furthermore, failed to solve the problem of the Irish Sweep, for whilst easing the way for smaller, local charitable lotteries it prohibited the advertising of foreign ones, and made sending tickets through the mail and buying them an offence. This halved the sales of tickets, but the average income was still over £5 million a year: in true British fashion 'offenders' were rarely prosecuted.[31]

Riding into the sunset

Gambling apart, more and more people, Priestley had noted, were taking up riding. 'The horse as a beast of burden may be at the end of his days, but as a sporting companion he is starting life all over again.'[32] The number of horses had fallen from 68,000 in 1924 to only 38,000 ten years later whilst motor cars were near the 2 million mark. But Minister of Transport Hore-Belisha's Highway code prescribed hand signals for horse-drawn vehicles with pictures showing arms rotating whips in various directions. Cars themselves were designed in imitation of a cart being pulled by a horse and they were categorised for tax purposes by horse-power. When Hore-Belisha became War Minister in 1937 he found horses no less dominant in military life. The official manual *Cavalry Training, 1937*, which had 23 pages of sword and lance exercises, included a brief supplement that stated 'Mounted drill (in armoured cars) is based on the same principles as that of cavalry.'

Hore-Belisha's assignment was to modernise the services, but he found a tradition of well-bred officers as well as well-bred horses. The two were frequently together. In 1938 he found himself presenting the Cavalry Open Cup to Captain C. B. Harvey who was pained to hear the Minister remark to the Senior Steward, 'Not a bad type for a professional jockey!' He said afterwards, 'I don't know if he was a good minister but he didn't know as much about the Army as he did about beacons.'[33] If he mistook their class Belisha could at least be forgiven for thinking that the likes of Harvey were full-time riders. As one of the many Etonian military men who graced the racing world explained, 'Although the number of cavalry regiments had been reduced, and there were signs that others, if not all, would eventually be overtaken by mechanisation, there was no lack of officers with the time, the money and the inclination to take up racing.'[34] The double Grand National winner of 1936, Reynoldstown, was ridden by Frank Furlong, of Sandhurst and the 9th Lancers, son of its owner and trainer, and when he had problems with his weight, the winning ride in 1937 went to his old Sandhurst classmate, Fulke Walwyn.[35]

Many more military riders competed in point-to-points, which depended heavily on military support for social tone and authenticity. Not all were rich, as distinct from leisured: two of the best, 'Perry' Harding and Peter Payne-Galwey, owned only a few horses. Army officers also dominated the world of equestrianism. In its latest and most popular branch, show-jumping, its earliest star, the outright winner of the King George V Gold Cup at the Royal International Horse Show, was Lieutenant J. A. Talbot-Ponsonby of the 7th Queen's Own Hussars. (Showing that the British Army was not alone in its equine orientation the Cup then went to officers of the Irish, French and Italian forces.) Indeed the BSJA was so sedately conscious of tradition that it overdid its work of standardisation and the organisers of events at the many agricultural shows, anxious to conform, found that the sameness of their programmes eventually began to lessen interest.

By far the greatest attraction in National Hunt racing was steeplechasing, and within that the spectacular uncertainties of the Grand National, and its excitements were further enhanced by the advent of the Irish Sweep. In 1931 the Aintree authorities, in an attempt to make the race less of a scramble, had increased the minimum jockey weight from 10 to 10½ stones, but commercial considerations including the enhanced appeal of bigger fields for lottery purposes led them to lower it again in 1937. The NH Committee had only limited success in trying to shift the balance towards more sporting, less chancy races, especially weight-for-age competitions. They owed much to the eccentric Dorothy Paget and her outstanding horse Golden Miller. The Miller won £9,000 from his single victory in the Grand National and only £6,000 from all his other races, including five consecutive Cheltenham Gold Cups from 1932 to 1936. Golden Miller was, and is, the only horse to win both in the same year (1934) and might have done it twice but for a sensational lapse – on whose part is still disputed.[36]

His usual rider (not invariable, for nothing was permanent with Miss Paget) was Gerry Wilson, champion from 1932 to 1937. Wilson was the son of a horse-dealer in the Whaddon Chase country. Billy Stott, his predecessor, was a former stable lad. The up-and-coming 'Frenchy' Nicholson got his nickname from his father, a professional huntsman in France. Trainers' sons were well placed to become professional riders and some did well, like Fred Rimell, champion in 1937 and 38, and Bruce Hobbs, only seventeen when he won the 1938 National on Battleship, until forced back into training early by injury, the chief occupational hazard. Paddy Prendergast, son of an Irish 'spotter', and Noel (later Sir Noel) Murless were amongst the less distinguished professional riders who became great trainers. Those who rode specifically for experience, like Staff Ingham and Jack Fawcus, tended to do so as amateurs, and it still caused remark when Fulke Walwyn turned professional and got his injury credentials for successful training.

In the social mix that came from love of a sporting chance Etonians were well to the fore. After Oxford, where he was a cricket Blue and half-Blue in rackets, real tennis and squash, Peter Cazalet inherited the Fairlawne estate in 1932 and began training and riding his own small string of horses. In Cazalet's house at Eton Anthony (Lord) Mildmay, a Cambridge polo-player and hunting buff, who left a post at Barings, the family bank, the following year to go into partnership with him, had no ambition outside riding. Soon, as his partner wrote of him, he was 'known and loved by the humblest to the greatest in the land'.[37] Everyone suffered with him when the reins of his horse, Davy Jones, became unbuckled and he ran off the course before the final fence in the 1936 Grand National.

The spreading chestnut tree

There had been an extra element of gloom for the racing establishment at the loss of George V. Though he left few entries in the annals of the Turf he had always shown a keen and amiable interest. His successor was an unknown quantity, though the omens were not good. Even as his father lay dying he had ordered the Sandringham clocks to be restored to Greenwich meantime from their traditional 'shooting time', an earnest indication of his intent to modernise his household, and harsh economies had followed at Balmoral. The royal horses had already been leased to Lord Derby by the time Edward paid his only visit to Ascot and the course authorities feared the worst when he turned the social occasion into a tour of inspection, looking into everything in detail, tight-lipped and taciturn. But the sunshine came back in 1937 as George VI and Queen Elizabeth drove the course together and the papers got lovely pictures of the family enjoying themselves at Windsor.

The British press, normally assiduous in the courtship of the common man, had been so muzzled by their proprietors that the rest of the world knew about Edward VIII's cavortings long before the British public. Now, having squeezed every bit of 'human interest' out of the abdication and its aftermath, they turned with equal delight to exploiting the accession of the thoroughly decent George VI with his bonny Scottish wife and two charming daughters, Elizabeth and Margaret Rose. The commercial benefits were enormous. The Coronation was *the* event of 1937. Every school had its Coronation celebrations, with commemorative medallions, mugs, spoons or whatever products the local council bestowed its favours on. The Royal Family, now with a real family at the heart of it, were themselves becoming part of the new Britain of the lower middle classes. They were the stars of an entertainment industry which even though the BBC's television service was barely operational, was already a dominant force in British life.

By great luck the country had hit upon the ideal man to heal the wounds left by the abdication. Even his defects were useful. He overcame his stammer well enough to perform rituals that had become essential to the job, like the Christmas broadcasts, but it inhibited any tendency towards the populist speeches of his elder brother. He stepped into the sporting role expected of him without difficulty. His youthful feats on the tennis court stood him in good stead, he was at home in hunting circles, and as the *DNB* puts it 'good at sports, an excellent shot and a skilled horseman, he was the country squire, the racehorse owner, the freemason'. But he displayed the common touch by continued visits to his summer camps. The King's enthusiasm for Scouting – Princess Elizabeth became a Girl Guide and her younger sister a Brownie – was thoroughly approved, and his manifest delight in the camp-fire song 'Underneath the Spreading Chestnut Tree' was recorded in a news-reel. The King, in an open-necked shirt, led the singing, opening his hands for 'spreading', touching his chest for 'chest', and his head for 'nut' and extending his arms for 'tree'.

Notes

1 H. Cleaver, *A History of Rowing*, London, 1957, p. 148.
2 F. Root, *A Cricket Pro's Lot*, London, 1937, p. 166.
3 ibid., p. 186.
4 ibid., pp. 187–8.
5 J. E. Greenwood, *A Cap for Boots*, London, 1977, p. 114.
6 K. C. Fyfe in H. B. T. Wakelam (ed.), *The Game Goes On*, London, 1954, pp. 160–2.
7 *Western Mail*, 23 December 1935, quoted by G. Williams in T. Mason (ed.), *Sport in Britain*, Cambridge, 1989, p. 330. For an account of the match by a participant see W. Wooller, 'Wales v New Zealand, 1935', in K. Wright and R. F. Wright (eds.), *I Was There*, London, 1966, Chapter Four.
8 *Ballymena RFC Centenary Handbook*, Ballymena, 1987, pp. 15, 101.
9 U. A. Titley and R. McWhirter, *Centenary History of the Rugby Football Union*, London, 1970, p. 150.
10 J. Burrowes, *Benny*, Edinburgh, 1982 (London, 1984 edn), p. 218.
11 J. Berthoud, 'Literature and Drama', in B. Ford (ed.), *Early 20th Century Britain*, Cambridge, 1992, p. 91.
12 S. G. Jones *Sport, Politics and the Working Class in Modern Britain*, Manchester, 1988, p. 186. Beckett was a celebrated Manchester speedway rider.
13 M. Polley, 'Olympic Diplomacy', *IJHS*, August 1992. p. 173.
14 Jones, *Sport, Politics*, p. 183.
15 Foreign Office minute July 1935, quoted in Polley, 'Olympic Diplomacy', p. 175.
16 Telegram, 8 January 1936, Polley, 'Olympic Diplomacy', p. 176.
17 Cleaver, *History of Rowing*, p. 142.
18 See, for instance, W. Hart-Davis, *The Berlin Games*, London, 1986; R. D. Mandell, *The Nazi Olympics*, Chicago, 1987.
19 Polley, 'Olympic Diplomacy', p. 183.
20 A. Brundage, 1949, quoted by J. Hargreaves, 'Women and the Olympic Phenomenon', in A. Thompson and G. Whannel (eds.), *Five-Ring Circus*, London, 1984, p. 61.
21 D. Wallechinsky, *The Complete Book of the Olympics*, Harmondsworth, 1988, pp. 135 and 154, gives details.
22 R. Graves and A. Hodge, *The Long Weekend*, London, d1940 (1971 edn), pp. 376–7.
23 *Hansard*, 11 November 1936.
24 See F. Donaldson, *Edward VIII*, London (1976 edn), for the details of the Welsh tour and of the Abdication crisis.
25 *Chips: The Diaries of Sir Henry Channon*, ed. R. R. James, London, 1967, p. 92.
26 Letter to W. Townend, 28 December 1936, in P. G. Wodehouse, *Performing Flea*, London, 1953, Chapter Three.
27 1937 figures quoted in J. Stevenson, *British Society 1914–45*, Harmondsworth, 1984, p. 271. For other useful background information see his Chapter Ten; G. D. H. Cole and R. Postgate, *The Common People*, London, 1938 (1961 edn), Chapter Forty-six; A. J. P. Taylor, *English History, 1914–45*, Oxford, 1965, Chapter Ten; H. Heald (ed.), *Chronicle of Britain and Ireland*, Farnborough, 1992, pp. 1080–96. For contemporary

views see G. D. H. and M. Cole, *The Condition of Britain*, London, 1937, J. Hilton, *Rich Man, Poor Man*, London, 1938, and G. Orwell, *The Road to Wigan Pier*, London, 1937.

28 Stevenson, *British Society*, pp. 116–24.

29 See G. Orwell, 'The *Road to Wigan Pier* Diary', in *Collected Essays, Journalism and Letters*, Harmondsworth, 1972, Vol. 1, pp. 199, 221, 244; and *Road to Wigan Pier*, pp. 79–81; Stevenson, *British Society*, pp. 385–6; M. Clapson, *A Bit of a Flutter*, Manchester, 1992, pp. 169–70; Heald, *Chronicle*, p. 1096.

30 Clapson, *Flutter*, p. 170.

31 See ibid., pp. 188–93.

32 J. B. Priestley, *English Journey*, London, 1934 (Harmondsworth, 1977 edn), p. 114.

33 J. Hislop and D. Swannell, *The Faber Book of the Turf*, London, 1990, p. 244.

34 R. Mortimer in M. Seth-Smith et al., *The History of Steeplechasing*, London, 1966, p. 115 Another Etonian, John Hislop, invalided out after Sandhurst became an assistant trainer and a noted amateur rider as well as a gifted journalist a skilful breeder and eventually a successful owner, notably of Brigadier Gerard. in the early 1970s.

35 Walwyn left the army and later turned professional. Injured in a fall, he became a trainer after the war, with prodigious success. Furlong was killed in the Fleet Air Arm.

36 See B. Briscoe, *The Life of Golden Miller*, London, 1939.

37 P. Cazalet, in *DNB*.

CHAPTER THIRTEEN

Changing the rules (1929–39):
fitness for what?

In July 1937 the Japanese resumed their quarrel with China and within a month had taken Peking. By November China was appealing to the League of Nations – with the usual results. These distant events attracted little notice in Britain: the RFU saw no reason to discourage plans for a 1940 tour of Japan. In Europe appeasement reached new depths. In February 1938 Chamberlain sought to persuade Mussolini out of Spain and to enlist his aid as a moderating influence on Hitler by recognising the Italian claim to Abyssinia. It did not work. Hitler annexed Austria and Mussolini sent more 'volunteers' to help Franco. Churchill warned the House that Europe was 'confronted with a programme of aggression, nicely calculated and timed, unfolding stage by stage'.[1] President Roosevelt talked airily of an international conference to settle everything, and Russia offered to discuss an alliance against the Germans. If the former was pointless the latter was unthinkable. Stalin's purges and mass trials of Trotsky supporters were alienating the sympathies of all but the most entrenched.

Joy through strength

Eden, the erstwhile supporter of the Tokyo Olympics, resigned over the Italian fiasco. The athletes themselves were still extending the hand of friendship. The AAA, under the presidency of Lord Burghley, now Marquess of Exeter, welcomed a small but impressive German team to its 1937 championships. If there were moral lessons to be drawn from the experience it is perhaps that sport, for all the British belief in its character-building qualities, is ethically neutral. It can build bad character as well as good. Nor were there any obvious political lessons. It was clearly possible for a fascist regime to produce not only medal-winners but sportsmen in the British sense. There was Luz Long, who had won great praise – but only a silver medal – for helping Jesse Owens with a temporary problem in the long jump. But there were also two gold medallists, a hammer-thrower and a shot-putter. The latter, Hans Wölke a Nazi policeman, was to be killed by the French Resistance for his crimes in concentration camps. There were mutterings that German athletes got more than intensive coaching in their training camps. Lord Exeter that year headed the first IOC investigation into drug-taking.

The British equivalent of the Nazi training camps was the prolonged leisure of an Oxbridge education, particularly now that it could be accompanied by expert coaching. The recent British backwardness in field events was put in perspective by the performance in the pole-vault of Achilles' Richard Webster, son of F. A. M., the sage of Loughborough. The services also provided plenty of leisure. Dublin-born Arthur Sweeney was one of Milocarians' stars in the sprints, RAF duties permitting, and D. O. Finlay continued to fly fastest over the hurdles. But there were hints of the new Britain – in Bill Roberts in the 440 yards and above all in Wooderson who later that year broke the world's record. The sprinter C. B. Holmes from Manchester University indicated that at last the provincial universities were beginning to make a mark in athletics, but they laboured under difficulties. The National Union of Students – a new phenomenon – in its booklet *Student Health* (1937) pointed out that of the 40,000 outside Oxford and Cambridge only about one-quarter took part in sport of any kind: there was no tradition, few residents and poor facilities.

The British Empire Games that winter were a pleasantly reassuring interlude, but they were held in Sydney, which did not make for strong British participation. However Roberts and Holmes confirmed their superiority and Jim Alford, in Wooderson's absence, got Wales's first gold medal. in the mile. Dorothy Odham, who won the high jump, kept on improving and two years later beat Didrikson's world record. In February even the AAA, pressed by the NWSA, voted against participation at the proposed Tokyo Olympics, and were no doubt greatly relieved when Japan withdrew.[2] (Helsinki volunteered to step into the breach but was denied the opportunity by Stalin's invasion.) That summer's AAA championships were remarkable for 12 overseas victories, 6 of them Italian. Britain entered the European championships for the first time, with fair success. Matches against Germany continued to the end, and a British team was in Cologne the week before war broke out.

Ironically it was the traditionally xenophobic FA that most notably supplemented the government's appeasement plans. The aspirant Stanley Rous was eager to perform acts of public service, but sending teams abroad was to enter a minefield nowadays. The civil servants, as in the Tokyo Olympics episode, were more cautious than the politicians. There had been embarrassing defeats in Prague, Brussels and Budapest in 1934 and again in Vienna two years later (offset only partly, even for chauvinists, by a win at Highbury in the return match with Hungary), and by 1938 the Foreign Office was trying 'to discourage the playing of football matches against foreigners and warning of 'the embarrassing situation created as the result of visits abroad by poor teams'. Losing gracefully was no longer fashionable as a diplomatic ploy. A show of strength was particularly indicated in the forthcoming return match with Germany in Berlin. Vansittart wrote to Rous in May 1938 telling him what the nation expected. It was a great triumph, from the English team's sheepish Nazi salutes to their highly satisfactory 6–3 win. Clearly British football, when we set our stall out, was still the best there was, and the Foreign Office was re-assured: 'the splendid game played by the English team was thoroughly enjoyed by the huge crowd and it is now recognised that the excellence of English football is still something to be admired and coveted'.[3] And any doubts occasioned by the continued British absence from the World Cup (won again by Italy) could be brushed aside after England's 3–0 victory over a (not very well) combined FIFA side.

Diplomacy apart, the Berlin Olympics had set alarm bells ringing in Westminster as well as Whitehall, and the National Fitness Campaign took on greater urgency and somewhat changed its character. A delegation of British educationists, mostly HMIs but including the Principal of Carnegie College, Ernest Major, visited Germany shortly after the Games. They were easy victims for Nazi propaganda and on their return produced a glowing report, sympathetic to the underlying values and ideals of the Nazi system.[4] Obviously the PE enthusiasts saw much to be said for a regime that valued 'action' rather than 'contemplation' and an element of their enthusiasm crept in to the government's next move. There had already been some mutterings about the CCPRT. In the charged atmosphere created by the Spanish Civil War nasty remarks were made about its chairman. Lord Astor, of American capitalist origin, the ultra-rich owner of *The Observer* had a country residence, Cliveden, at which he gave celebrated house-parties for an élite circle. 'The Cliveden set', despite loud protestations from Lady Astor, was rumoured by the Left to be pro-German. The CCPRT certainly took itself seriously but it was convoluted and bureaucratic rather than authoritarian. But sporting bodies did not like the idea of being co-ordinated in the name of a vague general concern for sport. What they wanted was money for their own hobby-horses and no interference.

Now, however, in January 1937, the government proposed a Physical Training and Recreation Act with £2 million to be spent over the next three years and set up a National Council for Physical Training and Recreation, with 22 subsidiary regional committees to administer the scheme. Criticism began during Parliament's second reading of the Bill, when the government spokesman, though reminding the House that its scope included recreation, laid stress on its training side and argued that it could do much to remedy the ills of industrial, urbanised society. Labour members, suggesting malnutrition as a more immediate evil, regarded the scheme as a concealed form of military training. So much the better, thought Sir Francis Fremantle, descended from a long line of admirals. Aneurin Bevan, MP for Ebbw Vale, delivered a two-pronged attack. The idea that we must 'seek the justification of national well-being' for playing games was 'one of the worst legacies of the Puritan Revolution'. Furthermore the government was pushing this training on the masses, getting 'all these boys and girls in rows like chocolate soldiers', as a cheap substitute for the playing fields and facilities for sport the upper classes already enjoyed.[5] But the ayes had it.

The National Fitness Council thus began in political ambiguity. Its moral integrity was made manifest through its Chairman, Lord Aberdare. A rackets and real tennis champion and a Middlesex cricketer, with a long record of service on such diverse bodies as the National Association of Boys' Clubs, the Miners' Welfare committee and the Queen's Institute of District Nursing, he declared in 1938 that his great ideal was to give everyone 'a chance of making the human body a fit instrument for the human soul'.[6] He was no Nazi but an old-fashioned muscular Christian. So, no doubt, was the idealist who excitedly wrote, 'the establishment of the National Fitness Council means much more than erecting a piece of machinery for giving grants to juvenile organisations and local education authorities. It signifies the advance of the educational army into the "no mans land" of adolescence.'[7] But the metaphor sent shivers down liberal spines. So did the talk that the Marquess of Exeter, who was high in the counsels of the NFC, was poised to become Britain's first Minister of Sport. And the CCPRT not only felt but *was* threatened: the NFC recruited a cadre of officials who promptly recommended that in the interests of efficiency they should take it over.

The reaction was swift, and not just from left-wingers. The voluntary principle was at stake. Sporting bodies and long-established youth organisations felt strongly that assisting them financially ought not to be relegated to a side issue by the advancing army. The provincial universities were anxious for assistance to help them with their embryonic plans, but on their own terms, and they concluded an arrangement whereby the NFC handed over £200,000 of their funds to the University Grants Committee for them to distribute. The CCPRT fought back strongly, on philosophical as well as organisational grounds, and stayed in being. The horde of gymnasts who attended the Lingiad in Stockholm in July, 1939, to do honour to P. H. Ling, the founder of Swedish gymnastics, showed by their very appearance what the British tradition was. Whilst the continentals sent massed teams, uniformly dressed and bearing national emblems, the separate little groups of the huge British contingent preserved their identities by a wide variety of garbs, some with Union Jacks but more with college or club badges and some with no badges at all. To the organisers they seemed such a shambles that they had to be hidden away, but to the British they showed the superiority of the approach through 'pleasant informality'.

If there was a growing corporateness in the recreations of the masses at this time it was that of the Boy Scouts not the Blackshirts, and it was shot through with Americanised commercialism and mass-production methods. The Canadian Ralph Reader's Boy Scout Gang Shows were regular West End attractions and their bouncy chorus numbers like 'We're Riding Along on the Crest of a Wave' were great hits. The Cup Final crowds continued to sing George V's favourite 'Abide With Me' but the new King's 'Chestnut Tree', jazzed up slightly, became a hit at the dance-halls. These, from village hop to palais de danse, were now enjoying a community phase, characterised by 'togetherness' numbers, such as the Palais Glide and the Paul Jones, often with strange gestures as in 'Chestnut Tree' and the hugely popular 'Lambeth Walk'. Thousands went to Butlin's new holiday camps, where guests were roused with stirring music and cries of 'Wakey, wakey!' and marshalled by men in red coats. There was even a vogue for formula jokes – 'Knock, knock, who's there?' and 'Little Audrey laughed and laughed' – in which some commentators have detected a faintly militaristic aura, like the hikers' uniforms. But the best-loved slogans were the daft ones of Arthur Askey and 'Stinker' Murdoch, stars of the BBC's 1938 *Band Wagon*, which truly united the nation – in escapist nonsense.

The best popular music was stylised but on American patterns: the crooning of Al Bowlly, the dance-music of Lew Stone and songs like Jimmy Kennedy's 'South of the Border'. It was American films the mass public wanted to see, from Disney's *Snow White* to the ultimate escape, *Gone with the Wind*. (The best British film of 1938, Alfred Hitchcock's *The Lady Vanishes*, made a joke of upperclass, cricket-mad insouciance in crisis-torn Europe.) And while Benny Lynch and his Glasgow cronies discussed the toughness of James Cagney, the Hollywood celebrity, as well as the crawl style of Johnny Weissmuller and Buster Crabbe inspired the youth of Ashton-under-Lyne to produce swimming and water-polo champions. Commercialisation had attractions of its own for the new British, and the most popular swimming 'baths' were those like Wakefield which became a venue for the surrounding mining villages for dancing on Saturday nights. Most obviously of all, whilst the IOC was investigating complaints that the leading ice-skaters were now signing professional contracts *before* competing, it was Sonja Henie on the silver screen, and the entrepreneurs who built rinks at places like Hammersmith and Golders Green to cash in on the vogue, that brought ice-skating to the millions.

Democracy – new style

The National Government, as it still called itself, was impelled increasingly by democratic concerns. This was in part because Chamberlain himself had something of his father's taste for social reform and in part because new concepts like planning, which were creeping in, were not party issues but more a sign of the progressive. But it was largely because the growing political necessity to have the people's backing was further increased when the nation's defence was at stake. Their needs and opinions were now studied more scientifically with the creation of the independent Mass Observation organisation in 1936 and the first Gallup polling by the British Institute of Public Opinion two years later. All these influences can be detected in the various measures enacted just before the war – the Factory Act bringing in a maximum 48-hour week, the Housing Act on rent controls, the nationalisation of mining royalties, and the Holidays with Pay Act (1938) which increased the numbers with paid annual holidays from 3 to 11 million. The government showed willing, too, on education. The Spens Committee recommended a tripartite system of secondary education – all free – with grammar, technical and 'modern' schools, They rejected 'multilateral' schools as standard provision 'with some reluctance' but urged experiments with this early form of comprehensive schooling The government accepted the plans and the local authorities looked forward to getting the money to implement them.

The new spirit that was in the air even penetrated the defensive screen of the rowing establishment. It did so in sedate fashion. On 7 April 1937 – somewhat belatedly – a question was raised in the House about the treatment of the Australian policemen. Three days later the President of Southampton University College Boat Club wrote to *The Times*. A cup had been presented for competition between all clubs on the Itchen, but most of them were NARA members so that if the students took part they risked expulsion from ARA activities. The time had come, he suggested, 'for real brotherhood in what is to many of us the finest sport for young men'. Other letters came from an old ARA man criticising its muddled thinking and an old NARA man pointing out that all the talent in Britain was needed if the foreign assault on Henley was to be withstood.[8] Few were aware that at a joint meeting of the two Associations the representatives of the ARA had agreed to the removal of the manual worker clause: it had to be kept secret because it needed approval of the full committee and the Henley Stewards. This took until June but at last the deed was done. And then – nothing very much happened. A Metropolitan Police Crew led the way for the artisans in the Thames Cup at Henley and an ARA eight entered (and won) the NARA championship. But there was no great intermingling of fraternal blood and no question of amalgamating the two organisations – they merely agreed to peaceful co-existence. Both remained implacably amateur.

The secretary of the NARA, Charles Tugwell, had invoked the new national spirit as exemplified by the PT&R legislation to persuade the ARA of its duty and it was no surprise when the National Fitness Council offered him a grant to work as a National Organiser of Rowing. This was no Hitler Youth style appointment. It was for 12 months only in the first instance and his work chiefly involved helping clubs find a way through the bureaucracy to get small grants towards the upkeep of their boathouses and so forth. He was able to prise £21,000 out of the NFC before the war. He skirted the edge of the professional world, such as it was, and the North-Eastern group sought his aid in getting help from the scheme. He responded by proposing a way in which those who had not rowed 'for personal profit' could apply for membership of the NARA, but did not find many takers.

In most athletic activities the professionals now unmistakably represented a more advanced stage, but there were some interesting variations, reflecting the sports' widely different histories. In boxing, for instance, where the ABA had based its highly successful expansion on open competition, although it still stayed aloof from the professional side, Petersen's example had shown that the transition could be made. One of the most exciting fights of the time was a professional contest in 1938 between Arthur Danahar, the previous year's ABA light weight champion, and Eric Boon. Danahar was 19, a splendid boxer and brave as a lion. Boon was only 18 and a country boy, but he was a fighter and too strong for Danahar, and it was Boon who advanced professionally until the relatively easy pickings of the British ring and exposure to the bright lights distracted him.

Waywardness was not a new phenomenon and it was admired rather than blamed in a fighter, provided it did not affect his performance. Benny Lynch, whose capacity for drink was enormous, got away with it for a time. But he was now an alcoholic. He stayed off the drink for a fortnight before his fight with Montana and managed to win but he was never able to show the same restraint again. He won more fights but lost some, too, and after an epic contest against Peter Kane relapsed into a sodden state, lost his title when he failed to make the weight and was on his way to an early grave. Kane, an apprentice blacksmith from industrial Lancashire, was almost as good as Lynch, and temperate. In the professional ring since 16 and before then a favourite at the local fairgrounds, Kane was still only 20 when he took the title in 1938, beating Jackie Jurich of Liverpool, and he held it for most of the war years.

Danahar v Boon was the first fight promoted by Jack Solomons, a fishmonger who sported a bigger cigar than Lord Lonsdale's, and it attracted enormous interest. But neither man was in the same class as 'Homicide' Henry Armstrong the black American champion. Britain had no black fighters of note. BBBC policy apart, there was only a trickle of immigrants so far. (From the peak of 200,000 in 1913 the number of immigrants of all races was down to less than 50,000 a year.) But there were other 'hungry fighters'. Hopes had been revived in 1937 for the British heavyweight – characterised by the *Daily Mail* cartoonist, Tom Webster, as irredeemably horizontal – by the splendid showing of Tommy Farr against Joe Louis, making the first defence of his title. The whole of Wales and most of Britain listened to that fight and were convinced, in the manner of such things, that their man had won, but though he gave Louis one of his hardest fights, he was up against something special. That was clear when Louis, motivated by a burning desire for revenge, turned his attention to Max Schmeling and struck a blow, at President Roosevelt's behest, for the credit of free America. At light heavyweight and middleweight there was another outstanding black American, John Henry Lewis. In the confusion following his retirement two Britishers, Len Harvey and Jock McAvoy of Rochdale, were matched in London in 1939 and Harvey was declared world champion. The message did not reach Pittsburgh where three days later Billy Conn claimed the title, perhaps more credibly, but the stylish Harvey was the essence of all the British admired and, everyone rather patronisingly agreed, a credit to his race.

Spice was added to the contests by home-town rivalry, often between the industrial areas of greatest deprivation, and it was a more genuinely local pride than that evoked by the itinerant soccer players who were obliged to follow the market. But the pattern of their origin was much the same as that of soccer. Thus Lancashire, with more overcrowded towns and cities in a smaller area – and greater economic hardship – produced more champions than Yorkshire. There were high hopes that the balance might be redressed, in the all-important heavyweight division furthermore, in the small South Yorkshire town of Doncaster. Good judges like Jimmy Wilde, now in plump retirement, felt that a promising lad called Bruce Woodcock, a member of the club at the local railway engine works who took the ABA light-heavyweight title in 1939, was destined for better things. That the better things were professional no-one doubted.

Similarly whilst amateur soccer was one of the chief beneficiaries of the National Fitness Campaign it was almost entirely subordinated to the Football League and its regional counterparts. The FA's highly-developed network in the state schools, built up by Rous, the former educator now prominent in the Fitness Campaign, was ideally placed to take advantage of the bounty of the NFC, the CCPRT and the voluntary agencies. The result could have been a system capable not only of contributing to the health and welfare of the nation's youth but of producing and sustaining national teams at various grades, amateur and professional. Unfortunately it became principally a conveyor belt for the League, making life easy for the clubs' all-pervading scouts. Their increasingly obtrusive presence turned yet more local authority grammar schools to rugger and the remaining public schools to despair. Boys from rugger schools could go on to first-class clubs and Old Boys' teams and the 'Varsity match offered a royal route to international selection, but the soccer schools had noshing comparable to offer their alumni.

In inter-school matches and in the Arthur Dunn Cup exclusiveness worked against high standards of play, and at University it was a similar trade-off between skill and social standing. As the Corinthians' chronicler recalled, 'the grammar schools were gently edging the traditional names from the annual 'Varsity match team lists although not from the public school fixture lists; and when representatives of the two . . . combined at University the lowering standards of the traditional schools retarded the progress of the less fashionable'.[9] (One less-publicised tradition survived. Resentful Victorian supporters of the professional game had drawn attention to the Corinthians' excessive reliance on physical force. League football in the thirties was much criticised for violence but Rous recalled that the Oxford and Cambridge matches were vicious, citing a Cambridge player who had been instructed to 'put the Oxford insides out of action in the first twenty minutes'.[10]) The Corinthians themselves went under in 1937 and pooled their dwindling resources with Casuals. The great G.O. Smith was one of the substantial minority who opposed the move, favouring complete disbanding rather than inevitable further decline. He had foreseen the consequences of joining in competition with the professionals – that they would be treated like professionals – and the last vestiges of special treatment went when the concession of delayed entry to the FA Cup was withdrawn. They had been forced to lower their social standards to try to keep up and the final flicker of Corinthian glory, when Bernard Joy was selected for the full England side against Belgium in 1936, was spoiled somewhat by the fact that he was already playing for Arsenal, the most professional club of all.

Herbert Chapman had been succeeded as manager by the smooth-talking Allison, who modelled his approach on the publicity men from Buffalo Bill's Wild West Show he had met in his impressionable youth. He took the team to Hollywood to make a film called *The Arsenal Stadium Mystery* and encouraged the players to market themselves; a group including the established internationals Hapgood, Bastin, Male and Drake and the young Compton brothers. Leslie and Dennis, were signed for a tour of the Butlin holiday camps. Allison also enthusiastically followed Chapman's policy of expensive purchase of players, offering it as a guarantee of quality. When he bought the hitherto unnoticed Welsh player Bryn Jones from Wolverhampton Wanderers in 1938 for a record £14,000, people were amazed, but Allison insisted, 'Bryn is a genius, a natural successor to Alex James at inside forward.'[11] He turned out to be nothing of the kind, partly because of the shower of publicity, but he had pulled in the crowds for a while which was what mattered.

The complement to Allison was Major Frank Buckley of Wolves who had sold Jones. His forte was discovering young talent and blending it into a team by coaching and hard training. This had its own publicity value: Buckley achieved great celebrity by his alleged 'monkey gland' injection of players, actually shots against the common cold, which apparently fortified them to the extent that they were runners-up in the League in both 1938 and 1939. But the champions were both big city 'chequebook' clubs, first Arsenal themselves and then Everton, who had acquired a genuine successor to their star 'Dixie' Dean in Tommy Lawton from Second Division Burnley. What Buckley demonstrated was what even a good small-town club had to do to survive. Sometimes it was the players themselves that wanted to move. There was no ostensible financial reason why an established player in a First Division side should want to move to another, especially if the first was in his home town. But although the maximum wage was unchanged, despite growing dissatisfaction as the contrast between players' publicity value and their earnings increased, there were under-cover payments – tax-free – houses and cars at the richer clubs and variations in the legitimate fringe payments, like benefits for five years' service.

It was an argument over a benefit that led to crisis at unfashionable Stoke when their young international Stanley Matthews asked for a transfer in 1938. He was offered £500 instead of the permitted maximum of £650. Since he had achieved the unlikely feat of making Stoke a household name he not unreasonably felt aggrieved, and his dispute with the club cost him three weeks' wages and deprived this stark and somewhat isolated Potteries desert of its one oasis. Priestley had found in the Six Towns, which had no monument even to Arnold Bennett, only 'an exceptionally mean, dingy provinciality, of Victorian indusrialism in its dirtiest and most cynical aspect', hellish in the depression.[12] Now the *Evening Sentinel* declared in an editorial 'Stoke City supporters and indeed the whole North Staffordshire community are deeply stirred by the possibility of Stanley Matthews leaving the club.'[13] Some 3,000 people attended a protest meeting at the King's Hall, and another 1,000 were left outside. Representations were made to the directors who refused his transfer request and persuaded him to stay. There were other loyal club men even amongst the stars, but they were getting fewer. For the Scots, migration was now the norm. When Scotland played England in 1938 eight of the team were playing in the English League.

Rugger had avoided such degrading developments, at a cost perhaps of a growing self-satisfaction. Even the young E. W. Swanton, 'the otherwise grateful guest at innumerable club dinners . . . sometimes felt that the maintenance of the spirit of the game was a sermon that might have been taken as read'.[14] He concluded that the middle-aged men who now ran the game were still sensitive about the question of amateurism, supposedly settled in 1895. Certainly the Rugby League were still there, annually invading the capital for their Cup Final: there were crowds of well over 50,000 in both 1938 and 1939. But there were nearly 70,000 at the 1939 championship play-off at Manchester City's soccer ground, showing where the game's real, strictly limited strength lay, and there was negative confirmation when yet another experiment in expansion, in Newcastle, failed in 1938. Australian tours had temporarily dried up, too, and there were no spectacular new signings to excite the fans. Nevertheless the RFU was alert enough to modern realities. Whilst the FA still bickered over broadcasting rights and allowed only limited access to the BBC these archetypal amateurs authorised counties and clubs 'to arrange for broadcasting of their matches in whole or in part'.[15] Perhaps realism also came into the 1939 decision of the four Home Unions to resume matches against France.

The price men's hockey paid for its even more purist attitude to amateurism was genteel obscurity. The biggest 'international' change in the game was that Ireland more than held their own with England in their annual encounters. England had played and beaten both Belgium and Holland in the early thirties and they played drawn games home and away with Germany, but the return match in 1936 was the last. Indeed it was their last venture abroad and they still had nothing to do with such dubious organisations as the FIH or the IOC. By contrast the women, now in full cry, were anxious so far as finances allowed to play abroad, and their fixture list showed a fine impartiality – South, Africa, Australia and the USA (very weak) as well as France, Belgium, Denmark, Holland and Germany. The AEWHA faced a general difficulty even before the crisis years in that in most European countries hockey was governed by a single, male body and affiliated to the FIH. The German ladies had been liberated enough to join the IFWHA, but this was abruptly stopped in 1938 when the German Hockey Association became a section of the Nazi Association for Physical Exercise with its own Sportführer. Hitler's annexation of Austria removed another member and only British Guiana and British Columbia were added to the original limited membership. Still, the triumph remained. Hockey was far the most successful women's game, with 1,500 clubs and schools in the AEWHA and a record 10,000 watching the home internationals in 1939. The matches were still one-sided in spite of a momentary lapse by England in 1933, but they were played with a sporting spirit the RFU would have drunk a toast to.

In croquet, with even fewer distractions of commercialism and spectatorship, women dominated the continued healthy revival. Miss D. M. Steel won the women's championship 12 times between 1925 and 1939 and took the Open 4 times. Apart from occasional friendly encounters with Australia and New Zealand it was a British, mainly English or Anglophile affair. In badminton, scorned somewhat less by the virility-conscious but similarly overshadowed by lawn tennis, the women were becoming at least equal to the men. The outstanding player was Mrs H. S. Uber who represented England 37 times and won the mixed doubles (unlike lawn tennis a respected event) 8 times. Denmark was the extent of international adventure so far for either sex, but badminton was played in various parts of the Empire, too, and when the All-England championships were opened to foreigners in 1939 two of the events were won by Danes, one by the Irish and one by a Canadian. In squash, on the other hand, tradition – public school, exclusive club and services – preserved its male orientation. It did not preserve its insularity, however, and the foremost player of the thirties, amateur or professional, was the Egyptian diplomat F. D. Amr Bey. He was so obviously superior and so much a part of the social scene that he was invited to captain the British team that played the USA at the Bath Club in 1935. Squash for women was largely a second string to lawn tennis and both Susan Noel and her successor as champion, Margot Lumb, were international tennis players.

Somewhat lower down the social scale, and not yet seriously challenged by its male counterpart, netball was progressing nicely, but though a county championship was started in 1932 it had not yet reached the stage of even home internationals. The county scene was dominated by Essex, Middlesex and the Civil Service, who merited county status on their own. Women's cricket, approaching even lacrosse for social cachet and the natural summer game for hockey players, was similarly oriented towards the south and the home counties. Its organisation was less advanced regionally than netball but it was much stronger, both numerically and socially. There were over 100 clubs and 8 schools in the WCA by 1936. Furthermore they had imperial aspirations. In 1934–5 there was a tour of Australia and New Zealand. They won all their matches but on a return visit in 1937 the Australian girls showed ominous signs of improvement, drawing the series. *The Times'* correspondent, viewing the final Test at the Oval, was only slightly facetious: 'Those who had not before been privileged to watch a cricket match between two teams of ladies of the highest class – and I admit that I had never attended such a ceremony – must have left the ground amazed at what they saw.'[16] His main criticism was a curious one: 'just too much leaping about to save overthrows'.

In none of these pursuits was there sufficient spectator interest in the women's game to bring commercialism and its attendant dangers. In golf, however, the signs were there. Pam Barton, at the height of her fame, fell foul of the LGU's amateur code when she published a book, *A Stroke a Hole* (1937) with obvious commercial intent, and soon she was making the most of her considerable physical assets by being photographed for the magazines in a short-sleeved shirt. Still, there were few Minoprios. Golf was not like that. Amongst the men the club member was still all-important. In 1938 Henry Longhurst described the average British golfer as 'dressed in a plus-four suit of brown Harris tweed, accompanied by red garters, and sometimes, alas, a stiff collar'. He drove a 10 hp family saloon and valued the game 'chiefly for the exercise it gives him and the pleasant social intercourse of the 19th hole, where his conversation turns on motor-cars, his day's play, income tax, his day's play, the Minister of Transport, his day's play . . .'[17]

Golf was not to be made a toil: 'He plays on Saturday afternoons, Sundays, and sometimes on summer evenings . . . he never practises and has never had a lesson or a game with the club professional . . . His explanation for the continual humiliation of British golfers in the Walker Cup matches is that they never practise and do not play enough with professionals.' So the Walker Cup gulf remained, and the average golfer stood 'in some awe' of his club professional. From the Oxbridge standpoint this must have seemed surprising. The diffidence that may have existed in the drivers of 10 hp family saloons was not shared by public school types. But all now acknowledged professional superiority. Fortunately the British pros had recaptured some of the lost ground. The Ryder Cup victory was not repeated and after Henry Cotton's win in the Open no-one expected more British triumphs But then came Perry (Alfred not Fred) followed by Padgham, Cotton again, Whitcombe and Burton. Only the churlish suggested that this was because fewer Americans were bothering to come.

In lawn tennis the professionals had no comparable chance to show their superiority, but it was no longer a question of whether the Wimbledon champion would turn professional, but when. Donald Budge, the 1937 winner, prudently waited for a year, whilst he took the Grand Slam, before crossing over. More seriously the shamateurism that had long been hidden now became blatant. The 1939 winner Bobby Riggs, whose memoirs were entitled *Tennis is My Racket*, showed that the amateur scene with fixing, gambling and appearance money – he reckoned to make £250 plus expenses from a week's tournament – was scarcely worth preserving. And women were on the same slippery slope. The reign of Wills-Moody and Jacobs was not yet quite over and Dorothy Round, who won Wimbledon again in 1937, was far too upright for undercover payments. She got 'about £15 and a medal' for her championships and the money had to be spent on suitably white tennis clothing. It was the photogenic Californian Alice Marble with stylish shorts and a peaked cap who signalled the change. The impact of her turning professional after Wimbledon in 1939 was muffled in Britain by the war, but it was considerable in the USA, which was where it mattered. Interestingly even Dorothy Round who married in 1937 and went to America during the war, turned professional. But she never played on Sundays.

In cricket, where the shamateurs were still called gentlemen, the backbone of Empire, G. O. Allen had sealed his popularity 'down under' by losing the last three Test matches and the Ashes. Bradman and Hammond both delighted the crowds by quick scoring. Even so Test cricket became increasingly a matter of huge scores on placid pitches. There was much interest nevertheless, particularly from the statistically-inclined, always an important element amongst cricket-lovers. There was also a new crop of young professional batsmen, of whom Compton and Hutton were the pick. In the anxious days of August 1938, British chests, particularly Yorkshire ones, swelled with pride as Len Hutton amassed his amazing score of 364 not out in the final Test.

For the favoured few parts of the match could be seen on television, a regular subscriber service by then, but millions listened avidly to the wireless broadcasts. The BBC had discovered that the appeal of the 'running commentary' (as distinct from the 'eye-witness account') could be extended to cricket, given the right approach. They found a compelling formula. The leading commentator, Howard Marshall, had an episcopal voice, reassuringly calm, yet with a gift of capturing the potential drama that lurked in every ball. His liturgical descriptions of the bowler's run up – 'One, two, three, four, five . . . over goes his arm, and . . . he's out!' – were amongst the treasured rituals of this era of formulas and incantations. All the broadcasters' skills were needed here, for it was a slow business. Hutton batted for over 13 hours as England compiled a record 903 for 7, beating Australia by an innings with Bradman hobbling off injured, reluctant to play a part in further butchery for this Roman holiday.

Britain enjoyed it hugely, but the *reductio ad absurdum* came in the 'timeless Test' that winter in South Africa, still unfinished after ten days when the England team had to leave to catch their boat. County cricket was marginally brisker but lacked competitive edge except in Yorkshire, always champions and Middlesex, always runners-up. Yet it still stirred schoolboys' blood, charmed the discriminating as a spectacle and produced fascinating literature, wonderful anecdotes and those endlessly fascinating score-sheets and lists of current averages. And county cricket held the loyalty of the professionals whether brilliant newcomers or gnarled veterans, making philosophers of them, one way or another. Harold Larwood, disillusioned though he was, declined offers from the leagues, preferring to stay on at Nottinghamshire for his benefit in 1938 – this raised only £2,000, but it was enough to allow him to buy a confectioner's shop in a Blackpool side-street when he retired the following year.

Socially the most remarkable development was the decision of Hammond (W. R.) in 1938 to become W. R. Hammond, Esq. His material rewards as a professional enabled him to turn amateur and thus qualify, according to the conventions of the day, to become captain of England, a position for which there were few credible contenders from the ranks of the gentlemen. For Lord Hawke, who died in October, the compromise seemed enough to safeguard the principle in a deplorably commercial world. Hammond found the convention offensive and said so – after his retirement: 'Apparently it is only the nominal status, not the man or his characteristics, to which objection is taken . . . I captained England, after most of a cricket life-time as a professional. I was the same man as before, or perhaps I even had a slightly declining skill by that time. But because I changed my label all was well.'[18] Herbert Sutcliffe, the other Savile Row nouveau-riche, was an example of more gradual but more permanent social progress. Rhodes and Hirst at the end of their playing days with Yorkshire had been content to become coaches at public schools like Cardus's old boss, Attewell, before them. In 1939 Sutcliffe, a successful business man, sent his son Billy to Repton School where a mixture of inherited talent and good coaching enabled him to go on to become W. H. H. Sutcliffe, a future captain of Yorkshire.

Umbrellas to swords

Hutton's Test match was a welcome distraction from the mounting crisis. Hitler, having dealt with Austria, had turned next to Czechoslovakia in whose Sudeten territory 3 million Germans lived. There was widespread feeling that the moment had come when he had to be resisted. The Czechs had treaties with France and Russia: with Britain's aid this admired little democracy could be saved and Hitler contained. Chamberlain believed he could be placated. Early in September he agreed to Hitler bidding for Sudetenland by negotiation with the Czechs, and a few days later flew to Godesberg to persuade him not to dispense with the formalities. Few believed that Hitler would keep his word. Air-raid precautions (ARP) had begun in 1937 and plans for voluntary evacuation of the cities had been laid. Now, as recruitment of ARP wardens and auxiliary firemen was stepped up, covered trenches were dug in public parks and a million and a half corrugated iron shelters were issued (free) to those with gardens. Thirty-eight million gas masks were given out. Barrage balloons were put up over London. After a meeting at the War Office the President of the RFU wrote to clubs near London urging players to join the Territorial Army or one of the Anti-Aircraft units that had been formed.

Yet with the air-raid sirens being tried out Chamberlain, too far into delusion to pull back, broadcast a siren message of a different kind; 'How horrible, fantastic, incredible it is that we should be digging trenches and trying on gas masks here because of a quarrel in a far away country between people of whom we know nothing.'[19] When he flew to Munich to sell out the Czechs and came back with Hitler's guarantee of future good conduct his 'peace with honour' was such a relief that he made it seem morally right. Philosophical sportsmen made the best of it, and the anglers even detected some of the fruits of exposure to their gentle art: 'Thank God our Prime Minister is a true angler! He possesses the patience, he strikes quickly at the right moment, he is willing to travel far for the fish he is after – whether the fish is salmon or Peace. His methods are always sporting and for the benefit of his brother anglers. He does not admit defeat.'[20]

Thank God, in fact, that Chamberlain's prudence had always included a belief in rearmament. Preparations had hitherto concentrated on the RAF and Royal Navy, but now the Army got its turn and 6 regular and 26 TA divisions were authorised. A Civil Defence complement of a million and a half workers was agreed including 400,000 full-timers. In March Chamberlain, now trying to bluff Hitler by sabre-rattling, signed a treaty with Poland and flirted, not very enthusiastically or successfully, with Stalin. More substantially a scheme of conscription for 20-year-olds was introduced. Service was intended to be limited to six months but before the first militia men had done their stint Hitler was into Poland and Britain was at war. Evacuation from the cities had begun in June and soon nearly 4 million men, women and children had transferred to safer areas. Two million made private arrangements. Most went to Wales, Scotland or the West Country; the well-to-do or well-connected to North America. Government Departments, the Bank of England, the BBC's Variety department and similar national treasures were scattered and hidden. Neville Cardus, who perhaps thought himself one of them, took ship for Australia.

Notes

1 Churchill, *The Gathering Storm*, London, 1948 (1950 ed), p. 228.
2 *Tribune*, 18 February 1938, quoted by S. G. Jones, *Sport, Politics and the Working Class in Modern Britain*, Manchester, 1988, p. 184.
3 Public Record Office FO 371/22591 and 395/568, quoted by Mason. 'Football' in T. Mason (ed.), *Sport in Britain*, Cambridge, 1989, p. 177.
4 *Physical Education in Germany*, London, 1937. For this and 'Strength Through Joy' generally, see H. Bernett, 'National Socialist Physical Education as Reflected in British Appeasement policy', *IJHS*, pp. 161–85.
5 7 April 1937, P. C. McIntosh, *Physical Education in England Since 1800*, London, 1974, pp. 242–4.
6 In a speech, quoted in *DNB*.
7 W. G. McEagan, *The Boy*, February 1938.

8 E. Halladay, *Rowing in England*, Manchester, 1990, p. 171.

9 E. Grayson, *Corinthians and Cricketers*, London, 1955, p. 174.

10 Quoted in S. Wagg, *The Football World*, Brighton, 1984, p. 63.

11 B. Butler, *The Football League*, London, 1993, p. 129.

12 J. B. Priestley. *English Journey* (Harmondsworth, 1977 edn), London, 1934, p. 201.

13 11 February 1938, quoted by Mason, 'Stanley Matthews', in R. Holt (ed.), *Sport and the Working Class in Modern Britain*, Manchester, 1990, p. 163.

14 E. W. Swanton, *Sort of a Cricket Person*, London, 1972, p. 207.

15 U. A. Titley and R. McWhirter, *Centenary History of the Rugby Football Union*, London, 1970, p. 151.

16 R. B. Vincent, *The Times*, 12 July 1937.

17 H. Longhurst, 'The Average British Golfer', *Evening Standard*, 21 December 1938.

18 W. R. Hammond, *Cricket's Secret History*, London, 1952, p. 55.

19 N. Chamberlain, broadcast on 27 September 1938.

20 *Fishing Gazette*, 8 October 1938.

CHAPTER FOURTEEN

Sport and the finest hour
(1939–45)

If any confirmation were needed that this would be a different war from last time it was the sight of schoolchildren with their teachers crowding the railway stations. This was the most ambitious part of the government evacuation scheme, taking the children from danger areas and billeting them on homes and schools in rural parts. The removal of 4 million had been planned for and 1.7 million actually went. The logistics of the move worked as well as could be expected but thereafter it was often a grim experience, particularly when city tenement children were quartered on the middle classes who had most room to spare. For their hosts' reaction varied from horror and disgust at the insanitary habits and dirty, sometimes verminous, state of the slum children to distress at their ragged and ill-shod condition. For the education authorities it was a revelation. As R. A. Butler recalled, it 'administered a severe shock to the national conscience' bringing to light 'the conditions of those unfortunate children of the "submerged tenth" who would also rank amongst the citizens of the future. It was realised with a deepening awareness that the "two nations" still existed a century after Disraeli had used the phrase.'[1]

The analysis was somewhat too crude. It is true that the deepening awareness led to pressure, even while the war continued, for major social reforms like the Beveridge Plan and Butler's own 1944 Education Act. Yet as Priestley had noted, there were not two nations but many. It was not enough for a conscience-stricken governing class to bestow blessings on the rest: they had ideas of their own of what was needed. They fought together, all these classes and conditions of men and women, united as never before, and they fought for a Britain they loved, but with a growing determination to put right her many imperfections. Meanwhile the middle classes debated what was best.

For some the jack-booted enemy was nearer home than Berlin. On the day before war was declared the CCPRT had received notice from an official of the National Fitness Council to quit its premises. The Council was not to be bullied. A delegation, including S. F. Rous who stood high in government regard, rushed off to see the President of the Board of Education.[2] He told the Council to ignore the edict and promised funds, emergency permitting. It was the NFC that was about to be wound up. Politics apart, the local authorities thought they could do the job better at less cost. The government wanted to concentrate on the needs of adolescents rather than the desires of sporting bodies and the Board of Education set up a branch for 'juvenile welfare'. Circular 1486 'The Service of Youth' expressed the government's determination 'to prevent the recurrence during this war of the social problems that occurred in the last'. It was the first time that fun as well as games had been prescribed for such a purpose.

A different sort of war

The sporting bodies themselves had sterner things in mind. The cricket season was all but over, yet there was no inclination this time to linger over it. The West Indies touring team had already left for home leaving seven matches unplayed and the few remaining county matches were abruptly cancelled. Sir Home Gordon delivered a message worthy of Newbolt himself:

England has now begun the grim Test match against Germany. We all echo the complete confidence of the Prime Minister as to ultimate victory. But we do not wish merely to win the ashes of civilisation. We want to win a lasting peace with honour and prosperity to us all.

Flt-Lt A. J. Holmes[3] has uttered a phrase which ought to be remembered by everybody: 'The Germans have as much chance of winning the war as a snowball would have in hell . . .'

. . . However long the period of strain, anxiety and conflict before first-class cricket is resumed, England knows that every cricketer and every lover of the game will do his duty. God save the King, God defend the Right. God bless us all.[4]

Unlike 1914 no-one believed that hostilities could be confined entirely to someone else's backyard or that civilians would go unscathed. Indeed the great fear was of massive air attacks. So it was a shock but not a surprise when minutes after the declaration of war the quiet of Sunday morning was disturbed by wailing sirens. It was a false alarm but it seemed a dreadful portent. A blackout descended on the land, and as people crashed into each other, on foot or in cars without headlights, the ARP Warden's 'Put that light out!' was the first popular rallying cry of the war. A cluster of new government departments had been set up in the light of Great War experience – Supply, Food, Home Security, Economic Warfare, Information, Shipping – and they were inevitably incurring odium as bumbling interfering nuisances. The BBC programme ITMA wrapped them all up in a comic Ministry of Aggravation beset by a German spy, Funf. Laughter took some of the pain away but it seemed a long time between programmes. People listened to their wireless sets a lot that autumn, many becoming addicted to the mixture of blood-curdling prophesy and blandishment of the Nazi propagandist 'Lord Haw Haw'.[5]

There was a war out there somewhere, but it was a low-key affair. Chamberlain strengthened his War Cabinet symbolically by including Churchill at the Admiralty and Eden at the Dominions Office. The Dominions, unlike India and the colonies, had been left free to make their own decision, but all – South Africa after a general election – came in. They began contributing at once, though with only vague ideas of what was required. The Allied military plans were based on attacking Italy, the weaker Axis power, whilst building up strength to take on Germany. But Mussolini declined the role of sacrificial lamb, proclaiming non-belligerence, so while Hitler dealt with Poland Britain's main effort on land was to send a token force to France. None of the services were called upon for aggressive initiative. The Air Minister was Sir Kingsley Wood, a son of the manse who thought it immoral to bomb private property. As the Luftwaffe might not be so scrupulous the RAF was restricted to dropping propaganda leaflets. The Navy was busiest, though still defensive. Its task was to blockade the enemy.

Conscription was extended to men between 18 and 41 but it proceeded at a measured pace. There were reserved occupations, at various ages, and employers could ask for deferment of key personnel. No danger this time of a glut of manpower ahead of equipment and training. Conscientious objections were few, and aroused little controversy. By the end of 1939 the Forces had been built up from 400,000 to 1.5 million men (mostly in the Army but with 200,000 each in the Navy and Air Force) and 43,000 women, all volunteers at that stage. There were volunteers in plenty. When the Australian Wallabies rugby team had to cut short their tour of Britain several stayed on and joined up. The cricketer I. A. R. Peebles and his flat-mate E. W. Swanton had enlisted in the last week of August 'fearful that, as so many others seemed also to be thinking, the army was a sort of club that might declare itself full up'.[6]

It was clubbier for some than others. Any public school man who went the right way about it could get a commission without too much formality. Sportsmen were especially well-placed. The Colonel of the Bedfordshire Yeomanry had told Swanton in March, 'When the war starts . . . you and Ian must join my regiment' and had suggested that meanwhile they might like to get some experience in the TA. Peebles's duties as captain of Middlesex and Swanton's journalistic career had made this induction impractical, but a quick telegram limited their stay in the ranks to a week or two. Though there were distinct similarities in this respect to 1914 it was otherwise quite different. Pebbles and Swanton went to face the Germans not in trench warfare but across the North Sea 'from the wind-swept promenades of Great Yarmouth and Lowestoft'.[7]

This time, too, although the cavalry élite were still at the helm socially and philosophically, mechanisation had reduced the horse to a subordinate role. Nevertheless the horsey types were swift off the mark. The fox-hunters, rushing to the colours once more, sometimes felt obliged to draw comparisons between their own patriotism and that of their townee critics. As one MFH noted afterwards, 'hunting men joined up at once, while urban intellectuals and clerks divided their time between calling for the destruction of all hounds and evading the indignities of uniform'.[8] But the phoneyness of the first months of the war obscured the argument. It also saved conscripts from the scorn of battle-scarred volunteers. Swanton's comment after months hanging about in England that 'the conscript batches' that came in 'were absorbed without detriment to the character and spirit of our close community' was merely patronising.

Most of the action was at sea. The editor of *Yachting Monthly*, Lieutenant-Commander M. Griffiths, RNVR, went off in October leaving the magazine to be run by his woman assistant. Its new proprietor took a sombre view of things, advising readers, 'Don't count on the war being over by next Spring; lay up your boats carefully; preserve them against decay.'[9] The blockade was not working very well. Asdic, Britain's secret submarine detection device, had been discovered by the Germans, and the U-boats sank the aircraft carrier *Courageous* and, having penetrated the defences of the Scapa Flow naval base, the battleship *Royal Oak*. As the Navy withdrew to the West of Scotland, the U-boats crippled the merchant fleet and the Luftwaffe laid floating minefields, so that it was the British who felt blockaded. Petrol rationing added to the impression that it was on the home front that the war was chiefly being waged.

Professional sport was switched off like the blackout. 'The people's war' began without 'the people's game', and not from government edict but voluntarily. The soccer authorities were jealous of its status as 'the national game' and aware of the responsibilities this entailed. At the time of Munich the FA had already laid plans for a joint meeting with the Football League to consider the immediate suspension of fixtures if war came. No-one had forgotten the bitter experience of 1914. The FA was determined not to be put in an embarrassing position this time by the professional side, but the League Management Committee had learned the lesson, too. On 8 September the FA announced the suspension of all football under its jurisdiction until further notice. Scotland and Wales made the same assessment of the public mood and only Northern Ireland carried on.[10]

As with the blackout it soon became clear that a total ban was an excess of zeal. Within days friendly matches were authorised except in a few prohibited areas, and shortly afterwards, following consultation with the Home Office, clubs were positively encouraged to play matches on Saturdays and public holidays, provided there was no interference with the war effort. No-one was interested in friendly matches and a new structure was devised with eight regional leagues in England and Wales and two in Scotland. Players were allowed fees of £1 10s a match. Of the 88 clubs 82 took part, but with no great conviction. Crowds were restricted to 15,000 in 'safe' areas and 8,000 elsewhere but the limit was academic for there was no great appetite for it at first. Even the pools were affected: their annual profits fell from £22 million to £5 million during the war years. The leading firms collaborated as Unity Pools and concentrated their activities around Liverpool. The value of postal orders issued by the GPO fell from £194 million to £29 million in 1940–1, thus helping to blunt some of the intermittent middle-class criticism of clogging the public services as well as squandering resources.[11]

Remarkably, soccer had closed down quicker than rugger. By 12 September the RFU had cancelled all fixtures (and declared a moratorium on clubs' debts), but there were no sheep and goats this time. The FA's action, the fact of conscription (which reduced the fervour of shirker-hunters) and the absence of bombing or military excitements greatly reduced the need for the rugger men to set a good example of patriotism. Twickenham itself was requisitioned as a Civil Defence headquarters but the game was soon underway again, even in London, where Richmond's Old Deer Park and Athletic Club grounds were mainstays. Murrayfield, Gloucester and Coventry were also particularly active. Many clubs, strengthened by servicemen seeking a game near their postings, resumed and kept up regular fixtures. Inter-service matches, in which the Civil Defence was prominent, the hospital teams, holiday games for schoolboys the Barbarians and Red Cross internationals were big attractions. The Middlesex sevens kept going. Oxford and Cambridge, which had many more students this time, played 'Varsity matches alternately home and away, the first at Cambridge on 6 December 1939.

Like soccer the Rugby League had avoided the criticism of 1914. Fixtures were cancelled as soon as war was declared and the New Zealand tourists had to go home after playing only two matches. But, as in soccer, friendly matches were soon allowed and within weeks two regional competitions were under way on either side of the Pennines, saving on travel, but arousing only modest interest. The RL relaxed its rules over registration to accommodate service and munitions workers' postings and some clubs built up strong teams based on guests: Dewsbury, for instance, had a good war. But the general standard fell as players joined up, either as volunteers or as conscripts. In November the RFU relaxed its ban on amateurs playing alongside professionals in the Forces. It was a people's war indeed.

The sports that found it easiest to carry on as if nothing had happened were those, spiced by gambling, that preserved the tradition of the Napoleonic Wars. Scottish fans found a successor to Benny Lynch when Jackie Paterson, took the British title in Glasgow on 30 September. Racing was logistically more difficult: the Jockey Club was obliged to suspend operations during September and the St Leger had to be cancelled. Some racecourses were taken over – Kempton Park by the Scots Guards, Sandown by the Coldstreams – but elsewhere restrictions were soon lifted, and racing outside prohibited areas resumed in October and continued until the last big event of the season, the Manchester November Handicap. Uniforms were much in evidence. The Doncaster Yearling sales had been lost with the St Leger but when Tattersall's held a substitute sale at Newmarket it was conducted by a Life Guards officer.[12] National Hunt racing was interrupted more, partly by frost, but it resumed in February and kept on until the Grand National.

A grave breach of etiquette occurred at Newbury in February when it was discovered that the winner of the United Services Steeplechase, Tom Hanbury, was not an officer. He was disqualified, but later atoned by taking a commission in the Household Cavalry and winning the MC. The racing men could fairly claim, in fact, that they were making an illustrious contribution to the war effort. Many of the National Hunt types were in the regular Army already and some like 'Perry' Harding and Peter Payne-Galwey earned great military distinction. With traditional cavalry opportunities limited many took their gifts to newer spheres: Frank Furlong joined the Fleet Air Arm and was killed in action. Lord Mildmay and Peter Cazalet joined the artillery – which usually meant the dreary business of anti-aircraft defence at that stage – until they found more belligerent assignments in the Guards. On the Flat it was mainly the trainers and officials who served, passing naturally like the National Hunt men into the commissioned ranks of the better regiments. Flat-race jockeys did not. Some could not pass the medical examination and were exempt; others were simply not officer material. There were exceptions like Billy Rickaby who became a major in the Royal Artillery, but the gulf is illustrated by the story of the professional jockey at one race meeting in the early weeks of the war who congratulated a race-course official on having joined the National Fire Service – he was a Coldstream Guards officer in his best blues.

Social class was still the most important factor in getting a commission, and this showed itself in all sports. Thus a higher proportion of rugger players became officers than soccer players, and hockey players did better still. Yet the grammar schools had made some inroads and the division between amateur officers and professional other ranks was less absolute, especially in the more meritocratic RAF. This showed clearly in cricket. Edrich, W. J., of Middlesex became a Squadron Leader and emerged as W. J. Edrich: Ames, L. E. G., achieved the same rank, remaining a professional and eventually became Kent's manager. The Army was more hidebound, but of the Yorkshire team not only the amateurs, Sellars and Yardley, were commissioned but also the professionals Verity, Bowes and Leyland.

There was another kind of warrior. Len Hutton became a physical training instructor with the rank of sergeant. So did Denis Compton and soccer professionals by the score. This major contribution to the war effort by the soccer professionals was another fruit of the virtuous involvement of the FA and Stanley Rous in government plans. The Army Physical Training Corps before the war had brought new dimensions to the traditional approach, emphasising physical fitness, and sport as well as gymnastics and drill was encouraged. Plans had been laid for the war-time expansion of the Corps, using FA coaches to train the new instructors, and in the autumn of 1939 many professionals and a few amateurs graduated as sergeant-PTIs after a short course at Aldershot. The FA was also brought in to advise the RAF on 'recreative welfare'. A small group was commissioned and 40 more were chosen to train as PTIs. The door opened wider as time went on. Meanwhile military service that winter was greatly enlivened by sport, not least for the instructors.

The dreariest hour

There was one naval success to lighten the gloom on the home front, the sinking of the *Graf Spee*. The stirring ballad, 'There'll Always Be An England' was top of the hit parade, and as the BEF nestled alongside the reputedly impregnable Maginot Line it was complemented by the inane 'We're Going to Hang Out the Washing on the Siegfried Line'. But there was no sign of it happening. Chamberlain did not mind the inaction: it gave us time to catch up. On 5 November he wrote to his sister predicting that the war would end in the spring, not by British victory but by the Germans realising that they could not win. Complications arose shortly afterwards – especially for left-wingers – when Stalin occupied the Baltic States and invaded Finland to protect Soviet borders against possible attack by Hitler. Much propaganda and production effort went into a campaign in support of the Finns. Scarce aircraft were sent and lost, and a ramshackle expeditionary force was on its way when the Finns made peace. The public was increasingly baffled. Vera Lynn sang 'We'll Meet Again', but 'When You Wish Upon a Star' from Disney's *Pinnocchio* was just as popular.

That first winter had not been the heroic one people had expected. When no air-raids came two-thirds of the evacuees returned home. Blackout restrictions were eased, dance-halls filled up again and cinemas flourished. So did dog-racing. In February the veteran Nel Tarleton showed all his old skills in taking the British featherweight title before a big crowd in Liverpool. Even middle-class sportsmen began to take a more relaxed view. The cricket historian Major H. S. Altham reported 'a general feeling that the game can and should be kept going whenever possible. With the military service act in operation . . . there is no room for the charge of skrimshanking, and where cricket can be played without interfering with the national effort it can only be good for the national morale.'[13] He was careful to add, 'Of course anything like county cricket is out of the question' but there were those who thought it possible to restore the championship relying on veterans, the medically exempt and servicemen on leave. In December 1939 Lancashire put forward an elaborate scheme of regional groupings involving the minor counties as well. MCC declined to have anything to do with such a scheme which, patriotism apart, many thought wildly impractical: 'three-day cricket, in peace, was scarcely main-taining the public interest . . . and how many are going to pay even sixpence to watch cricket for three days between scratch or constantly varying elevens?'[14]

There was not much money about and everything cost more. The government tried to restrict wage increases, but with Labour outside the government and the unions fiercely hostile some employers gave in and fuelled the inflationary spiral. The price of food was a particular problem. Public opinion favoured rationing and after weeks of indecision first bacon, ham and butter, then all meat except offal were rationed. (Reluctantly, to stave off a wage claim, the government also agreed to a 'temporary' subsidy on food: it became permanent and, though costly, avoided much unrest.) There were a few more jobs but in early 1940 a million were still unemployed, a drag on the Exchequer which helped put taxes up to 7s 6d in the £1. Munitions workers had increased by only 11%, about one-sixth of what was needed. Not much of their output was being expended as the Forces' strength built up and the troops hung about waiting. They sang 'Roll Out The Barrel' and read *Blighty* and by the end of March the prevailing mood was one of bored resignation.

Booksellers reported increased public interest in poetry as people sought spiritual uplift. But where was the inspiration to produce it? There were no Rupert Brookes or Julian Grenfells to stir the blood or wrench the heartstrings, no dashing young subalterns leading their men to action. Sir John Hammerton's *The War Illustrated* set out to parallel its First War original but its front-line pictures of sentries wearing gasmasks against surprise attacks that never came lacked conviction, and its poetry seemed similarly contrived. *Into Battle* had given way to laments for the League of Nations:

> Is there no power to break this chain of crime
> Will not the golden dawn of peace awake

> When gentle reason takes the place of hate
> And shadows cloud no more Geneva's lake.[15]

The monthly *Penguin New Writing* showed throughout the war the extent to which the new Britain was involved in it, and its many service contributors brought a fresh and lively eye to communicating their experiences, but its tone was documentary rather than inspirational. In January 1940, the aesthete Cyril Connolly, who must have been hard enough to bear even in peace-time, launched *Horizon* to uphold artistic standards in spite of the tiresome inter-ference of the war. It deplored the diffusion of culture through Penguin Books and the BBC. As Dylan Thomas, whose finest hour was spent at the BBC, built up his reputation in a shoddy imitation of Left Bank style, Robert Graves, the Great War veteran, offered an explanation for the absence of war poets. His argument was reminiscent of an old cricketer deploring a vanished golden age. Conscription, he reckoned, had made the 'volunteer pride' of Rupert Brooke 'irrelevant'.[16]

There had been casualties, of course, particularly at sea, but on nothing like the scale of 1914. The first rugger international to lose his life this time, in April 1940, was Alex Obolensky who was killed on a training flight with the RAF. Soon afterwards Wing-Commander Arthur Sweeney, the Milocarian sprinter, also died in a flying accident. It was bloodshed enough, but people almost seemed to need reminding that this was an authentic war. By then Chamberlain was claiming that Hitler had 'missed the bus' and there was a general disposition to believe him. A Poole correspondent of *Yachting Monthly* complained bitterly about new areas of prohibited waters in the harbour and feared that 'even more drastic restrictions of Hitler-like proportions are under consideration'.[17] Oxford and Cambridge held a Boat Race at Henley, and Eton which had taken over the war-time arrangements were busy organising a schools' regatta for the summer. The Racing Calendar announced that, as Epsom had been taken over by the military the Derby and Oaks would be held at Newmarket.

All in it together

So far from missing the bus Hitler promptly invaded Denmark and with a handful of troops took southern Norway, including Bergen, just 365 miles from Aberdeen. Britain's response to Norway's appeal for help was inept, with cabinet divisions mirrored by inter-service conflict over tactics. As Chamberlain reluctantly made way for Churchill Hitler's blitzkreig struck with devastating force. Neutral Holland went under on 15 May, Belgium on the 27th. Then France was overrun and on the 26th the Dunkirk evacuation began.

The poetry of the war came at last. Perhaps there was a faint echo of Brooke's feeling of purgation in Roy Fuller's

> At last the push of time has reached it; realer
> To-day than for centuries, England is on the map

but this particular Marxist in uniform saw no action.[18] It was old-fashioned rhetorical stuff, disguised as prose in Churchill's defiant speeches and Priestley's radio postscripts, and half-remembered snatches of *Henry V* that helped build up 'the Dunkirk spirit'. The Hollywood film *Mrs Miniver* helped keep it alive.

Meanwhile the speed of events took everyone by surprise, and there were some strange juxtapositions. As the remnants of the BEF and refugees poured in a volunteer returning to London from Guildford noticed that 'all along the line young men in flannels were playing cricket in the sunshine on beautiful tended fields shaded by stalwart oaks and poplar trees'.[19] But the only truly jarring note was sounded by the racing fraternity. The Derby was run as scheduled before 10,000 people and there were even special trains from London. A question in the Commons asked whether the Home Secretary would take steps 'to avoid squandering of war resources by prohibiting motor coach tours, horse-racing and hunting'. On 14 June a distressed reader wrote to the *Radio Times* 'I beseech you to cease broadcasting racing and sports news at such a time', and by the 19th the clamour was such that the Jockey Club announced that there would be no more racing 'until further notice'. It could not forbear, however, to refer to its responsibilities to the bloodstock industry and to the professionals who depended on the sport for a living. *The Times* was unimpressed by this hoary old chestnut, warning of widespread resentment and printing many indignant letters.

This apart it was a time to be proud of. Everyone was in the Battle of Britain, in spirit at least, and as the news hoardings described the day's encounter in sporting terms ('Biggest raid ever – Score 78 to 26 – England still batting') the many were inspired by the few to do their bit. Tax increases and further rationing were an incidental as gas masks came out again and invasion seemed imminent. There was a pride in standing alone, and in not being beaten, even if we could not win. Churchill was a reassuring figure; he made mistakes but he was a fighter. And Labour was in the war now, both politically and industrially. Ernie Bevin joined the team as Minister of Labour, mobilising the work force as only one of its own leaders could. At the other extreme Lord Beaverbrook transformed aircraft production. There was work for everyone, and as full employment returned the problem on the production lines became overwork. The Blitz made carrying on an act of heroism in itself. When all were in daily danger sport and recreation became less of an indecent indulgence, more of a legitimate solace. Maintaining high morale and physical fitness were seen as sport's essential contribution to the war effort.

There were some overtly utilitarian ventures. In June, 1940, for instance. the CCPRT, in harness with the FA, organised the first of a series of 'Fitness for service' programmes for those awaiting call-up. A total of 230 centres was set up at local football and recreation grounds and about 3,500 took part during the next two months. The CCPRT also put on special courses for Civil Defence workers. By the autumn the Council was operating in industry and offering short residential courses at Lowther College, a girls' boarding school in rural Wales. The Board of Education was busy, too, setting up a Directorate of Physical Education to work with its new Youth Branch. In November, 1940, Circular 1529 'Youth and Physical Recreation' outlined a purposeful develop-ment scheme. National Tests for youth leaders were introduced, not without controversy, for voluntary organisations like the Scouts and Guides had their own way of doing things.

Keeping fit apart, there was a saner, more positive attitude generally to all forms of recreation, professional as well as amateur. Cricket, of a casual kind, was played that summer as it had always been played, by clubs and schools, including not least servicemen. E. W. Swanton and Ian Peebles in remote parts of Norfolk managed only one game but the team they played against, full of the Edrich family, was determinedly carrying on. And in the north the Leagues flourished as they had done in the Great War, bolstered by servicemen and others on work of national importance posted to the area. Golfers, too, carried on, some taking gas masks round with them as they had been doing since Munich. The professional side was a major contributor to the war effort. Tournament play virtually ceased and many joined the services. (Of 667 PGA members who enlisted, 27 were killed; another 27 were taken prisoner and 23 invalided out, one of them Percy Allis who had re-enlisted as soon as war was declared. A further 250 took on war work, full- or part-time.) That left roughly half the membership, mostly too old or unfit, looking after the courses that escaped being requisitioned for agricultural purposes as 'digging for victory' became the patriotic thing to do. One of London's two municipal courses was kept open, signifying the general acceptance that taking healthy exercise was not the worst thing to do with time off in war-time. Similarly lawn tennis, with fewer professionals and less land, was able to set a fine example, suspending all tournaments of any significance but carrying on at club level. The All-England Club emblematically went on a war footing. Its premises, with gradually reducing staff, housed Red Cross, St John ambulance, ARP and FNS personnel and the Irish Guards occupied the neighbouring sports ground. The courts escaped bomb damage, but the stands were hit. Officers on leave, members or not, were welcomed for the duration and at least some pre-war luxuries, like having an attendant run a hot bath, were retained.

At provincial level, lawn tennis, like squash and Badminton, managed very well. Though individual clubs suffered others thrived, and the general level of participation, as in hockey, football and cricket, rose, for women as well as men, not least because of the influence and the facilities of the services. Athletics, too, brought more participation, for both sexes, at a generally higher standard than ever before. A strong domestic programme, in and out of battle dress, was in full swing by 1941. Apart from inter-service competitions AAA teams competed against Oxford and Cambridge and London University and service and Civil Defence teams. Sidney Wooderson, small, scrawny and with feeble eyesight, came to represent the British spirit, the indomitable underdog with unquenchable courage, overcoming superior forces against all the odds. In 1940 he was a member of the AFS, helping to fight the Blitz in his non-working hours. He was called up, but his eyesight was so poor that he was unfit for combatant service, and he became a corporal in the catch-all Pioneer Corps. He was soon in great demand for the array of charity meetings that studded the war-time programme, and by arranging his leave to fit them in he frequently appeared alongside more conventionally athletic figures such as C. B. Holmes, now a Company Sergeant Major in the Physical Training Corps.

Cycling, much less in the headlines, nevertheless was a notable feature of war-time sport. The bicycle itself obviously was much more prominent, politically correct both as a petrol-saving device and as an aid to fulfilling the national duty to keep fit. (This was now recognised for women as well as men, and the former were notably more enthusiastic adherents of the BBC's daunting *Up in the Morning Early* programme). Touring had always been popular, but the competitive side regained much of its early favour. Road-racing had never been technically illegal, but only because the NCU had banned it, lest it provoke legislation against even time-trials. In 1942 the first modern massed start race on public roads was staged, from Wolverhampton to Llangollen. At the same time track-racing enjoyed a revival, mainly through relatively modest local programmes, often at mixed athletics meetings on grass tracks or on shale tracks around cricket fields, The government's 'holidays at home' campaign, though not conspicuously popular in itself prompted local authorities and voluntary bodies to provide many more such meetings.

Professional sport also played a part in maintaining national morale. In the London of the Blitz soccer was an a oasis of normality. The troops in Egypt preparing to take on the Italians read in adjoining columns of their newspaper 'Britain can take it' and 'Football again' as West Ham played Spurs in the opening match of the season: they had 'already arranged a long list of fixtures including Clapton Orient and Southend'.[20] The Jockey Club for its part secured permission through the good offices of the Duke of Norfolk, a junior minister in Agriculture, to restart racing in September, albeit on a limited scale. They overcame criticism of potential danger from air-raids by arranging meetings in the rural parts of Yorkshire: the first was at Ripon and the St Leger was held at Thirsk. It was won by Gordon Richards riding the Aga Khan's Turkhan. The resumption had a revivifying effect on bloodstock prices. The Aga Khan chose this moment to sell the Derby winners Blenheim, Bahram and Mahmoud to the USA. This was viewed not only as an abuse of hospitality and an evident vote of no confidence in British survival but as a defilement. 'The dollar voice of the tempter is heard in the homeland', wrote one pundit. 'The sons and daughters of our true blooded Derby winners may . . . come back to us as half-breeds.'[21]

But the business provided ammunition for the familiar arguments. At the Thoroughbred Breeders' Association's annual dinner that December Lord Rosebery said, 'Even since war began sales . . . amounting to hundreds of thousands of pounds have been traded to purchasers in North and South America, South Africa, India and elsewhere . . . If there is no racing there is no acid test.' When there had been no racing breeders had been obliged to sell their yearlings 'at from five to ten guineas – largely to be slaughtered to feed greyhounds which were still allowed to race.' He was on firmer ground when he added, 'I also think a little relaxation one day helps people work harder at other times. This seems to be recognised by those in authority as otherwise they would not permit football matches, or dog-racing at which crowds collect in confined areas, as opposed to racing which takes place in open spaces.' The National Hunt season was curtailed – there were good crowds at Cheltenham, but no Grand National. When bombs fell on Newmarket that spring and seven people were killed it seemed like the end of the road, but in spite of public disquiet the Jockey Club went ahead with a limited programme, defiantly holding not only the Derby and the Oaks but the Royal Ascot programme at Newmarket. Again the crowds were full of uniforms: at Lincoln the Clerk of the Course wore the best dress of the Coldstream Guards and the Derby was won by Private Billy Nevett of the Royal Army Ordnance Corps.

And so the paradoxes multiplied. The war, enlarged by the Japanese attack on Pearl Harbor and the German attack on Russia, was going badly. In 1942 with setbacks in the Western Desert, Singapore fallen and the British man-power situation so acute that the Army had to be restricted to 2 million, women conscripted and civilian labour directed, there was grumbling in the popular newspapers at government attempts to curtail dog-racing and boxing. 'I was amazed at the re-actions of the Press generally,' wrote the sports writer of *Reveille*, the Forces' newspaper. Although in favour of professional boxing 'run as a sport for the entertainment of the troops and war workers' he was distinctly unimpressed at some of the so-called charity events the promoters made so much of: 'If promoters are so keen to help charity let them run shows for bare expenses.'[22] In fact boxing was amongst the most popular of war-time sports, not least in the services. Their own competitions were never stronger and the ABA resumed its championships after 1942. Bruce Woodcock, now a munitions worker, had his first professional fight in 1942, knocking out ex-Stoker Clark in three rounds, and was Northern area light-heavyweight champion by the end of the year. At the top of the division Freddie Mills and Len Harvey, both in the RAF, fought for the 'world title', British version, and in Glasgow Jackie Paterson disposed of Peter Kane in a single round. At all levels the uncertainties of war-time form and fitness made betting an even riskier business than usual, but it was all very exciting. That summer's flat-racing programme, at five centres, Newmarket, Salisbury and Windsor as well as Pontefract and Stockton, was also particularly well-patronised, with added public interest because of the emergence of HM the King as a leading owner. The National Stud was at last beginning to turn out horses worthy of the nation, and the colt Big Game and the filly Sun Chariot leased to the King won four of the five Classic races. And no-one doubted the King's patriotism, steadfastly remaining at his post with his family beside him, like millions of others.

The fact was that an ambivalence attached to all those who provided the sporting excitements that lifted the nation's spirits. The *Reveille* writer put his finger on it. 'Soccer football, like cricket, is a shining example of providing entertainment for war workers, except that some of the Service players might be quizzed on how much actual military duty they do in the course of a week.'[23] They were not all belligerents. Civil Defence was a favourite alternative for those with reason to stay at home. But this was unglamorous at best and famous sportsmen ran the risk of unkind remarks. 'Raich' Carter recalled wryly how he grew so tired of jibes from the press about his being in the AFS that he joined the RAF – and became a PTI. This was the best of all worlds, especially if the posting were to Blackpool, the RAF recruiting centre and the headquarters of its PT school. Stanley Matthews spent most of his war there. His wife and daughter went with him: 'all in all I had a comfortable billet. I ran the sports store on the pier and organised boxing tournaments and other activities for the troops.'[24]

The Blackpool professional soccer team was transformed by this sudden access of talent. It stood them in good stead for after the war, when Matthews himself, forsaking Stoke, took up permanent residence. Meanwhile they achieved great success in the war-time cups and leagues. So did the hitherto obscure Aldershot, close to the Army headquarters and, with normal registration suspended, the signings included Tommy Lawton, Cliff Britton and Joe Mercer (all of Everton), Stan Cullis (Wolves), Jimmy Hagan (Sheffield United), Tommy Walker (Hearts) and the ubiquitous Denis Compton (Arsenal). Compton recalled that for him 'Cup finals, League South matches and army representative games followed one on top of each other in a seemingly endless stream.'[25] Arsenal became an emblem of war-time endurance. Like Yorkshire in cricket they had encouraged their players to join up at the outset and they eventually lost all but 2 of their 44 regulars to war service. Highbury, like Twickenham and Wimbledon, was turned into a Civil Defence base and the club was obliged to share the ground of its North London rivals, Spurs. By 1943 the crowds were coming back to the terraces, albeit in some unexpected places.

Representative matches drew big crowds. The Army and the RAF both had teams of international strength with plenty of opportunities of playing together. The Inter-Allied Services Cup involved teams from the many countries whose troops were based in Britain, but England naturally had the best of it. In 1943 they beat the Scots 7–0 at Hampden Park in a war-time encounter and improved on that a year later. They were not doing so well in rugger: 'it is about time we had a resounding English rugger win for since the spring of 1940 the Sassenachs have lost [three] games in a row', reported *Parade*'s London correspondent.[26] Wales had been walloping them too. After a defeat the previous November only two players kept their places, one of them Lance-Corporal Ernest Ward the Bradford Northern Rugby League player. The RL was managing quite well, despite the siphoning off of its stars; better in Yorkshire than Lancashire. The Lancashire Cup was suspended and Barrow, Oldham, St Helens and Wigan played in the Yorkshire competition. The staple diet was the Emergency League Championship, with Dewsbury the surprise success along with Bradford, Wigan and Halifax. But Rugby Union, strengthened by its RL stars, was the big attraction; 20,000 watched Wales versus England at Swansea in 1943.

Bradford League cricket, as in the Great War, overshadowed the rest of the leagues. The Pope brothers and Wilf Copson of Derbyshire and Bill Voce of Notttinghamshire enlivened the bowling, and Len Hutton, invalided out of the Army when he broke an arm in the gymnasium, was amongst a score of Test and county batsmen. Even there, however, the array was not so glittering as in 1914–18. One reason was, as in soccer and rugger, the vast amount of services cricket that was played. Lord's, which escaped both requisition and bombing, set the tone with a strong programme. In 1943, for instance, 47 matches were played from 8 May to 11 September, mostly one-day but with a few two-day representative matches. Over 200,000 spectators, paying 6d a time, saw 17 matches, from which the proceeds went to charity. The services played a big part, with a few sergeants, like Cyril Washbrook and Alec Bedser and, of course, Denis Compton, amongst the officers. There was even the occasional private, like Leslie Compton, but even he soon managed promotion to lance-corporal. Amongst the most regular performers were the Civil Defence services, in various guises: Harold Gimblett, the Langridge brothers, Joe Hulme, J. H. Parks and Frank Lee seem to have got a full season in. A London Counties team was also active, calling on many of the same players, a British Empire XI played a heavy programme and there were internationals against a Dominions XI and the Royal Australian Air Force. In women's cricket, one of many sports to be taken up by the services, the ATS played both the WAAF and the WRNS, heavily defeating both. In the provinces Blackpool services had two sides, a workaday XI who regularly won the local Ribblesdale League and a battery of county players who performed in charity matches.

But for all the 'cushy numbers' and off-duty frolicking there was another side to the picture. Perhaps the most poignant story of all is that of Hedley Verity, a captain in the Green Howards, killed in the Eighth Army's attack on the German positions at Catania in Sicily. His platoon was trying to take the strong point, a farmhouse. 'The enemy fire increased and as they crept forward, Verity was hit in the chest. "Keep going", he said, "and get them out of that farmhouse." When it was decided to withdraw they last saw Verity lying on the ground in front of the burning corn.'[27] There was another kind of courage, that of the survivors. Bill Edrich, taking his squadron side to play against a local village team, had to find last-minute substitutes for the crews of two planes shot down over the North Sea. 'At times it seemed like a bad dream . . .' he recalled. 'Every now and then would come the old accustomed cry – "Owzatt?" – and then one's mind would flicker off to the briefing, and to joking with a pal whose broken body was now washing in the long, cold tides.'[28]

These gallant officers were both professional cricketers. It was a new kind of Britain coming through. What it retained of the old was a sense of the importance of playing the game, sustained and deepened by the string of Nazi atrocities from magnetic mines to the ultimate barbarism of the concentration camps. But when saturation bombing seemed the only way to win the war they took it up, reluctantly but purposefully. The Newbolt spirit and Rupert Brooke's ideal of self-sacrifice gave way to less high-flown sentiments. War was more than a game in fact: 'it's not cricket' did not cover all contingencies And fair play, it was now universally recognised, had a social dimension. The better world envisaged in the Beveridge plan and the Butler Education Act was one with fair shares for all. Sport would always be part of the precious heritage, worth fighting for, but it too had to change. The MCC and the Jockey Club were both hard at work on post-war planning long before the Germans were beaten. Only the soccer men were sure that all that was needed was a return to pre-war glory.

Notes

1 R. A. Butler, *The Art of the Possible*, London, 1971.
2 Earl De La Warr, an Etonian socialist who had followed Macdonald into government and had just been demoted for speaking in favour or resisting Hitler.
3 Captain of Sussex, A. J. Holmes had been in the RAF since 1925.
4 H. Gordon, *The Cricketer*, September 1939.
5 William Joyce, a former Mosleyite, of mixed Irish-American and British stock attracted an estimated 6 million regular and 18 million occasional listeners.
6 E. W. Swanton, *Sort of a Cricket Person*, London, 1982, p. 16.
7 ibid., p. 119.
8 R. Longrigg, *The History of Foxhunting*, London, 1975, p. 216.
9 G. H. Pinkard, October 1939; D. Sleighthome, in *Yachting Monthly*, 75th Birthday Issue, June 1981, p. 1259.
10 Conscription was not attempted in Northern Ireland out of deference to Eire. There were many volunteers from both sides of the border. Many Northern rugger clubs closed down, but otherwise, though things were not normal sport carried on.
11 M. Clapson, *A Bit of a Flutter: Popular Gambling and English Culture 1823–1961*, Manchester, 1992, p. 171.
12 Captain Terence Hall, who later lost his life.
13 H. S. Altham, 'Cricket in wartime', *Wisden*, 1940.
14 R. C. Robertson-Glasgow, 'The 1939 season', *Wisden*, 1940.
15 George Shelley, 'Shadows on the Lake', *The War Illustrated*, 16 December 1939. See also cover picture 9 December.
16 R. Graves, 'War Poetry in this War', *The Listener*, 23 November 1941.
17 D. Sleightholme, *Yachting Monthly*, 75th Birthday Issue, June 2982, p. 1259.
18 R. Fuller, 'August 1940', *The Middle of a War*, London, 1942.
19 Mrs Robert Henrey, *The Siege of London*, London, 1940, p. 100, quoted in A. Calder, *The People's War*, London, 1969, p. 128.
20 *Parade, the Middle East Weekly*, 28 August 1940.
21 'Tattenham' *Sunday Express*, 6 October 1940.
22 W. Evans, *Reveille*, 16 March 1942.
23 ibid.
24 S. Matthews, *Feet First*, London, 1948, p. 103.
25 Calder, *People's War*, p. 433.
26 *Parade*, 25 February 1943.
27 R. C. Robertson-Glasgow, *Wisden*, 1944, p. 41.
28 Calder, *People's War*, p. 435.

INDEX

Index

Index

Index

Puddefoot, Syd 178

Queen's Club 166

Racecourse Betting Control Board 157
Radcliffe, Sir Everard 25
Rainbow 257, 258
Ramblers' Rights Association 238
Rampling, Godfrey 289
Rangeley, Walter 218
Ranger 258
Rangers FC 87, 118, 183
Ranjitsinjhi, K. S. 60
Read, Charles 136, 166
Rees, F. B. 158, 160
Rees-Jones, G. R. 284
Resolute 149
Reynoldstown 295
Rhodes, Wilfred 94, 191, 227
Richards, Gordon 156, 233, 268, 329
Richardson, Vic 278
Rickaby, W. 322
Riddell, Lord 161, 162
riding *see* horse riding
Rieff, Johnny 16
Riggs, Bobby 312
Rimell, Fred 296
Risman, Gus 226
Rivett-Carnac, Mrs Francis Clytie 10
Roberts, Bill 289, 301
Robertson, Mrs Gordon 37
Robinson, Emmott 278
Roe, R. T. C. 271
roller-skating 135
Root, Fred 89, 185–7, 277, 278, 283
Rosebery, 5th Earl of 62, 67, 92, 154, 329
Rosenfeld, A. A. 51
Round, Dorothy 273–4, 312–13
rounders 204
Rous, Stanley F. 255, 276, 301, 317–18, 323
rowing 28–30, 40, 58, 110–11, 197–203, 236–7, 282,
    305–6
    Berlin Olympics 288–9
    betting 199
    women 202–3
Royal Ashdown Forest Golf Club 36
Royal Corinthian YC 9, 257
Royal Cornwall YC 9
Royal Eastbourne Golf Club 162
Royal Holloway College 40, 41
Royal International Horse Show 134, 295
Royal London YC 258
Royal Mid-Surrey Golf Club 162
Royal Yacht *Britannia* 8, 65, 112, 149, 150
Royal Yacht Squadron (RYS) 9, 232
Rudd, Bevil 214
rugby football 32, 45, 47–53, 109, 120–1, 225–6,
    284–5, 308, 310, 319, 321
    amateurism 47–50
    Ireland 44, 48, 83, 174
    middle class values 174–5
    professionalism 50–3
    Scotland 48, 50, 172, 173, 216–17
    social values 172–3

Wales 49, 50, 51, 59, 175, 182, 284
World War I 59, 75, 82, 97
Rugby Football Union (RFU) 48, 50, 59, 285
Rugby League (RL) 50, 51, 52, 75, 173, 176–7,
    226–7, 285, 310, 321
    see also Northern Union
Rugby School 172–3
Russia 106, 314, 329
Ryder Cup 163, 272, 312

sailing *see* yachting
St Leger, the 68–9, 153, 154
Sassoon, Siegfried 12–13, 58, 86, 94–5
Schmeling, Max 240, 286, 307
Schwartz, R. O. 93, 97
Scotland
    deer-stalking 147
    football 74–5, 87, 92, 108–9, 118, 177, 178–9, 183,
        241, 285
    golf 35, 161, 182
    lacrosse 41
    rugby football 48, 50, 172, 173, 216–17
    shooting prestige 145
Scott, Peter 259
Scott, Phil 240
Scouting 297–8, 304
Searle, Vera (née Palmer) 211, 212
Seawanhaka races 152
Segrave, Sir Henry 133
Selby-Lowndes, Colonel J. 107, 144
Shamrock IV & V 65, 149, 232, 256–7
Sheffield Angling Association 11
Sheffield United FC 74
Shirley Park Golf Club, Croydon 35
shooting 7–8, 19, 65, 107, 147–8, 261–2
shot-putting 290
show-jumping 134–5, 295
Shrewsbury, Arthur 23
Shrubb, Alf 215
Sinn Fein 123
ski-ing 135
slimming 137
Smallwood, A. M. 120
Smith, Dick 99
Smith, G. O. 308
Smith, Ian 174
smoking 131
Smyth, Miss D. M. 37
soccer *see* football
Solario 154
Solomons, Jack 306–7
Sopwith, T. O. M. 151, 256–8
South Africa
    cricket 25, 191, 313
    rugby football 48–9, 109, 172, 176, 284
Spartakiade, Moscow (1928) 220
speedboat racing 151
Spooner, R. H. 59–60, 116
squash 136–7, 296, 311, 328
stag hunting 147, 228, 261
Stalin, Joseph 300, 323
Stansfield, Margaret 41
Steel, D. M. 311
steeplechasing 13–14, 158, 159, 322

Index

Index